STRATEGIES FOR DEVELOPING EMERGENT LITERACY

STRATEGIES FOR DEVELOPING EMERGENT LITERACY

by **Wilma H. Miller, Ed.D.**
Professor Emerita,
Illinois State University

Boston   Burr Ridge, IL   Dubuque, IA   Madison, WI   New York   San Francisco   St. Louis
Bangkok   Bogotá   Caracas   Lisbon   London   Madrid
Mexico City   Milan   New Delhi   Seoul   Singapore   Sydney   Taipei   Toronto

KH

McGraw-Hill Higher Education

A Division of The **McGraw-Hill** *Companies*

STRATEGIES FOR DEVELOPING EMERGENT LITERACY

This book is printed on acid-free paper.

5 6 7 8 9 0 QPD/QPD 0 9 8 7 6 5 4 3

ISBN 0-07-289372-9

Editorial director: *Jane E. Vaicunas*
Sponsoring editor: *Beth Kaufman*
Developmental editor: *Cara Harvey*
Marketing manager: *Daniel M. Loch*
Senior project manager: *Kay J. Brimeyer*
Production supervisor: *Laura Fuller*
Coordinator of freelance design: *Michelle D. Whitaker*
Senior photo research coordinator: *Lori Hancock*
Compositor: *GAC–Indianapolis*
Typeface: *10/12 Times Roman*
Printer: *Quebecor Printing Book Group/Dubuque, IA*

Cover designer: *Sean M. Sullivan*
Cover image: *©Daniel Arsenault/Image Bank*

Library of Congress Cagaloging-in-Publication Data

Miller, Wilma H.
  Strategies for developing emergent literacy / Wilma H. Miller.—
1ˢᵗ ed.
    p.   cm.
  Includes indexes.
  ISBN 0-07-289372-9
  1. Language arts (Early childhood)   2. Language arts—Remedial
teaching.   3. Literacy.   I. Title.
LB1139.5.L35M55   2000
                                    372.6—dc21   99-26257
                                                CIP

www.mhhe.com

10/25/04

*To my dear friends Ted, Joan, and Becky Ichniowski
with my sincere gratitude*

CONTENTS

PREFACE

If you ever have worked with any children with special needs, you are well aware that they usually enter school not nearly so well prepared as many other children. You are probably also aware that in many instances these children are not able to catch up to their more advanced peers in the primary grades and may fall further and further behind as they progress into the intermediate grades, middle school, and secondary school. Yet children with special needs who have excellent kindergarten and first-grade teachers often can overcome their initial deficits and make satisfactory or good progress in school. Therefore, it becomes incumbent upon early childhood teachers to give such children along with all other children an emergent and primary-grade literacy program that provides many opportunities to develop listening, oral language, reading, writing, and spelling skills. This textbook has been written to help prospective early childhood teachers to accomplish this as effectively as possible.

In the past, developing beginning reading skills usually was called developing reading readiness. This concept stated that a child must master a specific number and type of readiness skills before he or she was considered to be ready for formal reading instruction in first grade, which was usually either a basal reader approach or some kind of phonics program. Today most early childhood teachers and specialists in beginning literacy accept the emergent literacy concept, which states that a child begins learning elements of literacy at birth and continues learning them mainly on an informal basis as he or she progresses through the preschool years into kindergarten and first grade. However, due to a lack of appropriate experiences in the home or in certain preschool settings, some children enter kindergarten with a very limited range of emergent literacy experiences which causes them to experience considerable difficulty with beginning reading, writing, and spelling skills in school.

This reader-friendly and practical book is designed to help all those who will work with young children to as-

sess, present, and reinforce emergent and primary-grade literacy skills effectively. Although the assessment devices and teaching strategies, games, and reproducibles included in this book may be especially useful with children who have been exposed to few emergent literacy experiences prior to school entrance, they should be equally helpful to all young children. This book has been written to be the major or a supplementary textbook for undergraduate students who are enrolled in a preservice or in-service reading or language arts course for preschool, kindergarten, and primary-grade teachers in four-year colleges, universities, or two-year colleges. This text also may be helpful in an undergraduate course for prospective special education teachers. In addition, it may be useful to family members of young children and some day-care or nursery school providers. It should save prospective early childhood educators much time and effort.

The book opens by providing a description of emergent literacy (listening, oral language, reading, writing, and spelling) in Chapter 1. The first chapter discusses why emergent literacy experiences should be provided in homes, preschools, kindergartens, and the primary grades and closes by explaining the relation of emergent literacy to success in primary-grade reading, writing, and spelling.

Chapter 2 describes the most commonly used approaches for teaching emergent and primary-grade literacy. The whole language philosophy is explained, as is its theoretical foundation. Also included are descriptions of the strategies and materials that often constitute whole language classrooms. This chapter explains thematic unit teaching and includes a comprehensive primary-grade unit entitled *Elementary Knowledge about Mammals*. Next, the chapter provides a description of the language-experience approach (LEA) and discusses its advantages and limitations for improving emergent literacy skills. Chapter 2 briefly describes the basal reader approach and its advantages and limitations. The chapter then describes a typical phonics program and summarizes its advantages and limitations. The chapter closes by describing a balanced primary-grade literacy program.

The third chapter is devoted to improving listening and oral language skills. It defines the term *listening* and then discusses some of the strategies and materials that can be used to improve competency in the listening skills. The chapter describes oral language and discusses the main theories of oral language development and then includes useful strategies and materials that can be used to improve oral language skills.

Chapter 4 is an extensive, practical chapter that is devoted to developing competency in letter-name knowledge and the word identification skills. The chapter explains letter-name recognition and letter-name identification and presents strategies and materials for improving ability in these skills. Next the chapter explains sight word recognition and sight word identification and includes a copy of *Fry's Instant Sight Word List* which the early childhood teacher may duplicate. The chapter also presents strategies, materials, games, and reproducibles for improving ability in sight word recognition and sight word identification.

The fourth chapter also contains much useful information about graphophonic (phonic) analysis. It presents information about the important phonic elements and useful phonic generalizations. In addition, it presents strategies, games, and reproducibles for improving ability in phonic analysis. Stress on important phonic elements and rules is in keeping with the emphasis currently being placed on teaching phonics in many states and school districts. The chapter also describes structural (morphemic) analysis and includes strategies, materials, games, and reproducibles for improving ability in this skill. Finally, this comprehensive chapter explains semantic (contextual) analysis and presents strategies and materials for improving ability in this most important word identification technique.

Chapter 5 is designed to help prospective early childhood teachers develop competency in teaching vocabulary and all the elements of comprehension. It explains the different kinds of conceptual (meaning) vocabularies and provides strategies, reproducibles, and games for improving ability in concepts and meaning knowledge. The chapter also presents a description of reading comprehension and includes a number of valuable activities for improving reading comprehension.

The sixth chapter describes ways to assess and develop writing and spelling skills. It provides a brief overview of children's writing and then summarizes the most important goals of teaching writing skills in the primary grades. Several ways of assessing and teaching writing skills are next presented. The chapter then describes the various stages of early childhood spelling and explains some ways in which spelling skills can be assessed in the primary grades. It includes a copy of the useful Developmental Spelling Test and provides some valuable strategies for improving spelling skills in the primary grades.

The seventh chapter describes various assessment devices and strategies that can be used in an early literacy program. It explains the differences between evaluation, formative and summative assessment, and authentic assessment and then explains the advantages and limitations of standardized and informal assessment. The chapter also explains the characteristics of standardized tests and how they may be used with young children and describes criterion-referenced tests, benchmarks, and rubrics. The remainder of the chapter is devoted to authentic or informal assessment of young children's reading strengths and weaknesses. It explains the relevance of using checklists and includes several reproducible checklists. It discusses the use of running records and miscue analysis. The chapter also contains a reproducible example of the El Paso Phonics Survey.

The last chapter of this book is an extremely important one. It is concerned with how any early childhood teacher can teach literacy skills to children who have special needs. It opens by describing how after the year 2000 children who are African American, Hispanic, Asian, and Native American will make up one-third or more of the school population. In addition, more and more children currently are being identified as having special needs of some type. The chapter describes the characteristics of the following children who have special needs:

> learning disabled (LD), attention deficit disordered (ADD), attention deficit/hyperactivity disordered (AD/HD), children who must learn English as a second language (ESL), children with limited English proficiency (LEP), bilingual children, children who are culturally or linguistically diverse, children with mild mental handicaps (EMH), children with visual impairments, children with hearing impairments, and children with speech or language disorders

The chapter explains the inclusion philosophy and provides numerous valuable guidelines and strategies for teaching literacy to all types of children with special needs. It concludes by providing a list of trade books for diverse learners, sources for multicultural aids, and a list of professional books for early childhood teachers of children with disabilities. The reader should find this chapter exceedingly timely, useful, and relevant.

Following the chapters is an activities index that provides a list of all the strategies, games, and reproducibles described in the book. This index should prove valuable and time-saving to prospective early childhood educators and other readers. In addition, there is a brief concluding statement intended to synthesize the main philosophy behind this textbook.

Literacy teachers will find the following items to be unique about *Strategies for Developing Emergent Literacy:*

- It contains an entire chapter devoted to general guidelines, strategies, trade books, and resource books for teaching and reinforcing emergent literacy skills to young children who have special needs of some type. This chapter will be extremely beneficial to early childhood educators.
- It describes the running record and miscue analysis strategies, which are effective ways of assessing a young child's reading strengths and weaknesses.
- It contains a wealth of classroom-tested strategies, games, and reproducibles for improving the emergent reading, writing, and spelling skills of young children.
- It emphasizes the whole language philosophy while also stressing the importance of teaching word identification and comprehension skills in isolation on occasion, especially to those children who seem to need it. Research consistently has indicted that children who are taught decoding (including graphophonic [phonic] skills) in a planned but meaningful way perform more effectively in reading and probably spelling and writing in the primary grades. Therefore, this textbook emphasizes using both the whole language approach and a skills-based approach in a balanced literacy program.
- It describes the basic characteristics, advantages, and limitations of the major programs for teaching emergent literacy skills—whole language, the language-experience approach (LEA), the basal reader approach, and a typical phonic program.
- It includes many strategies and reproducibles for improving competency in early writing and spelling and places much emphasis on the stages of emergent writing.

- It is the only text that contains some reproducible examples of strategies for improving emergent reading, writing, and spelling.

We are now failing to meet the literacy needs of a number of children in preschools, kindergarten, and the primary grades. Indeed, a number of them never become as effective in reading, writing, or spelling as their innate capabilities should enable them to be. In a democratic, technological society in which true competency in literacy is an absolute necessity, we must make every effort to help each young child reach his or her potential. We can afford to do no less. It is this author's sincere hope that this text can be beneficial to many young children and to their dedicated teachers.

In conclusion, I would like to gratefully acknowledge a number of people who have made it possible for me to write *Strategies for Developing Emergent Literacy*. I first would like to acknowledge the memory of my beloved late mother Ruth K. Miller, who worked with me on all my writing projects until the age of eighty. She remains an inspiration to me in all of my writing projects. I also would like to thank all of my former undergraduate and graduate students at Illinois State University for being a constant source of information, motivation, and renewal for me. I would also like to express my gratitude to Beth Kauffman, Cara Harvey, Kay Brimeyer, and Nikki Herbst, copyeditor, of McGraw-Hill for their valuable suggestions as well as to the reviewers who contributed greatly to making this a more readable, useful textbook.

Tony Stiefer, *Southeastern Oklahoma State University*
Deborah Ann Jensen, *Wagner College*
Nancy Clements, *University of St. Francis*

Wilma H. Miller
Normal, Illinois

INTRODUCTION TO EARLY LITERACY INSTRUCTION

CONCEPTS THAT YOU SHOULD LEARN FROM READING THIS CHAPTER

After reading this introductory chapter, you will be able to:

■ *Summarize the views that early philosophers and theorists held about early childhood education*

■ *Describe the historic maturational view and the reading readiness view*

■ *Provide a brief description of the emergent literacy model*

■ *Discuss some of the most important elements of emergent literacy that*

should be provided informally in homes and early childhood programs

■ *Explain why it is very important for kindergarten and first-grade teachers to provide each young child with all of the elements of emergent literacy in which he or she is weak.*

■ *Describe why young "at-risk" children may lack competence in some or all of the emergent literacy skills*

David Frazier Photo CD Library

Do you believe that a child entering kindergarten may be able to read on the second-grade level or better and may be able to write a well-constructed story with correct or nearly correct spelling? You may be somewhat surprised to learn that such children certainly do exist, although they may be quite unusual. In most cases no one has made a concerted effort to teach these children to read, write, and spell. So how do you think they learned these literacy skills? In most cases they have learned them informally in their home or an early childhood program of some type. All of these skills are called e*mergent literacy skills,* and they are the focus of this introductory chapter as well as the entire textbook.

A BRIEF HISTORY OF EARLY LITERACY INSTRUCTION

A number of philosophers, theorists, psychologists, and educators have studied early childhood and the appropriate strategies and materials that should be used with young children. Their concepts usually emphasize either the *nature* or the *nurture* of the child. The philosophies can also be called either the *transmission model* or the *transactional model.* The transmission model views children as empty containers into which knowledge must be "poured," and this model comes from behavioral psychology concepts. The transactional model, on the other hand, views children as already having prior knowledge and comes from the fields of cognitive psychology and psycholinguist learning about the acquisition of language (Weaver, 1994). Today some people call the transactional model a *constructivist view of learning,* and it is upon this model that the whole language philosophy is based as it is described in Chapter 2.

The earliest philosophers and theorists were Rousseau, Pestalozzi, and Froebel. *Rosseau* (1762) believed that a young child's education should essentially be natural. He strongly felt that children should not be pressured to learn things for which they are not developmentally ready. He thought that children should be allowed to grow and learn with the freedom to be themselves. Since Rousseau believed that children learn through their own curiosity, forcing education upon them interferes with both their learning and their development.

Although *Pestalozzi* (Rusk and Scotland, 1979) was influenced by Rousseau's emphasis on natural learning, he added another dimension to it. He began his own school and developed principles for learning that combined natural elements with informal instruction. He believed that parents and teachers should create the climate and conditions in which the reading process develops so that children can learn to read through natural exploration. Pestalozzi designed lessons that involved manipulating objects and learning about them through touch, smell, language, size, and shape.

The approach of *Froebel* (1974) was similar in some ways to those of his predecessors. Although he believed in learning through the natural unfolding of the child and also provided plans for instructing young children, he is best known for emphasizing the importance of *play* in learning. He stated that playing-to-learn requires adult guidance and direction and a planned environment. Therefore, Froebel thought that the teacher was a facilitator of learning and a designer of activities.

Froebel developed a systematic curriculum for young children involving objects and materials that he called *gifts* and *occupations.* It was Froebel who first used the term *kindergarten* which means "children's garden" to indicate that children are similar to plants in that they will grow properly only if they are tended and cared for.

In the twentieth century *Dewey* (1966) proposed a child-centered view of the beginning curriculum which led into the "progressive education" movement. He believed that the curriculum should be built around the interests of children. He agreed with Froebel that children learn best in real-life situations and by play. He did not believe that teaching skills should be the goal but rather the means toward the goal.

Froebel and Dewey were the primary influences in American preschools and kindergartens throughout the twentieth century, especially from the 1920s until around 1960. The typical preschool or kindergarten of that time

had areas for different activities such as an art center, a dramatic-play center, a block center, a center with manipulative toys, a science center, a music center, and a literature center. Most preschools and kindergartens of that time followed a similar schedule which included free play; circle time; snack time; a rest period; lessons in art, social studies, or science; outdoor play (weather permitting), and story time. They usually had a relaxed atmosphere free from pressure to learn true academics of any kind. A number of contemporary preschools and perhaps to a lesser extent kindergartens still incorporate this instructional model.

Montessori (1965) believed that children need early, systematic training in mastering one skill after another. Therefore, she supplied the teaching environment with materials for learning specific concepts in order to meet precise objectives. The materials then were the source of learning for the child. Children taught themselves by using these manipulatives, and because the materials were self-correcting the children could determine their own errors and make their own corrections.

Montessori called this type of education *auto-education,* and she also spoke of *sensitive periods* in which children are better able to learn certain concepts than other times. Therefore, parents and teachers should watch for these periods and attempt to take advantage of them by structuring the environment with appropriate materials and experiences so that children can learn. Work is important in Montessori's curriculum because play might waste opportunities for children to achieve important goals during their sensitive periods for learning.

Piaget (Piaget and Inhelder, 1969) provided a theory of cognitive development that has greatly influenced early childhood education. In explaining various stages of cognitive development, he stated that children at certain stages are capable only of certain types of intellectual endeavors. Piaget labeled these stages as the *sensorimotor stage,* the *preoperational period,* the *concrete operational period,* and the *formal operational period.* Piaget stated that the sensorimotor stage spans the period from birth to approximately age two. During this stage the young child learns that words are tied to activities. The preoperational period, which spans the ages two to seven years, is marked by the child's use of symbols to represent objects or experiences. Children in the concrete operational stage (ages seven through twelve years of age) can think about ideas from more than one point of view. Formal operations which allow abstract reasoning are attained by most children only after the age of twelve.

Educators who ascribe to Piaget's theory only involve children in problem-solving situations when they can assimilate new experiences into their existing knowledge. Piaget also believed that children are active participants in their own learning, constantly changing and recognizing their own knowledge. Piaget thought that young children should use their curiosity, inquisitiveness, and spontaneity to help themselves learn. In addition, Piaget emphasized the importance of decision making, problem solving, self-discipline, goal setting, planning one's own activities, and cooperation with teachers and classmates.

Vygotsky (1978) proposed a theory of intellectual development that has relevance for early childhood education. He believed that learning is acquired through social relationships, and that children learn by internalizing activities in the world around them. They also imitate behaviors and incorporate them into their existing base of knowledge. Vygotsky also used the term *zone of proximal development.* This is the "distance between the actual developmental level as determined by independent problem solving and the level of potential development as determined through problem solving under adult guidance or in collaboration with more capable peers (p. 84).

In summary, in this author's opinion a number of the philosophers and theorists of the past have accurately stated the following about early childhood education:

- A child's total level of physical, social-emotional, and intellectual development must be taken into account when planning a learning environment for him or her.
- Emphasis should always be on learning not on teaching.
- Each child needs social interaction with helpful adults and other children.
- Learning should always use real, not contrived, experiences.
- As much as possible, children should always participate in their own learning.

The Maturational View and the Reading Readiness View

Gesell (1925) was an early development psychologist who advocated *maturation* as the most important factor in a child's learning to read. Morphett and Washburne (1931) conducted a well-known research study that supported postponing reading instruction until a child had reached a mental age of 6½. Depending on a child's intellectual ability, she or he could reach this mental age as early as the age of about five, sometimes less, or as late as the age of about eight.

A number of the educators of that time felt uncomfortable with the concept of delaying literacy instruction until the child was "ready." They preferred to help children become ready to read. These educators supported the *reading readiness view,* which stated that early literacy is composed of a number of discrete, separate skills that the child must master in order to learn to read and write in school. It did not matter if the young child already could read and write at some beginning level. She or he still had to learn the different reading readiness skills. Here are some of the readiness skills that typically were taught in kindergartens and beginning first grade:

- *visual discrimination*—the ability to discriminate between similar and different geometric figures, patterns, colors, letters, and words
- *auditory discrimination*—the ability to identify and differentiate sounds, rhyme words, and understand beginning letter-sound relationships
- *picture interpretation*—the ability to interpret a picture in a reading readiness workbook or simple basal reader
- *left-to-right progression*—the ability to move the eyes from left to right as while correctly using a classroom calendar or reading readiness workbook page
- *visual-motor skills*—the ability to color within the lines of a picture or to cut effectively with a pair of scissors
- *laterality*—the ability to differentiate between the right and left hands and the right and left feet
- *large motor skills*—the ability to walk on a line, hop, skip, and jump

It was believed that children could not learn to read in first grade until they had mastered these prerequisite skills. The child's reading readiness skills usually were evaluated by standardized reading readiness tests that normally were given near the end of kindergarten. However, a few children who were already reading did not do well on a reading readiness test since the skills that such a test evaluated were very different from those required in actual reading of simple trade books. Teale (1982, p. 567), for example, has stated that a typical child does not learn in a part-to-whole manner and that sometimes isolated skills are harder to learn than is actual reading. This is the case, for example, of the typical young child who attempts to discriminate between the short /e/ and short /i/ vowel sounds, an example of using isolated phonic skills.

In summary, most of the recent research in early literacy instruction has supported a very different type of early childhood literacy instruction than that exemplified by the reading readiness view. This instruction is called the emergent literacy model and is described in the next section of this chapter.

WHAT IS EMERGENT LITERACY?

Emergent literacy is a contemporary theory that fits in well with the whole language programs and contemporary basal reading programs that are quite widely used in a number of today's preschools and primary grades. Very briefly, the emergent literacy philosophy states that *there is not a point in a child's life when literacy begins; rather it is a continuous process of learning.* Therefore, all aspects of literacy can begin in some form during infancy and proceed from that point forward. Emergent literacy is part of the *transactional model* which states that children have much prior knowledge that can be built upon. Clay (1975) and Holdaway (1979) are mainly credited with the concept of emergent literacy. However, emergent literacy as it is known today is also based on the work of Durkin (1966), Heath (1983), Hiebert (1981), Teale (1986), Sulzby (1989), and Morrow (1997), among others. These researchers have made the following general conclusions:

- All literacy begins at a very young age in some form and proceeds from that point forward at each child's own rate and in his or her own way.
- Most children who are brought up in a literate society begin to read, write, and spell in some form before formal schooling begins.
- Reading and writing are learned together, mutually reinforcing one another.
- Oral language serves as a predecessor to reading and later serves as a reinforcement of reading.
- Scribbling, random letters (letter strings), and invented spelling are considered valid ways to write and spell at various stages of a child's development.
- Literacy develops best in real-life situations, not in contrived settings, both in and out of school.
- Reading to children on a daily basis beginning in infancy is absolutely essential in helping them learn to read and write later.
- Learning to read and write is a complex task that requires work and energy for most young children.
- Learning to read and write effectively takes a long time.
- Children need meaningful, repetitive experiences while learning to read and write.

These concepts of emergent literacy have significantly altered the curriculum of a number of contemporary preschools, kindergartens, and primary-grade classrooms. Teachers are using these concepts to design early childhood literacy programs that are more transactional (child-centered) than they were in the past when the curriculum was primarily based on the transmission model (content-centered).

The typical contemporary preschool, kindergarten, and early primary-grade classroom may well reflect a number of the same type of strategies and materials that research has found early readers, writers, and spellers used in their homes to learn emergent literacy skills on a mainly informal basis. These typically are goal-oriented, purposeful activities for which the child sees real meaning and relevance. The typical early readers, writers, and spellers do *not* have anyone making a concerted effort to teach them literacy skills. Instead, these children learn beginning literacy skills by modeling family members and asking questions about letters, numbers and words. In such homes parents and children often interact around print. In addition, early readers, writers, and spellers often have an older brother or sister who plays school with them or reads to them.

Emergent literacy also entails the use of the appropriate *teaching point* at which the teacher provides meaningful opportunities for the child to expand and refine his or her early literacy skills. This is in direct contrast to the reading readiness model described earlier in this chapter

that required all children to learn all of the readiness skills whether or not they already were known or were relevant for the reading of actual material.

WHAT ARE SOME OF THE EMERGENT LITERACY EXPERIENCES?

Here is a very brief list of some of the emergent literacy experiences that a young child may have been exposed to before entering school. They are all discussed in greater detail in later chapters of this book.

- Listening to trade books (library books) of various kinds, nursery rhymes, poetry, and other material read aloud on a regular basis beginning during the child's infancy. Without a doubt, this is the single most important factor that influences a child's later primary-grade reading achievement. Unfortunately, today a number of children, especially children with special needs of various types (see Chapter 8 for a comprehensive discussion) enter either preschool or kindergarten never having heard a trade book, nursery rhyme, or poem read to them at home.
- Taking family outings with discussion before and after to encourage the development of vocabulary and concepts.
- Having a print-rich environment in the home and having questions about colors, letters, words, and numbers answered at home. Children who grow up in a print-rich environment learn some or all of the following concepts about print:

  - Print is different from pictures.
  - Print goes from left to right and top to bottom on a page.
  - A book has a title, an author, and perhaps an illustrator.
  - There are "white spaces" (word boundaries) between words in print.
  - A capital letter is different from a lower case letter.
  - A letter is different from a word.
  - Print can be found in many different types of media—paper, television, signs, or even can labels.
  - Print can be found in many places in the environment.
  - Grown-ups read different types of print in different ways. For example, they might read a book aloud to a child but read a magazine to themselves.
  - Adults are able to gain meaning from print in a "mysterious" way.
  - Print holds different kinds of information.
  - Anyone who is able can produce print.

Note: Obviously some children, especially "at-risk" children, do not grow up in a print-rich environment and therefore do not learn these concepts about print in their home. Instead, they need to learn them in an early childhood or kindergarten program.

- Listening to a trade book and then doing a reading reenactment (pretend reading) of the book. The child should be encouraged to use the pictures as an aid to this reenactment, and the child's rendition of the book should be welcomed even though his or her words may not exactly match the words in the book.
- Observing that parents, other family members, and friends value reading both for pleasure and information. Good reading models are considered to be a very important factor in influencing primary-grade reading achievement.
- Dictating language-experience stories and books to an adult who then helps the child to read them back while stressing left-to-right progression, letter names and letter sounds, sight words that are important to the child, and the understanding that reading mainly is talk written down. This valuable language-experience approach is described in detail in Chapter 2.
- Having access to writing materials in the home and being encouraged to participate in writing activities of all types such as making grocery lists, writing thank you cards, and writing notes and letters to relatives and friends. All types of writing including drawing, scribbling, letter strings (random letters), and invented spelling should be encouraged and welcomed. A word processing program on a computer can be used for this purpose if it is available to the child and seems relevant. Children as young as the kindergarten level or even younger can learn some rudimentary keyboarding skills, and they find it very motivational.
- Playing school with an older brother or sister. This is a very effective and interesting way for a young child to develop all emergent literacy skills.
- Actively participating in all types of art and construction activities.
- Participating in dramatic play either of a particular situation such as having a pretend grocery store or as a follow-up to listening to a trade book.
- Participating in block play (in many ways all kinds of play are a young child's work and add greatly to his or her prior knowledge and experiences).
- Viewing videotapes, computer software, films, pictures, demonstrations, scientific experiments, and other realia.

THE IMPORTANCE OF DEVELOPING EMERGENT LITERACY SKILLS IN EARLY CHILDHOOD PROGRAMS

It is essential for young children to be exposed to and learn the various elements of emergent literacy in their home and early childhood programs in order that they may experience the maximum amount of success in gaining literacy skills in kindergarten and the early primary grades. Family members and preschool workers play an extremely important role in informally helping children to develop the various elements of emergent literacy. Indeed, the importance of their role cannot be emphasized too much.

Unfortunately, children vary greatly in the amount of exposure that they have to emergent literacy skills in their home and early childhood programs, so their attainment of emergent literacy skills varies greatly upon school entrance. Some children enter kindergarten already reading at the upper primary-grade level, while other children have never listened to a trade book read aloud at home. They also may have had very few opportunities to go on family trips of any kind, even as simple as a picnic in a local park; have seen no reading or writing materials in the home; have no one that is either willing or able to answer their questions about letters, letter sounds, words, or numbers; and have received inadequate nutrition and rest. Instead they may spend a considerable amount of their time watching television programs of all kinds, including those that are not designed for young children and that may be harmful to them.

On school entrance, children with little or no exposure to emergent literacy skills may not be equipped to learn any beginning literacy skills, and they may fall further and further behind unless someone makes a concerted effort to help them.

Preschool, kindergarten, and first-grade teachers are able to compensate for a child's lack of emergent literacy experiences in the home, although it may be quite difficult for them to do this because of large class sizes, especially in kindergarten and first grade. It may be especially difficult in schools in which there are a large number of "at-risk" children. First-grade teachers may need additional help from other sources such as a Reading Recovery Program, a valuable early intervention program for "at-risk" first-grade children, a Title I (special) reading teacher, volunteer tutors from the community, or paid or unpaid parent volunteers. In any case, an exemplary kindergarten or first-grade teacher and emergent literacy program can enable a child with special needs to succeed as well or nearly as well as his or her peers. However, for this to occur, the teacher must work with each child at the child's current level of emergent literacy attainment and proceed at the child's own pace with a meaningful, well-designed literacy program that makes a concerted effort to help him or her attain competence in all of those emergent literacy skills in which she or he is currently weak. The literacy approaches, strategies, and materials in later sections of this textbook should help you to do this effectively.

It is absolutely essential that all children, whether they have special needs or not, have a kindergarten and primary-grade emergent literacy program that capitalizes on their strengths and compensates for their weaknesses; provides meaningful listening, oral language, reading, writing, and spelling instruction; enhances their self-esteem; and is highly motivating. I believe that in most instances this is some variation of a whole language program with meaningful skills and instruction that is designed for each child. Chapter 2 provides a description of one type of excellent kindergarten and primary-grade emergent literacy program. Although this type of program may be especially helpful for "at-risk" children, it also is an excellent program for all young children. Even though it is true that linguistically adept children may be able to learn literacy skills effectively with inadequate or improper instruction, they certainly should not have to do so.

IN CONCLUSION

Most young children enter school possessing a number of emergent literacy skills. I believe that the concept of emergent literacy is valid, and that early childhood teachers should informally stress all of the elements that were discussed in this introductory chapter. The importance of doing so cannot be stressed enough. Certainly literacy instruction cannot be delayed until first-grade entrance, as was the case in the past when the reading readiness view was commonly held.

Unfortunately, not all children have equal opportunities to engage in all of the activities that comprise emergent literacy. Since this is the case, it becomes incumbent upon early childhood providers, kindergarten teachers, and first-grade teachers to provide all of the elements of emergent literacy in which a child lacks competence. Only then can the child reach the ultimate level of literacy to which she or he is capable. The useful literacy approaches, strategies, and materials that are described and illustrated in the remainder of this book should help you as a future or in-service early childhood educator achieve this very important goal with the greatest amount of success.

SUGGESTED ACTIVITIES

1. Observe a preschool or kindergarten classroom for about 2–5 hours. Try to determine if this classroom is based on the older more traditional reading readiness view or the more contemporary emergent literacy model. Provide examples that help you to arrive at your conclusion.

2. Select a three-year-old child with whom you can interact a few times for a total of 2–3 hours. Choose three elements of emergent literacy that were presented in this chapter and try to improve this young child's competence in them. Be prepared to summarize orally or in writing the reasons why you chose these emergent literacy skills and how effective the experiences proved to be.

3. Choose a child in kindergarten and allow him or her to select a picture storybook for you to read aloud. After you have read this trade book, have the child demonstrate her or his competency in the following concepts about print:
   - Print is different from pictures.
   - Print goes from left to right and top to bottom on a page.
   - A book has a title, an author, and perhaps an illustrator.
   - There are "white spaces" (word boundaries) between words in print.

   - A capital letter is different from a lower case letter.
   - A letter is different from a word.

   If you want an example of how this can be done effectively, consult the following book:

   Clay, M. (1993). *An observation survey on early literacy achievement.* Portsmouth, NH: Heinemann.

   After your experience with the child, summarize orally or in writing how well the child demonstrated knowledge of these concepts and how you could help him or her to learn those concepts in which he or she was not competent.

4. After reading this chapter, think about your own preschool years. How much emphasis was informally placed in your home on the emergent literacy skills? In what ways do you think that the emergent literacy experiences provided in your home influenced your present enjoyment of reading for information and pleasure?

5. If you have the time and opportunity, volunteer in some type of community agency to present emergent literacy skills to young "at-risk" children.

SELECTED REFERENCES

Allen, J. (1995). Becoming readers and writers. In T. V. Rasinski (Ed.). *Parents and teachers: Helping children learn to read and write* (pp. 91–96). Fort Worth, TX: Harcourt Brace.

DeGraff, L. (1995). Using computers to promote literacy. In T. V. Rasinski (Ed.). *Parents and teachers: Helping children learn to read and write* (pp.131–135). Fort Worth, TX: Harcourt Brace.

Fields, M. & Spangler, K. (1995). *Let's begin reading right* (pp.14–16 & 20–22). Englewood Cliffs, NJ: Merrill.

Glazer. S., & Burke, E. (1994). *An integrated approach to early literacy* (pp. 1–8). Boston: Allyn & Bacon.

Gunning, T. (1996). *Creating reading instruction for all children* (pp. 23–76). Boston: Allyn & Bacon.

Holdaway, D. (1979). *The foundations of literacy* (pp. 38–63). Portsmouth, NH: Heinemann.

Hudson-Ross, S. (1995). Demystify the written word and make writing a lifelong adventure. In T. V. Rasinski (Ed.). *Parents and teachers: Helping children learn to read and write* (pp. 97–106). Fort Worth, TX: Harcourt Brace.

International Reading Association (IRA), & National Association for the Education of Young Children (NAEYC), (1998). Learning to read and write: Developmentally appropriate practices. *The Reading Teacher, 59,* 193–214.

Lancy, D. (1995). It's not just what you do, but how you do it that counts. In T. V. Rasinski (Ed.). *Parents and teachers: Helping children learn to read and write* (pp. 41–45). Fort Worth, TX: Harcourt Brace.

Machado, J. (1995). *Early childhood experiences in language arts* (pp. 384–391). New York: Delmar Publishers.

Mastain, M. (1995). Seven steps to creating a literate home environment. In T. V. Rasinski (Ed.). *Parents and teachers: Helping children to learn to read and write* (pp. 9–17). Fort Worth, TX: Harcourt Brace.

McGee, L., & Richgels, D. (1996). *Literacy's beginnings: Supporting your young readers and writers* (pp. 3–13 & 117–122). Boston: Allyn & Bacon.

Morrow, L. (1997). *Literacy development in the early years* (pp. 1–14). Boston: Allyn & Bacon.

Neuman, S., Caperelli, B., & Kee, C. (1998). Literacy learning, a family matter. *The Reading Teacher, 52,* 244–252.

Neuman, S., & Roskos, K. (1993). *Language and literacy learning in the early years* (pp. 33–39 & 64–97). Fort Worth: TX: Harcourt Brace.

Padak, N., & Rasinski, T. (1995). The role of lists in family literacy. In T. V. Rasinski (Ed.). *Parents and teachers: Helping children learn to read and write* (pp. 107–120). Fort Worth, TX: Harcourt Brace.

Reinking, D., & Pardon, D. (1995). Television and literacy. In T. V. Rasinski (Ed.). *Parents and teachers: Helping children learn to read and write* (pp. 137–145). Fort Worth, TX: Harcourt Brace.

Teale, W., & Sulzby, E. (1989). Emergent literacy: New Perspectives. In D. S. Strickland & L. M. Morrow (Eds.). *Emerging literacy: Young children learn to read and write* (pp. 1–15). Newark, DE: International Reading Association.

Wendelin, K. (1995). Children never outgrow "Read me another. . . ." In T. V. Rasinski (Ed.). *Parents and teachers: Helping children learn to read and write* (pp. 33–40). Fort Worth, TX: Harcourt Brace.

WORKS CITED IN CHAPTER 1

Clay, M. (1975). *What did I write?* Auckland, New Zealand: Heinemann Educational Books.

Dewey, J. (1966). *Democracy and education.* New York: First Press (original work published 1916).

Durkin, D. (1966). *Children Who Read Early.* New York: Teachers College Press.

Froebel, Frederick. (1974). *The education of man.* Clifton, NJ: Augustus M. Kelly.

Gesell, A. (1925). *The mental growth of the preschool child.* New York: Macmillan.

Heath, S. (1983). *Ways with Words.* Cambridge, MA: Cambridge University Press.

Hiebert, E. (1981). Using environmental print in beginning reading instruction. In M. R. Sampson (Ed.). *Reading Research Quarterly, 16,* 236–260.

Montessori, M. (1965). *Spontaneous activity in education.* New York: Schocken Books.

Morphett, M., & Washburne, C. (1931). When should children begin to read? *Elementary School Journal, 31,* 496–508.

Piaget, J., and Inhelder, B. (1969). *The psychology of the child.* New York: Basic Books.

Rousseau, J. (1962). *Emile* (ed. and trans. William Boyd). New York: Columbia University Teachers College (original work published 1762).

Rusk, R., and Scotland, J. (1979). *Doctrines of the great educators.* New York: St. Martin's Press.

Teale, W. (1982). Toward a theory of how children learn to read and write naturally. *Language Arts, 59,* 555–570.

Teale, W. (1986). The beginning of reading and writing: Written language development during preschool and kindergarten years. In M. Sampson (Ed.) *The pursuit of literacy: Early reading and writing.* Dubuque, IA: Kendall/Hunt.

Vygotsky, L. (1978). *Thought and language.* In J. J. Wertsch (Ed.) Cambridge, MA: MIT Press.

Weaver, C. (1994). *Reading process and practice: From socio-psycholinguistic to whole language,* 2nd ed. Portsmouth, NJ: Heinemann.

2

APPROACHES, STRATEGIES, AND MATERIALS FOR TEACHING EARLY LITERACY

CONCEPTS THAT YOU SHOULD LEARN FROM READING THIS CHAPTER

After reading this chapter, you will be able to:

■ *Provide a definition of the whole language philosophy*

■ *Explain the research and philosophy on which whole language is based*

■ *Describe a number of the most useful strategies and materials that can be found in whole language classrooms*

■ *Describe in detail the basic characteristics of thematic unit teaching and suggest a number of topics that are useful in kindergartens or primary-grade classrooms*

■ *Discuss the unique advantages of thematic unit teaching in kindergartens or primary-grade classrooms*

■ *Summarize the strengths and weaknesses of the whole language philosophy*

■ *Provide a brief history of the language-experience approach (LEA)*

■ *Describe in detail how to use dictation in homes, preschools, kindergartens, and first grades*

■ *Summarize the advantages and limitations of using the language-experience approach (LEA) in homes, preschools, kindergartens, and first grades*

■ *Briefly summarize the history of the basal reader approach*

■ *Contrast the basal readers of the past with those of the present*

■ *Describe the major elements contained in a typical basal reader series*

■ *Summarize the advantages and limitations of using the basal reader approach*

■ *Describe the characteristics of a typical systematic phonics program*

■ *Summarize the strengths and weaknesses of a systematic phonics program*

■ *Describe the characteristics of a good combination early childhood literacy program*

Many of you probably have seen or heard television or radio commercials for some type of phonics program. All of these commercials confidently state that if a family member uses this program with his or her child, the child will learn to "read" effectively. Several such commercials currently are heard on a regular basis in the area in which I live. Do you believe that this really is the case? Indeed, do you think that one reading program works equally well with all children no matter what inherent literacy strengths and weakness they have? If you answered "No" to these two questions, you are correct. According to many research studies done during the past forty years, perhaps the most extensive of which were the federally sponsored first-grade reading studies of the 1960s, no one method or type of materials is inherently superior to any other. That is why the most effective approach to helping children learn literacy skills is to understand and use the unique strengths of several different programs and materials. This chapter is designed to help you use the unique strengths of several literacy approaches so that you can provide the best possible literacy instruction for each child. Its major goal is to help you present a balanced, appropriate literacy program to young children.

THE WHOLE LANGUAGE PHILOSOPHY

What Is Whole Language?

Whole language is a philosophy based on the views and research of a number of psycholinguists and educators. Therefore, it is difficult to provide one single definition for this complex concept. Since this is the case, this textbook includes several different, but compatible, definitions. Stated very simply, *whole language is instruction in which language remains whole.* Bergeron (1990) defined whole language, after making a content analysis of sixty-five professional articles, in the following way:

> Whole language is a concept that embodies both a philosophy of language development as well as the instructional approaches embedded within, and supportive of, that philosophy. This concept includes the use of real literature and writing in the context of meaningful, functional, and cooperative experiences in order to develop in students motivation and interest in the process of learning (p. 319).

Whole language also can be defined as a philosophy concerning how children learn from which educators derive strategies for teaching. In addition, it can be defined as a philosophy which results in instruction that is child-centered and integrates all of the curriculum areas. One other definition states that no one becomes literate without being personally involved in literacy. According to this definition, this is why whole language is a philosophy, not a method (Crofton, 1991, p. 4). Whole language is based on the transaction theory explained in Chapter 1 which states that children bring prior knowledge to any learning experience that can be capitalized upon (Weaver, 1994).

Kenneth and Yetta Goodman (1986, 1989) were among the first educators to research and write extensively about whole language, and they are still among the major proponents of this philosophy. Whole language proponents believe that all language (including reading and writing) occurs, grows, and thrives while someone is preoccupied with the whole of life and that everyone learns to read and write to:

- connect with others
- understand our world
- reveal ourselves

By now you should be able to understand why it is difficult to provide one succinct definition for the whole language philosophy. Perhaps it is somewhat simpler to summarize the basic characteristics of whole language classrooms. However, you should remember that there probably are as many different whole language classrooms as there are whole language teachers. According to the basic philosophy, whole language programs should be different depending upon the unique needs, interests, and abilities of different children and teachers. You should keep in mind that there may not be one single whole language classroom that exemplifies all of the characteristics that are enumerated in this section. Perhaps the following diagram can best illustrate the different characteristics of a whole language classroom.

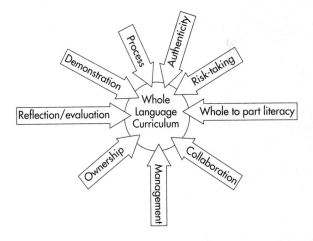

Major characteristics that *may* be found in a whole language classroom include the following:

- Since the classroom is child-centered and child-regulated, the children select the topics of the curriculum, the resources to attain the skills, knowledges, and attitudes involved that should be learned with that curriculum; the learning activities that are used; and the pace at which these activities take place there. The curriculum is entirely child-directed, not teacher-directed. The meaning and function of the curriculum are drawn from the child's life experiences at home or created at school. For example, when I was teaching second grade, a child brought in a Cecropia moth cocoon that he had found. A whole language teacher could build an entire unit of study on butterflies and moths as a result of his bringing this cocoon to school *if* the children in the classroom expressed an interest in doing so. All of the learning activities for this unit of study would be based on this cocoon, and the teacher as well as the children would have to do extensive planning and research to ensure that the unit was successful.

- Each teacher must show respect for each learner which should result in the child's independence and self-initiative as a learner.
- The teacher mainly is a facilitator of learning, not a director of learning.
- The students are active participants in the learning.
- All literacy skills, including listening, speaking, reading, and writing skills, are taught and practiced in the context of whole language when they are relevant, using environmental print, trade books of various kinds, informational books, textbooks, magazines, newspapers, poetry, and drama. They are not taught or practiced in solution such as in worksheets or reading games that isolate the skills. This is why the definition "whole language is instruction that remains whole" is so applicable. This is also the reason that this instruction is called holistic literacy instruction.
- All of the elements of literacy (listening, speaking, reading, and writing) are stressed in whole language classrooms because this creates a literate individual. In the past this type of program might have been called an integrated language arts curriculum.
- Themes for instruction are typically used. For example, the theme could be based on a trade book such as *The hungry caterpillar* by Eric Carle (New York: Collins, 1979). In this type of thematic teaching this picture storybook serves as the major resource, and all of the learning activities in literacy (listening, speaking, reading, and writing), social studies, science, arithmetic, drama, music, and art are related to it in some way if possible. In this case this method is called literature-based instruction. More typically a whole language classroom uses a theme derived from the content area of social studies or science, and all of the listening, speaking, reading, and writing activities as well as all of the other curricular areas are based on that theme. A very common theme, for example, in second grade is that of community helpers, a theme from social studies around which all of the learning activities would occur. This is the reason that not all whole language programs can be called literature-based instruction, although the two terms are sometimes used interchangeably, which is incorrect.
- Literacy instruction is embedded throughout the day, and large blocks of time are used for literacy.

- Various types of classroom organization are employed, depending upon the needs and interests of the children, not the teacher, including whole-group, small-group, partner (peer), and individualized instruction. Partner or peer groups (collaboration) are very common in whole language classrooms since the social aspect of learning is very important in the whole language philosophy, as you will learn from the next section of this chapter.
- Commercial materials do *not* dictate the curriculum. Instead, materials are only employed as a means to an end, not an end in themselves.
- All four of the following major cueing systems are emphasized:
  - semantic (meaning)
  - syntactic (grammar or structure)
  - graphophonic (visual/phonic)
  - pragmatic (the most effective cueing system at that time or a combination of several of them)
  Here is an illustration of the four cueing systems.

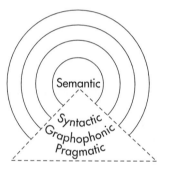

Note: Cueing systems are explained in detail in Chapter 4 of this book.

- Authentic, continuous assessment in the form of individual portfolios, daily performance samples, self-evaluation devices, videotapes, audiotapes, teacher observation checklists, and the like are used for evaluation. Informal assessment devices are the most effective ways of evaluating the outcomes of whole language programs. Standardized tests of any type are *not* considered compatible with whole language programs, since whole language stresses many concepts and attitudes that are not evaluated objectively by standardized means.

What Are the Foundations of the Whole Language Philosophy?

The whole language philosophy is based on the views of Rousseau, Pestalozzi, and Froebel as they were explained in Chapter 1. Pestalozzi and Froebel believed that learning should be active, through sensory experiences with materials. Dewey's Progressive Education model also contributed to the whole language philosophy with its child-centered approach to the learning of information and to literacy. In addition, the influences of Piaget and Vygotsky certainly can be seen in whole language classrooms through the emphasis on active learning and the belief that the adult is a facilitator of learning by guiding experiences in a social context (see the appropriate references in Chapter 1).

Whole language is based on the concept that literacy is student-centered, process-driven, and language-based. Therefore, whole language and traditional literacy programs stand as philosophical opposites. For example, Illinois Writing Project Co-Directors Steve Zemelman and Harvey Daniels (1988) have written:

> If I, as a teacher, spend the class period telling you rules for good writing, I am doing something profoundly different from what I do if I engage you as an active participant in a writing workshop, a growing community of writers. These are not minor differences of pedagogical styles; they are the essence of the matter (p. 12).

The philosophical foundation for whole language has been researched and written about by a number of interdisciplinary scholars. Some of these scholars are Brian Cambourne (1984), Carolyn Burke (1984), Kenneth Goodman (1986), Yetta Goodman (1967), Donald Graves (1983), Jerry Harste (1984), Shirley Brice Heath (1983), Judith Newman (1985), Frank Smith (1973), Gordon Wells (1986), Marie Clay (1991), and Linda Crofton (1991). Very briefly, here are some of the philosophical principles upon which whole language is based. These principles are a compilation of the research and views of these interdisciplinary specialists.

- **Language and Literacy Learning Must Be Socially Constructed.** Reading and writing are not solitary activities. Indeed, they are socialized learning events, since reading and writing are part of an ongoing dialogue between an author and a reader. Because learning is a perpetual social spiral, students need opportunities to learn from each other as well as from teachers. *Collaborative learning* is greatly encouraged and students talking with each other also is very important to learning.
- **Oral and Written Language Should Always Develop from Whole to Part.** All language is *whole* from the beginning stages of speech, and in literacy parts only have a meaning in relationship to the whole. Frank Smith (1986) has written that in an effort to make reading simple, we have made it hard. He also believes that the same thing has occurred with writing. Therefore, according to whole language proponents, materials for learning need to be whole, intact texts, and graphophonic (phonic) strategies are only meaningful in the context of whole language.
- **Literate Behaviors Are Only Learned Through Functional, Real-Life Experiences.** According to

this principle, young children always use language to achieve a desired result, and language in school should have the same real purposes as does language in other places. Children always want to use literacy (listening, speaking, reading, and writing) for their own *real* purposes. Therefore, in school, children need real personal, meaningful reasons to speak, read, and write (Halliday, 1975).

- **Demonstrations, Modeling, and Scaffolding Are All Essential to Learning.** Frank Smith (1986) has stated that process demonstrations are an essential component of learning. Demonstrations, modeling, and scaffolding (modeling and supporting the desired behavior) show novices how results can be accomplished; they show the process involved in achieving the end result desired. Therefore, whole language teachers need to read and write and learn *with* students so that students can share their thinking processes while they are engaged in these literacy activities. Whole language requires a shift from product to *process,* and students and teachers learn from each other.
- **All Learning Involves Risk-Taking and Approximation.** Since learning should be continuous and encourage risk-taking, students should be encouraged to take risks in reading and writing activities and approximations should be valued in both literacy skills. Risk-taking requires trust on both the teacher's and learner's part. This is the reason that in whole language programs words that the child guesses while reading silently and orally should be valued, especially if they are semantically acceptable (make sense). It also is the reason inventive spelling and rough drafts are considered acceptable in the process of writing. According to whole language proponents, word-perfect oral reading and the insistence on completely correct spelling, sentence structure, and grammar (mechanics) in written first drafts have limited students' ability to read and write as effectively as they might. However, students are eventually expected to use the conventions of print, and they are supported in this endeavor.
- **All Learners Must Take Responsibility for Their Own Learning.** According to whole language theorists, self-initiation results in ownership, commitment, and involvement. Therefore, the learning context should provide open-ended opportunities and student choice. Students should be given the opportunity to make choices in reading materials and in writing topics.

In summary, whole language is a perspective on language and learning that provides guidelines about how literacy instruction should occur. According to whole language proponents, these guidelines should always be modified in the light of the needs, interests, and abilities of students and teachers.

What Strategies and Materials Can a Whole Language Program Include?

Perhaps this part of the chapter should open with a caveat for the reader. Remember: whole language is a theory, not a method. Even though whole language classrooms incorporate strategies and materials of various types, whole language is not merely a collection of holistic strategies. It is, as stated earlier, a curriculum that is primarily based on the needs, interests, and abilities of the children in that classroom.

That is why the strategies and materials described in this section are merely suggestions of what can be included in any kindergarten or primary-grade classroom. All of the materials included in this section are for illustrative purposes and should be used or modified only in the light of any whole language teacher's class interests, competencies and weaknesses, and desires.

STRATEGIES THAT CAN BE USED IN A WHOLE LANGUAGE PROGRAM

Print-Rich Environment

It is essential for any preschool, kindergarten, or primary-grade whole classroom to have an abundance of print available around the classroom for the children to see. This print should be placed in a meaningful manner so that each child is able to associate print with meaning. For example, the equipment in the classroom can be labeled so that children can associate the abstract symbols with the concrete object, thus providing meaning for it. Although a print-rich environment is desirable in any early literacy classroom, it has perhaps most closely identified with whole language classrooms.

Interactive Story Reading

If possible, the early literacy teacher should read interesting trade books to a young child individually or in a very small group. It may be necessary to enlist the help of a teacher aid, a parent volunteer, or an unpaid or paid volunteer so that each child has the opportunity to hear trade books read only to him or her or to several children at a time to stimulate *interactive story reading*. Although it is true that children often gain much by being read to as an entire class, there are special advantages that can result only from being read to on an individual" or small-group basis. This type of reading simulates the bedtime story or lap reading that should take place in homes beginning in infancy.

In interactive story reading, a young child is encouraged to actively participate. The child can predict the book content from having the title read aloud, describe the pictures in the book, make additional predictions as the book is being read aloud, and comment on the book

both during and after the reading in any way she or he likes. It is obvious that this interaction cannot take place as effectively in a whole-class setting.

Perhaps interactive story reading will be made clearer if you examine the interaction between a kindergarten child and her teacher while the teacher read the trade book *The true story of the three little pigs* by Jon Sciezka (New York: Viking, 1989) aloud to her.

MS. SPELLMAN: Jessica, the title of this book is *The true story of the three little pigs,* and the author is a man named Jon Sciezka. Have you ever heard the book *The three little pigs?*

JESSICA: Yes, I think my father read that book to me when I was real little.

S: Well, this book tries to tell this story from the wolf's viewpoint. That means that this is how the wolf thinks that this story really happened. Since that's the case, what do you think that this book might be about?

J: Well, it probably may show how th e wolf isn't as bad as he was in the other book.

S: That's a very good prediction, and now I'll read the book to you and you can stop me whenever you want to say anything or ask me something.

J: OK. Oh, look, the wolf looks really hungry in that picture.

S: Yes, he does, doesn't he.

J: I'll bet he'll eat that first little pig cuz his house isn't built very well.

S: Yes, I think that he does.

J: I wonder what's gonna happen next in this book? Will he get caught by anyone, do you think?

S: I don't know, but let's read and find out.

J: I hope he does. It isn't nice for a wolf to eat a pig, do you think?

S: Maybe he feels that he has to eat something to live.

J: Oh, look, now he's going to get that second pig, I'll bet, isn't he?

S: Probably.

J: And he does. Oh boy.

S: Near the end of this book, the wolf says that he was "framed." What does that mean?

J: I think it means that he probably thinks he didn't do anything wrong, doesn't it?

S: Yes. Jessica, do you think that the wolf in this book was "framed" like he said that he was?

J: I don't think so. He really did eat those little pigs, but he had to have something to eat, I guess. He probably was pretty hungry. I really like that picture at the end of the book showing him in jail. I hope that he gets out since he had to eat something after all.

S: You don't think that he should be punished for what he did?

J: No, he was just hungry.

S: Do you believe the wolf's version of the story of the three little pigs?

J: Yes, I guess so.

S: Do you think that this book probably is real or made up?

J: I think that it's probably real because a wolf could really eat a pig.

S: What did you like best about this book?

J: I liked everything about it—especially how the wolf got to tell what really happened and how he had to eat those pigs.

S: I'm glad that you liked the book so much.

J: I really, really did!

Predictable Books

Predictable books usually are a very important part of an emergent whole language program. They may be used in shared book experiences (described later). However, they also are equally useful in small-group, partner, or individual reading. Predictable books are very useful for several reasons. They allow children to predict (guess) what will happen next in a book, thereby encouraging participation. They also are very easy to read because of the predictable language patterns, thereby providing concrete motivation especially to the children who need it the most.

Predictability can take many different forms. A very common form is through the use of repeated catch phrases such as, "Brown Bear, brown bear, what do you see? I see a yellow duck looking at me" from *Brown bear, brown bear, what do you see?* by Bill Martin, Jr. (New York: Holt, Rinehart and Winston, 1967). Predictable rhyme enables children to fill in words as in the book *Fox in sox* by Dr. Seuss (New York: Random House, 1965). Cumulative patterns also contribute to predictability with new events being added with each episode, as in the book *I know an old lady who swallowed a fly* by Nadine Westcott (Boston: Little, Brown, 1980). Conversation also can contribute to predictability as in *The three bears* by Paul Galdone (New York: Seabury Press, 1972).

All books become somewhat predictable as children become familiar with them, so repeated readings of a trade book makes it predictable at least to an extent. Since fairy tales may be familiar to many (but not all) children, many of them are predictable. Books that have familiar sequences such as the days of the week, months of the year, letters of the alphabet, and numbers are usually predictable to many children. Trade books also become familiar if they have good plots and familiar topics.

Books in which pictures exactly match the text usually are predictable to children, especially if all the children in the group can easily see the pictures in the book being read. Today some publishers are publishing simple trade books for young children that are very predictable and therefore easy to read. One publisher of very useful simple trade books is **Rigby.**

As stated earlier, predictable books are excellent for emerging and beginning readers because they enable a child's first experiences with reading to be satisfying and enjoyable with only a limited degree of effort. Here are some guidelines for using predictable books in any early whole language programs:

- Choose trade books to read aloud that you enjoy. Your positive attitude is important and will encourage your children to actively participate in the reading.
- Begin with books that have easily learned patterns, such as *Brown bear, brown bear, what do you see?* and gradually progress to books with a somewhat more complex structure, such as *Chicken soup with rice* by Maurice Sendak (New York: Harper & Row Publishers, 1962).
- Read the title and show the picture on the cover of the book to the children and ask "What do you think this book might be about?" You should encourage the children to use the title and picture to make the predictions.
- Read the book aloud to the children. When you come to a predictable line, use your voice and hands to encourage the children to read aloud with you.
- Allow the story lines and rhymes to carry the meaning. If you stop at various points in a predictable book, you may interrupt the flow of language and repetitive patterns, thus damaging the potential value of the book.

It is important for children as young as the age of three or four, depending on their ability, always to read the title, author, and illustrator of each book, including predictable books, before beginning to read or "pretend read" a book. Young children should get into the habit of doing this. It also is important to them to make predictions about the book content from the title. Such predictions will greatly add to their comprehension of the book. Here is an example of this activity before a first-grade child named Ray read the picture storybook *I know an old lady who swallowed a fly* (by Nadine Westcott) aloud to his reading partner Beth:

RAY: I'm going to read this book right now, Beth. See the name of it. It is called I know an old lady who swallowed a *fly*. I guess that it's going to be a make-believe story because who'd want to eat a fly?

BETH: Boy, I guess. I wouldn't want to eat a fly, all right. I wonder why she swallowed a fly. Maybe it just flew in her mouth when she had it open to talk. I swallowed a mosquito once when I was walking and talking at the same time. Oh, yuk.

RAY: I'm going to read it right now, and you can help me when I can't figure out a word.

BETH: Oh, Ray, remember you have to read the author's name and the illustrator's name before you begin to read the book.

RAY: Oh, I forgot. I'm glad you remembered. Look. The author's name is Na . . . . What is it, Beth?

BETH: I think it's Nadine or Nadden or something. I don't know. I never heard of any of those names. She drew the pictures for the book too. Let's ask Mr. Marino how it's said later. I want to read the book now.

RAY: So do I. We'll ask him later.

Here is a list of well-known predictable trade books that you may want to consider reading to your emerging and early readers or encourage them to read independently. Although they are integral to a whole language early literacy program, they also are equally valuable in other early reading programs such as the basal reading approach, a phonic approach, or a combination approach. Indeed, they are very commonly used in the Reading Recovery Program, an early intervention program for first-children with special reading needs.

Partial List of Useful Predictable Books

Aardema, V. (1981). *Bringing the rain to Kapiti Plain*. New York: Dial Books.

Aardema, V. (1975). *Why mosquitoes buzz in people's ears*. New York: Dutton.

Ahberg, J. A. (1978). *Each peach pear plum*. New York: Viking.

Arno, E. (1970). *The gingerbread man*. New York: Scholastic.

Aruego, J., & Dewey, A. (1989). *Five little ducks*. New York: Crown Publishers.

Asch, F. (1982). *Happy birthday, moon*. New York: Scholastic.

Bonn, R. (1961). *I know an old lady*. New York: Scholastic

Brown, M. W. (1942). *Runaway bunny*. New York: Harper & Row.

Cameron, P. (1961). *I can't said the ant*. New York: Coward, McCann & Geoghegan.

Carle, E. (1977). *The grouchy ladybug*. New York: Crowell.

Carle, E. (1984). *The very busy spider*. New York: Philomel.

Carle, E. (1979). *The very hungry caterpillar*. New York: Collins.

Cowley, J. (1986). *Greedy cat*. Welllington, New Zealand. New York: Richard C. Owen (distributor).

de Paola, T. (1978). *Pancakes for breakfast*. New York: Harcourt Brace Jovanovich.

de Regniers, B. S. (1967). *The day everybody cried*. New York: Viking.

de Regniers, B. S. (1968). *Willy O'Dwyer jumped in the fire*. New York: Atheneum.

Eastman, P. D. (1960). *Are you my mother?* New York: Random House.

Elting, M., & Folsom, M. (1980). *Q is the duck*. New York: Clarion.

Emberly, B. (1967). *Drummer Hoff*. Englewood Cliffs, NJ: Prentice-Hall.

Flack, M. (1932). *Ask Mr. Bear*. New York: Macmillan.

Fleming, D. (1993). *In the small, small pond*. New York: Henry Holt & Company.

Galdone, P. (1975). *Henny penny*. New York: Houghton Mifflin.

Galdone, P. (1973). *Little red hen*. New York: Scholastic.

Galdone, P. (1974). *Little red ridinghood*. New York: McGraw-Hill.

Galdone, P. (1975). *The gingerbread boy*. New York: Seabury.

Galdone, P. (1972). *The three bears*. New York: Scholastic.

Galdone, P. (1973). *The three billy goats gruff*. New York: Seabury.

Galdone, P. (1970). *The three little pigs*. New York: Seabury.

Guarino, D. (1989). *Is your mama a llama?* New York: Scholastic.

Hoberman, M. A. (1978). *A house is a house for me*. New York: Scholastic.

Hutchins, P. (1972). *Goodnight, owl!* New York: Macmillan.

Kasza, K. (1987). *The wolf's chicken stew*. New York: Putnam.

Keats, E. J. (1971). *Over in the meadow*. New York: Scholastic.

Krause, R. (1970). *Whose mouse are you?* New York: Macmillan.

Lobel, A. (1984). *The rose in my garden*. New York: Greenwillow.

Mack, S. (1974). *10 bears in my bed*. New York: Pantheon.

Mayer, M. (1975). *What do you do with a kangaroo?* New York: Scholastic.

McGovern, A. (1967). *Too much noise*. Boston: Houghton Mifflin.

Neitzel, S. (1989). *The jacket I wear in the snow*. New York: Greenwillow. (This book has the same pattern as *This is the house that Jack built*.)

Piper, W. (1954). *The little engine that could.* New York: Platt & Munk.

Poluskin, M. (1978). *Mother, mother I want another.* New York: Crown.

Rosen, M. (1989). *We're going on a bear hunt.* New York: McElderry.

Roy, R. (1980). *The three ducks went wandering.* New York: Scholastic.

Scheer, J., & Bileck, M. (1964). *Rain makes applesauce.* New York: Holiday House.

Seuss, Dr. (1965). *Fox in sox.* New York: Random House.

Seuss, Dr. (1960). *Green eggs and ham.* New York: Random House.

Seuss, Dr. (1940). *Horton hatches an egg.* New York: Random House.

Shaw, C. (1947). *It looked like spilt milk.* New York: Harper & Row.

Slobodkina, E. (1940). *Caps for sale.* New York: Scholastic.

Stevens, J. (1985). *The house that Jack built.* New York: Holiday House.

Tolstoy, A. (1968). *The great big enormous turnip.* New York: Franklin Watts.

Van Allsburg, C. (1987). *The Z was zapped.* Boston: Houghton Mifflin.

Weber, B. (1966). *"You look ridiculous," said the rhinoceros to the hippopotamus.* Boston: Houghton Mifflin.

Westcott, N. (1980). *I know an old lady who swallowed a fly.* Boston: Little, Brown & Company.

Wildsmith, Brian (1972). *The twelve days of Christmas.* New York: Franklin Watts.

Williams, L. (1986). *The little old lady who was not afraid of anything.* New York: Harper Collins.

Wood, Audrey. (1984). *The napping house.* San Diego: Harcourt Brace Jovanovich.

Zemach, Margot. (1965) *The teeny tiny woman.* New York: Scholastic.

Big Books (Oversized Books)

Big books are an essential part of an emergent literacy whole language program. Although they are valuable in any emergent literacy program, they have been the most often identified with whole language classrooms. Big books, which are sometimes called *oversized books,* are especially helpful in *shared book experiences* as that activity is described later in this chapter. A form of oversized books was used as part of a basal reader series in the 1930s and 1940s. However, they generally are considered to be contemporary.

Big books are oversized books that measure from 14″ × 20″ up to 24″ × 30″. They are appropriate for use from the preschool level through about the third-grade level. Because they are used in small- to large-group settings, active involvement by the group always should be encouraged. When using a big book, the teacher should place it on an easel, as it is very difficult to easily handle otherwise, and because an easel makes the print and pictures easily visible for the children.

Holdaway (1979) wrote that big books are especially useful because the enlarged print and pictures in these oversized books help children to become involved with concepts about books, print, and the meaning of text. He stated that:

> Reading to a group of children in school has little instructional value simply because the print cannot be seen, shared, and discussed. The parent is able to "display the skill in purposeful use" and at the same time keep before the [child's] attention the fact that the process is print-stimulated. Teachers can do the same by using enlarged print for the experience of listening to stories and participating in all aspects of reading (pp. 64–65).

Big books are effective because children need, benefit from, and enjoy repetition. Because the print and format are large in big books, children can easily participate in a sharing session. They also can recognize that pictures may be somewhat different in a smaller version of the book, but the words are the same but just smaller in size. Running your hand under each word, pointing to the white spaces (word boundaries), stressing unique words, pointing out the differences between letters and words, and demonstrating left-to-right progression probably are easier for young children to grasp while looking at a large book in comparison to a typical picture storybook.

As stated, big books are very effective mainly because of their size. As the teacher reads the page aloud and tracks the print from left to right across the page, children are aware that books are for reading and where to begin reading on a page. They also learn to differentiate between pictures and print. The connection is made that the oral language that they hear from their teacher is being read from print on each page. Since big books are large, it is easy for children to see the point on each page at which reading begins. Although many big books are predictable, not all of them are. Indeed, some of them are just large in size with no predictability. You can locate interesting informational big books on topics such as dinosaurs, a topic of great interest to young people. These books, of course, are not predictable. In many cases, small-sized copies of big books also are available as well as cassette tapes of a professional reading the book aloud. You also can make your own cassette tape of yourself reading a big book if you wish. Some of the commercial tapes are read at too rapid a rate for young children to keep up, especially if the child is not a fluent beginning reader. It is recommended that the teacher read a big book aloud several times to a class or a small group and then encourage children to read a small copy independently or with a partner. The child also can follow along in the small copy while he or she listens to the cassette.

In addition, big books can be used with groups for several days if children are enjoying them. They can be placed on the chart easel or some other convenient place after the actual sharing session with them. Individuals or small groups also can "play school" with them and read them to each other. Any trade book, certainly including a big book, should be read a number of times to children or read independently by themselves as this rereading helps them gain very important reading fluency and a feeling of success. Probably one of the most common errors a parent, preschool teacher, kindergarten teacher, or first-grade teacher makes is to read any type of book only once to a child or to encourage the child to read a book only once. **Repeated readings of all trade books are extremely important at both the emergent literacy and beginning literacy stages.**

The Wright Group was one of the first publishing companies to publish big books for shared reading. *Mrs. Wishy Washy* (Rigby Education, 1984) is probably one of their most popular books.

The Shared Book Experience

A very good way to help students gain concepts about print (for example, that words are made up of letters, sentences are made up of words, reading goes left to right and top to bottom, and other important understandings) is the *shared book experience.* A shared book experience is modeled on the bedtime story reading or lap reading in which a family member or friend reads to a child. Through observation and interaction the child discovers the purpose of print, the joy and satisfaction provided by books, and the basic concepts about print (Holdaway, 1979).

A shared book experience can effectively include the big books just described. An emergent literacy teacher also can use an opaque projector or an overhead projector and transparencies or carefully print parts of the book on chart paper or the chalkboard.

Before reading a big book or one of its variations in a shared reading experience, you should introduce the title, author, and illustrator and ask students to make predictions about the book content from the title and possibly some of the pictures. During this introduction, the teacher can also access (activate) prior knowledge and set purposes for reading. The purpose could be to enjoy hearing the book or to learn more about the story line or characters. As the teacher reads, he or she should glide his or her hand under the words so that the children can learn or review the concept that print moves from left to right and begin to understand that printed words have oral equivalents. Although the shared book reading should be interactive, with opportunities for children to make predictions, ask questions, or make comments, the story line should not be interrupted extensively. Punctuation marks and spelling conventions also can be discussed informally, if this does not interrupt the story line too greatly.

On a second shared reading experience, children can read aloud with you by reading refrains and by repeating familiar phrases, sentences, and words. In subsequent shared readings, point to each word or let your hand glide under the words in left-to-right progression.

You also can use one of the following strategies as you conduct a shared reading experience (Heald-Taylor, 1987):

- Read the story and encourage the children to read the refrain.
- Read one line of text at a time, and have the children repeat in unison first along with you and then alone as a group.
- Read most of each sentence, and pause for the children to fill in the missing word.
- Let the children read the text in unison, first with your help and then without it.

After one or several shared book experiences with a big book or an alternative, some follow-up activities in which children may engage are as follows:

- Read either the big book or its regular-sized counterpart individually, to a partner, or to a small group of children.
- Draw an illustration related to the big book.
- Look at another related book.
- Look at related CD-ROM disks, videotapes, films, or pictures.
- Have children write their own related story using invented spelling and drawings.
- Have the children dramatize or formulate a role play from the book.
- Encourage children to construct a simple puppet that is related to the book. (Chapter 5 provides many ideas for constructing various types of puppets.)
- Have the children respond to the material through art.
- Have the children write a personal version of the book.

You can periodically introduce other repetitive selections for a shared book experience. However, the shared book experience need not always be based on books. It also can be based on poems, rhymes, songs, or jump rope chants. These can be written in book form, on chart paper, or on the chalkboard.

Holdaway (1984) has suggested other shared reading experiences that you may want to consider. These activities are designed for children who are emerging into reading:

- *Tune In.* Write a well-liked but brief poem, song, or nursery rhyme on chart paper or the chalkboard and read, sing, or dramatize it yourself or with the class in unison. Alternatively, parts may be assigned.

- *Old Favorite.* Share a favorite tale in a big book or other format that can be read by the entire class.
- *Learning about Language.* Present a skill that may be related to the old favorite and may relate to the concept of word or sentence, alphabet knowledge, or beginning letter-sound relationships. For example, when reading the book *Duncan, the dancing duck* by Sydney Hoff (New York: Clarion Books, 1994), you might want to emphasize that this book contains many words that begin with the sound of /d/ such as is heard in the name Duncan. In addition, children may learn some common sight words such as *the* and *and* from this book. You can also have children predict (guess) words from a book that you have masked (covered with some type of opaque tape). Then unmask each word after the children have predicted it to determine whether or not they made a correct prediction. This very useful strategy helps young children to learn to use semantic (meaning) cues effectively. You can also use a shared book experience to discuss capital and lowercase letters and punctuation marks such as periods, commas, question marks, exclamation points, and quotation marks.

- *New Story.* You can use a new book in another shared experience one or several days later.
- *Independent Reading and Activity.* Students should be given a choice of follow-up activities. Some of these could be listening to a musical version of the book or viewing a videotape of the book.

A C T I V I T Y

Making a Big Book

Either the teacher or the class can make their own big books. Such a book can be an oversized copy of any picture storybook or simple informational book that the class has really enjoyed or a version of a class-dictated or class-written language-experience book. (**Note:** The language-experience approach is described later in this chapter.)

Here is one way that you and/or your class can make a big book:

- *Selections.* Make big books from selections that are fairly short and have repetitive language.
- *Format for the Book.* There are several different formats you can select.
  - Replica Book—an exact copy of the original
  - Different Illustrations—copy the text and let the children create new illustrations
  - Child-Composed Book—Here you can use a form of the book to create a new version. For example, you could create the big book *White dog, white dog, what do you see?* from the original book *Brown bear, brown bear, what do you see?* by Bill Martin, Jr.
- Write the text of the book. Write one or two sentences of the book on chart paper (about 12″ × 18″). For easy reading, put these sentences at the top of the page so that the children can see them easily. Include a title, author, and illustrator page.
- Leave at least three-fourths of the page available for illustrations.
- Bind the book by attaching the pages with heavy duty staples or preferably punching three holes and using metal rings to hold the book together.
- Protect the book by laminating at least the cover. Put an envelope in the back so that children can check the big book out to take home to read to their families and friends.

Below is an illustration of this type of big book.

Caps for Sale

ACTIVITY

Here is another way that you and/or your class can make a big book. These are the directions for this version:

Materials Needed
- two pieces of tagboard (14″ × 20″ to 20″ × 20″)
- 10 pieces or more of tagboard or chart paper of the same size as the tagboard used for the cover that will be used for the pages in the book
- 6 loose-leaf rings
- hole punch

Directions
- Punch three sets of holes in top, middle, and bottom of the cover and paper that are to make up the book
- Insert a loose-leaf ring in each hole. The big book should have a minimum of about ten pages.
- Print should be about 2 inches high.

Here is an illustration of this version of a big book:

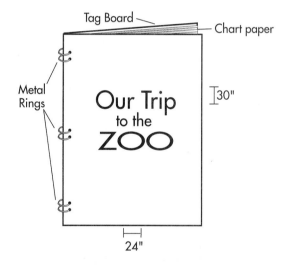

Note: Patterns for big book covers are found in the following teacher resource book:

Evans, J., Morgan K., & Moore, J. (1989). *Making big books with children.* Monterey, CA: Evan-Moor.

Wordless (Textless) Books

Wordless (textless) books are often identified with whole language. However, as in the case of many of the strategies and materials included in this chapter, they are equally useful in traditional reading programs as well. Wordless books are sometimes called textless books, although the former is the more common name.

Wordless books have definite story lines, but they use no words. Instead, the story is carried entirely by the pictures that comprise the book. Obviously, the child formulates the story by interpreting the pictures, many of which may be quite intricate. Wordless books are believed by many to be the most appropriate for very young children and are often thought of as just picture books. However, this is not the case, and they are designed for children at least three years of age. Indeed, some wordless books are applicable for students who are in the intermediate grades and beyond if they are significantly disabled in reading. You may be surprised that some of them even appeal to adults (Abrahamson, 1981).

Wordless books are exceptionally good in developing ability in oral language, picture interpretation, beginning story structure, creativity, and imagination. They also are very motivating for children, since they can use their innate creativity to formulate their own version of a book instead of merely reading an author's words.

Here is one procedure that you can follow in using wordless books in an early literacy program:

- Introduce the wordless book to a small group or to the entire class. Since these books are unique in that they contain no words, illustrate to the children how they will have to use their own creative storytelling skills while interpreting them.
- Guide the children through the book, encouraging them to interpret each picture and to predict what may happen next. You also should remind children of the basic story line of the book in order to help them successfully generate a reasonable story as they go along.
- Go through the wordless book several times, asking children to tell the story each time that the book is interpreted.

Since children enjoy telling stories again and again to accompany these interesting books, teachers can use special note paper with sticky backs (Post-its™) for writing stories in wordless books. Children stick a Post-it™ to each page of the wordless book so that their written text accompanies the pictures.

In another variation, have the children tape record their own interpretation of the book. Then place the wordless books and these tapes in the listening center for other children to listen to during free time.

You also can use an opaque projector to magnify each picture to encourage more group participation during the different retellings.

Many of the wordless books appeal greatly to children. For example, *Pancakes for breakfast* (de Paola, 1978) is very well liked by both preschoolers and older children. It illustrates the efforts of a little old woman as she makes pancakes. The series of wordless books about the dog Carl (*Good dog, Carl* by Day, 1985) are also highly motivating to young children, as is the book *Peter Spier's rain* (Spier, 1977).

Here is a fairly comprehensive list of wordless books that can be used effectively with young children for all of the purposes described above.

List of Wordless (Textless) Books

Alexander, M. (1968). *Out! Out! Out!* New York: Dial Press.

Alexander, M. (1970). *Bobo's dream.* New York: Dial Press.

Aruego, J. (1971). *Look what I can do.* New York: Scribners.

Day, A. (1985). *Good dog, Carl.* New York: Scholastic.

de Groat, D. (1977). *Alligator's toothache.* New York: Crown Books.

de Paola, T. (1978). *Pancakes for breakfast.* San Diego: Harcourt Brace Jovanovich.

Goodall, J. (1988). *Little red riding hood.* New York: McElderry Books.

Goodall, J. (1970). *Jacko.* New York: Harcourt Brace Jovanovich.

Hoban, T. (1988). *Look! Look! Look!* New York: Greenwillow.

Hoban, T. (1972). *Push—pull, empty—full.* New York: Macmillan.

Hoban, T. (1980). *Take another look.* New York: Greenwillow Books.

Hutchins, P. (1968). *Rosie's walk.* New York: Macmillan.

Keats, E. (1973). *Skates.* New York: Franklin Watts.

Mayer, M. (1967). *A boy, a dog, and a frog.* New York: Dial Press.

Mayer, M. (1974). *Frog goes to dinner.* New York: Dial Press.

Mayer, M. (1977). *Oops.* New York: Dial Press.

McCulley, E. (1985). *First snow.* New York: Harper & Row.

McCulley, E. (1984). *Picnic.* New York: Harper & Row.

McCulley, E. (1988). *New baby.* New York: Harper & Row.

Oxenbury, H. (1982). *Good night, good morning.* New York: Dial Press.

Spier, P. (1982). *Peter Spier's rain.* New York: Doubleday.

Turkle, B. (1976). *Deep in the forest.* New York: Dutton.

Ward, L. (1973). *The silver pony.* Boston: Houghton Mifflin.

Weisner, D. (1991). *Tuesday.* New York: Clarion.

Wezel, P. (1964). *The good bird.* New York: Harper & Row.

Winter, P. (1976). *The bear and the fly.* New York: Crown.

Reading Reenactment

A *reading reenactment* is a very valuable emergent literacy strategy that is commonly used in whole language programs, although it is equally as useful in any early literacy program. A child participates in a reading reenactment when the child retells the contents of a trade book as though he or she were actually reading it him or herself. In a sense it is a form of "pretend reading" and should be valued as a prelude to actual beginning reading. Children are actually trying out a behavior that they have seen around them and want to emulate.

When I was teaching an undergraduate early literacy course, I told the class that a reading reenactment can be called "reading in its emerging sense" and that it should be encouraged. Subsequently, one of my students with a four-year-old daughter told her husband that I said that "pretend reading" actually is reading. Therefore, she correctly said that Allison could read. Unfortunately, her husband did not agree and said that Allison could *not* read. They then had an argument and didn't talk to each other for several days! However, despite what her father believed, Allison really was "reading" when she engaged in reading reenactments.

Having books available both at school and at home encourages reading reenactments, as does an older sibling "playing school" with the young child. After reading a book aloud, teachers can ask children to "read" the story again. Sulzby (1985) has classified reading reenactments in the three following ways:

- descriptive comments governed by pictures but not telling a true story
- real storytelling governed by the pictures
- real storytelling governed by the print

At the first level of reading reenactment, children comment as though the action shown in the pictures was taking place right now and comment on the pictures as though to themselves. They may skip or repeat story parts, but they are becoming familiar with handling books and at a low level translating "book talk" into oral language.

At the next level a reenactment that takes cues from pictures can be of several types. Children can use "book talk" or speech-like language in the retelling or a combination of both. Book-like reenactments include phrases from the book and story patterns that sound like the book but were not found in the original book. This demonstrates that they understand that book language is considerably different from the spoken language that they hear every day. A good example of this is children's tendency to start a reenactment with the phrase "Once upon a time" even though it may not have been in the original book. Even when the reenactment does not exactly match the original book, it often is "read" in an intonation which is "reading-like" and very different from ordinary speech.

The highest level of reading reenactment is governed by the print. At this level, young children do learn to read independently, recognize common sight words, match letters with their corresponding sounds, and comprehend what they read. At this level children do not need extensive correction of their miscalled words nor an emphasis on word-perfect oral or silent reading. Instead, they need acceptance of what they are doing, enthusiasm for the progress that they are making, and help when they request it. This is an example of Vygotsky's (1978) concept, mentioned both in this chapter and Chapter 1, that the child should receive encouragement and support at the present time in preparation for independence in the future.

The last two versions of a reading reenactment provide different information about children. The first of the two indicates that the child primarily uses memory while "pretend reading" the book, while the second indicates that the child is learning about the matching of print and oral language. Either behavior is acceptable and should be encouraged, but both can be a source of frustration for the child if word-perfect reading is required from the beginning. It, therefore, should not be. And yes, Allison really was "reading," despite what her father believed.

Collaborative Learning

As stated earlier, *collaborative learning* is an integral aspect of whole language programs, although it also should play an important part in any early literacy program. It is obvious that collaboration is an important aspect of whole language. For example, Vygotsky (1981) has written that an adult should be a facilitator of learning by guiding experiences in a social context. The importance of collaborative learning also was represented by the principle about the philosophical foundation of whole language that states that *language and literacy must be socially constructed.*

Collaboration in whole language classrooms can take many forms. For example, the thematic unit teaching that is illustrated later in this section relies on collaboration between children as well as between teacher and children. In thematic units children work cooperatively with each other and with an adult(s) in satisfying their own formulated goals. They engage in various types of collaborative learning, including cooperative learning groups, buddy groups, literacy groups, cross-grade literacy partnerships, interest groups, and needs groups, during a unit of study in which they are actively involved in satisfying their own purposes. During a unit children should group themselves in ways that will be beneficial to them in fulfilling their own objectives. All of these collaborative groups are short-term, flexible groups that are disbanded when the purpose(s) for which they were formulated are completed.

A *cooperative learning group* usually is made up of two or three children with varying abilities in the literacy skills. The cooperative learning group normally is formulated by children themselves, and each child engages in those tasks in which she or he is able and then shares personal findings (product) with the others in the group and often the entire class. The group is child-directed, not teacher-directed, although the teacher may provide input if the children request it.

For example, if a third-grade cooperative learning group were studying the topic "wild animals of Africa," several of the children might read simple encyclopedia articles on this topic either from print or a CD-ROM disk or informational trade books about this topic. Perhaps they also could search the Internet to locate some easy-to-understand information. Better readers can provide scaffolding (support) to the children with reading difficulties. After finishing their research, the children then report to the class an oral and/or written summary of their findings. One or two children possibly could interview someone who has seen the wild animals in Africa. Any child in the group who wishes could collect pictures of these animals or perhaps could draw pictures of them. Children also could view videotapes or listen to audiotapes about the wild animals of Africa. At the conclusion of the study, all of the children share what they have learned with the class in any way in which they decide meets their own objectives.

Literacy partners also are very commonly used in whole language classrooms. *Partner reading* takes place when two children decide to be reading partners for a specified period of time. When the two children have decided together on a trade book that they both want to read and are able to read, they either push their desks or chairs together or simply sit on the floor near each other. They then each read their copy of the trade book either silently or orally depending on their purposes and preferences. When one of the children needs help either in decoding or in understanding, he or she simply asks the reading partner for help, and the other child provides the needed help. The reading partners can be children with similar or differing abilities, depending upon their needs and preferences.

Writing partners also can be used in whole language classrooms. Each writing partner can write his or her own rough draft of a story, or the initial writing draft can be a collaborative effort. In either case, the children help each other improve the rough draft in a nonthreatening, supportive writing conference by suggesting improved story structure, a more creative story line, or correct mechanics (spelling, grammar, and punctuation). As with reading partners, writing partners can be children of similar or different writing interests and abilities, depending entirely on their own preferences.

Note: Children can keep either their reading partner or their writing partner for an extended period of time or find a new literacy partner when one or both of the children think that it is desirable.

Cross-grade literacy partners also can be called *cross-age literacy partners.* In any case, the two partners obviously are not of the same age or grade. Instead, they are an older and a younger child who work together on all or some of the literacy skills. There are many variations of this type of collaboration. The partners can be composed of an older child who has literacy problems teamed with a young child with or without literacy difficulties. They can be two children of comparable abilities but of different grade levels. I believe that there might be unique advantages to partnering an older child who has literacy difficulties with a younger child either with or without such problems. For example, if a disabled reader in fourth grade had a first-grade child who was an average reader as his reading partner, he might choose to read the trade book *Frog and toad together* by Arnold Lobel (1972. New York: Harper & Row). Since this is a very easy-to-read chapter book, the fourth-grader should experience success in reading it, thus enhancing his self-esteem about reading. The younger child in turn has a good reading model to emulate, so the experience is a positive reinforcement for both children.

Interest and *needs groups* are similar in that they both should be formulated by the children themselves depending upon their interests and needs. Of course, the teacher may want to have some input into the selection of the needs groups, with much less, if any, input into formulation of the interest groups. Both of these groups are short-term, flexible groups that are disbanded when the interest or need that the group was formulated to fulfill is satisfied. As an example, if Ms. Beifuss, a second-grade teacher, determined that four of her children were still weak in applying semantic (meaning) cues while reading informational books on their level, she would plan a lesson to model this type of cue using appropriate informational books. This *mini-lesson* would be presented only to those children who had demonstrated a lack of this important reading skill.

Note: *Mini-lessons* are very common in whole language classrooms. They are very brief instruction including modeling, scaffolding for (supporting of) children, and demonstrations that are designed to present one or several very important reading, writing, or spelling skill(s). Each mini-lesson is presented only to the children that specifically need the literacy skill that the mini-lesson is designed to teach. It lasts only as long as is required to help the children gain competency in the literacy skill to which that mini-lesson was devoted. Usually a mini-lesson lasts only about five to seven minutes.

In summary, collaborative learning is very much identified with whole language classrooms and should be employed in them whenever and wherever possible. In fact, whole language cannot truly exist apart from constructive collaboration of all types between children and between teacher and children.

Message Boards and Mailboxes

Message boards and *mailboxes* are valuable in a whole language classroom, where children should experience the functional, interactive nature of writing. Both are helpful in emphasizing the social nature of written language, while engaging students in authentic written exchanges. Thus, they exemplify both the *social* and *authentic* aspects of the whole language philosophy.

A centrally located bulletin board can be designed as the class message board. A kindergarten or primary teacher also can set up class mailboxes and provide each child with an assigned space for his or her mailbox. Mailboxes can be constructed from cardboard dividers that are purchased in a discount or department store or clean empty milk or juice cartons that are stapled together.

When children enter a classroom at the beginning of the school year, they should find a note that the teacher has left for each of them on the message board, or the teacher should place a short personal letter in each mail slot. Teachers can informally discuss the notes and letters that children have received at home in the past, and then children and teacher together decide exactly how the message board and mailboxes will operate in the classroom. It is very important for the children to have much input in this discussion. The teacher can either include letter writing as one choice during the writing workshop time, or children can write letters at any free time during the school day. Students should be cautioned that all messages must be signed and that they must consider children's personal feelings so that no one gets hurt. If inappropriate messages or letters are sent, the teacher should close either the message board or the mailboxes for a short time so that the children are reminded of the rules that govern either of them.

Message boards or mailboxes are one way that teachers can informally keep in contact with children in a large classroom. Each child needs to know that he or she is a valued member of the class, and personal messages both from the teacher and from classmates helps children to remember this. Various children can be responsible for seeing that the message board and mailboxes are stocked with appropriate writing supplies such as notebook paper, personalized stationery that each child has made containing a personal emblem such as his or her picture, and envelopes.

Me Boxes

Me Boxes are collections of items that represent aspects of their owner—their interests, families, prior knowledge, and personal experiences. When children have the opportunity to share aspects of their own life, they can more effectively read and write material that reflect their experiences.

To begin this experience, the teacher should bring a small box filled with her or his personal items to share during the first week of class. The items should represent the teacher's unique interests, abilities, family, hobbies, trips, or any mementos that have a special significance. The number of items that the teacher brings should be fairly small for a class of young children. Then the teacher takes each item out of the Me Box and talks about its significance for her or him. At the bottom of the Me Box the teacher should include a short story or description that describes the items and experiences shared.

Next, the teacher asks the children to bring their own Me Boxes to school. Shoe boxes work well for a Me Box because they are easy to obtain and to handle. Each child will share his or her Me Box with the entire class or a small group of children. This sharing can take several days. It is very important that the teacher and other pupils develop some understanding about and appreciation for the life of each of the children in the class. After the Me Boxes are shared, have each child write a story or description about the items in the Me Box. Although all of the items in the Me Box do not have to be included in this story or description, the closer the match between the items and the text, the more predictable is the material in the story or description. After the children have finished their writing, they can share it with the class. The Me Boxes can be displayed with the writing located at the bottom of each box. All of the children in the class should be encouraged to examine the items in each Me Box and then read the accompanying story or description.

Here is an example of a story that accompanied a Me Box that was compiled by a third-grade girl.

> This is about me
> My name is Sue Ellen.
> I am in the third grade and I really like Beanie Babies. I have 37 of them now.
> I like to use the computer too a whole lot.
> I have a great family with a mother and two younger sisters.
> I like to swim and play basketball too.

Tell Me Something

Another opportunity for social exchange in a primary-grade whole language classroom is *tell me something,* an interesting strategy that can take place with a *literacy partner.* When this strategy is used in a whole language classroom, the teacher describes several reading selections to the class and asks each child to select one that she or he would like to read for pleasure or information. Then each child finds a partner who has selected the same reading selection, and they then read the selection together. They also should decide before beginning to read how much of the selection that they each will read before stopping to tell each other something about it.

During the stopping points in the reading each child may discuss what he or she just read, make a prediction about what may happen next in the material, describe any difficulty that she or he has in understanding the material, or tell how the material may relate to her or his own life. The primary-grade teacher must model this strategy many times before having the children try it independently. Once in a while the children should meet as a group to comment on their responses so that the teacher may suggest simple alternative prediction or comprehension strategies.

Talking about Reading

Since reading is a conversation between an author and reader (Goodman, 1986), the interaction that takes place as readers construct meaning consists of responses that are similar to the exchanges that occur when people are talking together. Such exchanges consist of predicting, agreeing with, disagreeing with, questioning, and summarizing, among others. The strategy of *talking about reading* is designed to help children become more active participants in the reading process by emphasizing the communication strengths that they have as speakers.

When this strategy is used, the primary-grade teacher introduces the characteristics of oral conversation. This discussion can include some items about how people interact with each other when they are talking together. Then the teacher and children summarize the items and write them on the chalkboard or on an overhead transparency. Each child independently or with a reading partner selects a reading selection from two or three choices. Before this time the teacher has cut each type of material into columns with enough space between them so that children can write in the margins while they are reading. In most cases the reading material should be very brief for primary-grade children.

While the children are reading the material independently or with their literacy partner, they should interact with the author's ideas by writing brief notes in the margin alongside the material. As an example, some third-grade children wrote these notes when they read a brief informational item about the tropical rain forest:

"People shouldn't cut it down so much."

"I would never want to go to a rain forest. It's too hot there."

"I didn't know that the rain forest was that important."

"It would be fun to visit a rain forest sometime."

Afterward, the children bring their notes to the whole class or to a small group and discuss them. Better writers may later want to expand some of their comments by writing a more extensive account of what they read and their reactions to it.

Bookmarks

As you are aware, the whole language philosophy emphasizes a child's interaction with print and the fact that reading always should be an act of constructing meaning. Good readers constantly should monitor their comprehension (know whether or not they are understanding and what they should do if they are not), ask questions while they read, and use their prior knowledge to help them understand the material. Of course, every good reader should employ all of these strategies no matter what reading approach is found in the classroom.

Using *bookmarks* is a strategy that encourages children to write their responses on small pieces of paper as they read. Children can use their bookmarks to write down difficulties that they have while reading and then keep on reading knowing that they will have the opportunity to talk about these reading difficulties later either with the teacher or with a classmate(s).

To use this strategy the teacher cuts notebook paper, construction paper, or tagboard into strips about two inches wide. Then the teacher should model this strategy by showing the children his or her own responses to reading on bookmark(s). Next, each child independently or with a reading partner should be given several bookmarks to use while reading material that she or he has selected. If the children use more than one bookmark per selection, they can staple them together later. The teacher must give the child or the two reading partners some uninterrupted time to read selected material and write their responses, comments, and questions about the reading on the bookmark(s).

Later, if they wish, the children can share their responses on the bookmark(s) with the teacher, a small group, or the entire class. If you wish, children can hand them in so that you can note what strategies they may need help with, not for grading them in any formal way. The teacher can also read the bookmarks thinking about answering the questions or comments directly on the bookmarks if she or he wishes.

Shown is an example of a bookmark that was written by a second-grade child named Fiona as she read the trade book *First grade takes a test* by Miriam Cohen (1980. NY: Dell Publishing Company).

First Grade
Takes a test
Why do rabbits
eat lettuce?
I don't under-
stand why Anna
had to leave.
Why did all the
Kids get
so mad?
Did they like
taking the test,
or not?
What did the
test tell
anyway?
I'm glad
that Anna
got to
come back.

The Book Talk

When a child is going to select a book to read independently or with a reading partner, he or she often mainly relies on other children for recommendations. Therefore, *book talks* can be used in primary-grade whole language classrooms to call attention to good books that other children may want to read for pleasure or information. Book talks should take place informally on a regular basis in classrooms in which children are surrounded by good literature of all kinds, and class time probably also should be given for more regularly scheduled formal book talks.

The primary-grade whole language teacher should introduce book talks with his or her own demonstrations from different genres. A book talk may consist of any of the following:

- a retelling of some of the main events, being sure not to include the ending
- an account of the child's favorite part of the book
- an account of the child's favorite character in the book and her or his reasons for choosing this character
- how the book may have changed the child's thinking of life
- how the book is alike or different from other books by this author
- why the child would or would not want to read another book by the same author

The teacher should explain why it is important for children to give book talks to their classmates. Children can give book talks on a regular basis after they have finished reading a book, either to a small group or to the entire class, depending upon the time restraints of that classroom. If the child wishes to do so, she or he can write brief notes about what she or he is going to say during the book talk, and a child also can make advertising posters for the book or put on a costume that represents her or his favorite character in the book.

Note: The message board, mailbox, me box, and bookmark strategies were adapted from the book *Whole language: Getting started . . . moving forward* by Linda K. Crofton (Katonah, NY: Richard C. Owen Publishers, 1991).

Thematic Unit Teaching

Thematic unit teaching undoubtedly is the cornerstone of every whole language classroom. The vast majority of the instruction and learning that occurs in a whole language classroom takes place through thematic units that are child-selected and child-driven. Dewey (1966) was primarily responsible for bringing the concept of an interdisciplinary approach to teaching to the attention of educators. The interdisciplinary approach presents skills from all content areas within the context of the unit topic that is being studied.

The themes that are studied at school should be derived from children's real-life experiences and should be topics that they really are interested in studying. Indeed, when the true whole language philosophy is followed, the children are totally responsible for selecting all of the themes that are to be studied in their classroom. In reality, however, the teacher usually must provide some input into the selection by attempting to guide the children's choice in a nonthreatening, supportive way. The learning experiences in thematic unit teaching also should be socially interactive and process-, not product-oriented. In addition, children also must be given sufficient time to explore the varied materials that are included in the theme. For example, if a second-grade class is studying the zoo theme, if possible the children should visit a zoo, have a zookeeper come to the class as a resource person, look at videotapes of zoo animals, talk about zoos, write about zoos and zoo animals, solve arithmetic problems that are related in some way to zoos, participate in art projects about zoos, and sing songs related to zoos.

Thematic unit teaching in a whole language classroom usually takes one or two forms. The unit normally is based either on the content area of social studies or science or on one of the following: one trade book, the trade books written by one author, or one genre of literature such as poetry that is appropriate for that grade level. In kindergarten or the primary grades most typically the unit is based on social studies or science.

When a unit is entirely based on literature, it is called literature-based instruction and also often features the following: reader response to literature, "read-alouds" in which teachers read aloud to students throughout the school day, sustained silent reading, and classroom libraries. However, all of these elements also should be found in any whole language classroom even if thematic units based on social studies and science are used. In both thematic unit instruction and literature-based instruction the literacy skills of listening, speaking, reading, and writing are integrated as much as possible throughout the school day.

Here are some possible thematic unit topics that are based on either social studies or science and may be appropriate for kindergarten and/or the primary grades:

- a dairy farm
- a grain farm
- animals that live in a zoo
- the pets that people may have
- neighborhood helpers
- community helpers
- plants that grow in the neighborhood
- healthy bodies and healthy minds
- school helpers
- tropical rain forest
- the environment
- the post office
- animals of the forest
- the veterinarian's office
- the airport
- dinosaurs
- animals

It is obvious that thematic organization has a number of advantages. Perhaps the main advantage is that it helps students make connections between listening, speaking, reading, and writing as well as between the content areas of social studies, science, arithmetic, art, music, drama, and play. However, Routman (1991) cautioned that before the language arts are integrated with content areas, they must first be integrated with each other. She also stated that some thematic units lack depth and "are nothing more than suggested activities clustered around a central focus or topic" (p. 277). She believes that this is *correlation,* not true *integration.* She believes that in order for true integration to occur, there must be some overall concept that the unit develops with activities that support these concepts. The unit must in all cases be developed around a genuine theme or core idea. "The presidents born in February," for example, is a topic not a theme, because it does not have a unifying idea.

After young children have selected a broad theme for a unit, with the teacher's help if necessary, they also should have an integral part in planning the learning activities and experiences for the unit. You first brainstorm with them what they already know about the theme of the unit, what they want to learn, and the learning activities in which they should engage to learn what they need to

know. (This is an adaptation of the K-W-L study strategy that is explained in Chapter 5.)

Next, summarize the overall concepts that you think the unit should emphasize. For example, several overall concepts for the theme *The zoo* might be: the animals that commonly live in a zoo, how a zookeeper cares for the animals that live in a zoo, the living conditions that make a zoo a good place for wild animals and birds to live, and the ways that people can help the animals that live in a zoo to have a better life. The teacher then formulates a list of objectives. These objectives should be related to the overall concepts of the unit. The objectives also should encompass all of the curricular areas that are to be involved in the unit. Since the unit is to be interdisciplinary, objectives should be formulated for each content area.

Here are a few trade books that could be used in a unit about zoos:

- Carle, E. (1989). *Animals animals.* NY: Philomel Books. (poetry)
- Crowther, R. (1982). *A jungle jumble.* Kansas City: Children's Hallmark Edition. (wordless moveable book)
- Emberly, R. (1986). *Jungle sounds.* Boston: Little Brown. (audiotape available)
- Fox, M. (1988). *Koala Lou.* San Diego: Harcourt Brace Jovanovich.
- Freeman, D. (1954). *Beady bear.* NY: Viking Penguin.
- Galdone, P. (1972). *The three bears.* NY: Scholastic.
- Hofmann, G. (1978) *Who wants an old teddy bear?* NY: Random House.
- Kaufman, E. (1987) *Bears: an animal information book.* Los Angeles: Price/Stem/Sloan.
- Mayer, M. (1989). *What do you do with a kangaroo?* NY: Scholastic. (big book)
- Minarik, E. (1957). *Little bear.* NY: Harper & Row.
- Prelutsky, J. (1983). *Zoo doings.* NY: Greenwillow Books.
- Tafuri, N. (1988). *Junglewalk.* NY: Greenwillow Books. (wordless book)

Teacher and children together should decide on the materials and activities to be included in the unit. As stated, normally all of the content areas should be integrated into the unit as much as possible. Each reading material, activity, or experience should advance the theme of the unit. In addition, materials, activities, and experiences should promote skill/strategy development in the language arts as well as the other curricular areas. Next, list and gather materials, audiovisual aids, guest speakers, and other resources that will advance the theme. You can enlist the help of the school or public librarian in gathering resources that can be used in the unit. The reading materials, for example, that can be included in the unit are trade books of all types including informational books at various reading levels, CD-ROM disks, materials found on the Internet, textbooks, children's magazines and newspapers, and posters, among many others.

Next the teacher plans a very motivating unit opener with the children's input. This can be a trip to the zoo, a zookeeper's classroom visit bringing some zoo animals with him or her, or viewing a videotape or a film about zoo animals. The opener also might be brainstorming with students to determine which aspect of the topic they would most like to study. The actual learning experiences and activities in the unit should evolve as the children participate in it. In a whole language classroom it is not necessary or desirable for the teacher to have carefully planned each aspect of the unit. Instead, the unit should evolve depending on the needs and interests of the children as they explore it.

When the children believe they have fulfilled their objectives and decide with the teacher's help that the unit is completed, the learning experiences should be evaluated in some informal ways that reflect authentic assessment, which is also a cornerstone of the whole language philosophy, as is explained later. This type of evaluation may take the form of portfolios, simple oral or written reports summarizing what was learned, self-evaluative checklists of learning, journal writing, or teacher checklists that assess whether or not each child has met his or her own objectives for the thematic unit.

Content Area Objectives

At this point it may be helpful to consider some of the most important objectives for the different content areas that should be considered when thematic units are used in whole language classrooms. Here is a very brief list of some of the objectives for early childhood education from each of the content areas, excluding those of the language arts which are mentioned throughout this book.

Social Studies

- improving self-esteem
- learning social skills for functioning well with others, including sharing, cooperating, and communicating well
- recognizing and respecting the similarities and differences between ourselves and others
- increasing knowledge and respect for other cultures and racial groups
- using the content of social studies to improve literacy skills
- increasing the understanding of the nature of our social world through the study of simple history, geography, and economics

Science

- observing, hypothesizing, recording data, summarizing, analyzing, and drawing conclusions
- using the content of science to promote literacy development
- increasing understanding in:
  - astronomy—heavenly bodies and their characteristics
  - biological science—the study of living things
  - chemistry—materials found on the earth and the changes that occur in them
  - meteorology—weather and air
  - physics—the nature of matter and energy

Arithmetic

- handling the materials and ideas of arithmetic
- learning to classify, compare, measure, graph, count, identify, write numbers, and perform operations with numbers
- moving from dependence on the concrete to more abstract ideas
- using the vocabulary of arithmetic
- using arithmetic to enhance literacy development

Art

- being exposed to different art materials
- exploring and experimenting with various art materials
- representing personal experiences through various art forms
- expressing feelings through art
- gaining an appreciation for the different art forms
- naming and discussing the content of art: line, color, form, texture, and shape
- experiencing literacy learning in art activities

Music

- experiencing music through listening, singing, moving, playing, and creating
- being involved in and responding to music
- being exposed to different types of music—instruments, singing, various kinds of music—so that one is able to discriminate between them and develop an appreciation for varied forms of music
- expressing feelings through experiences in music
- experiencing literacy learning in music activities

Play

- role playing real-life experiences
- solving problems
- dealing with situations that require sharing and cooperating
- developing language and literacy through play

Sample Thematic Unit that Can Be Used in a Whole Language Classroom

Following is a sample thematic unit about animals for use at the primary-grade level. You can use it in its present form or modify it in any way you want in light of the needs and interests of your whole language classroom. *It should be considered only as a sample unit in keeping with the whole language philosophy.* It should not be used at all if your children do not seem interested in it. In that case, it should serve only as a model of what this type of thematic unit might look like.

A THEMATIC UNIT: ELEMENTARY KNOWLEDGE ABOUT MAMMALS

Some Factual Background Information

What Is a Mammal and What Kinds of Mammals Are There?

An animal must have the following three characteristics in order to be classified as a *mammal:*

- It must be a *vertebrate.* A vertebrate is an animal with a backbone.
- It must have a four-chambered heart and must be warm-blooded. This means that its body temperature is kept fairly steady because it is regulated by insulating body coverings of fur, hair, or blubber.
- It must give birth to live young that are nourished by milk from the mother's mammary glands. Although the duck-billed platypus and the spiny anteater are two mammals that lay eggs, their young are nourished by their mother's milk.

There are about four thousand species of mammals in the world. Mammals can be divided into three main groups: the monotremes, such as the duck-billed platypus and the spiny anteater, the marsupials, such as the kangaroo and the koala, and the placental animals, which make up most of the animal species in the world today. The *monotremes* are mammals that lay eggs, while the *marsupials* give birth to their young when they are very small, like tiny pink worms. The young then climb through the mother's fur into a pouch where they feed on milk until they are large enough to leave. However, most mammals are *placental,* which means that they carry their young inside them in a placenta in which they are nourished, kept warm, and protected. The placenta is the organ that connects the mother and baby.

The most highly developed of all animals are called *primates.* They have a large brain; keen senses of hearing, touch, and vision; and a versatile skeleton. Some examples of primates are monkeys, chimpanzees, baboons, and humans.

Rodents are the most common group of mammals in the world. Examples of rodents are rats, mice, squirrels, beavers, and porcupines. Every rodent has chisel-shaped front teeth that are very effective for gnawing.

Animals that chew cud are called *ruminants.* They chew cud as a means of digesting fibrous plant material.

Some examples of ruminants are the giraffe, white-tailed deer, elk, cow, sheep, and goat.

Mammals can be both *wild animals* and *domesticated animals.* Wild animals are bred and born to live out their lives in their natural habitat. Some wild animals are *predators* that live by killing and eating other animals, while others eat mainly plants. Some wild animals eat both flesh and vegetation. Today a number of wild animals are *endangered species,* while some have already become extinct. Animals are endangered because of too much hunting, the destruction of their native habitat such as the rain forest for the use of humans, and pollution also often caused by humans. Some examples of endangered animals are the elephant, cougar, whale, cheetah, chimpanzee, leopard, giant panda, black rhinoceros, and tiger.

Domesticated animals are bred and born to live out their lives in various types of environments that are related to humans. Most of the domesticated animals that are known today had wild animals as their ancestors.

What Kind of Foods Do Wild Animals (Mammals) Eat?

Wild animals are *carnivorous, herbivorous,* or *omnivorous.* An animal that is carnivorous eats some type of flesh on a regular basis. Some carnivorous animals are predators, while some are mainly scavengers that eat the leftovers from the kill of predators. Some examples of carnivorous animals are the lion, the leopard, the cheetah, the spotted hyena, the jackal, the wolf, the fox, the mountain lion, and the tiger. A herbivorous animal eats some type of vegetation such as leaves, grasses, fruit, berries, riverside grasses and plants, bark, twigs, hay, or grain. Some examples of herbivorous animals are the wildebeest, the zebra, the hippopotamus, the elephant, the giraffe, the kangaroo, the wallaby, the koala, the giant panda, the jackrabbit, the white-tailed deer, and various kinds of antelopes and gazelles. The koala is unique in that it only eats one type of eucalyptus leaves. An omnivorous animal eats both flesh and vegetation, depending upon what is available at that time. For example, the baboon eats plants, small mammals, birds, and bird eggs. The black bear eats berries, roots, fish, and mammals. Although the coyote hunts and eats animals, it also eats fruit if it has the opportunity. The opossum eats small animals, insects, and fruit, while the raccoon eats rodents, corn, nuts, fruits, and berries.

What Kinds of Food Do Domesticated Animals Eat?

Although the ancestry of both dogs and cats is carnivorous, today most domesticated dogs and cats eat commercially prepared dry or canned dog food or cat food. Some dogs and cats prefer a combination of dry and canned food. The typical dog food today contains both meat and vegetable products, while the typical cat food contains some combination of fish, meat, and vegetable products. However, a typical barn cat often eats the flesh of small animals like mice or the flesh of birds.

Farm animals are domesticated animals that eat a variety of different foods. For example, cattle are ruminants whose stomachs have four sections. They eat alfalfa, hay, silage (fodder such as cornstalks, hay, or straw kept in a silo), corn, or grains of various kinds. Sheep are ruminants that eat grass, hay, silage, legumes, weeds, herbs, and shrubs. Special feeds also are manufactured for sheep ranchers to feed their animals. Goats also are ruminants that feed on alfalfa or a commercially prepared feed like Sweet Feed, a combination of oats, corn, and grain. They also graze on grass and other plants and like carrots and apples as treats. Horses are vegetarians that mainly eat grass and hay. They also enjoy special feeds of oats, nuts, bran, carrots, sugar beet pulp, and barley. Small, whole apples, apple slices, and an occasional sugar cube are a special treat for a horse. Pigs (swine) often eat commercially prepared pig feed or leftovers but are not overeaters, despite their reputation.

What Is the Habitat for Wild Animals?

Wild animals live in many different kinds of places. For example, different wild animals live in such varied places as a cave in a group of rocks, a hollow log, or beneath fallen trees. They also can live in a burrow (hole) in the ground, in a hole in a hollow tree, in a treetop, or among the grasses on a forest floor. Usually a wild animal lives in a habitat that seems relatively safe from the dangers of other animals and one that is suited to its unique requirements.

For example, a hippopotamus usually spends most of its time during the day in the water with only its eyes sticking out but spends more time on land at night. A white-tailed deer lives in the grasses of a woodland floor, while a black bear often has its den beneath some fallen trees. The typical lion tries to locate its den in a group of rocks. Monkeys spend their time in treetops, while the koala makes its home among the branches of a eucalyptus (gum) tree.

What Is the Habitat for Domesticated Animals?

As you know, a number of dogs and cats live inside their owners' homes. However, some domesticated dogs and cats live outdoors all or much of the time. For example, a dog may live all of its life outside sleeping in some type of doghouse, while a barn cat lives in a barn spending a good deal of its time outside also.

Horses, cattle, sheep, goats, and pigs usually live on a farm in a barn or some other special type of dwelling or on a ranch. They also may spend much of their time outside grazing. On a ranch, for example, the cattle and sheep may spend much of the time grazing outside except perhaps during the severest part of winter.

What Are Some of the Purposes of Wild Animals?

Wild animals sometimes kill and eat animals that otherwise would become overpopulated, potentially causing them to starve to death and perhaps destroy property such as trees or crops. In the past, but perhaps less at present, some wild animals such as minks, beavers, and foxes were trapped and killed for their fur. Today a number of people believe that this is not a valid reason for taking a wild animal's life.

Many years ago a number of wild animals were killed for necessary food for humans. This was the case with such wild animals as the white-tailed deer, jackrabbits, squirrels, antelopes, and buffaloes. Today, however, much of the hunting that takes place is for sport, not for food, although sometimes the food is eaten by the hunter. Carefully controlled hunting may have some purpose in that it may prevent the overpopulation of some animal species that would cause them to die from starvation.

Unfortunately, some animals have been killed for other portions of their body, such as the ivory tusks of African elephants and the horns of rhinoceros. Today, however, this practice is illegal in most places.

Perhaps a major role that wild animals play is simply to help humans become aware of their beauty, majesty, and uniqueness as we share the earth with them.

What Are Some of the Purposes of Domesticated Animals?

Dogs and cats have many important purposes. Perhaps some of their most important purposes are to provide love, companionship, and protection for humans. Both dogs and cats have been found to contribute greatly to the health and happiness of their owners because of their unconditional love and often playful attitude. Specially trained dogs also are used to lead the blind or help physically challenged people by pulling wheelchairs, picking up dropped objects, and turning light switches on and off. Of course, trained dogs also are used to locate missing people, including lost children, help police apprehend criminals, and locate illegal drugs.

Cattle, sheep, goats, and pigs usually are used for either their meat, their hides (wool), or their milk. Today horses are mainly used for recreation or sport, although they also sometimes can be used for transportation.

In any case, all domesticated animals add greatly to the quality of human life and should be very much appreciated by us.

What Should Humans Always Remember about Our Relationship with Both Wild and Domesticated Animals?

Both wild and domesticated animals play an important role in our environment and in our lives. Each member of the animal kingdom has a unique role that should be respected and appreciated. Although it is true that humans have a superior place in our environment to all animals, both wild and domesticated, all animals also have a unique place and are worthy of our care for their way of life and habitats. We also must learn to co-exist successfully with them in the environment. We need to clearly understand the importance of all wild and domesticated animals to our way of life. We must be especially aware of the need to protect the endangered animals that were mentioned earlier. We must not allow any more wild animals to become extinct, since it is a great loss for all of us.

Literacy Center Booklist for the Unit

Archambault, J., & Martin, B. (1994). *Beautiful feast for a big king cat.* NY: HarperCollins.

Arnowsky, J. (1987). *Raccoons and ripe corn.* NY: Lothrop, Lee & Shephard.

Asch, F. (1985). *Bear shadow.* Englewood Cliffs, NJ: Prentice-Hall.

Babbit, N. (1989). *Nellie, a cat on her own.* NY: Farrar, Strauss & Giroux.

Baker, K. (1990). *Who is the beast?* New York: Harcourt Brace Jovanovich.

Barrett, J. (1970). *Animals should definitely not wear clothing.* NY: Atheneum.

Berenstain, S., & J. (1966). *The bear's picnic.* NY: Random House.

Berenstain, S., & J. (1978). *The Berenstain bears and spooky old tree.* NY: Random House.

Besar, M. (1967). The cat book. NY: Holiday House.

Bolton, F. *Animal shelters.* NY: Scholastic.

Bonners, S. 1978). *Panda.* NY: Delacorte.

Bridwell, N. (1969). Clifford takes a trip. NY: Scholastic.

Bridwell, N. (1994). *Clifford the firehouse dog.* NY: Scholastic.

Bridwell, N. (1963). *Clifford the big red dog.* NY: Scholastic.

Brown, M. (1961). *Once a mouse.* NY: Scribners.

Brown, M. (1946). *The little fur family.* NY: HarperCollins.

Carle, E. (1989). *Animals, animals.* NY: Philomel Books.

Coffelt, N. (1995). *The dog who cried wolf.* San Diego, CA: Harcourt Brace Jovanovich.

Cooney, B., reteller. (1982). *Chanticleer and the fox.* NY: Harper & Row.

Cowley, J. (1988). *Greedy cat.* Katonah, NY: Richard C. Owen.

Crowther, R. (1982). *A jungle jumble.* Kansas City: Children's Hallmark Edition. (wordless moveable book)

Dreamer, S. (1986). *Animal walk.* Boston: Little Brown.

Dunn, J. (1984). *The little puppy.* NY: Random House.

Eichenberg, F. (1952). *Ape in a cape: An alphabet of odd animals.* NY: Harcourt Brace Jovanovich.

Emberly, R. (1986). *Jungle sounds.* Boston: Little Brown.

Flack, M. (1931). *Angus and the cat.* NY: Doubleday.

Flack, M. (1932). *Ask Mr. Bear.* NY: Macmillan.

Fox, M. (1988). *Koala Lou.* San Diego: Harcourt Brace Jovanovich.

Francine. (1985). *Francine sings a keepsake of favorite animals songs.* Berkeley, CA: Lancaster Productions. (audiocassette)

Gackenbach, D. (1984). *Poppy the panda.* NY: Clarion.

Gag, W. (1938). *Millions of cats.* NY: Coward-McCann.

Galdone, P., reteller (1979). *The monkey and the crocodile.* NY: Clarion.

Galdone, P. (1985). *The three bears.* NY: Clarion.

Galdone, P. (1979). *The three little pigs.* NY: Clarion.

Galdone, P. (1988). *The three little kittens.* NY: Clarion.

Goldstein, B. (1989). *Bear in mind.* New York: Viking Penguin.

Gregor, A. *Animal babies.* NY: Scholastic.

Hazan, B. (1988). *The gorilla did it.* NY: Aladdin Books.

Hoban, T. (1985). *The children's zoo.* New York: Greenwillow.

Hurst, M. (1986). *I love cats.* NY: Scholastic.

Jennings, L. (1995). *The brave little bunny.* NY: Dutton.

Johnson, D. (1995). *Never ride your elephant to school.* NY: Henry Holt.

Jones, T. (1994). *More wild critters.* Portland, OR: Graphic Arts.

Keats, E. (1972). *Pet show.* NY: Collier.

Kunhardt, D. (1942). *Pat the bunny.* NY: Western.

Kunhardt, E. (1984). *Pat the cat.* NY: Western.

Lane, M. (1981). *The squirrel.* NY: Dial.

Lewis, R. (1988). *Friska, the sheep that was too small.* NY: Farrar, Strauss & Giroux.

Lobel, A. (1979). *A treeful of pigs.* NY: Greenwillow.

Marshall, J. (1988). *Fox on the job.* NY: Dial.

May, J. (1969). *Living things and their young.* NY: Follett.

Mayer, M. (1971). *A boy, a dog, a frog, and a friend.* NY: Dial.

Mayer, M. (1989). *What do you do with a kangaroo?* NY: Scholastic. (big book)

McDermott, G. (1994). *Coyote: A trickster from the American Southwest.* NY: Harcourt Brace Jovanovich.

Patterson, F. (1987). *Koko's story.* NY: Scholastic.

Pearson, T. (1984). *Old McDonald had a farm.* NY: Dial.

Potter, B. (1902). *Tale of Peter Rabbit.* NY: Frederick Warne.

Prelutsky, J. (1983). *Zoo doings.* NY: Greenwillow.

Purdy, C. (1994). *Mrs. Merriweather's musical cat.* NY: Putnam.

Ranger Rick. *National Wildlife Federation.* 1412 16th Street, Washington, D.C. (magazine)

Reneaux, J. (1995). *Why alligator hates dog.* Little Rock, AR: August House.

Rey, H., & Rey, M. (1985). *Curious George visits the zoo.* NY: Scholastic.

Roy, R. (1982). *What has ten legs and eats cornflakes?* NY: Clarion.

Rylant, C. (1995). *Dog heaven.* NY: Scholastic.

Selsam, M. (1975). *How kittens grow.* NY: Four Winds Press.

Selsam, M. (1981). *How puppies grow.* NY: Scholastic.

Selsam, M. (1966). *When an animal grows.* NY: Harper & Row.

Shaw, N. (1994). *Sheep take a hike.* Boston: Houghton Mifflin.

Simon, S. (1979). *Animal facts/animal fables.* NY: Crown.

Skarr, G. (1966). *All about dogs.* NY: Young Scott Books.

Slater, T. (1994). *The lion king: Morning at Pride Rock.* Orlando, FL: Disney Press.

Smith, M. (1994). *Argo, you lucky dog.* NY: Lothrop, Lee & Shephard.

Stevens, J. (1971). *The tortoise and the hare.* NY: Holiday House.

Stevens, J. (1987). *The town mouse and the country mouse.* NY: Scholastic.

Tafuri, N. (1983). *Early morning in the barn.* NY: Greenwillow.

Teague, M. (1994). *Pigsty.* NY: Scholastic.

Waber, B. (1972). *An anteater named Arthur.* Boston: Houghton Mifflin.

Ward, L. (1972). *The silver pony.* Boston: Houghton Mifflin.

Weiss, N. (1989). *Where does the brown bear go?* NY: Viking.

Wildsmith, B. (1974). *Squirrels.* Oxford: Oxford University Press.

Your big backyard. National Wildlife Foundation, 1412 16th Street, Washington, D.C. (magazine)

Ziefert, H. (1987). *Where's the cat?* NY: Harper & Row.

Ziefert, H. (1987). *Where's the dog?* NY: Harper & Row.

Ziefert, H. (1987). *Where's the guinea pig?* NY: Harper & Row.

Zolotow, C. (1995). *The old dog.* NY: HarperCollins.

Zoo books. San Diego Zoo, San Diego, CA. (magazine)

Introductory Lesson

Objective

Children will engage in a highly motivating initiating activity for the thematic unit *Elementary Knowledge about Mammals.* This activity should begin the unit in an informative and motivating manner.

Activity

If the teacher thinks that he or she has enough expertise to organize it effectively, the class should take a school trip to one of the following: a local wildlife preserve, a local zoo, a pet store, a dairy farm, or a cattle ranch. Any one of these class excursions can provide children with much prior knowledge that they can bring to the study of the unit. The excursion should help children to be much more motivated to study the information, concepts, and attitudes that are to be learned from the unit, to realize opportunities for concept and vocabulary development, and to enjoy opportunities for social interaction and cooperation.

If a school trip is not practical or feasible, the teacher may be able to plan one of the following as initiating activities:

- having a resource person such as a local zookeeper and some zoo animals come to class
- having a member of the local humane society or animal shelter and one or several animals that are available for adoption come to class
- having a member of a dog training club and several of the dogs attending it come to class
- having a local veterinarian and/or veterinarian's helper along with several animals come to class
- having a salesperson from a local pet store and several of the animals that are for sale there come to class
- showing the class a videotape of the wild animals in East or South Africa, or Australia

The school trip or visit by a resource person(s) always should be preceded by a class discussion with an emphasis on the vocabulary and concepts of the unit. If you wish, the school trip, resource person(s), or videotape can be followed up by having the children engage in journal writing, chart writing, process writing, the use of art media, or some other related activity.

Objective (The children can engage in this activity either before or after the initiating activity.)

The children should formulate a simple *K-W-L chart—What I Know, What I Want to Learn, What I Have Learned.*

Activity

K-W-L Activity.   The children can have a discussion with the teacher about what they already know about mammals (wild and domesticated animals). The teacher then lists their responses on a piece of tagboard under the column *What I Know.* Next, the teacher asks the children what they would like to learn about this topic and lists their responses under the column *What I Want to Learn.*

The teacher goes on to introduce and read at least part of the related informational books and magazine articles that are found in the Literacy Center. Here are some of the titles of materials found in the Literacy Center that can be used for this purpose:

Animal shelter

Panda

Animals, animals

The little puppy

Jungle sounds

Animal babies

The children's zoos

Pet show

Zoo things

Ranger Rick (magazine)

How kittens grow

How puppies grow

Animal facts/animal fables (an excellent book)

Early morning in the barn

Where does the brown bear go?

Squirrels

Your big backyard (magazine)

Where's the cat?

Where's the dog?

Where's the guinea pig?

After several days of discussion and various activities related to these books, the teacher refers back to the first two parts of the K-W-L chart. Then the teacher writes a new heading, *What I Have Learned,* and asks the children to share concepts that they have learned about mammals, which the teacher then writes on the tagboard in the proper column on the third part of the chart. Next, the teacher compares this list to what the children wanted to know. She or he asks the children, "How are they different? What can you do to learn the things that you still want to learn?" The children can complete similar K-W-L charts related to the unit theme later.

Here is an example of a completed K-W-L chart:

What I Know	What I Want to Learn	What I Have Learned
Some wild animals are dangerous. Dogs are very smart. Cattle are found on a farm. Zoos have wild animals of all kinds	How are dogs trained to guide blind people? What are the animals in the zoo fed? How are baby pigs raised?	Dogs get trained by special people in different places. Zooos are not always good places for wild animals to live. We need to have respect for all animals.

Language Arts
Oral Language and Vocabulary

Objective 1

The children will improve their critical listening skills.

Activity

The children should listen carefully to the resource person(s) or visual aids that comprise part or all of the initiating activity. They then should orally summarize the main points in the initial presentation(s).

Activity

The children should listen to commercially available or teacher-made cassette tape recordings of various animal sounds and be able to correctly identify them.

Objective 2

The children will be able to correctly use the appropriate specialized vocabulary terms that are related to the names and characteristics of mammals, their foods, their habitats, and their purposes.

Activity

Children should engage in large-group, small-group, and partner discussions about the concepts of the unit using the appropriate vocabulary. As a result of their discussions, they should be able to construct semantic webs (maps) with a partner or independently using some of the specialized vocabulary related to the unit. At the bottom of this page is an example of this type of semantic web.

Objective 3

The oral communication skills of the children will increase through participation in a literature circle.

Activity

The children can sit in a small group with the teacher and discuss one or more of the books that they read related to the concept of the unit.

Objective 4

Children will have practice in creative oral sharing of what they have read related to the unit.

Activity

Each child should share the highlights of his or her reaction to a book that was read for this unit. If feasible, the sharing can be done with the support of props.

Objective 5

The children will be able to creatively dramatize one or more of the books that are related to the unit.

Activity

The children should dramatize one or more of the books that accompany this unit. Children can use simple costumes and props if they want to do so. Children should plan these dramatizations collaboratively, as is in keeping with the whole language philosophy. Here are several of the books that can be used for this purpose from those included in the Literacy Center:

> *Chanticleer and the fox*
>
> *Angus and the cat*
>
> *Millions of cats*
>
> *Friska, the sheep that was too small*
>
> *A boy, a dog, a frog, and a friend*
>
> *The tortoise and the hare*
>
> *The town mouse and the country mouse*

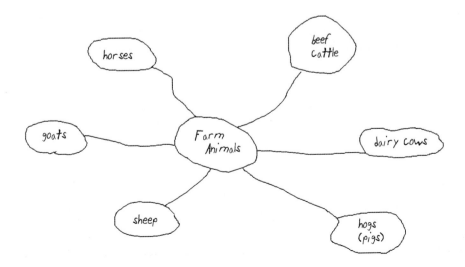

Reading

Objective 1

Children will use the three cueing systems—semantic (determining the meaning of an unknown word from context), syntactic (using word order or grammar cues to determine an unknown word), and graphophonic (using visual and/or phonic cues to determine the meaning of an unknown word)—within the context of the reading material of this unit. (See Chapter 7 for details about the three cueing systems.)

Activity

While reading materials related to this unit, children should use one or several of the cueing systems to determine the meaning and/or pronunciation of the unknown words in the material. If necessary, the teacher should assemble a short-term needs group to present those elements of the three cueing systems in which one or more children is weak. As much as possible, these cueing systems should be presented and practiced within the context of the actual reading material of the unit.

Objective 2

The children will learn about story structure by identifying the story elements (setting, theme, characters, plot episodes, and resolution).

Activity

After reading the picture storybook *The bear's picnic* by S. & J. Berenstain, the children should try to remember the time that the story takes place, where the story takes place, and who the story characters are. The children can engage in a similar activity with the other story elements such as the theme, plot episodes, and resolution. Next, the children can prepare a roll movie with the five headings. *Setting, Theme, Characters, Plot Episodes,* and *Resolution.* (A roll movie is a large piece of butcher paper that is attached to two wooden cylinders. It can be rolled to bring different elements into view.) They also can draw pictures and write a narrative for each section. Roll movies can, of course, also be constructed for other books related to the unit.

Objective 3

The children will retell a book from the Literacy Center that is related to the theme of the unit.

Activity

The children should select a book from the Literacy Center that relates to the unit and has a definite sequence. The child then retells this book in correct sequence either to the entire class, a small group, the literacy partner, the teacher, or on a cassette tape. Here are several books from

the Literacy Center that may lend themselves to retelling. However, others also may be used.

> *How kittens grow*
> *How puppies grow*
> *Little bear*
> *The three bears*
> *The three little pigs*
> *Clifford the big red dog*
> *Koko's story*

Objective 4

The children will demonstrate their comprehension of a book at the explicit (literal or factual) level by answering explicit questions about the book and then acting it out by using some simple type of puppet(s). (See the puppet patterns in Chapter 5.)

Activity

After several children have read the book *The three little pigs* from the Literacy Center, they can dramatize it using simple puppets they have made. Here are several other books from the Literacy Center that also can be used for this activity:

> *The three bears*
> *Animals should definitely not wear clothing*
> *Ten bears on my bed*
> *Greedy cat*
> *What do you do with a kangaroo?*
> *What has ten legs and eats cornflakes?*

Objective 5

The children should predict, draw conclusions and generalizations, problem solve, and critically analyze using the reading materials found in the Literacy Center and related to the unit.

Activity

Have the children predict the book content from the title of any of the books in the Literacy Center that relate to the unit. Several books that may be especially good for prediction are as follows:

> *Nellie, a cat on her own*
> *The Berenstain bears and spooky old tree*
> *Clifford takes a trip*
> *The monkey and the crocodile*
> *The gorilla did it*
> *What has ten legs and eats cornflakes?*

Children can also write a different ending for one of the appropriate books. Here are several books that lend themselves to this activity:

Chanticleer and the fox
Millions of cats
The three bears
The monkey and the crocodile
The tortoise and the hare
The town mouse and the country mouse

In another activity one child can portray the wolf and three children can portray the pigs in the book *The three little pigs.* An interviewer can interview the child portraying the wolf to gain his or her view of the story. The interviewer also then interviews each of the children portraying pigs in this book to gain their view of the story. As a follow-up, the children can read the book *The true story of the three little pigs* by J. Scieszka (New York: Viking, 1989) and compare the interviews with this book.

For an additional activity the children can read the fascinating book *Animal facts/animal fables* by S. Simon (New York: Crown, 1979). They then can engage in a critical discussion about which facts about animals are accurate and which are based on fantasy and tradition. As a follow-up, each child in the entire class or a small group writes his or her (or their) own sheet of animal facts/ animal fables for the other children to complete. A model of this type of activity sheet is found in the following source:

Wilma H. Miller, *Reading comprehension activities kit.* West Nyack, NY: The Center for Applied Research in Education, 1990, pp. 161–163.

Writing

Objective 1
Children will engage in journal writing of various kinds.

Activity
The children can keep a reading response journal for the books in the Literacy Center related to the theme of this unit that they have read. For each book that a child reads independently or with a partner, he or she should write a response to it. The responses can be written in a loose-leaf notebook or on note cards. Here is an example of a reading response journal entry:

> Tale of Peter Rabbit by Beatrix Potter
> This is a story about a rabbit who gets into lots of trouble. He likes to eat carrots from gardens. He better be careful or he'll get hurt.

Activity
Children should write in a dialogue journal related to the unit theme on a regular basis. A dialogue journal is a written interchange between a child and the teacher. When the dialogue journal is used in a unit, the subject of the dialogue can be the content of the unit. For example, at the bottom of this page is a very brief portion of Jeremy's dialogue journal during this unit.

Objective 2
The children should successfully engage in simple summary writing.

Activity
After researching any aspect of this unit, such as the food that domesticated animals eat, a small group of children can write a simple summary of what they have learned. If they wish, this summary can be in the form of a simple book with illustrations. The summary can be of any major portion of the unit.

> Dear Ms. May,
>   I really liked the man from Miller Park Zoo and all the animals that came to school. I like petting the ferret and the snake.
>   I liked the book I read named Zoo Doings. I can't wait till we go to the wildlife park next week.
>   Jeremy

> Dear Jeremy,
>   I am glad that you enjoyed hearing the zoo-keeper. I like animals too. Maybe you would like to look at one of the Zoo Books magazines. You could learn a lot from these magazines before our trip to the Prairie Wildlife Preserve.
>   Ms. May

Objective 3

The children should effectively participate in letter writing as an important form of communication.

Activity

The children can write thank-you letters to the guides at the zoo or wildlife preserve to which they took a school trip, or to the resource persons who came to class to speak, or to anyone else who has helped significantly with the planning or executing of this unit.

Activity

The children can write a group letter to the author of one of the books used for this unit in the hope that this letter may be answered by the author. Many times children's authors do answer the letters their readers write to them.

Objective 4

Children can engage in creative and functional writing that is related to the unit.

Activity

The children can write a self-selected creative story that is related to the unit. The topic should not be assigned to a child, as this is not in keeping with the whole language philosophy. Just as an example, one possible creative writing topic is "This Is the Animal that I Would Like to Be."

Activity

The children can design and make a bulletin board that is related to the unit. A nature bulletin board can be constructed on which children display their work as well as write and receive messages related to the unit in their space on the bulletin board. They can write a message about a very good book from the Literacy Center related to the unit as a recommendation or draw a picture related to a book or any other element of the unit.

Activity

The child can either individually or with one or more partners author an animal book. This book can be either fiction or informational and can be about any wild or domesticated animal(s). The book itself can be in the form of the animal about which it is written; for example, a book about dogs can be shaped as some type of dog. It can be a regular-sized book or a big book.

    Hint: Have the child construct the entire book first, including the blank pages, so that his or her writing will not go outside the book pages and be cut off when it is put together. The following two resource books contain some animal patterns either for regular sized or big books:

> Evans, J., & Moore, J. (1984). *How to make books with children.* Monterey, CA: Evan-Moor.

> Evans, J., Morgan K., & Moore, J. (1989). *Making big books with children.* Monterey, CA: Evan-Moor.

Play

Objective 1

The children will engage in creative dramatic play experiences.

Activity

Children can creatively dramatize one of the books in the Literacy Center that is related to the theme of the unit.

Activity

A play center can be constructed in one corner of the classroom with reading and writing materials and other props at which children can role play various situations related to the unit. Some of these may be as follows: a veterinarian's office, a dog obedience school, an animal shelter with pets available for adoption, or possibly a circus.

Objective 2

The children will have the opportunity to engage in meaningful block play related to the unit, especially using Legos.

Activity

Children can participate in block play that is related to the theme of the unit about animals to acquire new concepts and engage in collaboration. For example, the children can construct block representations of a cattle ranch, a dairy farm, or a circus.

Objective 3

The children will participate in various play activities that are related to the unit theme.

Activity

Children can do the "bunny hop," "kangaroo jump," "elephant walk," "snake crawl," "cheetah run," "chipmunk run," "horse gallop," or any other similar animal-related movement. These all are outdoor or gymnasium activities.

Art

Objective 1

The children will develop creativity and use various art media in relation to the theme of the unit.

Activity

The children can construct a diorama of a farm including the farmhouse, the farm buildings, and the animals. Oral or written language can be used for describing the diorama to enhance these literacy skills.

Activity

The children can construct a large mural for a bulletin board which shows: a farm in spring or summer, a jungle (tropical rain forest) with the appropriate animals, a savanna (grassland) of Africa including the various animals that are native to that area, a circus including all of the circus animals, or a wildlife preserve and all of the animals who live there.

Activity

The children can construct a puppet(s) representing one or more of the animals that are studied during the unit. The puppet can be a: garden glove puppet, box puppet, jumping jack puppet, hand or finger puppet, papier-maché head puppet, sock puppet, pop-up puppet, stuffed cloth puppet, tennis ball puppet, or potato puppet. Puppet patterns and directions for making all of these puppets are found in Chapter 5. Puppets are an excellent way to enhance oral language development.

Activity

Construct a simple set (scenery) to accompany the creative dramatization of one of the unit theme books from the Literacy Center. Tempera paint may be valuable for this purpose. Costumes also can be constructed for the dramatization using construction paper or cloth. Animal prints such as the leopard print or giraffe print can be made.

Activity

As one possible art project related to the unit theme, children can make three mouse friends. Here is how this project can be done:

1. The child draws the shape for a simple mouse on a plain sheet of paper, including a plan for the design of the face and tail. A second line is drawn all around the original, leaving ½″ of border.

2. The child lays the pattern on some scraps of plain cotton or silk material. The child must make sure that the straight edge lines up with the single thread in the weave. The child next pins the pattern in place and cuts around the edge. Two pieces of material should be cut for each mouse.

3. The child then cuts matching pieces for two more mice.

4. The child should place the two pieces for each mouse on a table, right side up and noses together, and draw the eye and ear on each one with a marker or crayon.

5. The child then stitches the eyes with a knot stitch and outlines the ears with a backstitch. The teacher will have to demonstrate these stitches first and give each child help as needed.

6. The child takes three short pieces of the decorative thread and braids them into some type of tail. Both ends should be knotted.

7. The child then places each pair of pieces right sides together and pins the tail in the proper place but *inside* the mouse. Next, the child stitches around the outline of the mouse, leaving the straight edge open. Then the right sides are turned out, and the tail is on the outside.

8. The child can fill each mouse about two-thirds full with small dried beans, rice, or sand. Then the open edges can be tucked in and closed up with an over-and-over stitch.

9. Last, the child fills the needle with 5 strands of decorative thread and sews these through the nose. The threads then can be tied into a reef (square) knot, and the thread is trimmed to make a type of whiskers. The child also can use markers to make the face and whiskers.

A simple illustration of the entire procedure follows on the next page. The teacher can change it in any way that he/she thinks is appropriate for his/her pupils.

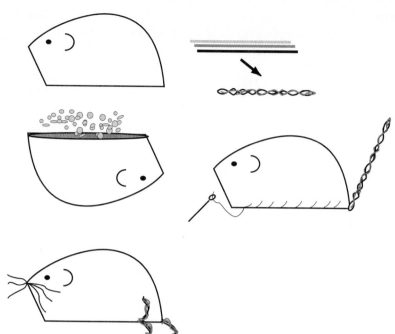

Activity

As another art activity related to the unit, the children can make animal seed pictures. These are animal collages made from various seed and grasses. Any number of animals can be made in this way, including badgers, squirrels, rabbits, horses, pigs, dogs, or cats. Here is one procedure for making an animal seed collage.

1. The child draws a picture of the animal that he or she wishes to make on a piece of cardboard. If the child wishes, he or she can draw it first on a heavy sheet of paper and then trace it onto the cardboard. Then the animal is ready to have the seeds glued onto it.

2. If necessary, the child colors the sunflower or pumpkin seeds the appropriate color for the animal that he or she wants to make with a felt-tip pen.

3. Next the child glues the seeds within the body shape by overlapping them as they are glued. The child also can glue various types of grasses onto the animal if she or he wishes it to resemble fur. The animal can be as realistic or as fanciful as the child wants it to be.

Here are some simple illustrations of how this art project can be done so that a child can make a cat collage.

Activity

An interesting resource book for helping children learn how to draw a number of different animals is:

> Ames, L. (1974). *Draw 50 animals: The step-by-step way to draw elephants, tigers, dogs, fish, birds, and many more.* NY: Doubleday.

Ames provides simple guidance for drawing various animals, although he makes it very clear that the use of this book is only one way of helping children learn how to draw and that their own creativity *always* should be encouraged. Therefore, the use of this book probably does not conflict with the whole language philosophy. Ames presents guidance for children in drawing the following animals: rabbit, squirrel, mouse, kitten, cat, leopard, tiger, lion, lion head, dog, horse, horse head, buffalo, elephant, camel, monkey, seal, deer, bear, dolphin, pig, cow, rhinoceros, giraffe, and kangaroo.

Objective 2

The child will illustrate a language-experience activity (LEA) (see a later section of this chapter) book or process writing book that is related to the theme of the unit.

Activity

The child can illustrate a dictated LEA book or process writing book related to the theme of the unit by using any of the following art media: markers (most popular with children), crayons, water colors, tempera paint, fingerpaints, colored pencils, colored chalk, materials such as macaroni, dried beans, or rice, colored construction paper, tissue paper, foil, or fabric scraps.

Music

Objective 1

The children will listen to and sing songs that are related to the theme of the unit. These songs also will enhance children's vocabulary knowledge.

Activity

The words and music of these songs which relate to the unit theme are found in the songbook *Disney sing-along song book* by R. Schroeder (ed.) (NY: Hyperion, 1995):

> "The Siamese Cat Song," 1953, p. 50
> "Mickey Mouse March," 1955, pp. 55–56
> "Winnie the Pooh," 1966, pp. 91–92
> "The Wonderful Thing about Tiggers," pp. 93–94
> "I Wanna Be Like You," pp. 98–99

Activity

The following are poems to read and songs, including words and music. They are related to the unit theme and

are found in the book *Raffi's top 10 songs to read* by Raffi. (NY: Crown, 1980–1993):

> "Baby Beluga," 1980, pp. 8–11
> "Down by the Bay," 1987, pp. 12–15
>   This song includes one verse about each of these animals: moose, whale, bear, and llama.
> "Tingalayo," 1989, pp. 36–39
>   This song is about a donkey.

The collection *Jane Yolen's Old McDonald Songbook* by J. Yolen (ed.), with musical arrangements by Adam Stemple and illustrations by Rosekrans Hoffman (Honesdale, PA: Caroline House, 815 Church Street, 1994) has the following traditional animal songs with words and music:

> "Old McDonald Had a Farm," pp. 8–9
> "Have a Little Dog," pp. 10–12
> "Bow-wow-wow," p. 13
> "Where, Oh Where Has My Little Dog Gone?" pp. 14–15
> "Old Dog Tray," pp. 16–18
> "Old Blue," pp. 19–21
> "Three Little Kittens," pp. 22–23
> "The Cat Came Back," pp. 24–25
> "Three Little Piggies," pp. 26–27
> "Sow Got the Measles," pp. 28–29
> "The Little Pig," pp. 30–31
> "The Old Woman and Her Pig," pp. 32–34
> "Lambs to Sell," p. 35
> "Sheep Shearing," pp. 36–37
> "I Wish I Had a Shepherd's Lamb," pp. 38–39
> "Black Sheep, Black Sheep," pp. 40–41
> "The Darby Ram," pp. 42–43
> "Bill Grogan's Goat," pp. 70–71
> "The Little Black Bull," pp. 74–75
> "The Cow," p. 77
> "The Old Cow Died," pp. 78–79
> "Shoe the Old Horse," pp. 80–81
> "My Horses Aren't Hungry," pp. 82–83
> "The Old Gray Mare," pp. 84–85
> "Hey, Little Boy," pp. 86–88 (about animals)
> "Donkey and Carrots," p. 89
> "Kicking Mule," pp. 90–91
> "Mules," pp. 92–93
> "Sweetly Sings the Donkey," p. 94

Objective 2

The children will be able to relate motivating music to art and writing on the theme of the unit. The music may be classical or pop music. Often music that best represents the teacher's own likes will be well accepted by children.

Activity

The children can listen to CDs, cassette recordings, or records while they are participating in creative writing or creative art activities related to the theme of the unit. Such music is both motivating and relaxing for young children while they are engaging in creative activities.

Social Studies

Objective 1

The children will develop an understanding about the native habitat of some well-known wild animals.

Activity

In small groups, children can look at maps or a globe to locate the native habitat of the following well-known wild animals:

> giraffe—Africa
>
> elephant—Africa, India, Thailand
>
> leopard—Africa
>
> rhinoceros—Africa
>
> hippopotamus—Africa
>
> tiger—India
>
> kangaroo—Australia
>
> koala—Australia

The children then can write what they have found out in their journal about the unit.

Objective 2

Children will increase their collaboration and cooperation while pursuing the activities of the unit.

Activity

The children should enhance their collaboration and cooperation with their peers by participating in many of the activities of the unit. Here are a few activities that already have been mentioned in other curricular areas of this unit that should increase collaboration and cooperation among the children.

- formulating a semantic web (map)
- engaging in a literature circle
- participating in creative dramatics
- participating in the K-W-L activity
- researching the content of the unit from various print materials, CD-ROM disks, and the Internet, and reporting back to the remainder of the class
- engaging in dramatic play
- participating in block play
- using art media to construct dioramas, murals, puppets, scenery, and the like
- engaging in music activities

Objective 3

The children will become aware of the positive and negative aspects to wild animals living in the wild, in a zoo, or in a wildlife preserve.

Activity

The children can brainstorm the advantages and limitations of wild animals living in various environments. While the children are brainstorming, the teachers write what the children say on the chalkboard or chart paper. Then either independently or with a partner, the children can write a short story pretending they are wild animals and stating in what environment they would rather live and the reasons for their preference. As an alternative, several children also could dramatize how wild animals in different environments feel.

Here is an example of such a chart with the information provided by a second-grade class.

Advantages	Limitations
Wild Natural habitat Free to live their own way	_Wild_ Can be killed by other animals Hard to find food Have to locate or make their home
Preserve Like natural habitat No predators Some freedom Plenty of food	_Preserve_ Not entirely free
Zoo Plenty of food Very safe life	_Zoo_ Artificial habitat Not a natural way for a wild animal to live

Objective 4

The children will learn more about the contributions of the various resource persons that have helped in implementing this unit.

Activity

Animal care and control resource persons can come to the classroom and share information about their career and its unique contribution to society. As a follow-up to each discussion, the children orally or in writing summarize the contributions of each resource person. The children also can either individually or as a group send a thank-you letter to the resource person. Possible resource persons include a hog (pig) farmer, dairy farmer, sheep rancher, cattle farmer (rancher), veterinarian or veterinarian's helper, zookeeper, employee of a local animal shelter, volunteer for the local humane society or animal shelter, and dog or cat breeder and/or trainer.

Objective 5

The children will learn about the specialized training that dogs receive who are to guide the blind or help the physically challenged. They will view a videotape (or see pictures) or read simple materials that show the activities of either or both of the following:

Leader Dogs for the Blind
PO Box 5000
Rochester, MI 48308
248 651-9011

Canine Companions
for Independence
PO Box 446
Santa Rosa, CA
95402
1-800-572-2275

The children can role play what it would be like to rely on a specially trained dog for help.

Science

Objective 1

The children will learn about how to care for a living animal—its food, its water, its housing, and its exercise. They will develop responsibility for caring for it satisfactorily.

Activity

The children should have a class pet such as a rabbit, guinea pig, or hamster. A small group of children can research from various sources its living requirements, record them on a simple chart, and report back to the class. A child can be assigned to be entirely responsible for the animal's care for one week. Each child then keeps a record in a chart of the food, water, and other care that they provided during the week.

Objective 2

The children will learn about the habitat, eating habits, young, and other characteristics of common wild animals that are being studied in the unit.

Activity

The children form cooperative learning groups, and each group selects what it is going to study and how they are going to do the research. Within each group the tasks are divided according to the interests and abilities of individual children. After the research is completed, each group shares it with the rest of the class.

Here are some of the animals that can be researched: kangaroo, koala, lion, giraffe, zebra, rhinoceros, leopard, hippopotamus, tiger, wolf, fox, deer, bear, and monkey. Here are some of the resources that can be used to conduct the research: scientific informational books, science textbooks, computer software, the Internet, CD-ROM disks, resource persons, and magazines.

Objective 3

The children will learn about endangered species and how they can protect them. They also will gain a greater appreciation for all the animals with whom we share our earth.

Activity

The children brainstorm what animals may be endangered and how everyone can better share our earth with all animals. They collaboratively research this topic and then share their findings with the rest of the class. The final product may look somewhat like this chart:

How We Can Share Our World
With Animals

1. Don't destroy where they need to live.
2. Don't let them be captured for zoos
3. Appreciate what they were born to do.
4. Treat pets kindly.
5. Don't kill an animal without a very good reason.

Arithmetic

Objective 1

The children will learn simple graphing skills.

Activity

A small group of children can make a simple line graph or picture graph (pictograph) showing how much food the class pet (such as a rabbit) ate during a week. They then can explain the graph orally or in writing.

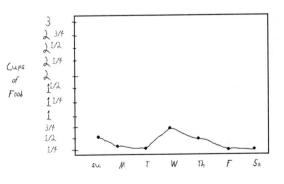

Objective 2

The children will have practice in solving simple arithmetic verbal problems that are related in some way to the theme of the unit.

Activity

The children independently or with a partner will solve such arithmetic verbal problems as the following:

Joel and his family owned 2 dogs. The dog named Honey had 4 puppies, and the dog named Buff had 5 puppies. How many puppies did the 2 dogs have?

> 9 puppies

While walking in the woods, Tim saw 2 bear cubs climbing a tree one day. He also saw a mother bear and her cub walking by the road. How many more bear cubs did Tim see climbing the tree than walking by the road?

> 1 bear cub

Each child in Mrs. Brown's class sent $1.00 to the zoo to feed zoo animals. There are 21 children in the class. How much money did the children in Mrs. Brown's class send to the zoo for food?

> $21.00

Objective 3

The children who need this activity will have practice in counting.

Activity

Have a small group of children count the total number of pets that the children in the class have in their homes.

dogs	cats	hamsters	guinea pigs	rabbits	snakes	lizards
9	12	16	12	3	1	2

Culminating Activity

If a school trip was not taken as the initiating activity, it can be taken as the culminating activity for this unit. The trip can be to: a zoo, a wildlife preserve, a pet store, a veterinarian's office, the local humane society shelter, a dairy farm, a cattle farm (ranch), a hog (pig) farm.

As alternatives, the children also can independently or as a group construct a book with simple text and illustrations summarizing the major findings of the unit. They may also orally summarize their findings or a portion of them for family members or other classes in the school in a creative skit or play that they have written with the teacher's help. In addition, they can creatively dramatize one or several of the trade books that they have read related to the unit. The children also can display art constructed for the unit, sing songs related to the unit, or bring their pets to school (have a "pet show").

Resource Books: Elementary Knowledge About Mammals

Christian, M. (Ed.) (1986). *The secret world of animals.* Washington DC: National Geographic Society.

Fields, D. (1989). *The kid's world almanac of animals and pets.* NY: World Almanac.

Staple, M., & Gamlin, L. (1990). *The Random House book of 1001 questions and answers about animals.* NY: Random House.

Note: The author wishes to thank Janelle Kohl of the Frank B. Koller Memorial Library, Manitowish Waters, WI 54545 for her help in choosing the resource books mentioned in this unit.

WHAT ARE THE ADVANTAGES AND LIMITATIONS OF THE WHOLE LANGUAGE PHILOSOPHY?

It may be helpful to conclude the discussion of the whole language philosophy by briefly summarizing some of the major advantages and limitations of this philosophy of instruction. Here are what I believe them to be:

Advantages

- It is very motivating to children.
- It is highly interesting to children.
- It involves students actively.
- It enhances the creativity of the children who are participating in it.
- It integrates the language arts of listening, oral language, reading, and writing very effectively and also can integrate all of the other curricular areas in thematic units.
- It makes all learning relevant to real-life situations.
- The skills are taught in a meaningful manner in the context of real materials as they are needed, not in an isolated manner in which they may have no true relevance.
- It represents child development principles very well, since the child's total development is considered when planning and implementing the program, not merely her or his intellectual development.
- It capitalizes on each child's teachable moment.
- It encourages a child to take the initiative for his or her own learning and to be a "risk-taker."
- It provides each child with considerable individual attention and support.
- It greatly encourages collaboration and cooperation among children.
- It allows the child to experience success—to perform at his or her own level of development.
- It does not use ability grouping, which may lead to a negative self-image especially for "at-risk" children of various kinds.
- Since it is not a prepackaged curriculum, it truly represents the children's own needs and interests.
- It allows the teacher to take each child from the point at which he or she currently is functioning and move forward at her or his own style and pace of learning.

Limitations

- Without a doubt, the major limitation of implementing the whole language philosophy in the classroom is that it does not provide children with sequential skills development of the literacy skills. However, an early childhood teacher can plan for systematic instruction in skills by careful choice of materials and planning of learning situations. Perhaps this limitation is the most significant with the graphophonic analysis skills and with children who have special needs of all types. Normally a child who has good linguistic aptitude develops the literacy skills, including graphophonic analysis, independently on a more incidental basis. For example, the state of California recently has been very concerned with declining reading test scores since whole language instruction has been so widely implemented in the state. Therefore, California is requiring school districts to implement more systematic teaching of graphophonic analysis (California Department of Education, 1995).

- It requires a well-trained, knowledgeable, and perceptive teacher to implement it successfully, since there are no written guidelines to follow as is true of a more traditional curriculum. The teacher must be knowledgeable about the reading process to be able to teach it effectively, especially if she or he has not had much experience in teaching that grade level or is a beginning teacher. Each teacher must have a planned set of objectives for skill development.

- It requires an adaptable person who is willing to alter the typical teacher's role of being a dispenser of knowledge to one who is willing to be a facilitator of learning. Not all teachers are able to adapt to this different role either willingly or successfully.

- It may be quite time-consuming to implement, especially until the teacher has acquired a cadre of strategies and materials that can be used.

- It may be too unstructured for some children. Some children seem to be more successful in a program that contains more structure, such as the basal reader approach or a modified phonics approach.

- It may be difficult for a child who transfers from a whole language classroom to a traditional classroom to adapt to a more structured traditional classroom.

- It may be difficult for a whole language teacher to adequately explain this philosophy of learning to administrators or parents. Today some parents are very cognizant of the well-publicized complaint that because schools are not teaching any phonics, children are not learning to read well. Certainly whole language programs can be explained effectively, but this requires some effort on the teacher's part.

- Even though a teacher may have a whole language classroom, he or she may be required by the state or school district to administer standardized tests. Since whole language is evaluated much more effectively by authentic assessment, standardized tests are not a true measure of what a child has learned in a whole language classroom. One reaction is that an early childhood teacher can direct his or her teaching toward the material that is to be evaluated, but to do so may well not be in keeping with the true whole language philosophy.

In summary, although I believe that the whole language philosophy does contain some significant limitations, it also has enough strengths to merit including it at least to some extent in the typical kindergarten and primary-grade classroom. All of its potential limitations, including that of insufficient sequential skill development, can easily be overcome with some type of balanced literacy program such as the one explained at the end of this chapter.

THE LANGUAGE-EXPERIENCE APPROACH (LEA)

A Brief History of the Language-Experience Approach (LEA)

The *language-experience approach (LEA)* may be considered a part of whole language, although I consider it a separate entity. LEA consists of two different aspects—*dictation* and *process writing*. Process writing is described in detail in Chapter 6. Dictation can begin as early as the age of three, while process writing with a completed product usually begins in first grade with children who are adept at writing.

The language-experience approach dates from the nineteenth century, and LEA charts were used at the University of Chicago Lab School in the 1920s. However, LEA as it is known today was chiefly researched and written about by the late Roach Van Allen, professor emeritus at the University of Arizona. In the 1960s Allen was researching and speaking about LEA in about the same way as it is conceptualized today. According to Allen (1976), the language-experience approach is mainly based on the following premise, all from the child's point of view:

What I think about is important.

What I can think about, I can say.

What I can say, I can write or someone else can write for me.

I can read what I have written or someone else has written for me.

Therefore, LEA is an integrated literacy approach which effectively relates listening, speaking, reading, and writing. Allen had seen LEA being used successfully in Harlingen, Texas, a Texas-Mexican border town, with Latino children. He said that it was very effective because these children with special needs dictated and read materials that reflected their own experiences and were written in their own language patterns. Therefore, they could read them very effectively. Allen then brought the concept of LEA to San Diego, California, where he became Director of Curriculum and conducted a number of research studies about it. He discovered that LEA was a very motivating way to teach beginning reading and writing skills. It also seemed to be as effective a beginning reading approach as were the basal reader approach or a systematic phonics approach. LEA was researched extensively in federally financed first-grade studies of the 1960s (Bond & Dykstra, 1967). In this large group of nationwide studies, the effectiveness of LEA was researched, as were the basal reader approach, systematic phonics approaches, and others. The majority of these studies found that the use of LEA resulted in very good first-grade reading achievement on about an equal basis with the more traditional and formal approaches. However, the studies also found that the use of LEA resulted in first-grade children who had a greater motivation to read for information and pleasure.

Some other researchers who have been associated with LEA are the late Russell Stauffer (1980), Mary Anne Hall (1976), Jeannette Veatch (1979), and Jerome Harste (1988).

How Is the Dictation of LEA Conducted?

LEA has been successful with children as young as three years of age who are linguistically adept and up to the age of seven or more with children who have special needs. Children who have dictated language-experience stories and charts usually find them highly motivating, interesting, and easy to read. They usually can read their own LEA dictated charts and stories more effectively than they can any print materials.

Here is the basic procedure that you can follow in implementing LEA dictation:

1. Provide some type of highly motivating experience so that the children will have an interesting experience about which to dictate. Although all children benefit from this, it usually is especially important for children with special needs. Here are some of the initiating experiences that can be used successfully with young children:
   - a trip to an interesting place such as the zoo, wildlife preserve, pet shop, museum, forest preserve, candy factory, glass-blowing studio, planetarium, pumpkin patch, children's section of a local public library, toy store, local mall, among countless others. Each community has its own unique attractions that can form the basis of a dictated LEA story.
   - an art or construction activity such as constructing a kite, making a snowman,

constructing a simple puppet (see the puppet patterns in Chapter 5), making a Thanksgiving turkey, carving a pumpkin, cutting out a snowflake, constructing a Valentine or Valentine box, cutting out shamrocks, and making a May basket. Of course, each early childhood teacher has her own repertoire of art or construction activities that can be used.
   - a cooking or baking activity such as frosting cupcakes, baking cookies of various types, making deviled eggs, baking a gingerbread person, making butter, baking bread, baking blueberry muffins, cooking vegetable soup, cooking applesauce, among many others. Each teacher of young children can add countless other cooking and baking activities that can be used as motivation for language-experience dictation.
   - a visual or aural activity such as looking at pictures, watching a videotape, listening to a book being read aloud, or listening to an audiocassette tape.

2. Have an interesting preliminary conversation with the children in which the motivation for the dictation is discussed in detail. As an example, if a child has taken a trip to a candy factory, the teacher and child can discuss the trip in detail using correct vocabulary and emphasizing the sequence in which the various concepts were seen at the factory.

3. Have the child or group of children dictate the language-experience chart (on chart paper) or book (on regular or oversized paper), trying to help the child dictate in complete sentences. It also can be transcribed in a blank book. Blank regular-sized and big books can be purchased from Bare Books, Treetop Publishing 220 Virginia Street, Racine, WI 53405. However, the teacher must be careful not to direct the dictation too much, or the LEA chart or book may belong to the teacher instead of the child or children. The language patterns of the child or children should be retained, including their unique dialect, although any clearly offensive language obviously should be altered. Most specialists in LEA believe that if the teacher alters a child's language patterns, the child may feel rejected because that is the only language that he or she has.

4. The next step in the procedure is as follows:
   - The teacher reads the LEA chart or story several times, placing his or her hand under each word as she or he reads it, being sure to stress one-to-one oral language and written word correspondence.
   - Next, the teacher asks the child or group of children to read the LEA chart or story with her or him several times as well as possible. The one-to-one correspondence should still be

emphasized, although the teacher can also stress left-to-right progression by moving a hand in a sweeping direction under each sentence as it is read aloud.

- The teacher presents and/or reinforces a number of beginning reading skills from each LEA chart or story. This stresses reading skills in context as is representative of the whole language approach. Some of the beginning reading skills that can be emphasized in this way are knowledge of both capital and lowercase letter names; concept of word and word boundaries; sight word recognition and sight word identification; beginning phonic analysis; knowledge of simple suffixes such as *ing, ed, s, es,* and *ly;* and use of semantic (contextual) analysis when alternative words are suggested for use in sentence context in the LEA chart or story.

- If the teacher wishes, the LEA chart or story can be used in a number of different ways. It can be duplicated for the other children in the class to "read." All of a child's stories over a time period can be bound into a book, reread a number of times, and then sent home with the child to read to the child's family. The LEA charts can be kept on a chart holder and reread a number of different times as a class or a group.

- Each child can illustrate each of his or her stories in a creative way using various art media such as markers, crayons, colored pencils, tempera paints, fingerpaints, or watercolors. Then all of the dictated LEA stories can be bound into a premade book (see the names of the two books mentioned earlier in this chapter that contain patterns for book covers). The books often are laminated to make them more durable and fastened with spiral binding (available in a number of different places such as Kinkos Printing or PIP Printing), three large rings, yarn, or a number of other creative, durable ways. It is important for the books to be as attractive as possible so that other children and the child's family find them interesting to examine and read. It also emphasizes the value that the teacher places on the child's words.

- Each of the "published" LEA books can be placed in the Literacy Center or library corner of the classroom so that other children can look at and read them. Many times children find dictated child-written books to be among the most interesting of the materials that they can read.

- Each child can construct her or his own *word bank.* A word bank is a collection of all the words that the child has found especially interesting and relevant from his or her LEA charts and stories. The child or the teacher prints

each of these words on a piece of tagboard about $1'' \times 3''$ with a dark-colored marking pen or crayon. All of the words are filed in the child's word bank container which may be a shoe box, a large brown envelope, or some similar easily available container. From time to time the child reviews these words, uses them in an oral or written sentence, and returns them to the word bank container to be studied again later. The word bank also serves as an easy-to-locate source for the spelling of some commonly used and meaningful words for the child. Here are some words from a LEA story about a trip to the lake that a child might include in his/her word bank:

lake, swim, boat, fish, dock, trees, sun, fun, summer, happy

These are the main steps in LEA dictation both of experience charts and experience stories. Of course, they should be modified depending upon each child's and each primary-grade class's unique literacy interests and needs. Here are several examples of actual LEA stories that were dictated by kindergarten children:

Frosting Cupcakes
Me and Beth frosted cupcakes for her birthday.
My mother made the cupcakes.
Then we opened the frosting up.
We put it on each cupcake with a knife.
It was hard to do.
We didn't do it very well, but it was good anyway.
We both licked the knives.
That was real good.
Then we both ate cupcakes.
It was lots of fun.

Our Trip to Florida
My family went to Florida for Christmas.
We went to Disney World first.
That was lots of fun.
We went on a bunch of different rides.
I saw Mickey Mouse.
Then we went over to the ocean, and I got to swim.
It tasted like salt.
I liked the trees there, and it was hot.
We all had fun in Florida.
I liked the plane rides too.

What Are the Advantages and Limitations of LEA?

LEA is an excellent way for family members (who are easily trained in the use of LEA), and preschool, kindergarten, and first-grade teachers to present the emergent literacy skills to young children. In fact, it may be the single best way. It also is very helpful in improving beginning reading and writing skills of older severely disabled readers, and in both young and older children with special needs of all kinds (see Chapter 8). It is the most common approach for teaching beginning reading skills to adult nonreaders because it uses their own oral language and prior knowledge. Some commercial beginning reading materials may appear somewhat uninteresting to such adults. Indeed, LEA probably has no weaknesses when it is used along with another somewhat more structured beginning reading approach such as basal readers and phonic instruction.

Here are the major strengths of using LEA as a major or supplementary way to present and/or reinforce emergent literacy skills:

- Since it capitalizes on the child's own oral language patterns and prior knowledge, children have no difficulty comprehending what they read.
- It integrates listening, speaking, reading, and writing very effectively.
- It enhances the child's creativity through illustrating LEA books and book covers.
- It is a highly motivating, interesting approach. It is a very rare young child who does not enjoy dictating and reading LEA charts and stories.
- The child learns the various beginning reading skills such as capital and lowercase letter names, concept of word and word boundaries, beginning phonic skills, beginning word structure skills such as simple word endings (suffixes), and semantic (contextual) analysis in a meaningful way within the context of actual words and sentences. LEA also stresses the relationship between spoken and written language as well as one-to-one oral language-word correspondence. All these literacy skills usually are learned very effectively.
- Since it uses the child's own language patterns and experiences, it is especially effective with many types of children with special needs, such as ESL (English as a Second Language) children or those with limited English proficiency (LEP), minority-group children, and children with other special needs such as learning disabilities or physical challenges. It may well be the single most effective way to teach emergent literacy skills to such young children.

Here are the major weaknesses when LEA is used as the sole approach for teaching beginning reading and writing skills. All of these weaknesses can easily be eliminated if LEA is used as an important approach along with some more structured approach such as basal readers or a phonic approach, both of which place more emphasis on skill development.

- It lacks sequential skill development of the various literacy skills, especially phonic analysis. This is the reason LEA has been criticized by those who also find weaknesses in whole language programs. It does not present the various phonic analysis skills in a structured way such as is typically done in the basal reading approach and phonic approaches.
- When it is used as the major approach for teaching beginning literacy, LEA requires a literacy teacher who can present the reading skills without the guidance of teachers' manuals.
- Since there are no materials that instruct a literacy teacher just exactly how to implement LEA, it requires considerable teacher time to present it as a major beginning reading approach.
- Some few students, perhaps especially children with learning disabilities, may need more structured presentation of the reading skills, especially of phonic analysis, than is presented in the LEA approach.

In summary, LEA is best used in combination with another more structured approach, as explained later in this chapter. If you want to learn more about how to implement LEA with any young child in any informal or formal program, you can consult the following sources, among others:

Allen, R. (1976). *Language experiences in communication.* Boston: Houghton Mifflin.

Hall, M. (1976). *Teaching reading as a language experience.* Columbus, OH: Charles E. Merrill.

Stauffer, R. (1980). *The language-experience approach to the teaching of reading* (2d ed.). NY: Harper & Row.

Veatch, J., et al. (1979). *Key words to reading: The language experience approach begins.* Columbus, OH: Charles E. Merrill.

THE BASAL READER APPROACH

A Brief History of the Basal Reader Approach

The *basal reader approach* traditionally has been the most commonly used kindergarten and primary-grade reading approach. Basal reading materials are designed to be the *basic* materials that are used in a classroom. They consist of children's readers, teachers' manuals, and many supplemental reading materials. Although it is not quite as widely used as it was fifteen or twenty years ago, it is still used at least to some extent in a number of primary-grade classrooms in the United States and Canada. However, it is not very common in Great Britain, Australia, and New Zealand, where whole language programs are widely used.

Basal readers have a long history of use in the United States. The contemporary basal readers in some ways are based on the *McGuffey Readers* of the nineteenth century. These were rather uninteresting children's reading books that had stories with a vocabulary controlled for graphophonic (phonic) regularity. They also taught moral values such as the importance of honesty, thrift, and good deeds, among others. One can look at an actual McGuffey Reader in the historical archives of some libraries (for example, Milner Library at Illinois State University has the McGuffey Readers).

Contemporary basal readers are based more on the basal readers of the 1930s and 1940s. The most popular basal reader publisher of that era was Scott, Foresman and Company of Glenview, Illinois, who published readers containing the main characters Dick, Jane, Sally, their parents, and their pets, a black and white cocker spaniel named Spot and a yellow kitten named Puff. They were supposed to be a suburban middle-class white family with a father who worked outside the home. The mother was a homemaker who stayed at home and raised the children. Although this stereotypical family persisted with some minor changes into the 1960s, it never was representative of most of the families of most of the children who had to learn to read using these books. However, the use of these rather uninspired materials taught millions of children to read more or less successfully. I, for example, learned to read very well using them. Although other basal series also were available, the Scott, Foresman basals were by far the most popular. The Public Broadcasting System had an hour-long special several years ago that explained the evolution of the Scott, Foresman basal readers over the years.

The basal readers of that time usually featured three rigid reading achievement groups—the above average, the average, and the below average groups. They also contained a very controlled vocabulary, especially in the beginning books, which were called *preprimers, primers,* and *first readers.* The first hard-covered book normally was the first readers. A typical story in a preprimer might be something like this:

> *Oh, look.*
> *Look at the dog.*
> *See Spot run.*
> *Look, look, look.*

This does not appear as though it would be very interesting to children.

The use of basal readers of that time also included the following:

- Short selections that were to be read in very short segments, such as a page at a time, followed by a number of comprehension questions usually of the factual type.
- Presentation of the new vocabulary for the story before it was read.

- Oral reading after the story which often was "round-robin" reading in which each child in the group read a short portion aloud while the rest of the group was supposed to follow along.
- The presentation of one or several reading skills after the story was read.
- A workbook page(s) or other seat work that the child was to do independently at his or her desk while the teacher worked with other reading groups.
- Enriching experiences such as the independent reading of a related supplementary reader story or trade book, a related art activity, a related music activity, or a related game activity.

Basal reader tests, which were achievement tests that a child should pass after a certain number of basal reader lessons were completed, also were included in the typical basal reader program.

The implementation of the entire basal reader approach often resulted in boring, unimaginative, repetitive reading instruction which could become very tiring after an entire school year. This especially was true if the teacher did not incorporate any of his or her own creativity into the lessons but rather just followed the teacher's manual in a rote, rather mindless fashion.

Contemporary Basal Readers

Gradually, basal readers have evolved in a number of ways from those of the past. The changes probably began in the 1970s but accelerated in the 1980s and 1990s mainly due to the whole language movement which recently had become popular. Although contemporary basal readers purport to reflect the whole language philosophy, they do not really do so. However, they do contain some elements that are more whole language related than they did in the past. Here are the major changes of contemporary basal readers in comparison to those of the past:

- They contain minority groups characters. For example, the typical basal reader today has main and minor characters that represent African Americans, Latinos, Native Americans, and Asians. Therefore, children from minority groups of various types have story characters with whom they can more easily identify. However, even contemporary basal readers have few physically challenged or elderly individuals as meaningful main characters.
- They portray women and girls in nontraditional roles. For example, the child may well see women doctors, firefighters, astronauts, construction workers, and police officers, among many others. These changes took place in the 1970s mainly due to the influence of the National Organization of Women (NOW), which stated that the basal readers of that time did not

portray women and girls accurately but rather in stereotypical roles.

- They contain more and longer excerpts of actual trade books than in the past. For example, today a basal reader may contain an excerpted version of *Little House in the Big Woods* by Laura Ingalls Wilder. They also contain more content (expository) selections, poetry, and realistic literature.

- Although basal readers today still employ vocabulary control, especially at the beginning stages of reading, it is not as rigid as it was in the past. While the stories in the preprimers, primers, and first readers are still rather boring due to their controlled vocabulary, they are somewhat more interesting than they were in the past.

- New vocabulary is often not presented in as formal a manner in the contemporary basals as it was in the past. In addition, reading skills such as graphophonic analysis and word structure are usually presented in the context of actual reading material more than was done previously.

- Although the basal reader teacher's manuals may be somewhat less prescriptive than they were in the past, they still are too prescriptive and rigid unless the early childhood teacher is willing and able to select the most relevant and meaningful suggestions found in them for her or his own pupils.

- Seat work may not be emphasized as much as it was in the past; however, workbooks still accompany basal reader series. If a workbook is to be used properly, a child should be required to complete only those workbook pages that have relevance for him or her. For example, a child never should be required to complete a workbook page that presents or reviews a reading skill in which the child already has competence. To do so is a waste of time and energy.

- Although ability groups may not be as commonly used as they were in the past, some primary-grade classrooms still use three achievement groups—the above average, the average, and the below average. Even though the manuals of all contemporary basal readers stress that such reading achievement groups should be flexible, allowing children to easily move from group to group, in fact they may well remain fixed. This usually is especially damaging to children in the below average group who often are stigmatized as being in the "dummy group," with a resulting effect on their self-esteem. Using collaborative grouping, partner reading, interest groups, and research groups (as described earlier in this chapter) can greatly help to eliminate this problem.

- Today basal readers usually are designated by level numbers instead of by grade level, to avoid the stigma that a child may feel from reading a book that is below his or her actual grade level. In the past the two basal readers for second grade, for example, were labeled as 2_1 and 2_2. However, today the second-grade basal readers might be labeled as Level 8, Level 9, Level 10, and Level 11. Since each set of basal readers differs somewhat on the levels that represent each actual grade level, the teacher must check the teacher's manual of the basal readers that she or he is using to find out what actual grade level the designated level refers to.

- Basal reader publishers today have made a concerted effort to publish materials that are as attractive and appealing to children as possible. On the whole they are much more attractive and interesting than they were in the past. Most of them appeal to children at least to an extent. However, whole language proponents still criticize them for their lack of intact quality literature and the use of vocabulary control, ability grouping, and overly prescriptive teacher's manuals.

Elements of the Typical Contemporary Basal Reader Series

A typical basal reader series costs significantly more than $10,000,000 to publish, which means the publisher must sell a great number of books before any profit will be made. This is one reason that every early childhood teacher must be certain to critically analyze any basal reader publisher's presentation at his or her school, at the exhibits at a professional convention, or in any other setting. The teacher should realize that the publisher has made a huge financial investment and wants very much to sell its product. The high cost of purchasing an entire basal reader series for a school or school district is one main reason why the typical series may be used in a school for as long as *ten years*. Therefore, it is very important for the early childhood teacher to select a basal reader series very carefully if she or he has the obligation or opportunity to do so.

A basal reader series usually has a number of different persons on its team of authors. For example, the team normally has several well-known literacy specialists as the major authors. These specialists usually write all or most of the material for the teacher's manuals and generally oversee the entire basal series. The team often consists of several specialists in children's literature and elementary classroom or reading teachers as well as the professional staff employed by the publisher. Since the production of an entire basal reader series is so time-consuming and costly, a company usually continues to publish a basal reader series for approximately six to ten years before significantly revising it. That is another reason that an early childhood teacher must select the series that is going to be used as a major or supplementary literacy approach very carefully.

The typical basal reader series has some type of material that is used in kindergartens. Although in the past this took the form of reading readiness workbooks, today other emergent literacy skills may be stressed as well. I recommend that the print materials of a basal reader series not be purchased for use in kindergartens, as I believe there are many better ways of improving emergent literacy skills. A number of these are whole language related. Many of them were described in the section on whole language earlier in this chapter, while others are discussed in later chapters of the book.

The reading books for use in the first half of first grade usually are paperback and are designated Level 1, Level 2, and so on. The books for the last half of first grade usually are hard-covered and may be given level designations such as Level 5, Level 6, and so on. The reading books for use in second and third grades are hard-covered and continue using the level designations, often Level 10, Level 11, and higher.

A teacher's manual accompanies each level of the child's reader, and each manual has countless suggestions for the following:

- presenting each story in the reader effectively
- using the accompanying workbook
- employing varied strategies for skill development
- using a *scope and sequence chart* that lists all of the literacy skills presented in the series
- extending each lesson such as related trade books for the children to read, related games to play, and related art, construction, and music activities

Basal reader series normally also consist of expendable workbooks of some type, supplementary readers of various types, basal reader tests that measure what a child is supposed to master after a certain segment of study, computer software, puppets, word cards and a card holder, games, videotapes, and pictures. The early childhood teacher can choose to purchase some, most, or all of these related materials, remembering that the additional purchases will cost his or her school district additional money. Much of this money may better be spent on purchasing multiple and single copies of interesting trade books for the children to read for pleasure and information.

The best way for a preservice or an in-service teacher to learn about a basal reader series is simply to go to a reading convention such as the annual International Reading Association Convention or a state or local reading association convention and examine several series at the publishers' booths there. Teachers also can go to the education center of the nearest university library and examine one or more basal reader series, carefully evaluating each series on a number of questions such as those included in the next section of this chapter. If the Dewey decimal numbering system is used in the library, the basal reader series should be found in 428 of the education center of the library. This center is called the Teaching Materials Center at Illinois State University and may also be called this at your local college or university library.

Evaluating a Basal Reader Series

The following are some general questions that you may want to ask yourself when evaluating any basal reader series for possible use in your early childhood classroom.

Basal Readers

Are the readers attractive and appealing to children?

Do the readers have a number of excerpted selections from actual trade books?

Do the stories in the readers seem as though they would interest children?

Do the readers contain a few informational selections as well as narrative selections?

Do the readers seem to have an adequate, but not excessive, amount of vocabulary control?

Is there a sufficient number of the following as major characters in the stories in the readers: members of minority groups (African Americans, Latinos, Asian Americans, and Native Americans), women and girls in nontraditional roles, persons with physical challenges of various types (visually impaired, hearing impaired, and physically challenged, among others), and elderly persons in nontraditional roles.

Do the readers seem as though they would be durable?

Teacher's Manuals

Are the suggestions in the manuals comprehensive and helpful?

Are a number of the strategies contained in the manuals reflective of the whole language philosophy?

Are the materials in the manuals easy to read and follow?

Do the suggestions in the manual help the teacher to integrate the language arts of listening, speaking, reading, and writing?

Do the manuals explain and reflect a certain philosophy of teaching literacy?

Do the manuals each contain a scope and sequence chart of the literacy skills presented and reviewed in the basal reader series?

Do the manuals recommend sufficient review activities and materials so that each of the important reading skills (especially that of graphophonic analysis) is thoroughly covered?

Do the manuals suggest additional ways of grouping children beside the most commonly used reading achievement groups?

Are the individuals on the authoring team reflective of the various groups that should be represented, that is, are they nationally known literacy specialists, specialists in children's literature, and classroom and literacy teachers?

Do the manuals suggest many valuable enriching experiences that are reflective of the whole language philosophy and would be truly motivating, challenging, and worthwhile?

Do the manuals contain a small representation of each of the pages in the reader that it is devoted to so that the teacher does not continually have to refer to the child's reader?

Basal Reader Workbooks

Do the workbooks provide meaningful independent activities, or are they merely a way to keep the children occupied?

Are the workbook pages challenging for the above average readers and yet able to be completed independently by the below average readers with a minimum of teacher or partner help?

Are the workbook pages attractive to children?

Can some of the pages be omitted if a child does not need the skill(s) emphasized on that particular page?

Are the workbooks fairly inexpensive for the school district to purchase so that the teacher does not have to be concerned about using every page with every child?

Are the workbook pages easy for the teacher to evaluate?

Basal Reader Tests

Do the tests assess those literacy skills that really are worth evaluating?

Are the tests easy for the teacher to evaluate?

Do the tests emphasize any aspect of authentic assessment as it was described earlier in this chapter, or are they merely standardized devices?

Would children have a fairly easy time understanding and carrying out the tasks that are evaluated by the tests?

Are the tests fairly inexpensive for the school district to purchase?

Do the tests take a reasonable amount of time for the children to take so that an excessive amount of time is not spent on assessment in comparison to teaching?

Supplementary Materials

Are the supplementary materials that accompany the basal reader series worthy of the money that would be spent on them?

Are the supplementary materials varied enough to meet the needs of all the children in a typical class, including computer software, games, word cards

and card holder, supplementary readers, pictures, puppets, and videotapes, among others?

Is it easy to locate the availability and price of the various supplementary materials in the teacher's manual or in a catalog that accompanies the basal reader series?

Note: A complete list of questions that an early childhood teacher can use to evaluate a basal reader series is found in the following professional book:

Aukerman, R. (1981.) *The basal reader approach to reading.* NY: John Wiley & Sons.

Basal Reader Publishers

Here is a comprehensive list of basal reader publishers. You should contact a publisher for complete information about the basal reader series that their company publishes. Usually a basal reader publisher also will give a presentation to one or more teachers in a school system. Each teacher must learn to be a critical, informed consumer when listening to the presentation.

Addison-Wesley

American Book

Ginn

Harcourt Brace Jovanovich

Harper & Row

D C Heath

Holt, Rinehart & Winston

Houghton Mifflin

Laidlaw

Macmillan

Riverside

Science Research Associates (SRA)

Scott, Foresman

Silver Burdett Ginn

Advantages and Limitations of the Basal Reader Approach

Here are the major advantages of using the basal reader approach as a main or supplementary approach for teaching early childhood literacy:

- Without a doubt, the main advantage is the sequential skill development. All of the word identification skills of sight word recognition and identification, graphophonic analysis, word structure, semantic (meaning) cues, and all of the elements of reading comprehension are presented in a sequential, developmental way. The scope and sequence chart that is part of a basal reader series indicates to the teacher the reading skills that are presented at all reading levels. Therefore, if the early childhood teacher uses a basal reader series, she or he can feel confident that all of the important reading skills have been presented, if not mastered.

- The teacher's manuals are comprehensive and provide exact direction to the teacher about how to implement all aspects of a basal reader lesson. The teacher who follows a teacher's manual carefully does not have to be knowledgeable either about the reading process or the strategies for teaching reading.
- The basal reader teacher's manuals and workbooks contain a myriad of materials that should save the busy teacher considerable time and effort in comparison to having to locate them on his or her own.
- The basal reader approach may be especially useful for beginning or fairly inexperienced teachers who need considerable direction and support. The use of this approach gives the inexperienced teacher great security.
- Since a basal reader series has been written by reading specialists and other literacy specialists who understand the literacy process and children's literature well, it generally contains accurate information.
- The contemporary basal readers reflect all of the minority groups very well, and women and girls are portrayed in nontraditional roles quite well.
- Most basal reader series utilize computer software in the literacy program.

Here are major limitations of using the basal reader approach as a main or supplementary method of teaching reading:

- Although the manuals state that the reading achievement groups used in this approach should be flexible, in practice they usually are fixed, causing a great deal of difficulty if a child wishes to move to a higher group. This can be especially damaging to a child in the below average group, who may develop a negative self-esteem about reading and a dislike for all literacy activities. No matter what names groups are given, even in the early stages of first grade children know exactly how well they read. In 1997 this author asked 212 first-grade children how well they thought they read, and all of them were able to tell me exactly how effective a reader he or she was (Miller, 1998).
- The teacher's manuals can be much too prescriptive, and the early childhood teacher must think of the suggestions and strategies that are included in the manual as only that. No teacher should ever ask all the questions, do all the activities, nor require all of the enriching experiences that are in the manual. Not only is this impossible, but it can be very detrimental to children. It may cause the literacy program to be extremely boring and unimaginative. The manuals must be considered as only a guide, with the teacher selecting only appropriate activities.

- The workbook pages often are not particularly creative or inspiring. No child should ever be required to complete a workbook page if she or he already has mastered the literacy skills being reviewed on that page. Some of the workbook pages do not reflect a child's unique interests or needs.
- Since some of the quality children's literature is excerpted for the basal readers, one must wonder if it is not much better for children to read the actual trade books from which the excerpts were taken.
- Some reading specialists believe that the basal reader approach does not include enough repetition of graphophonic analysis to ensure that all children master this important reading skill to the best of their ability.
- The beginning basal readers may contain so much vocabulary control that the stories are even more uninteresting than they need to be for beginning readers.
- The basal reader manuals should never be used as a definitive guide as to what selections, strategies, activities, or tests should be used with a child. The early childhood teacher is a professional who must choose all of the reading selections, strategies, activities, or supplementary materials that will be most beneficial to his or her pupils. I believe that basal reader manuals typically do not treat a teacher as the professional that he or she is.
- The entire basal reader series, including the readers, manuals, workbooks, tests, supplementary readers, and other supplementary materials, is very expensive. It may be more beneficial for the early childhood teacher to spend some of this money on multiple or single copies of good trade books for the class.
- Basal readers are weak in portraying all types of physically challenged individuals and elderly people as major characters. All types of physically challenged children need to have positive role models in their basal readers, and at this time this is just not the case. Neither do they have the opportunity to see older people in any but the stereotypical roles.

In summary, the basal reader approach never should be used without also using a significant amount of whole language and language-experience activities. The last part of this chapter provides you with detailed guidelines about how to do this effectively.

PHONICS PROGRAMS

The History of Systematic Phonics Programs

Phonics programs are another approach for teaching beginning reading. A systematic phonics program is a major or supplementary approach for teaching beginning reading skills that places great emphasis on using graphophonic analysis as the only important word identification technique. In the typical systematic phonics program, the other word identification techniques of sight word identification, structural analysis, and semantic (contextual) analysis usually receive little, if any, emphasis. The importance of reading comprehension also is de-emphasized to a greater or lesser degree, especially at the beginning stages of reading instruction.

Phonics reading instruction approaches have a very long history. Indeed, the first formal phonics program probably dates from the late eighteenth century when Noah Webster published his famous *American spelling book* (1798). Since that time, phonics programs have been in or out of fashion depending upon the climate of the times. Their popularity has come and gone in fairly regular cycles. For example, phonics programs were popular in the 1920s and unpopular during the 1930s and 1940s, when the whole word approach as used in the Scott, Foresman basal readers was in vogue. They were again popular in the late 1950s and the 1960s during which time Rudolph Flesch wrote the well-known book *Why Johnny can't read and what you can do about it* (1955). In this book Flesch equated pronouncing words (word calling) with reading and stated that if a person can pronounce a language such as Spanish or Finnish, he or she can read it. Of course, that is not true, since pronouncing Spanish is not really reading it. Reading always requires comprehension to be called true reading, according to most reading specialists. Phonics programs lost popularity as the whole language approach became increasingly popular in the late 1970s, 1980s, and 1990s. However, whole language is now subject to increasing criticism because of falling test scores, especially in the state of California, and phonics instruction is on the rise once again.

The one consistent major controversy in reading instruction always has been between those reading specialists who are in favor of a beginning reading approach that places a great deal of emphasis on graphophonic analysis and those who support the whole language approach. I have never understood why a professional early childhood literacy teacher cannot use whole language along with some structured skills instruction and reinforcement to provide young children with an optimum beginning literacy program. I do *not* see a need for a debate between the various philosophies of teaching beginning reading as was summarized in a very well known book by Jeanne Chall entitled *Learning to read: The great debate* (1967, 1983). Perhaps several of the best-known professional books that summarize the polarization between those literacy specialists that hold opposing views on this subject are the books *What's whole in whole language?* (1986) and *Phonics Phacts* (1993) by Kenneth Goodman, a whole language proponent, and *Beginning to read: Thinking and learning about print* (1990) by Marilyn Jager Adams, a proponent of a beginning reading approach that emphasizes decoding in beginning reading, especially graphophonic analysis.

How Is the Typical Systematic Phonic Program Different from Either Whole Language Programs or the Basal Reader Approach?

The typical systematic phonics program differs from other beginning reading instruction in that it teaches many more phonic elements and generalizations (rules) than does any other beginning reading approach of which I am aware, and it teaches them earlier in kindergarten and the primary grades. For example, *Alpha Time* (which has been a popular phonics program for use in kindergarten) teaches the sounds of the short vowels at that level. This is very different from even the basal reader approach that typically does not teach these sounds until later in first grade. *Alpha Time* uses varied strategies and materials to do this, including small or large inflatable "letter people," records, and other aids.

Although most of the kindergarten children with whom I have talked apparently very much enjoyed this formal phonics program, it is not recommended by any professional association of which I am aware. For example, neither the International Reading Association (IRA) nor the Association for Childhood Education International (ACEI) endorses its use.

It is difficult to accurately describe the basic characteristics of all systematic phonics programs, since they differ quite a bit, but it is correct to say that all of them teach more phonic elements and teach them earlier than do other reading programs. Most of them consider phonic analysis to be the most important technique for identifying words. The various programs do differ in the amount of emphasis they place on comprehension, with some of them emphasizing it quite a bit more than others.

Phonics programs also differ a great deal in the sequence in which they present the phonic elements and generalizations (rules). Some of them present initial consonants and consonant blends very early in the beginning reading program, while others present them later. Some systematic phonics programs teach the vowel sounds before they teach any consonant or consonant blend sounds. Some of these programs present the long vowel sounds first, while others present the short vowel sounds first. Therefore, it is difficult to generalize about the content of these programs. Indeed, some of them are much more like traditional approaches such as the basal reader approach than are others. Some of them are considerably more accurate than others. Some published formal phonics approaches contain significant errors that typical undergraduate early childhood education students might locate, while others are fairly accurate. Some of the programs are written by qualified literacy specialists, while it is quite obvious that some are not. That is why any early childhood reading teacher must carefully analyze any such program before deciding to use it.

Systematic phonics programs differ from either whole language programs or basal reader programs in a number of ways. As you remember, whole language programs teach phonic elements and generalizations (rules) only in the context of words, sentences, or passages, in other words, only as needed for effective decoding in whole language settings. Basal reader programs generally teach phonic elements in either word context or in portions of words such as *onsets* (consonants, consonant blends, or consonant digraphs) and *rimes* (word families). An example is the use of the rime *-all* making up the words *ball, call, fall, hall, small, tall,* and *wall.*

In addition, a phonics program may teach graphophonic analysis either analytically or synthetically. When it is taught *analytically,* a whole word is broken down into its parts, such as the word *let/ter.* However, when it is taught *synthetically,* individual phonemes (sounds) are blended to form a word such as "cuh-a-tuh" being blended to form the word "cat." On the whole, the analytic teaching of phonic analysis is much more effective because of the potential in synthetic teaching for the distortion of the consonant sounds such as "cuh" and "tuh" when the word "cat" is blended. It is almost impossible to pronounce a consonant in isolation without adding a vowel to it. Most children have a great deal of difficulty understanding that the word "cat" is sounded out when the three sounds "cuh-a-tuh" are put together.

The Strengths and Weaknesses of Phonics Programs

The proponents of systematic phonics programs present several advantages of using such a program to teach beginning reading in kindergartens and first grades. In most cases this in essence is only teaching phonic skills with a de-emphasis on comprehension of what is read. However, as stated earlier, some of the phonics programs do emphasize reading comprehension to a greater or lesser degree.

Here are what the proponents of these programs state are the advantages:

- Since they are taught so many phonic elements and generalizations (rules) early in the program, some children who are taught reading using this type of program in first and second grades achieve higher reading test scores through about the third-grade level than do those children who are not exposed to such a program.
- Children who learn phonics become independent in decoding (word attack) much earlier than children who are not exposed to such a program.
- Children who are taught many phonic elements and generalizations (rules) *may* be better spellers than those children who are not.

- Such a structured program may be especially helpful to children with learning disabilities and some children with other special needs.

Here are the major disadvantages of using any type of systematic phonics program in kindergarten or the primary grades:

- It can cause a child to become a "word-caller," that is, a reader who can pronounce words very effectively but has little or no comprehension of what he or she reads. This may result because the major focus of such a program is on word pronunciation, not on understanding what is read.
- It can result in a child who stops to analyze almost every word, even if some of these are words that he or she should know by sight. This not only slows down the child's rate of either oral or silent reading, but it also usually results in a child who cannot comprehend well, since the entire message is lost in the extensive sounding out of most words.
- It is very ineffective with and may well be very damaging to a child who does not have good *auditory discrimination,* the ability to hear the likenesses and differences in sounds. Most typically when a systematic phonics program is used in a kindergarten, first grade, or second grade, it is taught to all children without any regard for their auditory discrimination ability. This is a grave injustice to such children.
- Some phonic programs contain errors that the early childhood teacher must be aware of. The teacher must examine and evaluate any such program carefully before using it either as a major or supplementary approach for teaching beginning reading. I have found by reviewing many such programs that they typically contain a higher percentage of errors than do the typical basal readers teacher's manuals.
- Unfortunately, many of the systematic phonics programs are dull and uninteresting for children. They just are not very motivating. If the program does contain reading material on which the children should practice phonic analysis, this reading material too is often uninteresting. Most, if not all, of these programs are repetitive, sterile, and boring.
- Such phonic programs state that graphophonic analysis is the single most important, if not the only, valuable word identification technique for children. Indeed, most reading specialists believe that semantic (contextual) analysis perhaps in combination with graphophonic analysis is the most useful word identification technique. Certainly the use of semantic analysis provides the best way for children to determine the pronunciation and meaning of the unknown words that they meet while reading. This is especially true if the material does not contain more than one word in fifty that is an unknown word.

- As stated earlier, the use of analytic phonic analysis, in which the child begins with a total word and decodes it first into syllables and then into phonemes, is more useful than is synthetic phonic analysis, which begins with individual phonemes (sounds) and blends them together to form a word such as "buh-a-tuh" (bat). The use of onsets and rimes is more valuable than is synthetic phonic analysis. Therefore, if an early childhood teacher wants to use one of these phonic programs, she or he should select a program that employs some form of consonant substitution or analytic phonic analysis.

This author is not able to recommend any of the systematic phonics approaches as a major beginning reading program. Phonic elements and generalizations are taught and reviewed much better in context within whole language programs or in either context or isolation in basal reader systems. Perhaps some portion of a formal phonics program would be useful as a supplement to a whole language or basal program in a rare instance such as with a child who has special needs, such as a child with learning disabilities. In general, an early childhood teacher can design personalized phonic instruction and review by using the actual materials that the child is reading along with motivational activity sheets, useful computer software, and interesting games. Although phonic elements should be taught in the context of words as much as possible, it may be necessary to present and review them in isolation. This has especially been true with the short vowel sounds /a/, /e/, /i/, /o/, and /u/ which many children have a very difficult time hearing within word context. If the teacher decides to design his or her own phonics program, it also is more helpful to use analytic phonic analysis, as has been mentioned earlier.

A BALANCED EARLY CHILDHOOD LITERACY PROGRAM

An Introduction to a Balanced Early Childhood Literacy Program

A balanced literacy program or a variety of materials and approaches generally constitutes the best program for most children. Although this final part of the chapter very briefly suggests ways for doing this and presents a sample primary-grade schedule, each early childhood teacher is encouraged to design his or her own variation depending upon the needs and interests of a particular class. In fact, a teacher's literacy program may vary considerably from year to year depending upon the teacher's expertise in the field and the characteristics of his or her class. Therefore, the information presented in this part of the chapter must serve only as a general guide for what can occur.

A Preschool Literacy Program

The typical preschool literacy program should be very similar to the optimum early literacy activities presented in the home. They should be whole language oriented and directed toward the developmental level of each particular child. No type of formal instruction in any reading skill, including that of graphophonic analysis, should be presented in any preschool setting. Any literacy skills that are taught in a preschool setting should be informal, motivating, and beneficial to each individual child.

Although all of the literacy activities that can be informally presented in preschool settings are described and illustrated in other portions of this book, here is a very brief summary of them:

- Reading to the children on a daily basis from motivating materials of all types including picture storybooks, predictable books. Mother Goose books, poetry, and informational books, among others
- Having children listen to cassette tape recordings of interesting children's books read aloud by experienced readers
- Using language-experience approach (LEA) dictation on a regular, if not daily, basis
- Acting out trade books that the teacher has read aloud
- Engaging in dramatic play with props and costumes of various types
- Using puppets, stuffed animals, and felt boards to accompany the teacher's reading aloud of various trade books
- Engaging in block play of various types
- Going on school trips with accompanying prior and follow-up discussion of the experience, perhaps including an LEA dictation about the experience after returning
- Engaging in various informal activities to develop each child's concepts about print such as calling the children's attention to left-to-right progression, beginning and end of a printed page, concepts about words and letters, the concept of word boundaries, and the concepts of title, author, and illustrator of trade books
- Having writing materials of various types available, such as large unlined paper, markers, crayons, pencils, and blank books of various types
- Valuing all types of writing, including scribbling, random letters (letter strings), and invented spelling (although the latter is not likely to occur at the preschool level)
- Providing real-life reasons for writing, such as writing make-believe grocery lists, thank-you cards and letters, birthday cards, and get-well cards, and writing related to experiences occurring in the dramatic play center
- Providing many opportunities for improving oral language skills, such as sharing time, conversation,

informal discussions, LEA dictation, and "pretend reading" with buddies, among others

- Listening to all types of materials being read aloud, and cassette tape recordings of various types, and watching and listening to appropriate children's television programs such as *Sesame Street, Romper Room, Barney, Captain Kangaroo* (where available), and *Reading Rainbow,* among others
- Engaging in experiences to improve prior knowledge, such as going on school trips, having classroom visitors and parents in to talk about various occupations and vacations, and watching computer software, videotapes, films, and filmstrips
- Engaging in cooking and baking activities of all types
- Participating in all types of creative art activities, perhaps related to the theme of the whole language units
- Engaging in all kinds of construction activities, also often related to the theme of the whole language units
- Participating in all types of music and rhythm activities, often related to the theme of the whole language units

A Kindergarten Literacy Program

A kindergarten literacy program should be similar to a preschool literacy program in many ways. For example, all of the activities mentioned earlier in the section about preschool literacy programs are equally applicable in any kindergarten. The whole language approach with its emphasis on thematic unit teaching, active child involvement, child development principles, and all of its other characteristics described earlier are very applicable in any kindergarten.

In addition, the language-experience approach (LEA) is useful in any kindergarten literacy program. LEA should be used on an individual basis as much as is feasible. However, it also is very helpful in small-group and large-group settings. Obviously, each child has the opportunity to participate less in the dictation of a language-experience chart in a large-group setting than in a small-group setting. Children in kindergarten also very much enjoy writing their own LEA stories on sheets of paper, in blank books, or on sheets of paper that later can be bound into individual LEA books. Scribbling, random letters (letter strings), invented spelling, or traditional spelling all can be used in a child's LEA story (see Chapter 6). Individual or partner LEA stories also can be typed on a computer. As has been mentioned earlier, kindergarten children can learn basic keyboarding skills very well, and it is desirable for them to do so.

It cannot be stressed strongly enough how very useful LEA is for improving many aspects of emergent and beginning literacy. It stresses all of the language arts of listening, speaking, reading, and writing equally well, is

highly motivating to children, and greatly enhances their creativity.

Most kindergarten children need some primarily informal reading skill development, especially in very basic sight word recognition and identification, including environmental print, knowledge of both capital and lowercase letter names, very elementary graphophonic analysis, and use of semantic (meaning) cues. It is very important, for example, that all kindergarten children learn to recognize and identify all of the capital and lowercase letter names if possible. It also is helpful for them to learn a few basic environmental or sight words. Some kindergarten children who are ready for it can learn some easy-to-remember phonemes (sounds). Most often these are initial consonant sounds that are both easy to hear and regular. The initial consonants of /c/ and /g/ normally cause the most difficulty for young children since /c/ borrows either the sound of /k/ (hard c) or the sound of /s/ (soft c), while /g/ can either have a hard sound as in the word *goat* or a soft sound as in the word *gem.* Kindergarten children should not be exposed to any formal phonic program such as *Alpha Time.* Indeed, this program places great stress on the vowel sounds which are both hard to discriminate and irregular.

It must be stressed that any reading program in kindergarten should be informal, stressing interesting whole language activities with meaningful skill development (sight word recognition and identification and graphophonic analysis) for those children who are ready for it. Indeed, some kindergarten children already are reading at the beginning of the school year. These children should be allowed and encouraged to continue this reading at their own level whether it is the first-, second-, or even third-grade level. Phonic skills should be presented and reinforced for them in a meaningful way when they have a need for it in an individual or perhaps small-group setting. Although it is not desirable to teach reading in kindergarten per se, it is desirable to allow kindergarten children to learn to read if they are able and willing to do so. They also should be allowed to read at their own level, even if it is far above the kindergarten level. It can be very harmful, however, to pressure young children to learn any literacy skills for which they are not ready and in which they are not interested.

A Combination Approach for First, Second, and Third Grades

A balanced approach featuring many whole language activities and thematic unit teaching along with structured skill development (especially graphophonic analysis) as found in a basal reader system is the optimum literacy program for first-, second-, and third-grade children.

A sample daily schedule follows on page 57 that can serve as a model of how a primary-grade teacher can combine the best features of whole language (including

LEA and process writing) and some portion of a basal reader system. Of course, this daily schedule must be modified in terms of each elementary school's music, art, and physical education schedules and the length of the school day. It is simply included as a model of what a primary-grade schedule could be that attempts to blend both whole language and structured skills instruction using the basal reader approach. This chapter along with the others in this book provide guidelines and examples of how to present and reinforce all of the literacy activities that are included in this daily schedule.

TABLE 2.1	SAMPLE DAILY SCHEDULE			
	FIRST GRADE, SECOND GRADE OR THIRD GRADE			
Monday	**Tuesday**	**Wednesday**	**Thursday**	**Friday**
8:30–8:45 Opening activities Attendance Weather Calendar	8:30–8:45 Opening activities Attendance Weather Calendar	8:30–8:45 Opening activities Attendance Weather Calendar	8:30–8:45 Opening activities Attendance Weather Calendar	8:30–8:45 Opening activities Attendance Weather Calendar
8:45–9:15 Story time	8:45–9:15 Story time	8:45–9:15 Story time	8:45–9:15 Story time	8:45–9:15 Story time

9:15–10:30
Whole ianguage
  activities related
  to the unit theme—
  Oral Language
  Reading, Dictation/
  Writing (LEA)
	9:15–10:30
	Skill development using
	  modified basal reader
	  approach—Graphophonic
	  analysis, activity sheets,
	  Small group and
	  individual skill
	  development
		9:15–10:30
		Skill development using
		  modified basal reader
		  approach—Graphophonic
		  analysis, activity sheets,
		  Small group and
		  individual skill
		  development
			9:15–10:30
			Whole language
			  activities related
			  to the unit theme—
			  Oral Language
			  Reading, Dictation/
			  Writing (LEA)
				9:15–10:30
				Whole language
				  activities related
				  to the unit theme—
				  Oral Language
				  Reading, Dictation/
				  Writing (LEA)

10:30–10:45
Outside/inside
  playtime
	10:30–10:45
	Outside/inside
	  playtime
		10:30–10:45
		Outside/inside
		  playtime
			10:30–10:45
			Outside/inside
			  playtime
				10:30–10:45
				Outside/inside
				  playtime

10:45–11:15
Music related
  to the unit
	10:45–11:15
	Music related
	  to the unit
		10:45–11:15
		Music related
		  to the unit
			10:45–11:15
			Music related
			  to the unit
				10:45–11:15
				Music related
				  to the unit

11:15–11:45
Arithmetic related
  to the unit
	11:15–11:45
	Arithmetic related
	  to the unit
		11:15–11:45
		Arithmetic related
		  to the unit
			11:15–11:45
			Arithmetic related
			  to the unit
				11:15–11:45
				Arithmetic related
				  to the unit

11:45–12:30 Lunch	11:45–12:30 Lunch	11:45–12:30 Lunch	11:45–12:30 Lunch	11:45–12:30 Lunch
12:30–1:00 Story time	12:30–1:00 Story time	12:30–1:00 Story time	12:30–1:00 Story time	12:30–1:00 Story time

1:00–1:30
Science activities
  related to the unit
	1:00–1:30
	Science activities
	  related to the unit
		1:00–1:30
		Science activities
		  related to the unit
			1:00–1:30
			Science activities
			  related to the unit
				1:00–1:30
				Science activities
				  related to the unit

1:30–2:15
Whole language
  activities (same
  as a.m.)
	1:30–2:15
	Skill development
	  related to the basal
	  reader approach
	  (same as a.m.)
		1:30–2:15
		Skill development
		  related to the basal
		  reader approach
		  (same as a.m.)
			1:30–2:15
			Whole language
			  activities (same
			  as a.m.)
				1:30–2:15
				Whole language
				  activities (same
				  as a.m.)

2:15–2:30
Outside/inside
  playtime
	2:15–2:30
	Outside/inside
	  playtime
		2:15–2:30
		Outside/inside/
		  playtime
			2:15–2:30
			Outside/inside
			  playtime
				2:15–2:30
				Outside/inside
				  playtime

2:30–2:50 P.E.	2:30–2:50 P.E.	2:30–2:50 P.E.	2:30–2:50 P.E.	2:30–2:50 P.E.
2:50–3:20 Art related to the unit	2:50–3:20 Art related to the unit	2:50–3:20 Art related to the unit	2:50–3:20 Art related to the unit	2:50–3:20 Art related to the unit
3:20–3:30 Closing activities	3:20–3:30 Closing activities	3:20–3:30 Closing activities	3:20–3:30 Closing activities	3:20–3:30 Closing activities

SUMMARY

Despite what a number of people apparently believe, there is no single literacy approach or literacy strategies and materials that are equally effective with every young child. Although whole language is a valid philosophy, contains highly effective strategies, and suggests motivating materials, its sole use normally is not completely successful with all children. Although LEA also is very effective, used alone it is not a satisfactory literacy approach for most young children either.

Most young children achieve the greatest amount of success in emergent and beginning literacy by using some variation of a combination of approaches such as whole language, LEA, and some structured skills instruction such as those found in the basal reader approach. Of course, the kindergarten, first-grade, second-grade, or third-grade literacy program of each child always should be determined by considering his or her unique needs and interests and the expertise and interests of his or her teacher.

SUGGESTED ACTIVITIES

1. Observe a kindergarten or primary-grade whole language classroom for 2–5 hours. Observe the literacy strategies and materials being used in this classroom. Summarize orally or in writing which of these strategies and materials you would want to use in your own classroom, and provide your reasons for selecting them.

2. Conduct an interactive story reading and/or reading reenactment with a three-, four-, or five-year-old child using a predictable book. Summarize this experience orally or in writing in terms of the child's success with and enjoyment of the experience.

3. Construct your own big book following one of the sets of directions found on pages 18–19 of this book.

4. For a class project, independently or with a partner(s), construct your own thematic unit modeled after the one contained in this chapter for use in a kindergarten, first-grade, second-grade, or third-grade classroom. Try to include all of the curricular areas that were contained in the sample thematic unit found in this chapter.

5. Conduct LEA dictation with a three-, four-, or five-year-old child. Include all of the steps that were suggested in this chapter. Then write a brief summary of the experience and orally share with your classmates an account of the experience as well as the completed LEA book.

6. In a cooperative learning group, examine a set of contemporary basal readers. These may be found in the teaching materials center of a local university library or in an elementary school. As a group, evaluate this basal reader series using the questions contained in this chapter. Write a brief evaluation of the series, and be prepared to share your findings with your classmates.

7. Construct your own sample daily schedule for a first-grade, second-grade, or third-grade classroom. You may use the sample daily schedule included in this chapter as a model, but you can modify it in any ways that seem appropriate.

SELECTED REFERENCES

Allen, R., & Allen, C. (1982). *Language experience activities.* Boston: Houghton Mifflin.

Beggam, S. (1995). Understanding changes in beginning reading and writing instruction. In T. V. Rasinski (Ed.). *Parents and teachers: Helping children learn to read and write* (pp. 149–155). Fort Worth, TX: Harcourt Brace.

Cheek, E., Flippo, R., & Lindsey, J. (1997). *Reading for success in elementary schools* (pp. 11–14, 284–287, 290, & 440–458). Madison, WI: Brown & Benchmark.

Crofton, L. (1991). *Whole language: Getting started.* Katonah, NY: Richard C. Owen.

Fields, M., & Spangler, K. (1995). *Let's begin reading right* (pp. 104–107 & 345–348). Englewood Cliffs, NJ: Merrill.

Hall, M. (1981). *Teaching reading as a language experience.* Columbus, OH: Merrill.

Heilman, A., Blair, T., & Rupley, W. (1998). *Principles and practices of teaching reading* (pp. 300–358 & 374–408). Upper Saddle River, NJ: Merrill.

Holdaway, D. (1979). *The foundations of literacy* (pp. 24–30, 40–52, 64–80, & 134–138). Portsmouth, NH: Heinemann.

Machado, J. (1995). *Early childhood experiences in language arts* (pp. 391–395). NY: Delmar Publishers.

May, F. (1998). *Reading as communication* (pp. 335–364). Upper Saddle River, NJ: Merrill.

McGee, L., & Richgels, D. (1996). *Literacy's beginnings: Supporting your young readers and writers* (pp. 270–282, 309–319, & 341–349). Boston: Allyn & Bacon.

Morrow, L., Strickland, D., & Woo, D. (1998). *Literacy instruction in half- and whole-day kindergarten.* Newark, DE: International Reading Association.

Neuman, S., & Roskos, K. (1993). *Language and literacy learning in the early years* (pp. 236–240). Fort Worth, TX: Harcourt Brace.

Salinger, T. (1996). *Literacy for young children* (pp. 157–167 & 206–207). Englewood Cliffs, NJ: Merrill.

Scheckendanz, J. (1989). The place of specific skills in preschool and kindergarten. In Strickland, D., & Morrow, L. (Eds.). *Emerging literacy: Young children learn to read and write* (pp. 96–101). Newark, DE: International Reading Association.

Snow, C., Burns, M., & Griffin, P. (1998). *Preventing reading difficulties in young children.* Washington, DC: National Academy Press.

Temple, C., Martinez, M., Yokota, J., & Naylor, A. (1998). *Children's books in children's hands.* Needham Heights, MA: Allyn & Bacon.

WORKS CITED IN CHAPTER 2

Abrahamson, R. (1981). An update on wordless picture books with an annotated bibliography. *The Reading Teacher, 34,* 417–421.

Adams, M. (1990). *Beginning to read.* Cambridge, MA: MIT Press.

Allen, R. (1976). *Language experiences in communication.* Boston: Houghton Mifflin.

Bergeron, B. (1990). What does the term whole language mean? A definition from the literature. *Journal of Reading Behavior, 23,* 301–329.

Bond, G., & Dykstra, R. (1967). The cooperative research program in first-grade reading instruction. *Reading Research Quarterly, 2,* 5–142.

Burke, C. (1984). Linguistic data pool. In Harste, J., Woodward, V., & Burke, C. *Language stories and literacy.* Portsmouth, NH: Heinemann.

California Department of Education. (1995). *Every child a reader: The report of the California task force.* Sacramento, CA: Author.

Cambourne, B. (1984). Language, learning and literacy. In Butler, A. & Turbill. *Towards a reading-writing classroom.* Portsmouth, NH: Heinemann.

Chall, J. (1967, 1983). *Learning to read: The great debate.* NY: McGraw-Hill.

Clay, M. (1991). *Becoming literate.* Portsmouth, NH: Heinemann.

Crofton, L. (1991). *Whole language: Getting started . . . moving forward.* Katonah, NY: Richard C. Owen.

Dewey, J. (1966). *Democracy and education.* NY: First Press. (original work published in 1916).

Flesch, R. (1955). *Why Johnny can't read and what you can do about it.* NY: Harper & Row.

Goodman, K. (1986). *What's whole about whole language.* Portsmouth, NH: Heinemann.

Goodman, K. (1993). *Phonics phacts.* Portsmouth, NH: Heinemann.

Goodman, K., Goodman, Y., & Hood, W. (1989). *The whole language evaluation book.* Portsmouth, NH: Heinemann.

Goodman, Y. (1967). *A psycholinguistic description of observed oral reading phenomena in selected young beginning readers.* Unpublished doctoral dissertation. Detroit: Wayne State University.

Graves, D. (1983). *Writing: Teachers and children at work.* Portsmouth, NH: Heinemann.

Hall, M. (1976). *Teaching reading as a language experience.* Columbus, OH: Merrill.

Halliday, M. (1975). *Learning how to mean.* NY: Elsevier North Holland.

Harste, J., Short, K., & Burke, C. (1984). *Creating classrooms for authors.* Portsmouth, NH: Heinemann.

Heald-Taylor, G. (1987). *The administrator's guide to whole language.* Katonah, NY: Richard C. Owen.

Heath, S. (1983). *Ways with words.* Cambridge, England: Cambridge University Press.

Holdaway, D. (1979). *The foundations of literacy.* Portsmouth: NH: Heinemann.

Holdaway, D. (1984). *Stability and change in literacy learning.* Portsmouth, NH: Heinemann.

Miller, W. (1998). First grade children's perceptions of reading. *Arizona Reading Journal, 25,* 7–12.

Newman, J. (1985). Insights from recent reading and writing research and their implications for developing whole language classrooms. In Newman, J. (Ed.). *Whole language: Theory in use.* Portsmouth, NH: Heinemann.

Routman, R. (1991). *Invitations: Changing teachers and learners K–12.* Portsmouth, NH: Heinemann.

Smith, F. (1973). *Psycholinguistics and reading.* NY: Holt, Rinehart and Winston.

Smith, F. (1986). *Insult to intelligence.* NY: Arbor House.

Stauffer, R. (1980). *The language experience approach to the teaching of reading.* NY: Harper & Row.

Sulzby, E. (1985). Children's emergent reading of favorite storybooks. *Reading Research Quarterly, 20,* 458–481.

Veatch, J., Sawicki, F., Elliott, G., Flake, E., & Blakey, J. (1979). *Key words to reading: The language experience approach begins.* Columbus, OH: Merrill.

Vygotsky, L. (1981). The genesis of higher mental functions. In J. Wertsch (Ed.). *The concept of activity.* White Plains, NY: M. E. Sharpe.

Weaver, C. (1994). *Reading process and practice: From socio-psycholinguistics to whole language.* Portsmouth, NH: Heinemann.

Webster, N. (1798). *The American spelling book.* Boston: Isaiah Thomas & Ebenezer Andrews.

Wells, G. (1986). *The meaning makers: Children learning language and using language to learn.* Portsmouth, NH: Heinemann.

Zemelman, S., & Daniels, H. (1988). *A community of writers.* Portsmouth, NH: Heinemann.

3

DEVELOPING COMPETENCY IN LISTENING AND ORAL LANGUAGE SKILLS

© PhotoDisc/Education

CONCEPTS THAT YOU SHOULD LEARN FROM READING THIS CHAPTER

After you have finished reading this chapter, you will be able to:

■ *Define the term listening and provide a definition for some of the specialized vocabulary terms that are related to listening*

■ *List and describe some of the types of listening*

■ *Understand how to implement the following strategies and materials that can be used to improve competency in listening skills: the Directed Listening-Thinking Activity (DL-TA), listening centers (listening posts), nursery rhymes, counting rhymes, poems, jingles, songs, chants, finger plays, books with listening themes, and various listening games*

■ *List and describe the main functions of oral language*

■ *Describe the following theories of oral language development: the behaviorist theory, the nativist theory, the interaction theory, the Piagetian and Vygotskian theory, and the constructivist theory*

■ *Briefly describe the main stages of a child's oral language development from the age of two years through the age of eight years*

■ *Understand how to use the following strategies and materials that can be used to improve oral language skills: various types of conversations, wordless (textless) books, dictating language-experience approach (LEA) charts and books, direct and vicarious experiences, oral language modeling, dramatic play, dramatic play kits, costumes, show-and-tell, the daily news of the classroom, and various types of games*

I am well acquainted with a boy named Paul who recently entered first grade. When Paul was three years old, he could speak only a few words. Since I was rather concerned about Paul's delayed oral language development, I asked his mother why she thought he spoke so little. Since I knew he was not shy, I wondered why his oral language skills seemed to be delayed. Paul's mother told me that she was not concerned about him since he was the youngest of four children, and his three older sisters always took care of his needs so quickly that he probably did not need to talk. Now in first grade, Paul's oral language skills are excellent, and he speaks a great deal. This incident underscores the fact that the vast majority of children progress through the same stages of language development, although they may differ greatly at the rate at which they do so. Although a few children may not ever develop mature language skills due to a low intellectual level, severe hearing impairment, or some other cause, they are in the minority. Costa (1991) stated that intelligent behavior often is demonstrated in the speech of young children.

This chapter will help an early childhood teacher become aware of the importance of listening and oral language skills to the other literacy skills—reading, writing, and spelling. All of the elements of literacy are related, and improvement in one of them usually leads to improvement in all of them. Evidence that they are interrelated is found in the recent publication *Standards for the English Language Arts* (1996), a project of both the International Reading Association (IRA) and the National Council of Teachers of English (NCTE). This document reflects a contemporary view of literacy and presents standards defining what all children should know and be able to perform. As further evidence that these skills are interrelated, Ruddell and Ruddell (1995) stated that reading is the use of one's language to decode and comprehend.

Listening and reading are called the *receptive language arts,* while oral language, writing, and spelling are called the *expressive language arts.* All of them should be stressed at the appropriate time in preschool, kindergarten, and the primary grades.

WHAT IS LISTENING?

Listening is a learned behavior involving *hearing, attending, discriminating, understanding,* and *remembering.* The listening of both children and adults can be improved significantly with practice. For example, the typical person listens to about 50% of what he or she hears and comprehends about 25% of that. The listening skills of young children should be improved by well-structured and planned programs. Although improving listening skills was researched in the 1950s and 1960s, its improvement has not been researched a great deal in recent years. However, according to recent research, active involvement following listening activities may be more effective than passive activities (Pinnell & Jaggar, 1992). In contrast to listening, *hearing* is a process involving nerves and muscles and normally is fully accomplished by the age of four or five.

There are a number of terms related to the improvement of listening ability, including the following:

Auditory acuity—the ability to hear sounds at various levels of frequency. Hearing impairment of the high tones causes difficulty for a child in hearing consonant sounds, while impairment of the low tones causes difficulty for the child in hearing the vowel sounds.

Auditory memory—the ability to hear and remember a sequence of sounds. Auditory memory ability is most frequently evaluated by having the child repeat a series of numerals either in the same order in which they were given or in reverse order. The typical adult can repeat approximately seven numerals in the order in which they were given, although a few adults are able to repeat up to ten numerals correctly. A young child obviously is able to repeat significantly less than seven numerals correctly, since auditory memory is a skill that usually improves with maturation.

Auditory perception—the processing of sound in the brain and the ability to sustain attention span while listening. It also includes the skills of following directions and recognizing the intensity, pitch, and tempo of sounds.

Auditory discrimination—the ability to discriminate or note the differences between various types of sounds. While reading, auditory discrimination ability normally means the ability to differentiate between the various consonant or vowel sounds. Many young children have difficulty discriminating between the short vowel sounds, especially those of short /e/ and short /i/. This may be especially true of young children with special needs, especially those who speak a nonstandard dialect. No young child ever should use a beginning reading program that contains many phonic generalizations (rules) and elements such as a systematic phonics program unless she or he is very adept at auditory discrimination.

It also is useful to know that there are several types of listening. According to Scott, they are as follows:

Appreciative listening—The child finds pleasure and entertainment in hearing music, poems, and stories. It is useful to begin a listening program with this type of listening, since it is passive, but personal, for each child.

Purposeful listening—The child follows directions and then provides responses.

Discriminative listening—First the child becomes aware of changes in pitch and loudness, and then sounds become differentiated in the environment. Eventually, the child is able to discriminate between the speech sounds.

Creative listening—The child's imagination and emotions are stimulated by listening experiences. Thoughts are expressed spontaneously and freely through words or actions or both.

Critical listening—The child understands, evaluates, makes decisions, and formulates opinions. To encourage this critical listening, the teacher may pose such questions as, "What happens when we all talk at once?" or "What if everyone wanted to play in the playhouse at the same time?" The child must think through the responses, decide the most logical solution to the problem, and present a point of view (Scott, 1968).

STRATEGIES AND MATERIALS FOR IMPROVING COMPETENCY IN LISTENING SKILLS IN YOUNG CHILDREN

There are a number of different strategies and materials that can be used effectively to improve a young child's listening skills. Here is a sampling of them. All of them should be modified in terms of the needs and interests of any preschool, kindergarten, or primary-grade child.

Steps of Meaningful Listening Instruction

Meaningful listening instruction can be developed around the following five steps. Although you may have to simplify them for young children, they usually can make a beginning in learning effective listening strategies.

- *Identify the needed skill or strategy*—Through observation, teachers can identify listening needs, which helps children to activate their prior knowledge about what "good listening" is in relation to a specific strategy.
- *Teach the lesson*—Listening instruction should be integrated into daily teaching activities.
- *Supervise practice and debriefing*—At the end of lessons, teachers should engage children in discussions about how they were effective listeners.
- *Review skills and strategies that were previously taught*—Listening strategies that have been taught need to be reviewed and extended into other listening situations.
- *Select strategies for specific situations*—The ultimate goal of teaching listening skills is to help children analyze listening situations and adjust their listening strategies effectively (Brent & Anderson, 1993).

The Directed Listening-Thinking Activity (DL-TA)

The Directed Listening-Thinking Activity (DL-TA) strategy was developed by the late Russell G. Stauffer of the University of Delaware (Stauffer, 1980). It is a variation of the *Directed Reading-Thinking Activity (DR-TA)* which also was developed by Stauffer. DL-TA is designed to help young children derive meaning from stories and to develop story structure. It can be used either with fictional trade books of various types or with informational books. It consists of some variation of the following:

- Have the child predict the book (story) content from the title after it is read aloud to him or her.
- Have the child then pose appropriate questions before reading that can be answered from hearing the book (story) read aloud.
- The child actively listens to the book (story) being read aloud, verifying or changing the predictions that were made prior to the reading depending upon whether or not they were correct. During this part of DL-TA, the child should be engaged in interactive story reading (see Chapter 2) such as commenting on pictures, pointing to various words and letters, and interacting with the content in general.

The use of DL-TA not only stimulates active, involved listening, but it also encourages oral language development. In addition, it increases the story comprehension of young readers (Baumann, 1992). It is a very easy, yet effective, strategy to use with young children.

Here is a model DL-TA that was conducted with a first-grade child early in the school year. It is based on the picture storybook *The Foxbury force* by G. Oakley (NY: Atheneum, 1994). Very briefly, this interesting picture storybook describes a police force composed of foxes that has an arrangement with a group of foxes to "burgle" one shop a month so that the constables can get in some practice in chasing burglars. However, on one occasion the Foreman Burglar decided that the fox burglars would actually conduct a burglary and keep their loot. The plot unfolds with the constables chasing after the burglars and finally capturing and arresting them.

MS. CONTRERAS: Sami, the name of this book is *The Foxbury force.* From looking at the cover, what do you think that the book may be about?

SAMI: I think that it's about some foxes that look like policemen. It looks as if one other fox is going to take their picture while they are sitting down.

C: That's a very good guess, Sami. The author of this book is named Graham Oakley. Can you make any other predictions as to what this book may be about?

S: Well, maybe the foxes are going to have to chase after some other animals that have done something wrong, or maybe they're going to march in a parade. I don't really know.

C (after reading aloud the first four pages of the book): Well, Sami, do you think that your prediction about the policemen going after some other animals is right or wrong? What about the photographer who was going to take their pictures?

S: It doesn't say whether or not they got their picture taken. It does say that the burglar foxes are really going to steal some things and keep them. So I guess that at least one of my predictions probably was right.

C: That's right, Sami. Now do you think that the constables (policemen) are going to be able to catch the burglar foxes very easily, or will it be hard for them?

S: I think that it's going to be very easy for them to catch the burglars. They don't seem too smart to me.

C (after reading the next four pages of this book aloud): Well, the burglars really are trying to get away from the constables, aren't they? What do you think will happen next in the book?

S: I think that the policemen foxes will be able to catch the burglars real easy. They don't look very smart to me at all. I think that it'll be real easy for them.

C: That's a good prediction. While I read this next part of the book, let's see if you're right or not. (She reads the next four pages aloud.) Well, Sami, it looks as if the burglar foxes are not going to be so easy to catch as you thought. It looks as if the constable foxes had a pretty hard time getting to the castle. What do you think is going to happen now?

S: I think that they are going to go right in and arrest the burglars real easy. They won't have any trouble at all. I think that then they're going to have to go right to jail probably.

C: All right. I'll read you some more of the book and we'll find out, won't we? (She reads the next four pages of the book aloud.) Sami, was your prediction about the constables arresting the burglars and taking them to jail correct or not?

S: It was right, but they're going to have kind of a hard time doing it, I think. I think that the burglar foxes are going to be able to escape real easy.

C: Well, let's read some more of this book and find out. (She reads the rest of the book aloud to Sami.) Well, Sami, was your prediction right?

S: No, not really. The policemen were able to arrest the burglar foxes, but the burglars didn't get to escape after all.

C: Sami, did you like this book and think that most of your predictions about it were correct?

S: I liked it all right, and I think I made mostly good predictions, but some of them were wrong. But it wasn't my favorite book that you ever have read to me. I liked some of the other ones better, and my predictions about them were better too. But it was OK.

C: I thought that you made good predictions about the book, and I'll try to find a book to read to you next time that you might like better. I hope that it will be easier for you to make good predictions about it too.

S: Great.

Listening Centers (Listening Posts)

Listening centers, sometimes called *listening posts,* can be very useful in improving a young child's listening skills. They are often used in preschools, kindergartens, and first grades. A listening center or listening post is a part of a classroom in which a child can listen to various types of cassette recordings with headphones or where she or he can simply be alone. The typical listening center can contain phonographs, cassette tape recorders, picture sheets, and trade books of various kinds to follow along in.

Headsets plugged into a jack or terminal can help to block out room noise, while partitions can cut down on distractions. Listening places can contain the following:

- large packing boxes lined with soft fabrics and pillows
- old, soft armchairs
- a bunk or loft

A young child can either listen to commercially available tape recordings of professionals reading trade books aloud or teacher-recorded tape recordings of appropriate trade books. Either type usually are called *read-alongs.*

Cassette recordings of various types of music can be included in a listening center or the entire class can listen to them. The following songs are very popular with young children:

"Old McDonald Had a Farm"

"Noble Duke of York"

"Farmer in the Dell"

"Hokey-Pokey"

"The Wheels on the Bus Go Round and Round"

"London Bridge Is Falling Down"

Nursery Rhymes, Counting Rhymes, Poems, Jingles, Songs, Chants, and Finger Plays

Nursery rhymes, counting rhymes, poems, jingles, songs, and chants all can be used to improve a young child's listening skills. Most of these are equally useful in improving young children's oral language skills. Chants and choruses are mimicked, and sound and word patterns that have regularity and predictability are imitated. They usually involve a back-and-forth conversation and involve the rise and fall of accented sounds or syllables.

Here are several common *chants* that can be used to promote both listening and speaking skills:

It's Raining It's Pouring

It's raining, it's pouring
The old man is snoring
He went to bed and he bumped his head
And he couldn't get up in the morning.
Rain, rain go away—come again some other day.

Pancake

Mix a pancake.
Stir a pancake.
Pop it in the pan.
Fry a pancake.
Toss a pancake.
Catch it if you can.

The Grand Old Duke of York

The grand old duke of York
He had forty thousand men.
He marched them up the hill.
He marched them down again.
And when you're up, you're up!
And when you're down, you're down.
And when you're half-way in-between,
You're neither up nor down.

Who Ate the Cookies in the Cookie Jar?

All: *Who ate the cookies in the cookie jar?*

All: (Child's or teacher's name) *ate the cookies in the cookie jar.* (Teacher points to different child for each verse.)

Named person: *Who me?*

All: *Yes you.*

Named person: *Couldn't be.*

All   *Then who?*

Newly named person: *Who me?* (And so forth)

Little Brown Rabbit

Teacher: (Leader)   *Little brown rabbit went hoppity-hop,*

All: *Hoppity-hop, hoppity-hop!*

Teacher: *Into a garden without any stop,*

All: *Hoppity-hop, hoppity-hop!*

Teacher: *He ate for his supper a fresh carrot top,*

All: *Hoppity-hop, hoppity-hop!*

Teacher: *Then home went the rabbit without any stop,*

All: *Hoppity-hop, hoppity-hop!*

Finger plays are an enjoyable preschool and kindergarten group or individual activity that parents have often already introduced to children at home, like "peek-a-boo" or "this little pig went to market." Finger plays use words and actions (usually finger movements) together. Finger plays can easily improve both listening and oral language skills. They encourage careful listening, prepare children for sitting, keep children active and interested while waiting, and serve as transitions between activities.

An early childhood teacher should practice and memorize a finger play before attempting to present it to children. Each child learns finger plays at his or her own rate of speed and will join in the activity when ready. Here are some useful, common finger plays that you can use with young children to promote both listening and speaking skills.

Sleepy Time

Open wide your little hands,
Now squeeze them very tight.
Shake them, shake them very loose,
With all your might.
Climb them slowly to the sky.
Drop down like gentle rain.
Go to sleep my little hands,
I'll wake you once again.

Clap Your Hands

Clap your hands high,
Clap your hands low,
Pat your head lightly,
And down you go.
I'll touch my hair, my lips, my eyes,
I'll sit up straight, and then I'll rise,
I'll touch my ears, my nose, my chin,
Then quietly sit down again.

Hickory, Dickory, Dock

Hickory, dickory, dock!
(Rest elbow in the palm of your other hand and swing the upraised arm back and forth.)
The mouse ran up the clock.
(Creep fingers up the arm to the palm of the other hand.)
The clock struck one.
(Clap hands.)
The mouse ran down.
(Creep fingers down to elbow.)

Hickory, dickory, dock.
    (Swing arm as before.)

Firefighters

Ten little firefighters sleeping in a row,
Ding, dong goes the bell, down the pole they go.
Jumping on the engine, oh, oh, oh,
Putting out the fire, shhhhhhhhhhhhhhhhhh.
And home again they go.
Back to sleep again.
All in a row.

Two Little Apples

Two little apples hanging on a tree,
    (Put hand by eyes.)
Two little apples smiling at me.
    (Smile.)
I shook that tree as hard as I could.
    (Shake tree.)
Down came the apples.
    (Make falling motions.)
Mmmm—they were good.
    (Rub stomach.)

Five Little Astronauts

Five little astronauts
    (Hold up fingers on one hand.)
Ready for outer space.
The first one said, "Let's have a race."
The second one said, "The weather's too rough."
The third one said, "Oh, don't be gruff."
The fourth one said, "I'm ready enough."
The fifth one said, "Let's blast off."
10, 9, 8, 7, 6, 5, 4, 3, 2, 1,
    (Start with ten fingers and pull one down with each number.)
BLAST OFF!
    (Clap loudly with "BLAST OFF!!")

A Funny One

'Round the house
'Round the house
    (Put fingers around the face.)
Pop in the window
    (Open eyes wide.)
Listen at the door

    (Cup hand behind ear.)
Knock at the door
    (Knock lightly on the head.)
Lift up the latch
    (Push up nose.)
And walk in

Butterfly

Roly-poly caterpillar
Into a corner crept.
Spun around himself a blanket
A long time passed (Whisper)
Roly-poly caterpillar awakened by and by
Found himself with beautiful wings
Changed to a butterfly

Resource Books for Fingerplays

Here is a brief list of some of the books that contain fingerplays for young children.

Crowell, L., & Hibner, D. (1994). *Finger frolics.* First Teacher, Inc., PO Box 29, Bridgeport, CT 06602

Fingerplays for young children. (1996). Scholastic, 2931 East McCarty Street, Jefferson City, MO 65102

Glazer, T. (1973). Eye winker, Tom Tinker, chin chopper, *Fifty musical fingerplays.* NY: Doubleday.

Kable, Gratia. (1979). *Favorite fingerplays.* Minneapolis: T. S. Denison.

Books with Listening Themes

The young child also can listen to or read himself *books with listening themes.* These are books that emphasize listening carefully, critically, or appreciatively. Their use may stimulate young children to improve various levels of their listening skills. They also can be good springboards to discussions about listening. Here is a partial list of books with listening themes that can be used in any early childhood literacy program:

Aliki. (1974). *Go tell Aunt Rhody.* NY: Macmillan.

Brooks, L. (1977). *Ring 'o roses.* NY: Frederick Warne.

Brown, M. (Ed.). (1985). *Hand rhymes.* NY: Dutton.

Brown, M. (Ed.). (1985). *Party rhymes.* NY: Dutton.

Brown, M. (Ed.). (1985). *Play rhymes.* NY: Dutton.

de Regniers, B. (1988). *Sing a song of popcorn.* NY: Scholastic.

Eastman, P. (1960). *Are you my mother?* NY: Random House.

Eichenberg, F. (1952). *Ape in a cape: An alphabet of odd animals.* NY: Harcourt Brace Jovanovich.

Fox, D. (Ed.). (1987). *Go in and out the window.* NY: The Metropolitan Museum of Art & Henry Holt and Co.

Gag, W. (1928). *Millions of cats.* NY: Coward, McCann & Geoghegan.

Galdone, P. (1984). *The tenny-tiny woman.* NY: Clarion.

Galdone, P., reteller and illus. (1968). *Henny penny.* Boston: Houghton Mifflin.

Geisel, T. (Dr. Seuss). (1968). *The foot book.* NY: Random House.

Geisel, T. (Dr. Seuss). (1957). *The cat in the hat.* NY: Random House.

Geisel, T. (Dr. Seuss). (1983). *Hop on pop.* NY: Random House.

Hayes, S. (1990). *Nine ducks nine.* NY: Lothrop, Lee & Shephard.

Hayes, S. (Ed.). (1988). *Clap your hands: Finger rhymes.* NY: Lothrop, Lee & Shephard.

Hennessy, B. (1989). *A, B, C, D, tummy, toes, hands, knees.* NY: Viking Kestrel.

Hoban, T. (1978). *Is it red? Is it yellow? Is it blue?* NY: Greenwillow.

Hoban, T. (1986). *Red, blue, yellow shoe.* NY: Greenwillow.

Hopkins, L. (1979). *Go to bed! A book of bedtime poems.* NY: Knopf.

Hopkins, L., collector. (1988). *Side by side, poems to read together.* NY: Simon & Schuster.

Keats, E. (1964). *Whistle for Willie.* NY: Viking.

Kovalski, M. (1987). *The wheels on the bus.* Boston: Little, Brown.

Kuskin, K. (1956). *Roar and more.* NY: Harper & Row.

Langstaff, J. (1974). *Oh, a'hunting we will go.* NY: Atheneum.

Lear, E. (1987). *The owl and the pussy cat.* NY: Clarion.

Lindbergh, R. (1990). *The day the goose got loose.* NY: Dial.

Martin, B., & Archambault, J. (1989). *Chicka chicka boom boom.* NY: Simon & Schuster.

Oxenbury, H. (1985). *The Helen Oxenbury nursery storybook.* NY: Knopf.

Prelutsky, J. (1986). *Read-along rhymes for the very young.* NY: Knopf.

Quakenbush, R. (1975). *Skip to my lou.* Philadelphia: Lippincott.

Rae, M. (1988). *The farmer in the dell: A singing game.* NY: Viking Penguin.

Smith, J. (1986). *The Jessie Willcox Smith Mother Goose.* NY: Derrydale.

Spier, P. (1967). *To market, to market.* NY: Doubleday.

Spier, P. (1985). *London Bridge is falling down.* NY: Doubleday.

Tripp, W. (1976). *Granfa Grig had a pig and other rhymes without reason from Mother Goose.* Boston: Little, Brown.

Wells, R. (1973). *Nosy Nora.* NY: Dial.

Wildsmith, B. (1982). *Cat on the mat.* NY: Oxford.

Wright, B. (1916). *The real Mother Goose.* NY: Macmillan.

Yolen, J. (Ed.). (1986). *Lullaby songbook.* NY: Harcourt Brace Jovanovich.

Zemach, M. (1965). *Teeny tiny woman.* NY: Scholastic.

Zuromskis, D. (1978). *The farmer in the dell.* Boston: Little, Brown.

An excellent source of all types of children's books is the following:

Trelease, J. (1995). *The read-aloud handbook.* NY: Penguin.

ACTIVITY

Games for Improving Listening Skills

Here is a brief description of some of the games that can be used to improve young children's listening skills. You can adapt any of them as you wish to fit the interests and needs of your own students. They are presented as examples of the types of games that can be used to effectively improve listening skills in any early childhood program.

Recognizing the Voices in School

Objective

This game is designed to improve auditory memory skills and discriminative ability.

Materials Needed

You will need to collect individual photographs of different school staff such as the principal, the custodian(s), the secretary(s), the nurse, the art teacher(s), the music teacher(s), the media resource specialist, and the physical education teacher(s). You will also need to have each of them tape record their voice reading the paragraphs in a book in correct order.

Game Activity

After the children identify each of the photographs, place the photos in a line and tell the children that they are now going to listen carefully and try to identify each of the voices on the tape recording. When a child is able to correctly identify a voice correctly, have him or her place the photograph face down. You then continue to the next voice. At the end of this game, show the photographs one by one and give the name of each person pictured. Each child's voice can instead be guessed as a variation of this game.

Try and Guess What This Is

Objective

The purpose of this game is to identify common sounds.

Materials Needed

Assemble various items such as an alarm clock, a bell, a noisemaker, sandpaper, a rattle, a drum, a tambourine, paper to crumple, a doll that cries, and so on. Stand behind a screen or a blanket that is fastened across a doorway so that the children cannot see any of the objects that you will use to make the various sounds. This activity can be placed on a cassette tape for an independent listening activity.

Game Activity

In each case ask the children to guess what you have behind the screen that makes the sound that they hear. As a variation, you can clap rhythms behind the screen and have the children imitate them. You can use patterns of loud and soft claps or slow and fast claps.

What Sounds Crunchy to You?

Objective

This game is designed to provide practice in listening in a discriminative manner and to improve auditory memory skills.

Materials Needed

You will need to assemble carrot sticks, celery sticks, marshmallows, uncooked macaroni, cotton balls, and other materials that you wish to use.

Continued

Continued

Game Activity

Place all the materials in a bag that you hold behind your back. Then reach in and get out a carrot stick as you begin to sing "Carrot sticks are thin and orange, thin and orange, thin and orange" (to the tune of "Mary Had a Little Lamb"). Then pass out a carrot stick to each child and sing the song again crunching the carrot stick when you reach the end of the song. You can follow up with "What else is crunchy?" You can then introduce the other objects to the children along with the appropriate songs in each case:

"Celery sticks are long and green. When you eat them they can crunch."
"Marshmallows are big and soft. When you squeeze them, they feel soft."
Spaghetti is long and thin. When you break it, it goes snap."
"Cotton balls are soft and white. When you touch them, they feel soft."

Using Cans for Sounds

Objective

The purpose of this game is to match similar sounds by using discriminative listening skills.

Materials Needed

You will need to collect cans with press-on or screw-off lids. You also need cards large enough to hold two cans. Outline circles of can bottoms with a dark marking pen. You drawn two circles for each can. Large different colored index cards work well. You should use cans that are impossible for students to open, or else you need to tape the cans shut securely. You then fill the pairs of cans with some materials such as sand, paper clips, rocks, rice, beans, nuts, and bolts.

Game Activity

This is an activity that a child can play independently or with other children. It can easily be used in a learning center. You need to use an introduction such as this: "Here are some cans and cards. The way you play this game is to shake one can and then shake all the rest to find the one that sounds the same as the first can. Let's listen to this can." Shake it. "Now I'm going to try to find the can that sounds the same as this one when I shake it." Then pick up another can and ask, "Does this one sound the same to you?" Shake the first can and the second can. "No, this one sounds different, so I'm going to shake another can." Keep doing this until the mate is found and placed beside the first can on the card. Since this activity is very common, many sound sets are found in preschool programs and also are manufactured commercially.

Make a Hamburger

Objective

This game is designed to provide practice in purposeful listening.

Materials Needed

You will need to assemble cutouts of foods that are added to hamburger buns—slices of onion, lettuce, slices of tomato, slices of cheese, pickles, meat patties, bacon, mayonnaise, mustard, and catsup. You also need to cut out paper buns or make clay bun halves.

Game Activity

You first can ask the children what kind of food they like to have on their hamburgers. After the group discusses the foods they like, you can say, "I'm going to show pictures of some of the foods that you liked on your hamburgers and some of the foods that I like. Here are onion slices; Jerry said that he liked them." Then show and name all of the cutouts. Choose three children to start the activity and have them sit facing the other children. One child holds two bun halves, the next child holds a flat box lid with all the hamburger foods, and the third child names all the foods that the first child selected when his or her hamburger is completed. The second child hands the first child the cutouts that he or she names and places them between the bun halves. At different times the teacher asks various children in the group whether the second child has selected the item that the first child has named. The children also can be encouraged to say "Hamburger, hamburger, yum, yum, yum." I want that hamburger here on my tongue." After each hamburger is completed and the food items are named, the children to play the game in the second round are selected by the children in the first round.

I'm Going on a Trip

Objective

The objective of this game is to provide children with practice in very careful listening.

Materials

There are no materials needed for this game.

Game Activity

One child in the class says, "I'm going on a trip, and I'm taking markers with me." He or she then selects another child to continue the game. That child says, "I'm going on a trip, and I'm taking markers and a book with me." The game continues with children trying to remember all of the previous items that are going to be taken on the trip in addition to their own item. The winner is the child who is able to name the most items in the correct order without forgetting any of them.

WHAT IS ORAL LANGUAGE?

Oral language is an integral part of literacy. Humans are programmed to need to communicate, and communication by speech enables the members of the human community to connect with others for professional and personal reasons. Oral language therefore occurs as a part of life enabling humans to interact with others, understand the world, and reveal ourselves. Human beings have an innate sense of the rules that govern language. In other words, most children possess an intuitive set of rules indicating when different parts of speech can occur. Oral language also has an interactive aspect in that it primarily occurs so that humans can communicate with others. Therefore, oral language is *constructive, interactive,* and *functional*. Oral language also has *stability, versatility,* and *predictability*.

Several important relationships between oral language and literacy are that (1) oral language capabilities develop to a fairly high degree of proficiency before written language capabilities develop; (2) oral and written language share the same grammar (syntax) and vocabulary; (3) knowledge of oral language is used extensively by children in learning to read and write; (4) oral language and literacy are keys to developing more complex cognitive capabilities (Raphael & Hiebert, 1996).

Halliday (1973) proposed the following main functions of language:

Instrumental language satisfies wants and needs.

Regulatory language exerts control over others.

Interactional language establishes and maintains contact with others.

Personal function language expresses and asserts individuality.

Heuristic function language assists in learning and describing.

Imaginative function language creates images and aids in pretending.

Informational (representational) language informs.

It may be useful at this point to provide some examples in which an early childhood education teacher can promote these various functions of language.

Instrumental Language

1. Be as responsive as possible to all of the children's requests.
2. Enhance each child's use of instrumental language with other children by encouraging him or her to provide support to classmates.

Regulatory Language

1. Gather a list of discussion rules from the children.
2. Enable children to contribute to a list of classroom policies.

Interactional Language

1. Create opportunities for children to share work areas in the classroom and talk about how this can be done.
2. Have informal times in the classroom for children to talk with each other.
3. Discover ways of encouraging small group discussions, especially involving only two or three children.

Personal Function Language

1. Use language to share personal thoughts and ideas.
2. Read books aloud that encourage personal responses from children.
3. Be willing and able to listen and talk on a one-to-one basis with children during transition times in the classroom.
4. Provide appropriate and inviting areas in the classroom where children can talk quietly with each other.

Heuristic Function Language

1. Create real, meaningful problems for the children to solve.
2. Structure experiences in the classroom to satisfy the natural curiosity of the children.
3. Allow children to work collaboratively with a partner or a small group of children to solve problems.
4. Motivate heuristic language use in children, by saying, for example, "I'd like to know why. . ." Such problems always should be relevant for children.

Imaginative Language

1. Structure classroom situations that motivate dramatic play; for example, include a classroom grocery, a playhouse corner, and a block area.
2. Read books aloud that are designed to develop the imagination, and then relate them to appropriate discussions about art, music, and drama.
3. Provide time for children to interact with a partner or with a small group of children of the same or a different age.
4. Encourage language play—help children notice the sounds of words and the images that they create.

Informational (Representational) Language

1. Use questioning strategies that encourage complex forms of providing information.
2. Design activities that require children to observe carefully and objectively. They then should have the opportunity to summarize and draw conclusions from the observations. Going on school field trips is very effective for this purpose.

3. Keep records of events over a period of time, and then look back on them and draw appropriate conclusions. As one example, with the teacher's help the children can keep records about what kind of food and how much food a classroom pet eats over a period of time (loosely adapted from Pinnell, 1985).

THEORIES OF ORAL LANGUAGE DEVELOPMENT

There are several different theories about how children develop oral language skills. Although each of these theories contains aspects that are correct, no single theory can provide a complete explanation for the oral language development of young children. Rather it appears as if a combination of several of these theories provides the most nearly accurate explanation of how a young child develops oral language. In any case, here is a very brief description of the major theories related to the oral language development of young children.

The Behaviorist Theory

The *behaviorist theory* presents an accurate, but incomplete, view of how young children develop oral language skills. For example, the psychologist Skinner (1957) defined language as the observed and produced speech that occurs in the interaction of a speaker and a listener. He stated that thinking is the internal process of language and that thought is initiated through interactions with the environment—interactions between a parent and a child, as one example. Therefore, according to the behaviorists, a child's acquisition of language is encouraged and developed by imitating the language of the adults and other children around him or her and by the positive reinforcement that they give to the young child.

Of course, babies and young children do learn many spoken words by listening to an adult or to older children and imitating their language, even though the imitation has no meaning for them whatsoever. For example, when I was in kindergarten many years ago, my class recited the Pledge of Allegiance every morning. I believed throughout kindergarten and probably also during the primary grades that one part of the Pledge said: "One nation invisible" instead of "One nation indivisible." I wondered for several years how a country such as the United States could be invisible, which I knew meant that nobody could see it. I did not completely understand the Pledge of Allegiance until I was in the fourth grade, although I had recited it each morning for four years.

It also is obvious that young children learn some oral language by constructing it instead of merely imitating it; otherwise one cannot account for a young child using a word such as "goed" for the verb "went" as he or she well may do.

The Nativist Theory

The *nativist theory* also attempts to provide an explanation about how young children develop oral language skills. Although this theory also is partially correct, it too is an incomplete explanation. Chomsky (1965), Lennenberg (1967), and McNeil (1970) described the nativist theory of oral language acquisition. These linguists stated that language develops *innately*. In other words, young children discover for themselves how language works by internalizing the rules of grammar, which allows them to say a number of different words and sentences. They are able to do this, according to the nativists, without the modeling, practice, and reinforcement provided by the adults and older children in their environment. Therefore, the nativists believed that the ability to develop oral language is innate to humans. They stated that language growth depends upon maturation, since a child's oral language skills increase as she or he matures. In general, the nativists believed that children learn new patterns of language and generate new rules for new elements of language.

This theory is at least partially accurate, since an animal such as a dog obviously cannot speak. Therefore, oral language as we know it is innate only to humans. Although a house dog has heard oral language all of its life and can understand a great many words as well as the tone of a person's voice, no dog can speak. However, the nativist theory cannot account for the imitation that is present in oral language learning nor for the part that social interaction and construction of oral language plays in speech. Therefore, the nativist theory also is a partially correct, but incomplete, theory of oral language development, as was the behaviorist theory.

The Interaction Theory of Language Development

Oral language also is *interactive* which means that it is mediated through interactions designed to elaborate and extend meanings (Neuman & Roskos, 1993). For example, when infants make cooing or other verbal sounds, the majority of family members are thrilled and answer with words of encouragement. The baby then responds to the positive reinforcement by repeating the cooing sounds. As babies mature, they usually are able to formulate both consonant and vowel sounds. For example, the typical six-month-old baby often makes sounds such as *ma, ma, ma; ba, ba, ba;* and *da, da, da.* Most parents believe that *ma-ma* really means *Mommy* and are very excited. They usually encourage the child to continue saying *mama,* and the child is receiving positive reinforcement which promotes continued similar oral language play. These prelinguistic "chats" form the foundations of listening, speaking, and writing (Menyuk, 1991).

As the child continues to develop oral vocabulary, he experiments with more words. For example, when the young child is playing with a stuffed toy dog, he or she may say "doggie, doggie, doggie" over and over. An adult or other child then often says "Yes, that's a pretty, brown dog."

Through the expansion and positive reinforcement of words by an interested adult or older child, the child is able to acquire oral language skills. The adult also often extends on the young child's words by asking questions such as, "What else can you tell me about your pretty, brown dog? What do you like to do with it?" Such extension encourages a young child to think and understand. This type of oral language development may be called the *elaborated language code (style).* In this type of oral language development, an interested adult or older child elaborates on, extends, and clarifies the speech of a young child. This type of oral language development often leads to a higher degree of emergent literacy ability and more success in beginning reading activities both at home and at school (Bernstein, 1961, and Miller, 1967).

On the other hand, in some families the baby's cooing and babbling may be considered a nuisance, and infants' attempts to use oral language may not be considered important. Without interaction and positive reinforcement, a young child may use a predominantly *restricted oral language code (style)* which may lead to a lesser degree of emergent ability and less success in beginning literacy activities (Bernstein, 1961, and Miller, 1967).

The Piagetian and Vygotskian Theory

Piaget's theory of cognitive development is based on the principle that children develop through their activities. He believed that children's understanding of the world is related to their actions or sensory experiences as in the environment. According to this theory, a child's first words are *egocentric,* or centered on her or his own actions. Young children primarily talk about only themselves and what they do. Therefore, their beginning oral language as well as their development in general is related to the events, objects, and events that they have experienced directly through seeing, hearing, touching, tasting, and smelling (Piaget & Inhelder, 1969).

On the other hand, *Vygotsky's theory of basic learning* is related to oral language development. According to him, children learn higher cognitive functions by internalizing social relationships. For example, adults first give children the name of objects and they direct them and make suggestions. Then when children become more competent, the adults and older children they interact with gradually withdraw the amount of scaffolding and support that they give. Vygotsky also describes the *zone of proximal development,* a range of social interaction between an adult and a child. Theoretically, the child can perform within that range but only with support (Vygotsky, 1978). In summary, adults need to interact with children by encouraging, motivating, and supporting them (Sulzby, 1986).

The Constructivist Theory

The *constructivist theory* of language acquisition is a contemporary theory emerging from the work of Piaget and Vygotsky but described and supported by such linguists as Brown, Cazden, and Bellugi-Klima (1968) and Halliday (1975). Constructivists view children as the creators of language using an innate set of rules or underlying concepts. Therefore, language is an active and interactive process. As the child constructs language, she or he may well make errors that exemplify the rules that the child already knows. Adults including teachers need to accept errors as a necessary part of a child's learning how language works, especially when she or he is young.

For example, even if a language development chart tells adults what is "normal" in language development for a child, adults must accept each young child's individuality in speech and his or her right to grow at his or her own pace of development. We also must remember that the process of acquiring language is interactive and continuous and takes place in the social context of each child's interaction with others. Children learn oral language by playing with language themselves. They try out new words, may formulate new words, engage in monologues, and practice what they have learned. Therefore, oral language acquisition varies from child to child, depending upon his or her social and cultural background (Jagger, 1985). Certainly, a young child does not simply imitate the language of others. If that were the case, a child never would use such terms as "goed" for "went," "runned" for "ran," or use any of the other interesting language constructions that they try out. As an example, a young child may say, "Look at that snow. It looks like the roasted marshmallows that we ate last night," or "The sun came out today and swallowed up all the snow."

STAGES OF ORAL LANGUAGE DEVELOPMENT

As stated earlier, most young children progress through approximately the same stages of oral language development, although they may progress at different rates. In general, infants advance from cooing, to babbling, to single words, to two-word utterances sometimes called telegraphic speech, to complex sentence structure. Normally this progression is made by the time a student enters kindergarten. Obviously, some children progress through these stages at a much more rapid rate than do others. In addition, the forty-four *phonemes* (sounds) in the English language also are mastered in a predictable fashion from *bilabial sounds* such as /m/, /p/, and /h/ to the consonant sounds. A portion of a child's oral language development also is related to how *kernel* (basic) *sentences* can be transformed into *question, negative,* or *passive form.*

Very briefly, here is a description of the stages of a young child's oral language development:

Age of two years—Children create many two-word sentences (telegraphic speech) and often chant favorite nursery rhymes (if they have been exposed to them).

Age of three years—Children have about a 300-word vocabulary. However, at this age a young child's vocabulary grows very quickly and soon may approach the 900-word vocabulary that is achieved by age four.

Age of three and a half years—The /b/, /m/, /p/, /v/, and /h/ sounds develop.

Age of four years—Children have about a 900-word vocabulary.

Age of four and a half years—The /d/, /t/, /n/, /g/, /k/, /ng/, and /y/ sounds develop.

Age of five and a half years—The /v/, /sh/, /za/, and /l/ sounds develop.

Age of seven and a half years—The /s/, /w/, /r/, /ht/, and /wh/ sounds develop.

Age of seven to eight years—Sentence foundation is mastered (pronouns and prepositions).

Age of eight years—All sounds have been developed, and speech should be readily intelligible.

STRATEGIES AND MATERIALS FOR IMPROVING ORAL LANGUAGE SKILLS

The chapter now contains a number of strategies and materials for improving the oral language skills of children at the emergent and beginning literacy levels. In keeping with the whole language philosophy (see Chapter 2), the strategies and materials included in this section should be considered only as guidelines for optimal ways of improving oral language skills. You should modify any of these suggestions and materials in the light of the interests and needs of your own pupils.

Various Types of Conversations

Different types of conversations can be very beneficial in improving a young child's skill in oral language as well as motivating her or him to speak and improving her or his confidence while speaking.

Adult conversations with children help the children to become more proficient in oral language as well as providing valuable interaction. As an adult talks with children, he or she should pay careful attention to them, try to sit at their eye level, listen respectfully to what they say, and ask questions that encourage them to think and to use additional language. The adult also should elaborate on a child's comments by extending his or her statement, elaborating on the idea, and using additional language. For example, when Bobbi told Ms. Ichniowski that she

got a new puppy for her birthday, Ms. Ichniowski first asked her to tell more about the puppy. After Bobbi's description, Ms. Ichniowski commented, "I think that you are going to be able to play lots of games and have loads of fun with that adorable black and brown puppy."

If a teacher has difficulty understanding a young child, especially a preschool child, because of the child's immature language skills, his or her use of a nonstandard dialect, cultural differences between the teacher and child, or the teacher's lack of the appropriate prior knowledge, it still is very important for the teacher to show respect for and acceptance of each child's oral language skills and his or her contributions. The teacher of young children should try to listen carefully to them and question them with respect as well as asking them relevant questions rather than questions such as "What color hair ribbon are you wearing today?"—a question to which the teacher obviously already knows the answer.

The teacher should follow these guidelines when engaging in a conversation with young children:

- Always focus on the child's agenda.
- Treat all children with respect.
- Have genuine concern for each child which you clearly indicate to her or him.
- As much as possible, allow the young child to touch, taste, see, feel, and smell what you are talking about while he or she is listening to you.
- Try to speak in simple sentences as much as possible while still conveying the meaning of what you are saying.
- Watch each child for nonverbal reactions. You can watch the young child's face and body actions to detect fear, interest, and happiness, among other emotions.
- You should talk to a nonverbal child slowly while emphasizing key words such as nouns and verbs. You also can repeat them if the child does not seem to understand them.
- If you cannot understand a word that a child is saying, repeat it back to the child in a nonthreatening way.
- Accept a child's attempt to say a word. If a child says, "*wabbit*," you can say, "Yes, our rabbit likes to eat carrots." As stated earlier, correct articulation usually improves with maturation and proper speech modeling.
- If a child seems to be interested in some object or activity, you can talk about this using simple sentences such as "Your new puppy is cute," or "You like the swings," or "That's a pretty dress."
- Make commands and requests easy to understand. For example, "Put the blocks in that box," or "Please get into line," or "Please look at me."
- Pause and wait patiently for a child's response to a question or request.
- Correct incorrect oral language overgeneralizations such as "goed" or "runned" by tactfully using the

correct word in a sentence such as, "Yesterday you went to Billy's house," or "You just ran very fast in the race."

- Accept hesitant speech and stuttering in an interested, patient manner. When a young child is very excited or anxious, he or she may not be able to develop ideas into words properly.

- Wait patiently while a child is trying to speak. Although his or her thoughts may not be expressed properly or at all at first, if you respond with interest and encouragement to what she or he said, the child probably will try again.

- Use conjunctions (*and, but, or*), possessives (*Mother's, yours, mine, their*, etc.), contractions (*don't, can't, doesn't, we'll, I'm, they're*, etc.), and prepositions (*at, to, into, on, under, over*, etc.), in your speech to encourage young children to use them correctly.

Dramatic Play

Dramatic play is extremely motivating and useful in improving the oral language skills of young children. With young children, dramatic play involves acting out and repeating the words and actions of others. Research has found that dramatic play has many important benefits for young children (Fein, 1981). For example, dramatic play helps children to:

- improve their conversational skills and their ability to express ideas in words.
- understand the feelings and roles of other people, both adults and children.
- improve their vocabulary.
- greatly enhance creativity since children imagine, act, and make up events as the dramatic play continues.
- participate in social interaction with other children.
- attempt to deal with various life situations by acting out different emotions. As an example, two children can play a father and a mother engaging in an argument.
- assume both leadership and group participation roles.

Dramatic play is enhanced by using props and using learning centers in a preschool, kindergarten, or early primary-grade classroom. Thus, teachers can encourage dramatic play by providing such props as adult clothing, materials that suggest such activities as a doctor's office, a veterinarian's office, a travel agency, a grocery store, or a home, among many others. Since dramatic play develops from the imitative actions of younger preschool children to the more sophisticated dramatic play of four-, five-, and six-year-old children, teachers can support each step by providing the necessary props and materials that will enhance dramatic episodes.

One type of dramatic play that four- and five-year-olds often participate in is called *superhero play*. Superheroes are powerful figures that are able to do many of the things that children and ordinary adults cannot do. For example, some superhero figures may be the good guys and the bad guys, the police and the robbers, cartoon characters who are themselves superheroes, and robots and space aliens.

According to Segal (1987):

. . . Superhero play is the child's way of restructuring his {or her} world according to his {her} own rules. By dubbing himself {or herself} a superman a four-year-old can instantaneously acquire major powers and awesome strength. This strength represents access to a powerful force that is missing in their adult-controlled everyday lives.

Although superhero play may have some positive characteristics such as encouraging a certain kind of limited, although repetitive, creativity on a child's part, it also may have limitations. Since superhero play may be fairly violent, the teacher should have group discussions with his or her children emphasizing that although superhero dramatic play may sometimes be fun, the violent behavior that is portrayed in it is only make-believe and should not be used in real-life situations. In most cases, superhero dramatic play in early childhood probably only lasts for a limited time and is not particularly harmful to a young child who seems generally well adjusted.

As was the case in overall oral language improvement, the following also are useful in encouraging young children to engage in dramatic play:

- direct experiences such as school trips to different interesting places
- classroom visitors
- reading a wide variety of picture storybooks, poems, and informational books aloud to a large group, a small group, or an individual child
- vicarious experiences such as pictures, videotapes, films and filmstrips, simple scientific experiments, demonstrations, and realia
- boxed kits (see the next section of this chapter)
- classroom centers

Dramatic Play Kits

Dramatic play kits can be very helpful in motivating young children to engage in various kinds of dramatic play. A dramatic play kit contains some items that are related, are boxed together, and are motivational for encouraging a definite type of dramatic play. Here are some ideas that can be used for kits that encourage dramatic play:

- *Doctor/nurse*—Stethoscope, bandages, Band-Aids, tongue depressors, red stickers for play wounds, play thermometer, paper pad and pencil for writing prescriptions, adhesive tape, cotton balls, paper hospital gown, and white shirt.
- *Post office*—Used postcards and letters, Christmas stamps, "Love" stamps or wildlife stamps, large index cards, mail boxes (shoe box with slot cut in front and name clearly printed), old shoulder bag purses for mailbags, and shirts.

- *Teacher*—Chalk, bell, picture storybooks or simple informational books, notebooks, pencils, plastic glasses, and flannel board with cut-out figures of various kinds.
- *Grocery store*—Play cash register, play money, empty food cartons, play grocery cart or rolling laundry cart, wax fruit, old purse or wallet, and paper bags.
- *Service station*—Bucket, sponges, tire pump, squirt bottle, paper towels, sign that says "Gas for Sale," short length of hose and cylinder (for gasoline pump), and gas cap.
- *Airplane*—Some chairs in rows, trays, plastic eating utensils, play food, little pillows, blankets, headphones, tickets, magazines, a rolling cart of some type, napkins, and flight attendant clothing of some kind.
- *Beauty shop*—Plastic combs, plastic brushes, cotton balls, colored water in old nail polish bottles, curlers, water spray bottle, old hair dryer or old curling iron (no electric cord), curlers, hairpins, and mirror.
- *Camping*—Flashlight, old pots and pans, backpacks, blankets, short lengths of logs, old pup (small) tent, food, old camp stove (not operable), canteen, and portable radio.
- *Restaurant*—Old order pads, wax food, napkins, paper or plastic plates, plastic utensils, an apron or some other type of server uniform, play cash register, and play money.

Costumes

Costumes and clothing props also help children transform themselves into a character easily. If the costumes and clothing have snaps and strong ties it will help children use them independently. Clothing with elastic waistbands also is helpful. Clothing that is cut down to the proper size so that it doesn't drag on the floor also is useful. Here are some clothing items that can be used to motivate various kinds of dramatic play:

- wigs
- work clothes
- hats
- shoes, boots, and slippers
- discarded fancy adult clothing of various kinds
- accessories such as scarves, purses, ties, old jewelry, aprons, and badges

Note: Wigs, hats, caps, and other headgear may not be practical in classrooms if any of the children have had head lice. One way to stop the spread of head lice is to give each child a shower cap, like those available in hotels, which he or she keeps stuffed into a paper tube and stored in his or her own cubby or desk. The shower cap is then worn under any headgear that the child puts on.

Show-and-Tell

Show-and-tell is probably the most common activity that is used with older preschool children, kindergarten children, and children in the early primary grades to stimulate oral language development. Although it certainly can be helpful, it also can be boring, tedious, and a great waste of time. However, if it is structured correctly, it can help some children, especially shy children, develop the self-confidence to speak with greater ease before a large group or small group of children. Here are some aspects of show-and-tell that should be avoided so that it does not become a time-wasting, boring routine:

- It probably should not be done on a daily basis, but rather on a scheduled basis that occurs only one or two days each week.
- Children should not be allowed to bring the same item to show more than once.
- The items that children bring should be truly worthy of showing and talking about—not merely an item that is uninteresting.
- A child who does not want to talk on any specific day should not be forced to do so.
- The length of a child's sharing should be limited to several minutes. She or he should not be allowed to ramble on and on as some children may want to do.
- Show-and-tell items should not be so valuable that if they are lost or damaged it would create a real loss to either the child or his or her family.
- All children in the audience should be required to listen carefully and with respect to the child who is speaking. The teacher also should give the child his or her undivided attention.

Here are some suggestions that may help show-and-tell be a more worthwhile activity for improving oral language skills than it has been in the past in some early childhood programs.

- Show-and-tell items should be related to the theme (topic) that the class is studying at that time.
- Children should be taught to tell three things about the topic.
- If a child does not want to talk, she or he should be encouraged just to show what she or he has brought to school.
- The children in the audience should be encouraged to ask the child some relevant questions about what she or he has brought.
- Sometimes the child can hide the item behind his or her back while describing it to the other children in the group. Then the other children can guess what the item is.
- Allow the child who is doing the showing to stand near the teacher for security if this is required.
- Limit the time for the activity so that the children do not become bored. Thus, it is helpful to have some type of flexible schedule for the show-and-tell period.
- Limit the time for children who are likely to talk too long by using an egg timer.

- Have the children who are to share on a particular day exchange their items if this seems feasible so that they must talk about each other's items.
- Bring in a surprise item yourself once in a while to share with the children.
- Display all of the articles that were brought in one day and have the children try to guess who brought them.

As stated earlier, although show-and-tell can be boring and time-wasting, it also can be profitable when some of the above-mentioned modifications are made. For example, Oken-Wright (1988) has written that show-and-tell can be:

- a good way to develop expressive and receptive language
- an activity for *closure* that can bring activities to an ending in a positive way
- a way for children to learn and practice brainstorming and idea expansion
- an opportunity to reflect and engage in group problem-solving

- a way for teachers to learn about children's thoughts and feelings

The Daily News

Many preschools, kindergartens, and early primary grades participate in a daily news or recap group that focuses on sharing the important or interesting events of each day. During this time both teachers and children share news, happenings, and anecdotes from both their school and home lives. An early childhood teacher can begin this activity by saying: "Tamika told me today about something exciting that just happened at her house. Would you like to tell us your news, Tamika?" or "Mario and Ramon built something really interesting today during center time. Would you like to tell the class about it, Mario and Ramon?" As is the case with show-and-tell time, the teacher must be cognizant of the children's interest in and reaction to this activity to ensure that it does not become a boring, time-wasting activity. However, it can be beneficial under the right circumstances.

SUGGESTED ACTIVITIES

1. Select a four- or five-year-old child and use the Directed Listening-Thinking Activity (DL-TA) while reading an appropriate picture storybook to him or her. Summarize orally or in writing how successful this strategy was with the child. Why do you think that this may be a good strategy to use to promote both listening skills and prediction abilities?

2. Construct your own version of a chant or fingerplay that can be used with young children and then share it with other early childhood teachers or children.

3. Construct (implement) one of the listening games that were included in this chapter or your own listening game. You can play it with one child or a small group of young children.

4. Tape record the oral language of a young child from three to seven years of age. Then summarize orally or in writing

the main characteristics of child's oral language. Does her or his own language at that age exemplify the characteristics of children's oral language at that age mentioned in this chapter?

5. Select one of the wordless (textless) books that were included in Chapter 2. Have a young child of the appropriate age narrate this wordless book to provide him or her with practice in oral language skills. Describe orally or in writing how successful this experience was and your view of the reasons for its success of lack of success.

6. Construct (implement) one of the oral language games included in this chapter, or construct (implement) one of your own oral language games. You should play it with one child or a small group of children, if possible.

SELECTED REFERENCES

Berk, L. (1996). Infants and children: Prenatal through middle childhood. Boston: Allyn & Bacon.

Fields, M., & Spangler, K. (1995). *Let's begin reading right* (pp. 12–18, 46–51, & 72–82). Englewood Cliffs, NJ: Prentice-Hall.

Glazer, S. (1988). Oral language and literacy development. In D. Strickland & L. Morrow (Eds.) *Emerging literacy: Young children learn to read and write.* Newark, DE: International Reading Association.

Glazer, S., & Burke, E. (1994). *An integrated approach to early literacy* (pp. 9–15, 55–57, 82–87, 104–105, 131–132, 154–155, 168, 194–198). Boston: Allyn and Bacon.

Holdaway, D. (1979). *The foundations of literacy* (pp. 19–23 & 147–160). Portsmouth, NH: Heinemann.

Hoyt, L. (1992). Many ways of knowing: Using drama, oral interactions, and the visual arts to enhance reading comprehension. *The Reading Teacher, 45,* 580–584.

Mayesky, M. (1995). *Creative activities for young children.* Albany, NY: Delmar Publishers.

Morrow, L. (1997). *Literacy development in the early years* (pp. 86–123 & 199–200). Boston: Allyn and Bacon.

Neuman, S., & Roskos, K. (1993). *Language and literacy learning in the early years* (pp. 5–10, 28–35, 75–86, & 272–273). Fort Worth, TX: Harcourt Brace Jovanovich.

Pinker, S. (1994). *The language instinct.* NY: Harper Perennial.

Salinger, T. (1996). *Literacy for young children* (pp. 109–130). Englewood Cliffs, NJ: Prentice-Hall.

Snow, C., Tabors, P., Nicholson, P., & Kurland, B. (1995). SHELL: Oral language and early literacy skills in kindergarten and first-grade children. *Journal of Research in Childhood Education, 10,* 37–48.

ACTIVITY

Games to Promote Oral Language Skills

There are a number of interesting games that can be used in an early childhood program to develop the children's oral language skills. Here are a few such games that you may want to consider using. As was the case with the strategies and materials included in this section, each early childhood teacher should modify any of these games in the light of the needs and interests of his or her children.

Grocery Guessing Game

Prepare a brown paper bag with a number of grocery store items. Pull out one of the items and describe it. Then have the children take turns pulling out an item and describing it. The teacher can make a shopping list of the items named and explain the purpose of a shopping list. If you want, for a related activity, you then can have each child who is interested write (scribble) his or her own shopping list.

The Mystery Bag

In this game the teacher can collect a group of common objects. She or he then turns away from the group and puts one of the objects into another bag. Then have a child reach (without looking inside) into the second bag and describe the object. The child then pulls the item out of the bag, and the item is discussed in ways such as this: "What can we do with this object? What is its name? What other, if any, object in this room does it look like?" Since it is hard for a young child to wait for his or her turn, the group of children playing this game should be fairly small. Some examples of objects that can be used are an apple, an orange, a stuffed animal, a small model, a rock, a feather, a whistle, a brush, a comb, and a hand or finger puppet.

The Letter Game

Bringing a large bag of letters into the classroom. Take one letter out. Then talk about the letter that you are going to send to a child in the group. For example, you can say, "I'm going to give this pretend letter to Artiz and tell him about my new puppy," or "I'm going to send a thank-you letter to Lawanda because she did such a good job last week taking care of the hamsters in our classroom," or "Who would like to pull out one of these letters and tell us the person that they would like to send the letter to and what the letter will say?"

Tell about a Child

Select a child from the group to stand beside you. Then describe three of the child's characteristics, for example, her red hair, black shoes, nice smile, etc. Then ask what child in the group would like to pick another classmate and tell three *positive* things about that person. Before playing this game, the children should be reminded that they need to mention only positive things that will not be offensive to the chosen child.

WORKS CITED FOR CHAPTER 3

Baumann, J. (1992). Effect of think aloud instruction on elementary students' comprehension monitoring ability. *Journal of Reading Behavior, 24,* 143–172.

Bernstein, B. (1961). Social class and linguistic development: A theory of social learning. In B. Bernstein (Ed.). *Education, economy, and society.* NY: The Free Press, 288–310.

Brent, R., & Anderson, P. (1993). Developing children's classroom listening strategies. *The Reading Teacher, 47,* 122–126.

Brown, R., Cazden, C., & Bellugi-Klima, U. (1968). The child's grammar from one to three. In J. Hall (Ed.). *Minnesota symposium on child development.* Minneapolis: University of Minnesota Press.

Chomsky, N. (1965). *Aspects of a theory of syntax.* Cambridge, MA: MIT Press.

Costa, A. (1991). The search for intelligent life. In *Developing minds: A resource book for teaching thinking.* Alexandria, VA: Association for Supervision and Curriculum Development.

Fein, G. (1981). Pretend play: New perspectives. *Child Development, 30,* 681–693.

Halliday, M. (1973). *Explorations in the functions of language.* London: Edward Arnold.

Halliday, M. (1975). *Learning how to mean: Exploration in the development of language.* London: Edward Arnold.

Jagger, A. (1985). Allowing for language differences. In G. Pinnell (Ed.). *Discovering language with children.* Urbana, Illinois: National Council of Teachers of English.

Lennenberg, E. (1967). *Biological foundations of language.* NY: John Wiley.

McNeil, D. (1970). *The acquisition of language: The study of developmental psycholinguistics.* NY: Harper & Row.

Menyuk, P. (1991). Linguistics and teaching the language arts. In J. Flood, J. Jensen, D. Lapp, & J. Squire (Eds.). *Handbook of research on teaching the English language arts* (pp. 24–29). NY: Macmillan.

Miller, W. (1967). *Relationship between mother's style of communication and her control system to the child's reading readiness and subsequent reading achievement in first grade.* Unpublished doctoral dissertation at the University of Arizona, Tucson.

Neuman, S., & Roskos, K. (1993). *Language and literacy in the early years.* Fort Worth, TX: Harcourt Brace Jovanovich.

Oken-Wright, P. (1988). Show and tell grows up. *Young Children, 43.2,* 52–63.

Piaget, J., & Inhelder, B. (1969). *The psychology of the child.* NY: Basic Books.

Pinnell, G. (1985). Ways to look at functions of children's language. In A. Jaggar, & M. Burke (Eds.). *Observing the language learner.* Newark, DE: International Reading Association, and Urbana, IL: National Council of Teachers of English.

Pinnell, G. & Jaggar, A. (1992). Oral language: Speaking and listening in the classroom. In J. Flood et al. (Eds.) *Handbook of research in teaching the English language arts.* NY: Macmillan.

Raphael, T., & Hiebert, E. (1966). *Creating an integrated approach to literacy instruction.* NY: Holt, Rinehart & Winston.

Ruddell, R., & Ruddell, M. (1995). *Teaching children to read and write.* NY: McGraw-Hill.

Scott, L. (1968). *Learning time with language experiences.* NY: McGraw-Hill.

Segal, M. (1987). Should superheroes be expelled from preschool? *Pre-K Today, 1.8,* 37–45.

Skinner, B. (1957). *Verbal behavior.* NY: Appleton-Century-Crofts.

Standards for the English language arts. (1996). Urbana, IL: National Council of Teachers of English, and Newark, DE: International Reading Association.

Stauffer, R. (1980). *The language experience approach to the teaching of reading.* NY: Harper & Row.

Sulzby, E. (1986). Children's elicitation and use of metalinguistic knowledge about "world" during literacy interactions. In P. Yaden and S. Templeton (Eds.) *Metalinguistic awareness and beginning literacy.* Exeter, NH: Heinemann Educational Books.

Trealease, J. (1995). *The new read-aloud handbook.* NY: Penguin.

Vygotsky, L. (1978). *Mind in society: The development of psychological processes.* Cambridge, MA: Harvard University Press.

DEVELOPING COMPETENCY IN LETTER-NAME KNOWLEDGE AND THE WORD IDENTIFICATION SKILLS

CONCEPTS THAT YOU SHOULD LEARN FROM READING THIS CHAPTER

After you have finished reading this chapter, you will be able to:

■ *Differentiate between the terms* letter-name recognition *and* letter-name identification

■ *Explain some valuable strategies and materials that can be used to help children learn to identify the capital and lowercase letter names*

■ *Suggest some games that will help children learn to identify the capital and lowercase names*

■ *Differentiate between the terms* sight word recognition *and* sight word identification

■ *Describe sight word lists and provide the names of several useful sight word lists*

■ *Describe some strategies and materials that can be used to help children improve sight word recognition and identification*

■ *Suggest some interesting games that will help children learn to identify important sight words*

■ *Provide the definition of* graphophonic (phonic) analysis

■ *Explain some of the basic principles of phonics instruction and the two main approaches to teaching phonics in the primary grades*

■ *Explain the most common phonic elements and generalizations*

■ *Describe some useful strategies for improving ability in phonic analysis*

■ *Suggest some useful games that can be used to improve competency in phonic analysis*

■ *Explain* structural or morphemic analysis

■ *Describe some strategies for improving ability in structural (morphemic) analysis*

■ *Suggest some useful games for improving ability in structural (morphemic) analysis*

■ *Provide a description of* semantic (contextual) analysis

■ *Discuss some useful strategies and materials for improving ability in semantic (contextual) analysis*

© PhotoDisc/Education

Do you believe that parents of young children should make a concerted effort to teach them the various consonant and vowel sounds before they enter school? Although some parents apparently believe that this is a desirable practice, many reading specialists believe that letter-sound relationships should be presented and practiced only after young children have learned a number of words by sight and have learned to identify the capital and lowercase letter names.

If a child cannot effectively identify the words that are met while reading, he or she cannot understand the material successfully. Many readers with reading disabilities undoubtedly could understand what they read if they had effective word identification strategies. This chapter presents many useful strategies and materials that you can use with young children for this purpose.

LETTER-NAME RECOGNITION AND LETTER-NAME IDENTIFICATION

Letter-name recognition and letter-name identification are both important for achieving success in beginning reading activities. However, these two reading skills are *not* a prerequisite to successful beginning reading. For example, most young children learn a number of environmental print and sight words such as *STOP, McDonalds, Hardees, dog, cat, mom,* and *dad* from having these words pointed out to them by adults and other children and having their questions about these words answered. In addition, the use of the language-experience approach (LEA) and various types of writing activities all usually should precede direct instruction in the letter names. Because the alphabet traditionally has been very important in early reading instruction, it probably always will be an integral part of beginning reading programs. However, it should not be overemphasized in terms of the time devoted to it or the expectations held for children about learning it.

Before children learn to name or write any alphabet letters, they are able to discover a great deal about alphabet letters and written language. Young children must learn that alphabet letters are a special category of visual graphics that can be named. For example, Lass (1982) found that her son began calling each of the letters in his alphabet books or in environmental print signs *B* or *D* when he was a toddler. Apparently Jed had learned to recognize the unique category we call *letters.* Therefore, he

called all the visual graphics (letters) that he saw *B* or *D,* two letters he could say aloud.

Young children also should learn that alphabet letters are associated with important people, places, or objects. As an example, a young child named Giti is reported to have noticed the letter *M* in *K-Mart* and called it *McDonalds.* She also noticed the letter *Z* on one of her blocks and said, *"Look, like in zoo"* (Baghban, 1984, pp. 29–30). Giti did not call *M* or *Z* by their names, but she associated their unique shapes with two meaningful places where she had seen those same shapes.

Young children also should have *metalinguistic awareness* about letters. For example, a young child may attempt to write the sentence: "I like my new puppy. His name is Boots." After writing this sentence, the child may say, "Mommy, look! I just wrote three p's." This indicates that the child knows what the letter *p* looks like and how it is written. This type of awareness of his or her own knowledge about the alphabet names is called metalinguistic awareness and is important to a child's subsequent reading success in the primary grades.

When they are writing, some young children may use *mock letters* (see samples at bottom of this page), which are letterlike shapes that seem to have many of the properties of real letters except that they are not actual letter names. They often are a stage between a young child's scribbling and the actual letters he or she later writes.

As preschoolers, some children learn the names of a number of letters and also are able to write some of the letters. By the age of three, a few children can name as many as ten alphabet letters (Hiebert, 1981; Lomax & McGee, 1987), while by the age of four, some children can write some recognizable letters, most commonly those letters found in their first name. Even precocious children who may be able to read and write prior to kindergarten entrance often have taken as long as six months to learn all the letter names (Anbar, 1982; Lass, 1982). Children may take two or three years to be completely adept at writing their names (Hildreth, 1936). Therefore, there is wide variation in the ability of children to learn the letter names (Morgan, 1987), and some children entering kindergarten and even first grade are not able to identify any capital or lowercase letter names.

It is important for children in kindergartens and beginning first grades to master all of the capital and lowercase letter names for several reasons. Parents, for example, put great emphasis on this knowledge, and research has found that the knowledge of letter names in later kindergarten and beginning first grade is the single most important predictor of subsequent first-grade achievement (Durrell, 1980). In addition, a child cannot always call the letter *a*, for example, "a circle and a stick" (that is, the description of its appearance). The child needs an arbitrary but consistent name to assign to it.

Even so, it is important to remember that the child who can identify the letter names probably has come from a home environment in which all literacy activities such as reading on a regular basis to the child, scribbling and writing activities, and development of prior knowledge has been encouraged. Therefore, the child learns both letter names and sight words fairly easily, especially if he or she has a good linguistic aptitude.

Although *letter recognition* is easier for most young children than is *letter identification,* it also is less significant to reading achievement. For example, the following is an example of letter recognition.

Put an X on the capital S.
F S Y O

and here is an example of letter identification:

What is the name of this letter?
S

It should be obvious that letter identification, not letter recognition, is required in actual reading. Therefore, although letter recognition activities such as the one illustrated above may have some value as a beginning point, letter identification should receive the primary stress in initial reading instruction.

A child obviously needs to have 100 percent competency in the identification of both the capital and lowercase letter names. Letter-naming is a very easy task for a child who has a good linguistic aptitude, and this kind of child seems to learn the letter names effortlessly primarily by being read to and engaging in other informal emergent literacy activities. However, it can be a very difficult and time-consuming task for some children with special needs, especially children with learning disabilities and those who learn slowly. For example, it is not uncommon for a special needs child to learn to identify only four or five letter names in an entire semester of working with an adult individually for approximately twenty 30- to 40-minute sessions.

If the child seems to have great difficulty learning the letter names, it is important to teach only one letter at a time. Tactile strategies such as those described in the next section of this chapter may be the most helpful, although this is not always the case. If a child does not have a great deal of difficulty, it may be possible to teach two letter names at a time. If you decide that this is feasible, select two letters that do not resemble each other. For example, you could teach these two letters at the same time:

h s

but you should not, for example, teach these two letters in the same lesson:

c e

Research has not found any single correct sequence in which to teach the letter names. Usually the child is taught to recognize, identify, and write the letters in his or her own first name first, for example:

Kersti

After that, a few kindergarten or first-grade teachers prefer to teach the child to identify all of the lowercase letter names first, followed by the capital letter names. Most teachers, however, present matching capital and lowercase letters in pairs such as the following:

P p

This may be the most common way of presenting letter names, but some teachers prefer to present letter names in terms of their usefulness. For example, such a teacher probably would present the letters *s* and *t* before presenting the letters *v* and *z,* since the latter two letters are seen less frequently. One possible exception to this would be the letters *X* and *x,* which are uncommon but often needed to complete beginning reading workbooks and tests.

It is important that children learn letter names that are meaningful at first. That is why the letters in the child's own first name are so often presented and practiced. Letters that relate to the thematic unit that is being presented in a kindergarten or beginning first-grade classroom also are meaningful to young children. For example, in a unit about zoo animals, the letters *m* for *monkey* and *l* for *lion* could be among those presented.

The child also should learn the differences between a *letter* and a *word*. This author has asked kindergarten children to point to a word on an experience chart, and some of the children have pointed to a letter. Some children do not completely understand this concept unless it is explained and illustrated for them.

It also is important for a young child to use the proper terms for the letters For example, most kindergarten and first-grade teachers use the terms *capital* and *lowercase,* although the term *uppercase* also may be used instead of the term *capital*. Young children should not be allowed to use the terms *big* and *little* (or *small*) in place of the proper terms, as this may be confusing for them. For example, the letters *b* and *k* can justifiably be called big letters because they are ascenders (that is, they have a part that rises above the main body of the letter), although they obviously are lowercase letters.

A number of teachers in contemporary kindergartens teach the letter names in *D'Nealian script* because of the potential help this may give the children in later making the transition to cursive handwriting. However, a number of early childhood educators prefer *Zaner-Bloser hand-writing* (block handwriting) because family members can teach it properly in the home, it better matches the print found in the books that the children read, and it is usually easier for young children to learn.

STRATEGIES AND MATERIALS FOR IMPROVING ABILITY IN LETTER-NAME RECOGNITION AND LETTER-NAME IDENTIFICATION

The chapter now contains a number of classroom-tested strategies and materials for improving ability in letter-name recognition and letter-name identification. You are encouraged to modify any of these suggestions as you believe necessary in the light of the needs and interests of your own pupils, which is consistent with the whole language philosophy (see Chapter 2) and is equally important in any more traditional literacy program.

Reading Activities of All Types

In keeping with the whole language philosophy, all kinds of reading activities are the most effective way of presenting letter names to most children. Such whole language presentation is effective with many, but not all, children. As much as possible, however, children should learn and practice both capital and lowercase letter names in the context of meaningful words, stories, books, rhymes, and fingerplays.

The language-experience approach (LEA) (see Chapter 2) is a very effective way of helping young children recognize and identify letters. As a matching activity, for example, the teacher can prepare capital and lowercase letter cards which children can match to the appropriate letters in an experience chart or story. Children can be asked to circle or underline designated letters in an experience chart or story or to spell any word in the story that they wish or are asked to spell. They also can be asked to point to capital or lowercase letters in an experience chart or story. Letter matching and letter identification activities within the context of experience charts or stories is very effective because it is in the context of the child's own experiences and language. LEA should be used on a regular basis for this purpose in older preschool settings, in kindergartens, and in beginning first grades.

Many trade books have been published that are designed to emphasize a certain letter of the alphabet in context. They are very helpful if the preschool, kindergarten, or first-grade teacher wishes to stress a certain letter of the alphabet with the entire class, a small group of children, or an individual child. Most of these books also are beautifully illustrated and therefore motivating to young children. Here is a partial list of trade books that can be used for this purpose with young children. Many of them also can be used to present and/or review the sounds of the letters in context.

The Letter A

Barry, K. (1961). *A is for everything.* NY: Harcourt Brace Jovanovich.

Boynton, S. (1983). *A is for angry: An animal and adjective alphabet.* NY: Workman.

Ferguson, D. (1977). *Ants.* NY: Wonder Books.

Guilfoile, E. (1957). *Nobody listens to Andrew.* NY: Scholastic.

McMillan, B. (1979). *Apples: How they grow.* Boston: Houghton Mifflin.

Scarry, R. (1976). *About animals.* NY: Golden Press.

The Letter B

Baker, A. (1982). *Benjamin's book.* NY: Lothrop, Lee, & Shephard.

Bottner, B. (1992). *Bootsie Barker bites.* NY: Putnam's.

Flack, M. (1932). *Ask Mr. Bear.* NY: Macmillan.

Gretz, S. (1981). *Teddy bears' moving day.* Chicago: Follett.

Gretz, S. (1971). *The bears who stayed indoors.* Chicago: Follett.

Kessler, E., & L. (1957). *Big red bus.* NY: Doubleday.

Lindenbaum, P. (1992). *Boodil my dog.* Elgin, IL: Child's World Publishing.

McLeod, E. (1975). *The bear's bicycle.* Boston: Little, Brown & Company.

McPhail, D. (1972). *The bear's toothache.* Boston: Little, Brown & Company.

Moncure, J. (1984). *My "B" sound.* Elgin, IL: Child's World Publishing.

The Letter C

Bridwell, N. (1972). *Clifford, the small red puppy.* NY: Scholastic. (All of the other Clifford books also are appropriate.)

Carle, E. (1969). *The very hungry caterpillar.* NY: Scholastic.

Crews, D. (1982). *Carousel.* NY: Greenwillow Books.

Freeman, D. (1977). *Corduroy.* NY: Penguin Books.

Keats, E. (1970). *Hi, cat!* NY: Macmillan.

Mandel, P. (1994). *Red cat white cat.* NY: Henry Holt & Company.

Rounds, G. (1991). *Cowboys.* NY: Holiday House.

Schecter, B. (1967). *Conrad's castle.* NY: Harper & Row.

The Letter D

Berenstain, S. & J. (1980). *Dinosaur bone.* NY: Beginner Books.

Colbert, E. (1977). *The dinosaur world.* NY: Stravon Educational Press.

Cole, B. (1994). *Dr. Dog.* NY: Knopf.

Cole, J. (1974). *Dinosaur story.* NY: Morrow.

Geis, D. (1959). *Dinosaurs and other prehistoric animals.* NY: Grosset & Dunlap.

Hoff, S. (1994). *Duncan the dancing duck.* NY: Clarion Books.

McCloskey, R. (1941). *Make way for ducklings.* NY: Viking.

Moncure, J. (1984). *My "D" sound.* Elgin, IL: Child's World Publishing.

Pringle, L. (1968). *Dinosaurs and their world.* NY: Harcourt, Brace and World.

Steig, W. (1982). *Doctor Desoto.* NY: Farrar, Strauss & Giroux.

The Letter E

Eve, E. (1971). *Eggs.* NY: Wonder Books.

Ginsburg, M. (1980). *Good morning chick.* NY: Greenwillow Books.

Lobel, A. (1981). *Uncle elephant.* NY: Scholastic.

Piper, W. (1961). *The little engine that could.* NY: Scholastic.

Tresselt, A. (1967). *The world in the candy egg.* NY: Lothrop, Lee, & Shephard.

The Letter F

Dennis, W. (1973). *Flip.* NY: Scholastic.

Galdone, P. (1975). *The frog prince.* NY: McGraw-Hill.

Hoban, R. (1968). *A birthday for Francis.* NY: Scholastic.

Leaf, M. (1936). *The story of Ferdinand.* NY: Viking.

Lionni, L. (1967). *Frederick.* NY: Pantheon.

Ryder, J. (1979). *Fog in the meadow.* NY: Harper & Row.

Zolotow, C. (1965). *Flocks of birds.* NY: Thomas Y. Crowell.

The Letter G

Arno, E. (1967). *The gingerbread man.* NY: Scholastic.

Blair, S. (1967). *The three billy goats gruff.* NY: Scholastic.

Carle, E. (1977). *The grouchy ladybug.* NY: Thomas Y. Crowell.

Harrison, S., & Wilks, M. (1980). *In Granny's garden.* NY: Holt, Rinehart, & Winston.

Keats, E. (1969). *Goggles.* NY: Holt, Rinehart, & Winston.

Weatherill, S. (1982). *Goosey, goosey, gander.* NY: Greenwillow Books.

Zolotow, C. (1974). *My grandson Lew.* NY: Harper & Row.

The Letter H

Brown, M. (1969). *How, hippo!* NY: Charles Scribner's Sons.

Burton, V. (1969). *The little house.* Boston: Houghton Mifflin.

Hadithi, M., & Kennaway, A. (1994). *Hungry hyena.* Boston: Little, Brown & Company.

Galdone, P. (1973). *The little red hen.* NY: Scholastic.

Jeffers, S. (1974). *All the pretty houses.* NY: Macmillan.

Nodset, J. (1963). *Who took the farmer's hat?* NY: Harper & Row.

Rose, D. (1983). *It hardly seems like Halloween.* NY: Lothrop, Lee, & Shephard.

Weatherill, S. (1982). *Humpty Dumpty.* NY: Greenwillow Books.

Zion, G. (1965). *Harry by the sea.* NY: Harper & Row.

Zion, G. (1956). *Harry the dirty dog.* NY: Harper & Row.

The Letter I

Bornstein, R. (1973). *Indian bunny.* NY: Scholastic.

Brown, M. (1949). *Important book.* NY: Harper & Row.

Manley, D. (1977). *Let's look at insects.* NY: Derrydale.

Martin, B. (1966). *Knots on a counting rope.* NY: Holt, Rinehart, & Winston.

Waber, W. (1972). *Ira sleeps over.* Boston: Houghton Mifflin.

The Letter J

Bartocci, B. (1991). *Jungle jumble.* Kansas City, MO: Hallmark.

Degan, B. (1983). *Jamberry.* NY: Harper & Row.

Hennessey, B. (1990). *Jake baked the cake.* NY: Viking.

Hoban, R. (1964). *Bread and jam for Francis.* NY: Harper & Row.

Kalan, R. (1981). *Jump frog jump.* NY: Greenwillow Books.

Keats, E. (1966). *Jennie's hat.* NY: Harper & Row.

Simon, I. (1979). *This is the house that Jack built.* NY: Dandelion Press.

Steadman, R. (1970). *Jelly book.* NY: Scroll Press.

Stobbs, W. (1965). *Jack and the beanstalk.* NY: Delacorte Press.

The Letter K

Chance, E. (1970). *Just in time for the king's birthday.* NY: Scholastic.

Holmelund, M. (1968). *A kiss for little bear.* NY: Harper & Row.

Mayer, M. (1973). *What do you do with a kangaroo?* NY: Scholastic.

Payne, E. (1972). *Katy-no-pocket.* NY: Scholastic.

Rockwell, H. (1980). *My kitchen.* NY: Greenwillow Books.

Sendak, M. (1970). *In the night kitchen.* NY: Harper & Row.

Shapiro, A. (1978). *Kenny's crazy kite.* Los Angeles: Price/Stern/Sloan.

Wood, A. (1985). *King Bidgood's in the bathtub.* NY: Harcourt Brace Jovanovich.

The Letter L

Carle, E. (1977). *The grouchy ladybug.* NY: Alfred A. Knopf.

Cosgrove, S. (1977). *Leon the lop.* Bothell, WA: Serendipity Press.

de Regniers, B. (1989). *Laura's story.* NY: Atheneum.

Keats, E. (1968). *A letter to Amy.* NY: Harper & Row.

Kraus, R. (1971). *Leo the late bloomer.* NY: Windmill Books.

London, J., & Long, S. (1994). *Liplap's wish.* San Francisco: Chronicle Books.

Moncure, J. (1984). *My "L" sound.* Elgin, IL: Child's World Publishing.

Waber, B. (1969). *Lovable Lyle.* Boston: Houghton Mifflin.

Zolotow, C. (1980). *If you listen.* NY: Harper & Row.

The Letter M

Allen, J. (1990). *Mucky moose.* NY: Macmillan.

Bemelmans, M. (1977). *Madeline.* NY: Puffin Books.

Burton, V. (1939). *Mike Mulligan and his steam shovel.* NY: Houghton Mifflin.

Eastman, P. (1960). *Are you my mother?* NY: Random House.

Felix, M. (1980). *The story of a little mouse trapped in a book.* La Jolla, CA: Green Tiger Press.

Fleischman, S. (1978). *McBroom and the beanstalk.* Boston: Little, Brown & Company.

Kraus, R. (1980). *Mouse work.* NY: Windmill.

Lobel, A. (1977). *Mouse soup.* NY: Harper & Row.

Lobel, A. (1981). *On Market Street.* NY: Scholastic.

Moncure, J. (1984). *My "M" sound.* Elgin, IL: Child's World Publishing.

Numeroff, L. (1991). *If you give a moose a muffin.* NY: HarperCollins.

Rockwell, A. (1973). *The awful mess.* NY: Parents Magazine Press.

Segel, L. (1970). *Tell me a Mitzi.* NY: Farrar, Straus, & Giroux.

Seuss, Dr. (1948). *Thidwick: the big hearted moose.* NY: Random House.

Walter, M. (1971). *The magic mirror book and magic mirror tricks.* NY: Scholastic.

The Letter N

Allard, H., & Marshall, J. (1977). *Miss Nelson is missing.* Boston: Houghton Mifflin.

Brown, M. (1939). *The noisy book.* NY: Harper & Row.

Gag, W. (1941). *Nothing at all.* NY: Coward, McCann, & Geoghegan.

Masner, J. (1989). *Nicholas Cricket.* NY: Harper & Row.

Mayer, M. (1968). *There's a nightmare in my closet.* NY: Dial Books.

McGovern, A. (1967). *Too much noise.* NY: Scholastic.

Selsam. M. (1979). *Night animals.* NY: Scholastic.

Skofield, J. (1981). *Nightdances.* NY: Harper & Row.

Sugata, Y. (1971). *Good night 1, 2, 3.* NY: Scroll Press.

Wells, R. (1973). *Noisy Nora.* NY: Scholastic.

Wezel, P. (1967). *The naughty bird.* Chicago: Follett.

The Letter O

Hall, D. (1979). *Ox-cart man.* NY: Viking.

Hoff, S. (1960). *Oliver.* NY: Harper & Row.

Keats, E. (1971). *Over in the meadow.* NY: Scholastic.

Marestro, B., & G. (1981). *Traffic: A book of opposites.* NY: Crown.

Turkle, B. (1981). *Thy friend, Obadiah.* NY: Viking.

The Letter P

Ahlberg, J., & A. (1978). *Each peach pear plum.* NY: Scholastic.

Bonners, S. (1981). *A penguin year.* NY: Delacorte Press.

Brown, R. (1973). *Pig in the pond.* NY: David McKay.

de Paola, P. (1978). *The popcorn book.* NY: Holiday House.

Dillon, I. (1957). *Policemen.* Chicago: Melmont.

Duvoisin, R. (1950). *Petunia.* NY: Alfred A. Knopf.

Flack, M., & Wiese, K. (1933, 1961). *The story about Ping.* NY: Viking.

Galdone, P. (1970). *Three little pigs.* NY: Scholastic.

McDermott, G. (1980). *Papagayo: The mischief maker.* NY: Windmill/Wanderer.

Rockwell, A. (1993). *Mr. Panda's painting.* NY: Macmillan.

Roth, S. (1966). *Pick a peck of puzzles.* NY: Arnold Norton.

Sendak, M. (1962). *Pierre: A cautionary tale in five chapters and a prologue.* NY: Scholastic.

Wolcott, P. (1975). *Pickle, pickle, pickle juice.* NY: Scholastic.

The Letter Q

Brown, M. (1950). *The quiet noisy book.* NY: Harper & Row.

Carle, E. (1990). *The very quiet cricket.* NY: Philomel.

de Paola, P. (1977). *The quicksand book.* NY: Holiday House.

Eltings, M., & Folsom, M. (1980). *Q is for duck: An alphabet guessing game.* NY: Clarion Books.

Fleisher, R. (1978). *Quilts in the attic.* NY: Macmillan.

Freeman, D. (1969). *Quiet! There's a canary in the attic.* San Carlos, CA: Golden Gate Children's Books.

Johnston, T., & de Paola, T. (1985). *The quilt story.* NY: Putnam's.

Mayer, M. (1971). *The queen wanted to dance.* NY: Simon & Schuster.

Rothman, J. (Spanish words by Palacios, A.) (1979). *This can lick a lollipop.* Garden City, NY: Doubleday.

Zolotow, C. (1963). *The quarreling book.* NY: Harper & Row.

The Letter R

Bate, L. (1975). *Little rabbit's loose tooth.* NY: Scholastic.

Baylor, B. (1974). *Everybody needs a rock.* NY: Charles Scribner's Sons.

Buringham, J. (1974). *The rabbit.* NY: Thomas Y. Crowell.

de Paola, P. (1992). *Rosie and the yellow ribbon.* Boston: Joy Street Books.

Fisher, A. (1983). *Rabbits, rabbits.* NY: Harper & Row.

Heilbroner, J. (1962). *Robert and the rose horse.* NY: Random House.

Kellogg, S. (1981). *A rose for Pinkerton.* NY: Dial Press.

Kent, J. (1982). *Round robin.* Englewood Cliffs, NJ: Prentice Hall.

Rockwell, H. (1974). *The compost heap.* Garden City, NY: Doubleday.

Sendak, M. (1975). *Really, Rosie.* NY: Harper & Row.

Shulevitz, U. (1969). *Rain rain rivers.* NY: Farrar, Straus, & Giroux.

Thaler, M. (1974). *How far will a rubber band stretch?* NY: Parents Magazine Press.

Thayer. J. (1980). *Applebaums have a robot!* NY: William Morrow.

Watts, M. (1979). *Little red riding hood.* Racine, WI: Golden Press.

Zion, G. (1958). *No roses for Harry!* NY: Harper & Row.

The Letter S

Ayliffe, A. (1992). *Slither, swoop, swing.* NY: Viking.

Berenstain, S., & J. (1981). *The Berenstain bears and the sitter.* NY: Random House.

Brown, M. (1947). *Stone soup.* NY: Scribner's.

Hill, E. (1980). *Where's Spot?* NY: G. P. Putnam's Sons.

Jordan, H. (1960). *How a seed grows.* NY: Thomas Y. Crowell.

Keats, E. (1976). *The snowy day.* NY: Puffin Books.

Kessler, E. & L. (1973). *Slush, slush!* NY: Parents Magazine Press.

Krauss, R. (1945). *The carrot seed.* NY: Scholastic.

Lionni, L. (1973). *Swimmy.* NY: Random House.

Shapiro, A. (1978). *Squiggly Wiggly's surprise.* Los Angeles: Intervisual.

Stadler, J. (1985). *Snail saves the day.* NY: Thomas Y. Crowell.

Ungerer, T. (1962). *Snail, where are you?* NY: Harper & Row.

Zolotow, C. (1967). *Summer is. . . .* NY: Thomas Y. Crowell.

The Letter T

Burney, B. (1994). *Tyrassosaurus.* Boston: Houghton Mifflin.

Cosgrove, S. (1984). *Tee-tee.* Vero Beach, FL: Rourke Enterprises.

Ehrich, A. (1977). *The everyday train.* NY: Dial Books.

Lexau, J. (1971). *T for Tommy.* NY: Garrard.

Lobel, A. (1979). *A treeful of pigs.* NY: Scholastic.

McPhail, D. (1972). *The bear's toothache.* NY: Penguin Books.

Mosel, A. (1968). *Tikki tikki tembo.* NY: Scholastic.

Preston, E. (1969). *The temper tantrum.* NY: Viking.

Seuling, B. (1976). *Teeny-tiny woman.* NY: Viking.

Udry, J. (1956). *A tree is nice.* NY: Harper & Row.

Wolfe, R. (1981). *The truck book.* Minneapolis, MN: Carolrhoda Books.

The Letter U

Anderson, H. (1965). *The ugly duckling.* NY: Scribner's.

Anno, M. (1971). *Upside-downers.* NY: Walker/Weatherhill.

Bright, R. (1959). *My red umbrella.* NY: William Morrow.

Tashima, M. (1971). *Umbrella.* NY: Viking.

The Letter V

Carle, E. (1969). *The very hungry caterpillar.* NY: Philomel.

DeArmond, F. (1963). *The very, very special day.* NY: Parents Magazine Press.

Duvoisin, R. (1961). *Veronica.* NY: Knopf.

Elke, E., & T. (1981). *The night vegetable eater.* NY: Dodd, Mead & Company.

Goldreich, G., & E. (1972). *What can she be? A veterinarian.* NY: Lothrop, Lee, & Shephard.

Jasapersohn, W. (1978). *A day in the life of a veterinarian.* Boston: Little, Brown & Company.

Leithauser, G., & Breitmeyer, L. (1978). *The rabbit is next.* Racine, WI: Golden Press.

The Letter W

Carlstrom, N. (1993). *How does the wind walk?* NY: Macmillan.

Freschet, B. (1972). *The web in the grass.* NY: Charles Scribner's Sons.

Isadora, R. (1977). *Willaby.* NY: Macmillan.

Keats, E. (1964). *Whistle for Willie.* NY: Viking.

Kennedy, M. (1980). *Wings.* NY: Scholastic.

Nyblom, H. (1968). *The witch of the woods.* NY: Knopf.

Ross, C. (1993). *The Whiryls and the west wind.* Boston: Houghton Mifflin.

Sendak, M. (1963). *Where the wild things are.* NY: Harper & Row.

Zolotow, C. (1962). *When the wind stops.* NY: Abeland-Schumann.

Zolotow, C. (1972). *William's doll.* NY: Harper & Row.

The Letter X

Bartkowski, R. (1975). *Little Max, the cement mixer.* Chicago: Rand McNally.

Maloney, C. (1978). *The box book.* Racine, WI: Golden Press.

Moncure, J. (1979). *My "X, Y, Z" sound book.* Elgin, IL: Child's World Publishing.

Robbins, J. (1985). *Addie meets Max.* NY: Harper & Row.

Thomas, P. (1979). *There are rocks in my socks said the ox to the fox.* NY: Lothrop, Lee, & Shephard.

The Letter Y

Battles, E. (1978). *What does the rooster say, Yoshio?* Chicago: Albert Whitman.

Lionni, L. (1959). *Little blue and little yellow. A story for Pippo and Ann and other children.* NY: I. Obolensky.

Marshall, J. (1973). *Yummers.* Boston: Houghton Mifflin.

Seuss, Dr. (1958). *Yertle the turtle and other stories.* NY: Random House.

The Letter Z

Bunting, E. (1974). *We need a bigger zoo.* Lexington, MA: Ginn.

Modesitt, J., & Johnson, L. (1990). *The story of Z.* Boston: Picture Book Studio.

Rojankonsky, F. (1972). *Animals in the zoo.* NY: Alfred A. Knopf.

Seuss, Dr. (1950). *If I ran the zoo.* NY: Random House.

Seuss, Dr. (1955). *On beyond zebra.* NY: Random House.

Tallon, R. (1979). *Zoohapets.* NY: Scholastic.

There also are some *alphabet trade books* that stress all of the alphabet letter names. Here is a partial list of some of these alphabet books:

Agard, J. (1989). *The Calypso alphabet.* NY: Henry Holt & Company.

Alexander, A. (1971). *ABC of cars and trucks.* NY: Doubleday.

Anno, M. (1974). *Anno's alphabet: An adventure in imagination.* NY: Thomas Y. Crowell.

Base, G. (1986). *Animalia.* NY: Henry N. Adams.

Beisner, M. (1981). *A folding alphabet book.* NY: Farrar, Straus, & Giroux.

Boynton, S. (1983). *A is for angry: An animal and adjective alphabet.* NY: Workman Publishers.

Brown, R. (1952). *Alphabet times four.* NY: Dutton Children's Books.

Duvoisin, R. (1952). *A for the ark.* NY: Lothrop, Lee, & Shephard.

Elting, M., & Folsom, M. (1980). *Q is for duck: An alphabet guessing game.* NY: Clarion Books.

Feelings, M. (1974). *Jambo means hello: A Swahili alphabet book.* NY: Dial Books.

Gag, W. (1971). *The ABC bunny.* NY: Coward, McCann, & Geoghegan.

Hague, K. (1983). *Alphabears.* NY: Holt, Rinehart, & Winston.

Isadora, R. (1983). *City seen from A to Z.* NY: Greenwillow Books.

Kitchen, B. (1984). *Animal alphabet.* NY: Dial Books.

Lear, E. (1965). *Lear alphabet—Penned and illustrated by Edward Lear himself.* NY: McGraw-Hill.

Montresor, B. (1969). *A for angel: Beni Montresor ABC picture stories.* NY: Alfred A. Knopf.

Musgrove, M. (1976). *Ashanti to Zulu: African traditions.* NY: Dial Books.

Niland, D. (1976). *ABC of monsters.* NY: McGraw-Hill.

Provenson, A., & Provenson, M. (1978). *A peaceable kingdom. The Shaker abecedarius.* NY: Viking.

Sendak, M. (1962). *Alligators all around: An alphabet book.* NY: Harper & Row.

Shannon, G. (1996). *Tomorrow's alphabet.* NY: Greenwillow Books.

Tallon, R. (1989). *An ABC in English and Spanish.* NY: Lion Press.

Wegman, W. (1994). *ABCs.* NY: Hyperion.

Yolen, J. (1991). *All in the woodland early: An ABC book.* Honesdale, PA: Boyds Mill Press.

Teaching and Reinforcing Letter Names in Isolation

For many children letter name recognition and identification are most effectively presented and reviewed in the context of actual reading. However, for a number of children with special needs, the letter names must be isolated in order for them to be able to either recognize or identify them. Such strategies are very effective with children who cannot easily learn the capital and lowercase letter names in the context of reading materials.

Tactile Strategies

Tactile (VAKT [visual-auditory-kinesthetic]) strategies undoubtedly are the single most effective way of presenting letter names to children who have shown they are having great difficulty in learning them. They are especially useful with helping children who have learning disabilities to remember the letter names. However, you should remember that all tactile strategies are fairly time-consuming.

A C T I V I T Y

Tactile Strategies

Here are some tactile strategies that have been found to be effective with children with special needs.

Instant pudding—This tactile strategy usually has been very motivating and effective. Prepare a package of instant pudding and place it in a flat pan (like a cake pan). Have the child draw the target letter name in the pudding, saying its name aloud as he or she does so. Have the child use the terms *capital* or *lowercase*. The child may lick his or her fingers after each letter is made. Although chocolate pudding usually has been the favorite of young children, strawberry pudding also has been used successfully.

Colored chalk and sand tray—Place sand in a flat pan such as a cake pan. Grind a piece of colored chalk and add it to the sand to make the sand more attractive. Have the child draw the target letter in the sand, saying its name aloud as he or she does so. Have the child use the terms *capital* and *lowercase*. You can buy commercially colored sand instead of coloring your own if you wish.

Colored chalk and salt tray—This tactile strategy is identical to the previous one except that salt is used instead of sand. Both seem to work equally well.

Finger paints—Have the child spread finger paint over a sheet of butcher (shiny) paper. Have the child draw each target letter in the finger paint, saying the letter name as he or she does so. The child should indicate whether the letter is a capital or lowercase letter. Finger paints are fairly messy, and therefore many early childhood educators prefer to use instant pudding, which is less messy. The child also can lick his or her fingers with the pudding. Still, you may prefer to use finger paints, at least some of the time. Here are two recipes for finger paints.

Finger Paint Recipe #1

½ cup lump starch
½ cup cold water
1½ cups boiling water
½ cup white soapflakes
1 tablespoon glycerin
food coloring

Dissolve the starch in cold water. Add hot water and cook the mixture until it is clear, stirring constantly. Add soapflakes and stir, and remove from heat immediately. When cool, stir in glycerin and enough drops of food coloring to give the desired shades.

Finger Paint Recipe #2

½ cup cornstarch
1 cup cold water
1 envelope unflavored gelatin
2 cups hot water
½ cup mild soapflakes or detergent
Rit™ dye (powdered form)
If liquid Rit™ dye is used, increase the cornstarch to ¾ cup.

Combine cornstarch and ¾ cup of the cold water in a medium-sized saucepan. Soak gelatin in remaining ¼ cup cold water. Stir hot water into the starch mixture, and cook over medium heat until the mixture comes to a boil and is smooth, stirring constantly. Remove from heat, and blend in softened gelatin. Add soap

or detergent, and stir until thoroughly dissolved. Divide into portions in jars or bowls. Stir in about 1 teaspoon Rit™ powder or 1 tablespoon Rit™ liquid dye for every cup of mixture. If not used immediately, cover mixture tightly for storage. This recipe makes about 3 cups and can be multiplied.

- **Finger painting letters**—The young child also can use finger paints to paint the target letters on paper at an easel. This is an easy-to-use strategy for tactile reinforcement of the capital and lowercase letter names.
- **Oobleck**—This is the name for a gooey substance that children love to work with.

Oobleck Recipe

6¾ cups water
4 boxes cornstarch

Mix the ingredients together. A half batch is usually plenty. Then have the child draw each target letter in the oobleck which is spread on a sheet of heavy paper such as butcher paper. Read the book *Bartholomew and the Oobleck* by Dr. Seuss (NY: Random House, 1950), either before or after the oobleck is used for letter naming. This has been a very popular tactile strategy with older preschool children and kindergarten children.

- **Shaving cream**—The child also can draw the target capital or lowercase letters in commercially available shaving cream. Shaving cream is less messy than are either finger paints or oobleck.
- **Hair gel**—Place some hair gel in a Zip-Loc™ freezer bag. Spread some of the hair gel on a piece of paper with a shiny finish. Have the child draw each target letter in the hair gel, saying the letter name as he or she does so. Have the child indicate whether it is a capital or lowercase letter.
- **Clay**—Have the child form each target letter out of clay, saying the letter name aloud as he does so. Have the child indicate whether the letter is a capital or lowercase letter.
- **Pipe cleaners**—Have the child bend a pipe cleaner into the shape of each target letter. Then have the child trace over the pipe cleaner saying the letter name aloud as he or she does so. Have the child indicate whether it is a capital or lowercase letter.
- **Playdough and Magic Modeling Clay**—The child can form the target letter(s) with either play dough or magic modeling clay for tactile reinforcement.

Playdough or Magic Modeling Clay Recipe

2 cups salt
⅔ cup water
1 cup cornstarch
½ cup cold water

Mix salt and ⅔ cup water in a saucepan. Place pan over low heat, stirring constantly until mixture is thoroughly heated. This will take 3 or 4 minutes.

Remove from heat. Immediately mix cornstarch and ½ cup cold water and add this all at once to the hot salt and water mixture. Stir quickly to combine. Mixture should thicken to about the consistency of stiff dough. If the mixture does not thicken, place the pan over low heat again and stir about 1 minute or until the mixture starts to thicken.

Turn out on board or work surface and knead as you would bread dough to form a smooth, pliable mass. It can be used immediately, and it will keep pliable indefinitely if it is stored in a tightly closed container or wrapped in plastic or foil. This recipe makes 1¾ pounds.

Continued

Continued

Double Batch

Double recipe ingredients. Follow the directions given, except keep saucepan over heat when adding cornstarch and water to the hot salt mixture.

How to Color

Food colors or tempera paint may be added while cooking, or they may be kneaded into the pliable base. Modeled objects may be painted when hard and dry to give the surface color.

How to Dry

Objects will dry and harden at room temperature in about 36 hours, depending on the thickness. To speed drying, preheat oven to 350 degrees. Then turn the oven off and place object in oven on the wire rack to allow air circulation. Leave in oven until the oven is cold. When dry, surface may be smoothed by rubbing with sandpaper.

- **Alphabet Pretzels**—Making pretzels in the shape of alphabet letters is a very good way to have children experience the formation of each letter.

Alphabet Pretzels (Edible) Recipe

1 cup lukewarm water
1 cake active yeast or 1 package dry yeast
4½ cups all-purpose flour
2 teaspoons sugar
¾ teaspoon salt
1 egg yolk beaten with 1 tablespoon water
coarse salt

Preheat oven to 475 degrees. Grease a cookie sheet. Slowly stir yeast into 1 cup lukewarm water, following package directions. Set aside.

Combine flour, sugar, and salt. Add to yeast mixture to form stiff dough. Turn dough out onto floured counter and knead 8 to 10 minutes or until it is smooth and elastic.

Oil a large bowl. Turn dough in bowl to oil both sides and then cover with clean damp cloth. Let rise in warm place until double in size.

Punch down and shape into letters. Place on cookie sheet. Baste each pretzel with egg yolk mixture. Sprinkle with salt. Let rise again almost double.

Bake for 10 minutes or until golden brown and firm.

Letters of Dough (Inedible) Recipe

1 cup salt
2 cups flour
1 cup water

Put the ingredients in a mixing bowl. Mix together and then knead for ten minutes.

Have the child shape each target letter, saying its name as he or she does so. (The child's own first name often is used in this tactile activity.) Place the letters on an ungreased cookie sheet and bake 40 minutes at 325 degrees. When the letters have cooled, have the child paint them with watercolors. Bake again for 10 to 15 minutes, then varnish and mount them on a board with white glue. Have the child trace each letter mounted on the board for additional tactile reinforcement.

ACTIVITY

Cooking and Baking Activities

There are a number of cooking and baking activities that can be used to stress both letter identification and letter-sound relationships. Most of these cooking and baking activities are very motivating and therefore very effective for this purpose. A number of these activities also can be used to promote a child's understanding of letter-sound relationships. Here is a sample of the cooking and baking activities that can be used for this purpose. There also are a number of other ones that you easily can use.

Recipes for all of the starred foods can be found in *Cook and learn* by Bev Vietch and Thelma Harms Menlo Park, CA: Addison-Wesley, 1981).

The Letter A
apple salad*   applesauce*

The Letter B
banana bread   biscuits*
bean salad*   butter*

The Letter C
cole slaw*   cupcakes*

The Letter D
doughnuts (Have one tube-type refrigerator baking biscuit per child. Have the child gently flatten the biscuit and push his or her fingers through the center to make a hole. Then heat one inch of cooking oil in an electric fry pan to hot, which is about 375 degrees. Place the doughnut in the cooking oil and fry it on both sides until it is golden brown. Remove the doughnut from the oil with cooking tongs and have the child shake it in a brown paper bag with powdered sugar.)

The Letter E
eggs*

The Letter F
French fries   fruit salad*
fritters*

The Letter G
gingerbread man*   grilled cheese sandwich

The Letter H
hamburgers   hush puppies*

The Letter I
ice cream*   Irish soda bread*

The Letter J
jam sandwich   juice*
jelly beans

The Letter K
kabob (Have the children thread cut pieces of fruit on a straw.)

The Letter L
lasagna   lemonade*
latke* (potato pancake)

The Letter M
macaroni salad*   muffin*
meatballs

Continued

Continued

The Letter N
navy bean soup
noodles
nachos (Place tortilla chips in a single layer on a cookie sheet. Sprinkle them with grated cheese and bake in a
    400-degree oven until the cheese melts, usually in about five minutes.)

The Letter O
oatmeal ("Three bears' porridge")   orange juice
omelet

The Letter P
pasta   pizza*
peanut butter*   popcorn

The Letter Q
quesadillas   quince jelly
quick bread   (Any food that the child thinks is "fit for a queen.")

The Letter R
raisins   hot rice salad

The Letter S
salad*
stone soup (Make stone soup as described in the book *Stone soup* by Marcia Brown (NY: Charles Scribner's Sons,
    1947).
soup*

The Letter T
tacos*   tortillas*
tomato catsup*

The Letter U
upside-down cake (use a packaged mix)

The Letter V
vanilla ice cream*   vegetable soup*

The Letter W
waffles*

The Letter X
Have the child mix fruits or vegetables.

The Letter Y
yogurt*   yogurt shake*

The Letter Z
zucchini fritters*   zucchini muffins*

Another resource book for food items beginning with each letter of the alphabet is *Eating the alphabet*
by L. Ehlert (NY: Red Wagon, 1996).

Letter Cut-Outs

Letter cut-outs are a very useful strategy for emphasizing various capital letter names. Cut target capital letters out of construction paper or poster board. Each letter should be about ten inches high. If the child is able
to do so, he or she can cut the target letter him- or herself. Then have the child look through old magazines to

ACTIVITY

locate pictures of objects that begin with the target letter; e.g., pictures for the capital *B* might be of a baby, bicycle, boy, balloon, and ball. Have the child glue each of the pictures to the large cut-out letter. As an alternative, have the child draw a picture of each of the objects that is to be included on the cut-out letter. Place a string on a large cut-out *B* with the glued-on or drawn-on pictures to make a necklace that the child can wear.

Stringing Letters

To make stringing letters, obtain a box of large macaroni (ziti or rigatoni). With fine-line felt-tipped pens, write large capital and lowercase letters on the macaroni. Make five of each capital and lowercase letter. Paint the consonants in black and the vowels in red. Dip the ends of pieces of heavy yarn into glue and while they are still somewhat wet, roll the ends of the yarn to form permanent points to make the letter stringing easier.

Have the child string the letters of the alphabet in correct order on the yarn—all capital letters and all lowercase letters. Have the child subsequently pair the letters and make words of the letters on various pieces of yarn.

Continued

Continued

Newspaper Letters

Provide the child with various pages of a daily newspaper in order to locate a target letter or letters. Have the child circle each letter with a felt-tipped pen. An alternative is to let the child cut out the target letters or letters and paste each letter to a sheet of paper to form a collage.

Pig

Have the child trace and cut out a large pig. Have the child then use a felt-tipped pen to write as many words as he or she can that begin with the letter *p*. The child should be allowed to use invented spelling.

Octopus

Have the child trace a circle about six inches in circumference and then cut it out. Then have the child paste on eight round stickers around the circle. The circles show the child where to paste the tentacles. Have the child paste on eight strips to form tentacles. This requires one-to-one correspondence. Then the child can draw a large letter *O* on the body of the octopus. Then have the child glue confetti on the letter *O*. This is a very effective way to become familiar with the letter *O*.

Visual Closure Cards

Cut strips from white poster board about 5 inches by 20 inches and "begin" four letters per card. Make only the first stroke. Make dots to show the remaining strokes in the following color coding: 1—green, 2—blue, 3—red, and 4—brown. Cover each card with clear self-stick vinyl. Have the child complete each incomplete letter by connecting the dots in the same color code as the writing strokes. Here are several examples of this type of closure activity.

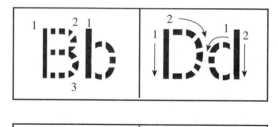

Back

Magnetic Letters

Magnetic letters also are very useful in helping young children to learn letter names. They are commercially available through many teachers' catalogs as well as at many teacher stores. The child can easily manipulate them to match capital letters with their corresponding lowercase counterpart. In addition, the child also can later formulate words by moving them around. They are used extensively in the Reading Recovery Early Intervention Program for first-grade children with special needs. They are adaptable for use in many ways in older preschool classrooms, kindergarten classrooms, and first-grade classrooms and even occasionally in second-grade classrooms.

One catalog from which early childhood teachers can purchase magnetic letters can be obtained from:

Dominie Press
5945 Pacific Center Boulevard
Suite 505
San Diego, CA 92121

This company sells both magnetic spelling boards and magnetic letters, and they are priced fairly inexpensively. Most teacher stores in your local community also sell both magnetic letters and magnetic spelling boards.

An Alphabet Worm

An *alphabet worm* is an interesting teaching tool for both preschools and kindergartens. The children in your class can name the alphabet worm anything that they wish. An alphabet worm can be constructed of tagboard circles covered with different colors of felt. The size of the circles depends upon the space that you have in your classroom for displaying the worm. If you place the worm on a large bulletin board or the chalkboard, the circles can be six inches in diameter.

To construct an alphabet worm, cut twenty-seven circles—one for each alphabet letter and one for the worm's head. The circle for the head can be larger than the others if you wish. Then cut twenty-seven circles of felt in a variety of colors or twenty-seven circles of wallpaper in different patterns and glue these on the pieces of tagboard. Cut a set of capital letters from felt in various colors. Then glue a different letter on each felt circle or wallpaper circle. Next, cut a set of lowercase letters from the corresponding color of the capital letters and another set of lowercase letters from one color of felt not used for a body part. Do *not* glue the letters on the worm's body parts. If the worm is to be used on the chalkboard, glue small pieces of magnetic tape on the back of each circle. To finish the head, add felt eyes, a pom-pom nose, a felt smile, and antennae made of two pipe cleaners with pom-poms glued to one end. Tape the other ends to the back of the head.

The alphabet worm can remain in a classroom as long as the boys and girls need help with letter identification, and later it can be used for letter-sound (phonic analysis) games.

Here are some ways in which an alphabet worm can be used:

- Have children sit in a circle. Throw all of the worm's body parts except the head into the middle of the circle, and tell the children that when the worm woke up that morning and shook itself, its body fell apart. Then you can say, "Who can help put our alphabet worm named _____ together again? Can anyone find the first letter of the alphabet? Does anyone see the letter that comes next? What letter comes after M? What letter of the alphabet is the last one?"

- Mix up the body parts on the chalkboard or bulletin board and have the children place them in the correct order.

- Have the child select the letter that his or her first name begins with and take that body part to the art table where he or she can draw pictures of things that begin with that letter.

- Talk with the children about how they might check out an alphabet worm body part. They should sign their name and selected letter on a large sheet of chart paper and take that letter home to share with their family overnight or for the weekend. When they return the letter, they might talk about what they saw in their house that began with that letter or what letter games they played with their families.

- Construct a paper alphabet worm that the children can work with during free choice time. Each child can make his or her own paper alphabet worm which he or she can name to take home by tracing a tagboard circle pattern on different colors of construction paper. The children can also practice letter formation by

Continued

ACTIVITY

Continued

writing the letters on the body parts. The worm can be placed in an envelope with the child's name written on the front.

- Make a human alphabet worm. Give each child a large paper circle with a letter printed on it and ask the children to arrange themselves in alphabetical order. The child who is the "head" can wear a headband made from a strip of paper with two pipe cleaner antennae sticking up at the top and also have a big smile. Then the class can sing the alphabet song and each child can sit down (or stand up) as his or her letter is sung in the song.

Here are illustrations of the alphabet worm and a child pretending to be the head of the worm.

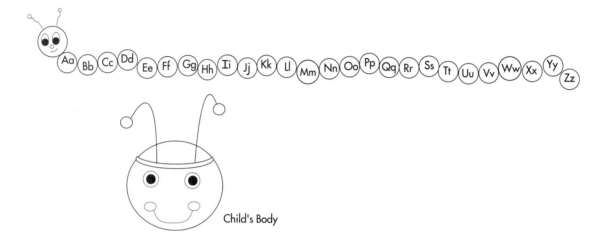

Child's Body

An Alphabet Train

An *alphabet train* can be constructed from half-pint milk cartons, which usually can be obtained from an elementary school lunchroom. Use a knife or sharp scissors to cut off the pointed top of each milk carton, leaving an open box. Then cover twenty-six milk cartons with prepasted paper or brightly colored wrapping paper. Attach cardboard wheels to two opposite sides of each milk carton with paper fasteners. Either print or glue construction paper letters to the sides of the milk cartons. The engine can be another milk carton lying on its side with its wheels attached and a paper smokestack on the top. Have the children cut pictures from magazines and put them in the car with the appropriate beginning letter. They also could bring small objects from home to put in the train. The children also can play "engineer" and try to remember the objects or pictures that belong with each letter. If you wish, you can bring an engineer's cap to be worn by the children who are working on the train.

A C T I V I T Y

Special Activities for Each Letter of the Alphabet

There are a number of interesting activities that can be used for the teaching and/or reviewing of the various alphabet letters. This part of the book presents one of them for each alphabet letter to serve as a model. There also are many others that are equally useful and motivating.

The Letter A
Cut an apple horizontally so that the "star" shows. Have children dip the apple half in thick paint and then make a print on a piece of construction paper.

The Letter B
To make a *bubble painting,* mix tempera paint and liquid soap to a thin consistency. Pour into yogurt or cottage cheese containers. Provide a short length of straw for each child. Let the children blow bubbles in containers so that the bubbles froth and then have them lay a piece of paper lightly over the container. The bubble design will transfer onto the sheet of paper.

The Letter C
To make a *crepe paper collage,* have each child paint liquid starch on construction paper and attach crepe paper while the starch is wet.

The Letter D
Each child can make a *daisy letter D* out of construction paper by using the following pattern:

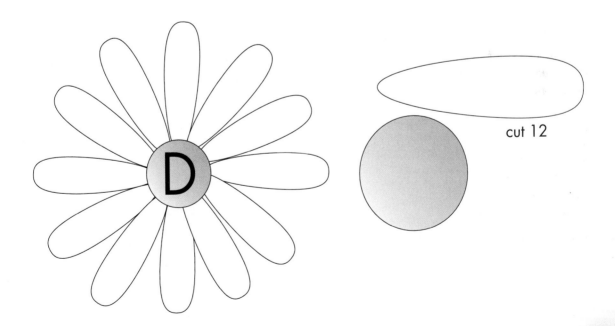

cut 12

Each child then can print the letter *D* on the daisy after he or she has finished cutting and pasting it.

The Letter E
Have the children make an *elephant letter E* of construction paper by using the following pattern:

Continued

A C T I V I T Y   *Continued*

Then the child can print the letter *E* on the elephant.

The Letter F

Have the children do *feather painting* instead of brush painting by using feathers to paint pictures.

The Letter G

Fold a large sheet of paper in half. Then each child selects a bow for the front and then opens it to dictate or write about what they would like to *give* (and to whom).

The Letter H

Have children cover half-pint milk cartons with black construction paper. Then have them decorate the milk cartons and dictate or write a scary story on them with a light-colored marker or crayon to make a variation of a *haunted house*.

The Letter I

Have each child make an *iguana letter I* out of construction paper using the following pattern. After a child has cut out the iguana, he or she can make a large letter *I* on it by gluing seeds to it.

ACTIVITY

The Letter J

The children can make their own simple *jigsaw puzzles* by either drawing a picture on a piece of cardboard or by gluing a picture to a piece of cardboard. Then the child can cut the piece of cardboard into four or six parts to make a simple jigsaw puzzle that he or she or a friend can put together. Several children can exchange their cut-apart puzzles to have practice in reassembling someone else's puzzles.

The Letter K

If you think that it is appropriate, you can apply a light coating of lipstick to children and have them print *kisses* on light-colored paper. If you don't think this is an appropriate activity, you can have children make a *king's crown* from yellow construction paper and wear it on their heads.

The Letter L

To make a *lion puppet,* have the child paste a circle face on a small paper bag. Then the child can add yarn to make the mane and draw in its features. If the child wishes, the features can be humorous.

The Letter M

To make a *marble painting,* put paper in a large, shallow box. Show the children how to dip marbles in paint and tilt the box so that all the marbles roll across the paper to make an interesting painting.

The Letter N

To make a *bird's nest,* mix pine needles and shredded wheat and white glue. Then have the children mold it into a nest's shape. Let it dry and have the children fill the nest with "eggs" made from cornstarch dough.

The Letter O

Have the child string *o-shaped cereal* to make an o-necklace for him- or herself or a friend.

Continued

ACTIVITY *Continued*

The Letter P

Have the child make a *pinwheel* by marking an *X* from corner to corner on a square piece of paper. Cut on the lines almost to the center. Then help the child to attach every other corner piece to the center. Fasten a pin through the center of the pinwheel into the eraser of an unsharpened pencil, which will serve as the stick to hold when blowing the pinwheel.

The Letter Q

To make a *paper quilt,* draw lines making four columns and four rows on a piece of paper. In the top row of squares, place a circle, square, triangle, and rectangle, each of a different color. Then ask each child to complete the patterns by pasting the appropriate shapes on their quilts.

The Letter R

Have each child locate a large smooth rock on his or her own and then bring it to school. The child then can paint it in any way he or she wants to have a *painted rock.*

The Letter S

To make a *sand painting,* have the child mix dry sand and dry paint. Then have him or her make a pattern with glue. Shake the sand/paint mixture on glue and blow or shake off the excess.

The Letter T

Place a pencil through a cardboard circle to make a *top.*

The Letter U

To make an *undershirt,* take a brown grocery bag and have the child decorate it with crayons. Then cut arm holes on the sides and a neck hole from the bottom of the sack.

The Letter V

Have the child make a *volcano* out of papier-mâché placed around a glass jar. Have the child paint the outside of the volcano. When this is finished, the child can make his or her volcano erupt by doing the following:

1. Mix ¼ cup vinegar, ¼ cup liquid detergent, and red food coloring in the jar.
2. Add 6 tablespoons baking soda that has been dissolved in warm water.

The Letter W

To make a *wizard hat,* have each child make sponge prints on a large sheet of construction paper. Roll the paper into a pointed hat, and then staple it to keep the shape.

The Letter X

To make a *treasure box,* have the children paint egg cartons and then sprinkle glitter on while the paint is still wet.

The Letter Y

Have each child make a design by sewing yarn on a piece of burlap.

The Letter Z

To make *zoo pictures,* have each child cut out zoo animals. Then staple paper fence bars over the animals to make a zoo.

ACTIVITY

Games for Improving Ability in Letter-Name Recognition and Letter-Name Identification

There are many games that early childhood teachers can use to improve a young child's ability in letter-name recognition and letter-name identification. This part of the chapter briefly summarizes a few of them. Many others can be found in teacher resource books of various kinds.

Memory (Concentration)

Constructing the Game

This game has been very well liked by young children. To construct it, use a marker to make capital and lowercase letter cards out of tagboard. Make two sets of identical cards.

To Play the Game

Place the letter cards in two sets face down on a flat surface. Have the child turn up a card in one set and try to find the card that matches in the other set. When a match is made, have the child say the letter name and keep the card. Points or prizes can be given for the number of cards that each student has.

Bang

Constructing the Game

Cover a Pringle™ potato chip can or a similar container with red self-stick vinyl or red construction paper. Attach a piece of heavy string about 1 inch by 2 inches to the top of the can and use aluminum foil to form a "firecracker" wick. Then print the capital and lowercase letters with a marker on small cards made of tagboard. However, print the word **BANG** on a few of the cards. The can should be shaken often to mix up the cards.

To Play the Game

Have the child take turns drawing a card and saying each letter name. If the child can correctly say the letter name, he or she can keep the letter card. If a child draws the word BANG, he or she must return all the cards to the can. The first child to collect ten cards is the winner of the game.

Alphabet Bingo

Constructing the Game

Cut cardboard to make enough 8½″ × 11″ sheets for each child (any similar size also is all right). Then each sheet is divided into 9 or 12 sections. An alphabet letter is printed on each section. Make sure that each sheet contains a different combination of letters. Then cover the sheets with clear contact paper. For markers, you can use small pieces of paper, poker chips, or bottle caps.

To Play the Game

As the caller says a letter name, have the child place markers of some type on their card. When a complete row—either horizontal, vertical, or diagonal—is covered, the child calls out "Bingo." To win the game, the child must be able to identify each letter name as he or she takes off the chips to prove that he or she has won. As an alternative, you can hold up a card with a letter name on it and ask whether any child has that letter on his sheet. This version of the game ends when the first child playing the game has "covered" his sheet. The first version reinforces letter-name identification, while the latter version stresses letter-name recognition.

Continued

Continued

"Old Maid" Letter Name Game

Constructing the Game

To construct the game, print the uppercase and lowercase letter names on 2″ × 2″ colored construction paper or tagboard cut into cards. Make a card with an "Old Maid' on it.

To Play the Game

Have the children take turns picking a card and saying the letter name on it. If the child can give the letter name correctly, he or she is able to keep the card. If not, the card goes back into the pile. If a child picks the "Old Maid" card, he or she must put all of his or her cards back into the pile. The winner is the child who has the most cards after a certain number of rounds or a given time limit.

The Letter Chair Game

Constructing the Game

Line some chairs up behind each other. Make letter cards with either an uppercase or a lowercase letter printed on each one.

To Play the Game

Have children sit on the chairs that have been lined up behind each other. Begin at the front of the line and show a card with an uppercase or lowercase letter name printed on it. If the child can give the letter name correctly, he or she is able to stay in the chair. If a wrong answer is given, the child goes to the end of the line, and all of the other children move up. Children try to stay at the front of the line to be the "captain."

Alphabet Feet

Constructing the Game

Write the different uppercase letters on "feet" made from posterboard. Then place the "feet" on the floor in a line to represent an alphabet path.

To Play the Game

Two or more players participate in this game, trying to follow the alphabet path by saying the name of the uppercase letter on each "foot" before stepping on it. If a player misses a letter, he or she must start back at the beginning. Anyone who successfully follows the path receives one point. The player with the most points at the end of the game wins. The "feet" can be replaced by other "letter feet," or the order can be changed.

Twin Letters

To Construct the Game

To construct the game, write various lowercase letters on 3″ × 5″ index cards or cards of tagboard. There should be two cards of each letter. Place the cards face down on a table. Five or six sets of the cards should be used at a time.

To Play the Game

Two or more children can play this game. The players take turns turning over two cards at a time to see if they can get a match. If they are able to get a match, they are able to keep the cards. The game continues until all the cards are gone. The child with the most cards at the end of the game is the winner.

Superman or Superwoman

To Construct the Game

Write each of the uppercase letters on a 3″ × 5″ index card or a card made of tagboard. On one card glue a picture of Superman or Superwoman.

To Play the Game

To play the game, each child is dealt an even number of the letter cards. The children then take turns drawing a card from the child to the right. When a player gets a match, he or she must lay it down. The first player to get rid of all his or her cards except the Superman or Superwoman card, which he or she must have, is the winner of the game.

Find the Letter

To Construct the Game

Trace and cut out the uppercase letters of the alphabet on sandpaper. Glue the letters to separate sheets of tagboard. One letter should be glued to one piece of tagboard.

To Play the Game

Each child should be given those uppercase letters of the alphabet that he or she does not know. (Do not give him or her more than five letters at a time.) The child then is allowed to study the pile of letters, and then he or she is blindfolded. While the child is blindfolded, he or she is asked to feel the letters and tell what they are. When more than one child is playing, the first player to correctly identify the letter is awarded the point. The child with the most points is the winner.

Tennis Ball Alphabet Game

To Construct the Game

Collect twenty-six tennis ball cans and lids. You may be able to obtain them from a tennis club in your local area. Then cover the cans with self-stick vinyl or prepasted paper. Use a marker to print a capital letter on the side of each can. Gather twenty-six old tennis balls (you might ask a tennis club for these also), and print a lowercase letter on each one.

To Play the Game

Have the child match each lowercase tennis ball with the corresponding capital letter can and put the ball inside. Lined up in a row under a chalkboard, the tennis ball cans do not take up much room. As the children sit in a circle, roll a ball to each. The child should identify the letter and put it in the right can when the letter name is called.

Find the Missing Letter

Constructing the Game

To construct this game, you will need 8 pieces of posterboard that are about 4″ × 10″ and 26 pieces of posterboard that are 2″ × 2″, a ruler, a marker, and scissors. Fold the 4″ × 10″ pieces of posterboard to make 2″ × 10″ rectangles. Then, using a ruler, draw a line every two inches as shown in the illustration on the next page.

Continued

ACTIVITY

Continued

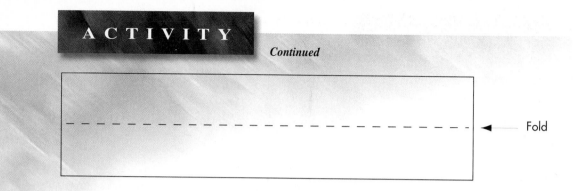

Fold

Copy letters on the pieces of posterboard as shown in the illustration. Next, cut out the squares that would cover the letters if they were folded over. On the back of the blank letter spaces copy the letter that has been omitted so that if it is folded over it will show the correct letter. Here are illustrations of this.

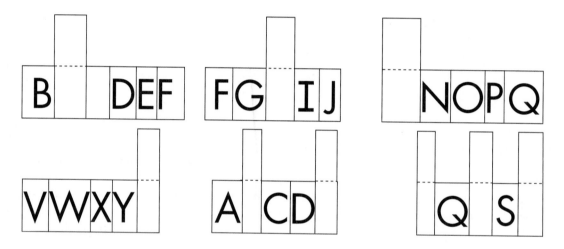

To Play the Game

Have the child take one strip at a time and look at the letters. He or she should see that there are one or more letters missing in the order that they are in. The child has to find the missing letters from the letter cards and place them in the blank spaces. Then the child should fold the squares over to see if he or she is correct. A child can play this game independently or with a partner.

The Letters of the Alphabet Oak Tree

Constructing the Game

To construct this game, you will need one 12″ × 8″ piece of posterboard, 26 pieces of posterboard that are 1¼″ × 1″, a marker, and scissors. First you cut a tree design using the 12″ × 8″ piece of posterboard. Print the

uppercase letters of the alphabet on the tree using the marker. Next, cut each of the small pieces of poster-board into the shape of an acorn and print a lowercase alphabet letter on each one. Here are some patterns that you can use for this game.

To Play the Game

Put the tree on a flat surface such as a table or desk. The child tries to match each acorn letter with the corresponding capital letter on the tree. Another child or the teacher can check his or her work when the child is finished. Thus, this game can be played independently or with a literacy partner for help or checking.

Reproducibles for Improving Ability in Letter-Name Recognition and Letter-Name Identification

The chapter now contains several ready-to-use reproducibles that any early childhood teacher can use to improve either letter-name recognition or letter-name identification. Any of them can be used in their present form or modified in any way in which you want in the light of the needs and interests of your children. It is important to modify any reproducible if necessary to be compatible with the whole language philosophy and also to be useful in any traditional reading program. You should remember that the use of activity sheets is not in keeping with the whole language philosophy. They may be of some use if they are not overused. Some young children apparently enjoy completing activity sheets, contrary to the beliefs of some of the proponents of the true whole language philosophy (Miller, 1998).

Continued

Name _____

Tracing Hard Letters

These letters may be hard for you to remember. If you <u>trace</u> them on this sheet, it may help you to remember them.

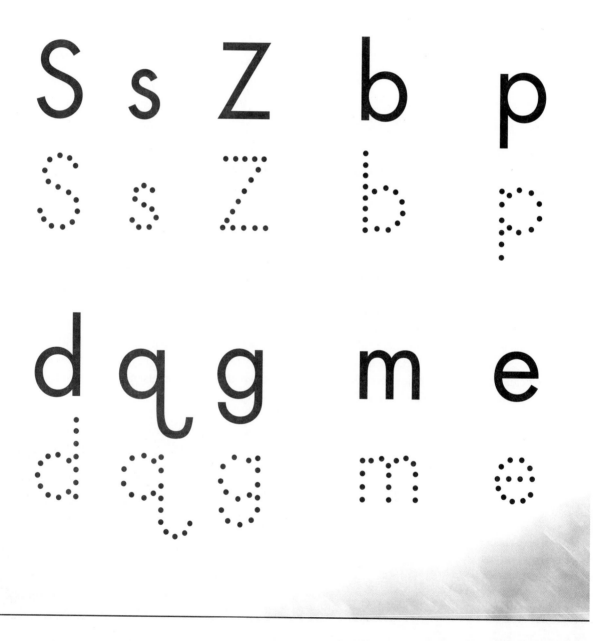

ACTIVITY

Name _____

The Lost Puppy

Fill in the missing letters to help the <u>puppy</u> find its way home.

Continued

ACTIVITY *Continued*

Name _____

Be My Alphabet Valentine

a b c d e f g h
i j k l m n o p
q r s t u v
w x y
z

Fill in the missing alphabet letters to be a real "sweetheart"

A B ♡ ♡ E ♡ ♡ H ♡ J

♡ L ♡ ♡ O ♡ Q ♡ ♡ ♡

U ♡ ♡ X ♡ Z

a ♡ c d ♡ ♡ g ♡ i ♡

k ♡ m n ♡ p ♡ r ♡ t

♡ v w ♡ y z

Name _____

Whose Mittens are These?

Draw a line from each mitten to the other mitten that will make a <u>pair</u>.

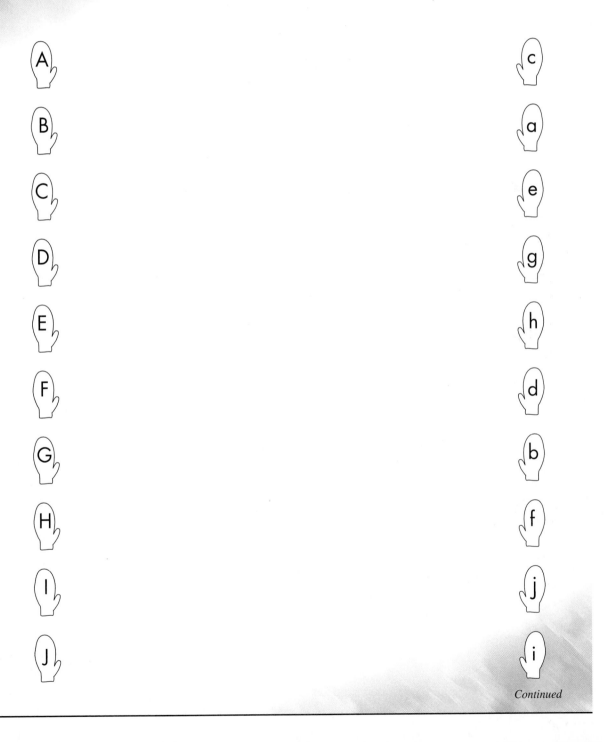

Continued

Name _____

Squirrels and Acorns

Match each squirrel and acorn.

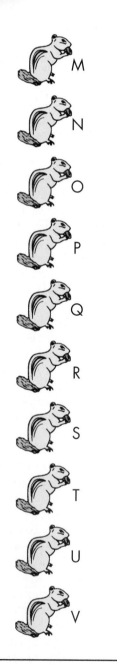

M

N

O

P

Q

R

S

T

U

V

r

u

q

m

v

t

n

o

p

s

SIGHT WORD RECOGNITION AND SIGHT WORD IDENTIFICATION

Sight word recognition is simply recognizing or being able to pick out a word immediately when it is located with other similar appearing words. On the other hand, *sight word identification* is being able to identify or pronounce (actually say) a word immediately when it is encountered while reading. It is obvious that sight word identification is the more difficult of the two activities, and it is the one that is required in actual reading.

It is also important to note that many sight words do not have a regular *phoneme-grapheme (sound-symbol) relationship* and therefore cannot be analyzed phonetically. Such words are more effectively learned as a total unit. Several examples of such sight words are *mother, father, of, off, dog, through,* and *though.*

Sight vocabulary also can be thought of as all the words that a reader can identify with automaticity, or immediately upon seeing them. Although a reader often first had to analyze many of these words phonetically, structurally, or contextually, he or she now has them in his or her stock of sight words. It is obvious that a child must have a large sight word bank so that he or she does not have to stop and analyze most of the words while reading, which would interfere with the comprehension of the material being read. It is especially important that children have mastered all of the basic sight words by the end of third grade so that they can read all grade-appropriate materials with ease and fluency. In addition, they need a mastery of the basic sight words so that they can effectively read the content materials they will encounter in the fourth grade and above. An insufficient sight word bank is one major reason why a child who has been an adequate reader in the primary grades may begin to have difficulties in reading activities in fourth grade.

It also is important for a child to master the basic sight words because a small subset of them comprises a large proportion of the words found in everyday reading for both children and adults. For example, the following ten words comprise at least 20 percent of all of the words found in print material:

the	of
and	a
to	in
is	you
that	it

In addition, the most common twenty-five words found in the English language comprise about one-third of all print materials (Fry, Kress, Fountoukidis, & Polk, 1993).

For most children the easiest way to learn unknown words is simply to memorize them (Richek, 1997–1998). However, memorization also is the most limiting way, since children have a finite limit as to how many words

that they can remember without using any graphophonic (phonic) or structural clues. This limit may be around forty words for some children, a very small number in comparison to all of the words that they must learn.

Sight word identification consists of such subskills as recognizing a word by its total shape, its first few letters, its special characteristics such as *ascenders (b, d, h)* or *descenders (g, p, q),* or its length. *Configuration* or *drawing a frame* around the word is another skill of sight word identification. Here is an example of configuration:

However, you will notice that configuration is not an effective word identification technique in words such as these, since they have no unique configuration or shape:

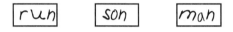

You should understand that some subskills of sight word identification may provide unimportant or irrelevant cues to word identification. For example, the double *o* in the word *look* is sometimes said to "appear to be two eyes." However, a number of other words, such as *book, cook, hook, shook, took, goose, spoon,* and *moon,* also have a double *o* in the same position. One other incorrect cue is the somewhat common practice of having a child look for the small words in a larger word. Although this technique is acceptable in the case of the word *into,* for example, it certainly is incorrect in locating the words *fat* and *her* in the word *father.*

Unfortunately, some of the most common words found in reading also are among the most irregular and therefore potentially difficult for young children to learn. Many reading teachers, for example, believe that a child may need as many as 120 to 140 meaningful exposures to a sight word before it becomes part of his or her sight word bank. Some disabled readers and children with learning disabilities may need more exposures than that before a sight word can be recognized instantly.

When selecting words from a sight word list to present to young children, probably the two most important factors in deciding which words to present are *utility,* or usefulness, and *ease of learning.* For example, although the sight word *one* is very difficult for young children to learn, it also is a common and useful word. Therefore, the word *one* probably should be presented and practiced fairly early in the reading program. Sight words also often are *structure* or *function* words, which means that they have no real referent or do not represent any object. Such words are often difficult for children to remember, since the child cannot associate such a word with any concrete entity. On the other hand, a few sight words are *content* words and therefore theoretically are easier for children to remember. The words *mother* and *father,* for example, are examples of content sight words that are common in beginning reading materials.

Sight words should be presented both in context and in isolation so that most children can learn them effectively. The presentation of sight words in context is most representative of the whole language approach (see Chapter 2), but many children, certainly including children who are not linguistically adept, also should meet sight words in isolation both for presentation and practice. When words are taught in isolation, children often note the way they are formed (Samuels, 1967; Singer, Samuels, & Spiroff, 1973–1974). When words are presented in context, children usually pay more attention to word meanings and the way in which they are used. Teaching articles, prepositions, and conjunctions in context is especially important, since the most effective way to understand function or structure words is to see how they are actually used. Presenting sight words in context and in isolation helps children both learn their meanings and their pronunciations. However, if children already know the meaning of a sight word, the early childhood teacher should spend most of the time teaching the distinctive features of the word, including how it is spelled and noticing the pronounceable word parts. Knowing how to spell and/or sound out a word partially or completely helps students learn and remember new words (Ehri, 1991), but time spent discussing known definitions may be wasted for the child.

Automaticity and accuracy are both extremely important in identifying sight words (Samuels, 1994). In order to reach an effective level of accuracy, children must actively process words. They must pay attention as they look at words. Of course, children need varying amounts of time to reach a high level of accuracy. Once they have reached an acceptable level of accuracy in identifying sight words, they seem to gain automaticity at similar rates (Samuels, 1994). According to Samuels, "The critical test of automaticity is that the task, which at the beginning stage of learning could only be performed by itself, can now be performed along with one or more other tasks" (1994, p. 819). You may remember how carefully you tried to remember all of the necessary tasks when you were first learning to drive an automobile. However, now that you have gained both experience and confidence in driving, you perform many of those same tasks without ever thinking about them. This automaticity is what children should also achieve when they are reading sight words.

You may be surprised to learn that good readers often can learn *four times* as many sight words in a specified time period as can poor readers. Disabled readers and other special needs children such as children with learning disabilities often need extensive meaningful practice to master useful sight words. Later sections of this chapter present many strategies and materials for helping

inadequate readers achieve the necessary accuracy and automaticity in sight word identification that will help them become successful readers.

A Brief Description of Sight Word Lists

The most common sight words are found in a number of different sight word lists. Although the lists differ somewhat depending upon the sources from which they were taken (children's reading, writing, or a combination of both), there is considerable overlap among all of the lists.

Probably the most common and one of the most useful sight word lists is the *Dolch Basic Sight Word List,* which was formulated by the late Edward Dolch of the University of Illinois in 1941. Although it might seem to be outdated, it is not, since the words contained in it are comparable to those contained in the newer word lists. This list of 220 service words is supposed to make up about 70 percent of the words found in most first readers and about 65 percent of the words contained in many second and third readers. As is the case with all the sight word lists, many of the words contained in the Dolch Basic Sight Word List are structure or function words with no referent. As you know, structure or function words usually are more difficult for most children to remember than are content words that have a concrete referent. Children with learning disabilities and other special needs children usually find those words especially difficult to remember.

You may obtain the Dolch Basic Sight Word List for a very nominal cost from the following address:

The Garrard Press
1607 North Market Street
Champaign, IL 61820

Counting the number of words recognized is one way to ascertain a child's approximate *instructional reading level* (the level at which he or she can read material with some teacher assistance) as determined by his/her performance level on the Dolch Basic Sight Word List (McBroom, Sparrow, & Eckstein, 1944). Although this application has not been researched, these numbers probably also may be used with the *Instant Word List* found later in this chapter to determine a child's approximate instructional reading level. The author has found these numbers to be quite applicable to other sight word lists since the content of the sight word lists overlaps a great deal.

Words Recognized	Reading Level
0–75	Preprimer
76–120	Primer
121–170	First Reader
171–210	Second Reader
Above 210	Third Reader or Above

Edward B. Fry, Professor Emeritus of Rutgers University, has compiled an updated version of the Instant Word List, which he first compiled in 1957. This word list was revised in 1980 based on a modification of the Carroll (American Heritage) data. The first 100 words make up half of all written material, and the 300 words together comprise 65 percent of all written materials.

The first hundred sight words should be mastered by the end of the first grade, while both the first and second hundred sight words should be mastered by the end of second grade. It is very important for a child to have mastered **all** of the words on the Instant Word List by the end of third grade. If he or she has not done so, the child well may have considerable difficulty with reading activities in the fourth grade and above.

Here is a copy of Fry's Instant Word List which you can reproduce in any way that you wish.

The Instant Words*

First Hundred

Words 1–25	Words 26–50	Words 51–75	Words 76–100
the	or	will	number
of	one	up	no
and	had	other	way
a	by	about	could
to	word	out	people
in	but	many	my
is	not	then	than
you	what	them	first
that	all	these	water
it	were	so	been
he	we	some	call
was	when	her	who
for	your	would	oil
on	can	make	its
are	said	like	now
as	there	him	find
with	use	into	long
his	an	time	down
they	each	has	day
I	which	look	did
be	do	more	get
this	how	write	made
have	their	go	may
from	if	see	part

Common suffixes: -s, -ing, -ed, -ly, -est

*If you want more than the 300 sight words, the following is a list of 3,000 sight words: Sakiey, E., & Fry, E. (1984). *3000 instant words.* Providence, RI: Jamestown Publishers.

Second Hundred

Words 101–125	Words 126–150	Words 151–175	Words 176–200
over	say	set	try
new	great	put	kind
sound	where	end	hand
take	help	does	picture
only	through	another	again
little	much	well	change
work	before	large	off
know	line	must	play
place	right	big	spell
year	too	even	air
live	mean	such	away
me	old	because	animal
back	any	turn	house
give	same	here	point
most	tell	why	page
very	boy	ask	letter
after	follow	went	mother
thing	came	men	answer
our	want	read	found
just	show	need	study
name	also	land	still
good	around	different	learn
sentence	farm	home	should
man	three	us	America
think	small	move	world

Common suffixes: -s, -ing, -er, -ly, -est

Third Hundred

Words 201–225	Words 226–250	Words 251–275	Words 276–300
high	saw	important	miss
every	left	until	idea
near	don't	children	enough
add	few	side	eat
food	while	feet	face
between	along	car	watch
own	might	mile	far
below	chose	night	Indian
country	something	walk	really
plant	seem	white	almost
last	next	sea	let
school	hard	began	above
father	open	grow	girl
keep	example	took	sometimes
tree	begin	river	mountain
never	life	four	cut
start	always	carry	young
city	those	state	talk
earth	both	once	soon
eye	paper	book	list
light	together	hear	song
thought	got	stop	being
head	group	without	leave
under	often	second	family
story	run	late	it's

Common suffixes: -s, -ing, -er, -ly, -est

STRATEGIES AND MATERIALS FOR IMPROVING SIGHT WORD RECOGNITION AND SIGHT WORD IDENTIFICATION

This chapter now includes a number of classroom-tested strategies and materials that can be used for improving ability in sight word recognition and sight word identification. You should modify any of these suggestions and materials as you need to in the light of the needs, interests, and abilities of your own pupils. This is in keeping with the whole language philosophy (see Chapter 2) and is equally important in any traditional literacy program.

All Types of Reading Activities

All types of *whole reading activities* undoubtedly are the most effective way of presenting sight words to the majority of young children. Whole language presentation and reinforcement is successful with many, but certainly not all, young children. However, as much as possible children should learn and practice sight words in the context of meaningful words, stories, books, and rhymes.

The language-experience approach (LEA) (see Chapter 2) is one of the most effective ways of teaching sight words to young children. As a matching activity, the teacher can make word, phrase, and sentence cards that children can match to the appropriate words, phrases, or sentences in the LEA chart or story. In addition, children can be asked to circle or underline target words or phrases in an experience chart or story. The teacher or child can print important or meaningful sight words from a language-experience chart or story on 3 × 5 cards to make a *word bank.* The sight words in a child's word bank can be kept in alphabetical order in a shoe box, a large brown envelope, or any other practical container. The child then can practice identifying the sight words in his or her word bank either independently or with a partner, classify them into different categories, use them for writing stories, or use them in any other way in which he/she or the teacher wants. All types of sight word activities using language-experience stories or charts are especially useful for children because they are the children's own words.

Wide reading of all types of materials undoubtedly is the single most effective way for children to practice sight word identification. However, some special needs children including some children with learning disabilities apparently do not enjoy reading any type of material even if the reading material is easy for them. Therefore, it is extremely important for the early childhood teacher to provide such children with a wide variety of very easy, highly motivating books to read and to give them choices about the books they are to read. These books usually should be on the child's independent (easy) reading level.

The chapter now includes a list of easy-to-read trade books that should be helpful in motivating young children to identify sight words in a meaningful way. Since this is not a comprehensive list, you also are encouraged to consult many other sources, including other professional books and *Children's Choices,* a feature of *The Reading Teacher* that appears in each October issue. The trade books included here are presented in an easy-to-hard sequence, with the books found near the beginning of the list most appropriate for beginning readers and those found near the end of the list most suitable for children reading at approximately the second reader level. Other appropriate trade books are listed in the various lists of books that were included in Chapter 2.

Aruego, J. (1971). *Look what I can do!* NY: Scribner.

Carle, E. (1971). *Do you want to be my friend?* NY: Crowell.

Carle, E. (1987). *Have you seen my cat?* NY: Scholastic.

Hoban, T. (1972). *Push, pull, empty, full.* NY: Macmillan.

Maestro, B., & Maestro, G. (1978). *Busy day: A book of action words.* NY: Crown.

McLenighan, V. (1982). *Stop-go, fast-slow.* Chicago: Children's Press.

Scarry, R. (1963). *Richard Scarry's best word book ever.* Racine, WI: Golden.

Maris, R. (1983). *My book.* Chicago: Children's Press.

Wildsmith, B. (1983). *All fall down.* NY: Oxford.

Cole, J. (1976). *Fun on wheels.* NY: Scholastic.

Eastman, P. (1960). *Are you my mother?* NY: Random House.

Gordon, S. (1980). *What a dog!* Mahwah, NJ: Troll.

Hutchins, P. (1972). *Good-night, owl.* NY: Macmillan.

Kraus, R. (1970). *Whose mouse are you?* NY: Macmillan.

Lesieg, T. (1963). *Ten apples up on top.* NY: Random House.

Raffi. (1988). *One light, one sun.* NY: Crown.

Ziefert, H. (1985). *A dozen dogs.* NY: Random House.

Blocksma, M. (1992). *Yoo hoo, moon.* NY: Bantam.

Brown, M. (1952). *Where have you been?* NY: Scholastic.

Cebulash, M. (1972). *Willie's wonderful pet.* NY: Scholastic.

Hoff, S. (1988). *Mrs. Brice's mice.* NY: Harper.

Lobel, A. (1972). *Frog and toad together.* NY: Harper & Row.

Martin, B. (1967). *Brown bear, brown bear, what do you see?* NY: Holt, Rinehart, & Winston.

Martin, B. (1972). *Polar bear, polar bear, what do you see?* NY: Holt, Rinehart, & Winston.

Phillips, J. (1986). *My new boy.* NY: Random House.

Robart, R. (1986). *The cake that Mack ate.* Toronto: Kids Can Press.

Seuss, Dr. (1960). *Green eggs and ham.* NY: Random House.

Williams, V. (1990). *More, more, more said the baby.* NY: Scholastic.

There also are several series of children's books that are specifically designed to give children practice in sight word identification. Here are some of them:

Reading corners. San Diego, CA: Dominie Press. This series features several different basic patterns such as I do _____, I have _____, and I like _____. Since these books each have only eight to twelve pages of material, they are very easy for young children to read.

Read more books. San Diego, CA: Dominie Press. This series of books emphasizes a number of basic sentence patterns. They have limited text and explicitly illustrated color photographs and are therefore very easy to read.

Seedlings. Columbus, OH: Seedling Publications. This series of books includes sixteen-page booklets in which each page contains one line of material accompanied by an illustration. The vocabulary is somewhat varied.

Predictable books also are very helpful in presenting and reinforcing sight words because they employ repetitive sentence patterns that are easier for young children to read than are many other sentence patterns. The following is a simple strategy that you can use for helping your children acquire various sight words while reading predictable books.

Step one—Choose a book that children will enjoy and that contains the sight words you want to reinforce. If possible, obtain a big book version of the trade book so that young children will be able to easily follow along as you read aloud.

Step two—Preview the book with the children, read it to them, and then discuss it. Point to each word as you read it aloud.

Step three—Reread the book. Invite children to read the repeated parts or other easy parts.

Step four—After several rereadings of the book, copy the text onto chart paper or cover the illustrations in the big book. With the pictures covered up, your pupils can concentrate on identifying the words. Have children read the version without the illustrations, with your help if necessary.

Step five—Duplicate the story, and cut the duplicated versions into sentence strips. Have children match the individual sentence strips to those contained in the chart version. Then have the children reassemble the story, sentence by sentence. Sentences can be cut up into individual words also, which gives children the opportunity to match the individual words with the words in the chart story. Have children reconstruct each individual sentence by placing the cut-out words in the proper order.

Chapter 2 of this book contained a comprehensive list of predictable books, and you are encouraged to consult that list if you want to locate valuable predictable books for your pupils.

All Types of Tracing Activities

Most of the *tracing strategies* that were described in detail earlier in this chapter for helping children to remember difficult-to-retain letter names are equally applicable in helping children retain difficult sight words. These tracing strategies are usually most helpful for children with learning disabilities or severe reading disabilities along with other children who have special needs. These are the children who often cannot seem to remember sight words taught by a conventional method. Since tracing is time-consuming, it should only be used with sight words that seem especially difficult for a child. For the same reason, tracing should only be used as long as absolutely necessary.

The following are several tracing strategies that were described earlier in the chapter that can be used to help children remember difficult sight words:

- *Instant pudding* (the favorite with most young children)
- *Shaving cream*
- *Colored chalk sand tray*
- *Colored chalk salt tray*
- *Playdough*
- *Modeling clay*

When using instant pudding, shaving cream, or a sand or salt tray, the child should print the target sight word in the material, saying it aloud as he or she forms it. Have the child trace the word in the material as many times as necessary to remember the word. In each case have the child also use the word in a sentence. In using modeling clay and Playdough, the child can form the target sight word out of the material. Have the child trace the word enough times to ensure mastery and then use each sight word in a sentence. You should refer to the earlier part of this chapter for additional substances that can be used in tracing.

A *screen board* is a tracing device that can help children remember difficult sight words. A screen board is made by attaching wire screening to a frame made of four boards and securing the screen with masking tape to cover the rough edges. The child then puts lightweight blank paper on top of the screen board. The child copies the selected sight word by writing it on the paper with a crayon. Writing with crayon on paper on top of the screen provides a raised texture that the child can trace with a finger while saying the sight word. Here is an illustration of a screen board:

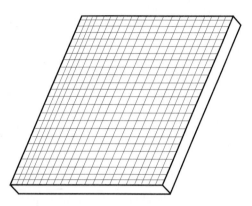

Magnetic letters also can be used as a variation of a kinesthetic technique. The child should form each target sight word out of commercially available magnetic letters, saying the sight word aloud as he or she does so. Each sight word also should be used in a sentence. If desired, the child also can form an entire sentence using magnetic letters. This type of activity is used in the contemporary Reading Recovery Program, an early intervention program for first-grade children with special needs.

The "Drastic" Technique

If a student has a great deal of difficulty remembering certain sight words and you do not want to take the time to use a tracing strategy, Cunningham (1980) has described a very useful strategy called a *"drastic" technique* that you may want to consider using. Here is a very brief description of this technique, and you are encouraged to modify it if you would like.

Step one—Write the sight word on cards, and give one to each child.

Step two—Tell a story in which the word is used several times. Children hold up their cards every time they hear the word.

Step three—Children make up their own stories using the word. As one child reads his or her story, the others hold up their cards when they hear the target word.

Step four—The word is cut into separate letters. Children reassemble the letters to form the word.

Step five—The word is written on the board. Children memorize the word and spell it from memory three times.

Step six—The word is put into story context.

Another Teaching Strategy for Sight Words

Here is a useful three-step strategy for teaching difficult sight words to young children.

1. *Seeing.* Write the word on the chalkboard and pronounce it. Call attention to such features of the word as initial consonants and word endings that are similar to words that have been presented earlier. Use each word in a sentence so that its meaning can be deduced from the sentence. When children are more proficient readers, they will not need such a detailed introduction to new words.
2. *Discussing and Defining.* When the meaning of the new word is unfamiliar to the children, you should discuss the word in detail. Students should draw upon their prior knowledge to determine the meaning of the word, and they should consult the dictionary if they are not sure of the meaning of the word.
3. *Using and Writing.* Have the children use the new word in their speaking and writing. Ask one or more children to make up a sentence containing the word, and write each of these sentences on the chalkboard, chart paper, or overhead projector transparency. Children at the beginning stages of reading may want to include the words in their word banks. New words become mastered in two main ways: through repeated exposure when they recur frequently in sentences and stories that the children read and when they are used often in children's writing.

Animal Tachistoscope

Using a *hand tachistoscope* is a very effective, motivating way to enable children to practice sight words. Although a tachistoscope can be constructed without the animal theme, most children find it more interesting if it is made in the shape of any animal such as a dog, monkey, bear, or giraffe. It also can be made to reflect a holiday theme by using, for example, a ghost, pumpkin, snowman, or heart.

How To Construct a Tachistoscope in the Form of a Dog

Trace a dog pattern on a sheet of tracing paper. Place the tracing paper on top of a sheet of carbon paper. Place these on top of a piece of white posterboard. Trace over the tracing to transfer the dog drawing onto the posterboard. Remove the tracing paper drawing and carbon paper. Color the dog with marking pens or colored pencils, and then cut out the dog and laminate it. Trim the laminating film from the cut-out dog. Using an art knife, cut two horizontal slots, about 2½″ long and 1″ apart, on the dog's chest. Cut a piece of white tagboard into strips about 2″ × 12″ and laminate them. (See the illustrations on the next page.)

How to Use the Dog Tachistoscope

Select some sight words with which the child needs practice. Using a marking pen, print the sight words on the laminated paper strip, one under the other and about 1″ apart. Place the word strip behind the dog tachistoscope and thread it through the bottom slot and then back through the top slot. To use it, slide the word strip up to expose a word. Have the child identify the word. Then pull the word strip up to expose the next word and ask another child to identify that word. Continue in this manner.

When you are finished with the sight word practice using the dog tachistoscope, remove the word strip and wipe off the words with a damp paper towel. New words then can be written on that word strip. After some practice, a child can use the tachistoscope for independent practice or for work with a reading partner(s).

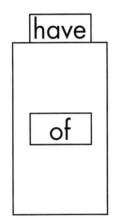

A Magnetic Card Reader

A magnetic card reader is a very useful device for reinforcing sight words. Containing a strip of magnetic tape on the bottom and a surface for writing on the top, the cards can have a word or phrase recorded on the tape and also written on the upper portion of the card. As the card passes through the reader, its taped message is read. Children therefore can both hear and see the sight word or sight word phrase and so may practice sight words on their own in a motivating way.

Computer Software

Many different types of computer software also lend themselves to meaningful, motivational practice in both sight word recognition and sight word identification. Since sight word knowledge is a low-level reading skill, it is easily practiced using computer software. When evaluating computer software for this purpose, the early childhood teacher should make certain that the practice is meaningful and relevant for his or her own pupils. There is no point in spending money for software that does not really provide worthwhile, appropriate practice.

Since computer software packages are being developed and also are becoming obsolete on an almost daily basis, this textbook does not list any of them. Such a list would become out of date almost as soon as it was written. Instead, you are encouraged to consult the appropriate software catalogs or attend reading conferences when you are ready to select such software for your pupils.

Two Unique Strategies for Learning Difficult Sight Words

This chapter now includes two useful strategies for learning difficult sight words that you may want to consider using in some form. You should modify either of them to suit the needs and abilities of your own pupils.

Lapp and Flood (1986) have suggested the following procedure for improving sight word identification:

1. If it is appropriate, use pictures to illustrate the target sight word. Ask the children to study the picture and then predict what is included in the selection.
2. Ask the children to read along with you as you read the various words. This will help them in determining whether their predictions are correct or incorrect.
3. Have the children follow along as you reread the passage and point to the picture.
4. Encourage the children to read the passage with you.

5. While the children are following the story visually, ask individual children to read a sentence.
6. When you have finished reading a sentence, reinforce the individual words by pointing out each of them to the children.
7. Discuss the meaning of each word, and explain that some words, such as *a, the,* and *am,* serve as helping words to finish sentences.
8. Emphasize those words with irregular spelling patterns such as *laugh, one, who,* and *of.*
9. Frame each word with your hands for your pupils so that they can familiarize themselves with its length, configuration, beginning letters, and other unique features.
10. Have children reread the sentence with you.

May (1994, pp. 161–162) has presented a very effective meaning-based interactive, useful procedure that you can use in this form or modify to develop your pupil's sight word identification abilities. Here are the ten steps in this procedure:

1. The teacher should select enjoyable predictable books such as Martin's (1967) *Brown bear, brown bear? What do you see?* or Guarino's (1989) *Is your mama a llama?*
2. The teacher reads the book out loud.
3. The teacher reads the book aloud again with the children joining in whenever they can predict what comes next.
4. The children take turns with *echoing* (the teacher reads aloud first and then the children repeat what he or she has read) and *choral reading.*
5. The teacher reads the text from teacher-made charts with no pictures.
6. The children place matching sentence strips on the charts. (The teacher should make the charts so that a sentence strip can be taped under each sentence in the chart.)
7. The children later place matching word strips on the charts, saying the words in order the first time that this is done and in random order later.
8. The children and teacher chorally read the entire story.
9. The teacher places word strips in random order at the bottom of the chart. The children then come up and match the strips to words in the story, saying each word as they match it to the one in the story.
10. The children write the target words as well as read them. This will help them commit the words to their sight vocabulary.

Configuration Clue Activities

Although using *configuration* as a sight word identification technique for beginning readers was not recommended by reading specialists for a number of years, with the resurgence of the whole language philosophy it is again considered to be a useful technique. Configuration involves drawing a "frame" around a word to emphasize its unique shape as an aid to remembering it. This is, of course, useful if the word has a unique shape but of no value if it does not. In any case, here are several configuration clue activities that you may want to consider using with beginning readers, especially if they seem to have a difficult time remembering some sight words.

- Use the chalkboard or newsprint to make a large wall chart called a *My Name Puzzle.* Place it so that all the children can see it. Make the configuration outline of the teacher's name and each child's name.
- Introduce the activity to the children by printing your last name on a strip of colored paper. Then outline the name as shown in the illustration and cut it out. Then go to the chart and find the matching shape. If photographs of the children are available, paste these above the shape after the child has pasted his or her configuration name shape over the matching chart shape.

The Cloze Procedure

The *cloze procedure* is a very useful strategy for improving contextual analysis and comprehension ability. It features the deletion of every *n*th word in print with the

exception of the first and last sentences, which are kept intact. The cloze procedure was developed by Taylor (1953) and is based on the psychological theory of *closure,* which presumes that a person wants to finish any incomplete pattern. Therefore, the cloze procedure is based on the *prediction aspects* of reading which indicate that a reader wants to predict the unknown words that he or she may encounter in a passage.

Word masking can be used as a variation of cloze when children begin to acquire some reading skills. For example, the children can follow along as a big book is being read during the first reading. During the second reading some of the words are covered over by masking tape or sticky notes. When the teacher gets to one of them, he or she pauses and the children try to predict what it might be. After they respond, the word is uncovered, and the children are asked if they were correct or not. In the word masking cloze procedure, sight word identification, contextual analysis, and comprehension all are used.

Other Strategies for Improving Ability in Sight Word Identification

The remainder of this section very briefly describes a number of other classroom-tested strategies that can be used for improving ability in sight word identification. You are encouraged to use them in their present form or modify any of them to meet the unique needs and interests of your pupils.

- *Word window.* Cut a window either in a 3″ × 5″ index card or a small card of posterboard so that the child can hold it directly over words in dictated language-experience charts to frame or isolate the target sight word. A similar window also can be made to frame target sight words in children's picture storybooks if you wish, although a word window probably is not as effective in the case of a book as it is with an experience chart because the print in the book is much smaller. Here is an illustration of a word window:

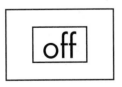

- *Writing a sight word story.* Have children create stories about target sight words or draw pictures illustrating them.

- *Categorization.* If possible, have the child categorize the sight words in his or her word bank. They can be categorized as animals, color words, words related to school, words related to family, words that tell how many, etc. Of course, not all words in the sight word bank can be categorized.
- *Flash cards.* Encourage children to test each other on target sight words using flash cards.
- *Sentence strips.* Have students write a sentence strip from a language-experience chart or from one of the trade books that they have recently read. Then have them cut the sentence strip apart into words and try to reassemble the sentence in correct order.
- *Cut-outs.* Have the children look in old newspapers and magazines for target sight words and cut them out after finding them. Then have them make a collage using the cut-out sight words.
- *Framing.* Have the child "frame" the sight word found on an experience chart to isolate it and make it easier to remember.
- *Word wheels.* Construct a word wheel to provide practice in determining difficult sight words.

    To do so, cut one circular disk about 6″ to 8″ in diameter and a somewhat larger circular disk. Print target sight words with a marker on the larger of the two disks. Cut a sight word window on the smaller disk so that each sight word on the larger disk is visible as the smaller disk is turned. Fasten the two disks with a brad so that the smaller disk can easily be turned, exposing each of the sight words. The child is to immediately pronounce each sight word as it appears in the word window.

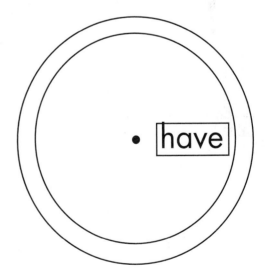

A C T I V I T Y

Games for Improving Ability in Sight Word Knowledge

The chapter now includes several games that early childhood teachers have used to improve sight word knowledge. Such games are not in keeping with the true whole language philosophy, but nonetheless they can be motivating and effective. Research has shown that children demonstrate a 53 percent greater gain in knowledge when they participate in active games in comparison with practice using worksheets. Even passive games result in a 30 percent better gain than does the use of worksheets (Dickerson, 1982). The games included in this part of the chapter have proven to be especially successful with young children.

Fishing for Words

To Construct the Game

Print the target sight words with a black marker on individual fish about 1″ × 2″ made out of construction paper or posterboard (laminated for extra durability). Attach paper clip to the head of each fish. Construct a fishing pole by using a ruler or stick of a similar length with a string tied to it. Tie a small magnet to the end of the string, which will let children "catch" the target sight words.

To Play the Game

Place all of the fish containing the sight words into a container such as a shoe box. Then have the child fish for each sight word using the fishing pole. As the child is able to "land" a fish, he or she must identify the sight word. If he or she can do so, the child keeps the fish. If the child cannot identify the sight word contained on a fish, he or she should throw it back into the box. If you wish, two or more children can take turns fishing for sight words, and the child who has caught the most fish after a specified time period is the winner.

Bang

To Construct the Game

When used for sight word identification, *Bang* is constructed and played in a very similar way as when it is used for letter name identification. Cover a Pringle™ potato chip can with red self-stick vinyl or red construction paper. Attach a piece of heavy string through the plastic lid and use aluminum foil to make a firecracker wick. Print the letters B A N G on the can. Cut posterboard into cards about 1″ × 2″, and print the target sight words on these word cards. Print the word *BANG* on several of the cards. Then shake the can often to mix up the words.

To Play the Game

Have the children take turns drawing a card and identifying each sight word. If a child can correctly identify the sight word, he or she is able to keep the word card. If the child is not able to identify the sight word or draws the word BANG, he or she must return all of the cards to the can. The first child to collect ten cards (or any other arbitrary number of cards) after a specified time period is the winner of the game.

Memory (Concentration)

To Construct the Game

Make target sight word cards out of posterboard. Make two sets of identical cards, being certain that the writing does not bleed through and make the word visible on both sides. Then place the cards face down on a flat surface such as a table or large desk.

To Play the Game

The two sets of cards are shuffled and placed separately on the table. Then have the child turn up a card on one set and then try to find the card that matches in the other set. When he or she has made a match, have the

child say the word and keep the card. Points or prizes can be given for the number of cards that each child has identified or that the teacher and the child have identified.

Bingo

To Construct the Game

When used for sight word identification, Bingo is played in about the same way as it is when it is used for letter-name identification. Construct Bingo cards out of posterboard divided into 8 or 16 squares. Write a target sight word in each square with a black marker. Each card should have the words in different order from the other cards.

To Play the Game

As the caller says a sight word, have the child place markers of some type on his or her card. When a complete row—either horizontal, vertical, or diagonal—is covered, the child calls out "Bingo!" The child must be able to identify each sight word as he or she takes off the markers to prove that he or she has actually won the game.

As in actual Bingo, a variation is **Cover the Card** or **Cover All.** In this variation, a child places his or her markers on the Bingo card until the entire card is covered to win the game. Then the child must be able to identify all of the sight words on his or her Bingo card while removing the markers to win the game.

Triangle Words

To Construct the Game

To construct this game, you need 5 pieces of 4″ × 4″ blue posterboard and 15 pieces of 4″ × 4″ yellow posterboard. You also need a ruler, a pair of scissors, and a marker. Cut triangles from the posterboard pieces using the following pattern:

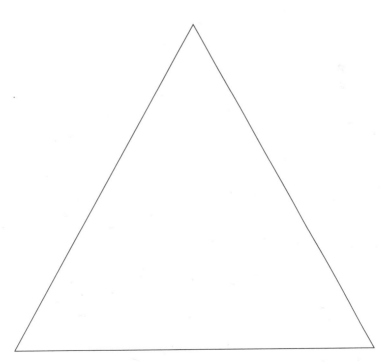

Print the following words on the blue triangles as illustrated. Print one definition on each of the yellow triangles as illustrated.

Continued

A C T I V I T Y

Continued

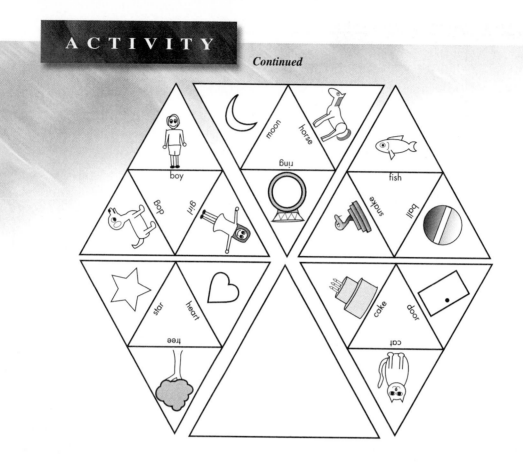

To Play the Game

The child should take a blue triangle out of the box and place it face up on his or her desk. Next the child should place the yellow triangles face up on his or her desk. The child then selects one of the words on his or her blue triangle. He or she should find a picture on the yellow triangle that shows what the word means. Then the child places the yellow picture triangle next to the blue word triangle as illustrated below:

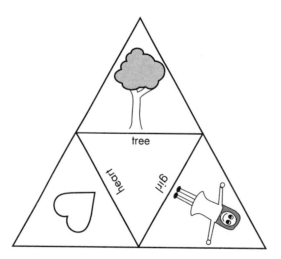

The child continues this procedure until all of the yellow triangles have been matched with the blue word triangles. This game can easily be made self-checking.

ACTIVITY

Word Checkers

To Construct the Game

You will need 6 pieces of posterboard about 8″ × 8″, 16 poker chips (8 of one color and 8 of another color), and a marker. Using the six pieces of posterboard, lay out six game boards similar to the one illustrated. You should use a different list of sight words for each of the boards.

two	who	any	one	of	there
which	love	off	why	this	what
when	than	by	how	where	then
orange	stop	with	dog	jump	boy
brown	spot	the	man	fall	girl
can	cold	but	tell	said	goat

To Play the Game

The child should select one of the word checkerboards and choose a friend to play the game with him or her. Each child takes a set of the colored chips. In order for the child to be able to move his or her chips, he or she must be able to identify the word he or she has landed on. The other child should be listening to make sure that the word is pronounced correctly. A child may jump his or her friend's chips just as if the game of checkers were being played. The child with the most chips of the opposite color at the end of the game is the winner.

Sight Word Basketball

To Construct the Game

Obtain a soft foam basketball and hoop and hang the hoop in an appropriate place for the children. Divide the class into two teams. You should make target sight word cards, each containing a single word.

Continued

Continued

To Play the Game

Hold up a sight word card for the first team member of Team A. If the child can correctly identify the word and use it in a sentence, he or she is allowed to attempt to shoot a basket. If the child makes the basket, he or she earns two points for his or her team. If the child hits the rim of the basket, he or she earns one point. Continue this same procedure with Team B. Keep playing until all of the team members have had a chance at the basket.

Reproducibles that Can Be Used to Improve Ability in Sight Word Knowledge

The chapter now contains several ready-to-use activity sheets that you may want to use to improve your pupils' ability in various elements of sight word knowledge. You can duplicate and use any of these activity sheets in their present form or modify them in any way you wish. You should remember that the use of such activity sheets is not in keeping with the true whole language philosophy, but they may be of use with some children if they are not overused. Some young children enjoy completing activity sheets (Miller, 1998).

ACTIVITY

Name _____ Grade _____

Which Word is Right?

First Grade, Second Semester Level

<u>Circle</u> the word in each sentence that fits.

1. This is a picture _____ a lion.
        off, of

2. Is that lady _____ mother?
        their, them

3. Rosa is playing with her _____ kittens.
            there, three

4. _____ will have fun when they go camping
    Them, They   next summer.

5. Betsy will give her dolls to _____.
                then, them

6. _____ do you think those boys are going?
    Where, Were

7. I always feed my dog Lady very _____.
                will, well

8. _____ one of your friends will you take with you
    Which, With   to the park?

9. What will Jenny do _____ she gets there?
            what, when

10. That boy is the tallest _____ in our class.
            one, on

ACTIVITY

Name _____   Grade _____

Can You Solve this Thanksgiving Puzzle?

Second-Grade Level

Use the words <u>in the box</u> to solve this puzzle.

DINNER	FRIENDS
TURKEY	STUFFING
PUMPKIN	THANKS
PIE	FAMILY
HAPPY	GRATEFUL
GRAVY	STOVE

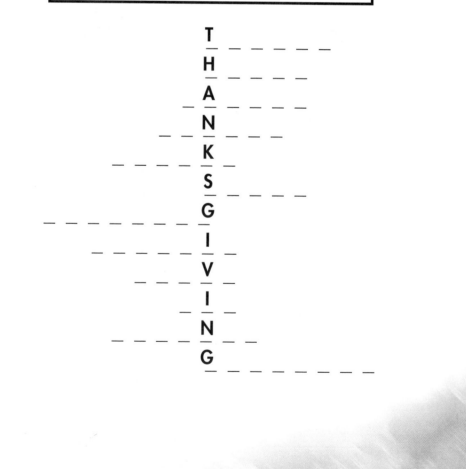

T _ _ _ _ _

H _ _ _ _

_ _ A _ _ _

_ _ N _ _ _ _

_ _ _ _ _ K _

S _ _ _ _

_ _ _ _ _ _ _ G _

_ _ I _ _

_ _ _ V _

_ _ _ _ I _

_ _ _ N _ _

G _ _ _ _ _

A C T I V I T Y

Name _____   Grade _____

Where are the Animals?
Second-Grade Level

<u>Find the names of the hidden animals</u> in this puzzle. All of the animal names that you should find are printed on the lines below the puzzle.

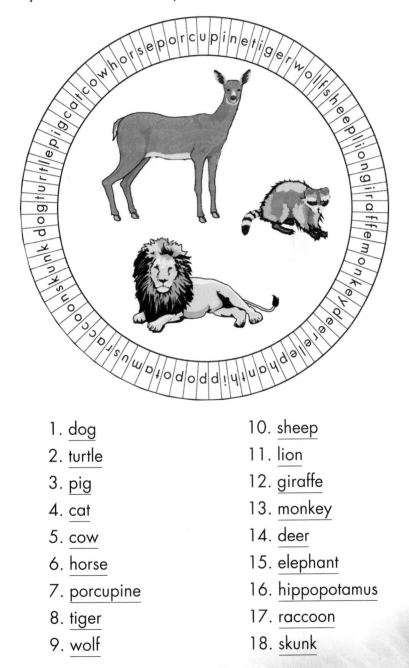

1. <u>dog</u>	10. <u>sheep</u>
2. <u>turtle</u>	11. <u>lion</u>
3. <u>pig</u>	12. <u>giraffe</u>
4. <u>cat</u>	13. <u>monkey</u>
5. <u>cow</u>	14. <u>deer</u>
6. <u>horse</u>	15. <u>elephant</u>
7. <u>porcupine</u>	16. <u>hippopotamus</u>
8. <u>tiger</u>	17. <u>raccoon</u>
9. <u>wolf</u>	18. <u>skunk</u>

WHAT IS PHONIC (GRAPHOPHONIC) ANALYSIS?

Phonics (also known as *graphophonics or graphonics*) is the study of speech sounds that are related to reading. It is often identified with decoding, which is emphasized in the early primary grades, and which literally means to "break the code," which in the case of reading refers to the alphabetic code. Many reading specialists, including this author, believe that some competency in phonics is necessary to ensure a child's adequate success in reading in the primary grades. For example, Adams (1990) stated the following after completing a comprehensive study on beginning reading that was commissioned by Congress:

> In summary, deep and thorough knowledge of letters, spelling patterns, and words, and of the phonological translations of all three, are of inescapable importance to both skillful reading and its acquisition. By extension, instruction designed to develop children's sensitivity to spellings and their relations to pronunciation should be of paramount importance to the development of reading skills (p. 416).

In summarizing Adams' research, Stahl, Osborne, and Lehr (1990) stated the following:

> Insufficient familiarity with the spellings and spelling-to-sound correspondences of frequent words and syllables may be the *single most common source of reading difficulties* (emphasis mine) (p. 115).

Other research studies also have indicated that children who are taught through an approach based on decoding achieve better results in reading than do those who are not taught to decode (Snow, Burns, & Griffin, 1998; Anderson, Hiebert, Scott, & Wilkinson, 1985; Chall, 1967, 1983; Dykstra, 1974). However, the research studies disagree on exactly how phonics should be taught, except in very general terms. For example, Adams (1990) stated, "The best way to build children's visual vocabulary is to have them read meaningful words in meaningful contexts" (p. 156). This suggests that phonics can be taught successfully within the context of the whole language philosophy.

In any case, teachers and children always should understand that phonics is a means to an end, not an end in itself. Phonic analysis is only one technique that children should use in identifying words, although it is an important one. Contextual (semantic) analysis, especially along with phonic analysis, is the most effective way to identify unknown words. The following statement made by Adams (1990) summarizes the usefulness of phonic (graphophonic) analysis:

> The goal of teaching phonics is to develop students' abilities to read connected text independently. For students, however, the strongest functional connection between these two skills may run in the reverse direction. It is only the nature of reading that can make the content of a phonics lesson seem sensible; it is only the prospect of reading that can make them seem worthwhile (p. 272).

PRINCIPLES OF PHONICS INSTRUCTION AND THE TWO MAIN APPROACHES TO TEACHING PHONICS

The main purpose of teaching phonics is to teach the skills necessary for decoding words. There is no real purpose in knowing that the /e/ in the word *let* is short unless the child is able to successfully decode the word. Most importantly, the phonic skills being taught should always be related to reading tasks in which children are currently participating or in which they will soon be participating. For example, an excellent time to teach the sound of the consonant *b* is when the children are going to read the very interesting trade book *Bootsie Barker bites* (by B. Bottner, NY: Putnam's, 1992). Sometimes children are taught phonic skills before they are given the opportunity to use them, or at some time after the instruction would have been truly relevant, so there is no real opportunity to use them. Research has shown that children do not use or internalize phonic information unless the skills that they have been taught are applicable to the present reading instruction (Adams, 1990). To summarize, phonic instruction must not only be systematic but also meaningful, functional, and contextual.

The two main approaches to teaching phonics are *analytic* and *synthetic*. In *analytic phonic analysis,* which also is called *implicit phonics,* consonants usually are not taught in isolation, since researchers believe that in isolation the consonant sounds are distorted. Instead, consonants are taught within the context of an entire word. As an example, the sound /d/ would be referred to as the sound that is heard at the beginning of the words *dog, duck,* and *doll.* In analytic phonics the sound /d/ is not pronounced in isolation, as *duh,* because that is distorted (that is, there is no "duh" syllable in dog, or doll).

In *synthetic phonic analysis,* which also can be called *explicit phonics,* each word is decoded sound by sound, and both consonant and vowel sounds are pronounced in isolation. For example, a child pronouncing the word *dig* would say *duh-i-guh.* In this approach the consonant sounds often are distorted because they cannot be pronounced without a vowel sound being added. A number of children have great difficulty determining how a word is pronounced by using synthetic phonic analysis, since they are not particularly proficient in *auditory blending,* and because the consonant sounds are distorted.

Ehri (1991) has stated that the synthetic blending of sounds into words may be a necessary help to beginning readers as they begin to successfully decode words. Groff (1986) has written the following on this subject:

> For over 40 years linguists have protested that isolating speech sounds was improper and contrary to the productive development of children's word recognition skills (Bloomfield, 1942). . . . Linguists who have opposed the teaching of explicit phonics apparently have failed to understand the difficulty that young children have in identifying and reproducing (segmenting) separate speech sounds when these phonemes are heard within words. Telling children to listen to the first sound in *fed,* for example, and to say another word that begins with the sound (implicit phonics), does not teach children to segment speech sounds. Instead, this direction presupposes that the child already knows what it intends to teach. Explicit phonics instruction makes no such presumption (p. 922).

Although most contemporary basal series recommend using only analytic phonic analysis, this textbook recommends using a combination of analytic phonic analysis and synthetic phonic analysis. Some children simply are unable to discriminate the individual sounds unless they are presented and practiced in isolation. This is especially true in the case of the short vowel sounds, and it also is the case to some extent with consonant sounds. A number of reading specialists including this author believe that the single best way of teaching young children to decode words is by using *analogy (word families).* Analogy involves using *onsets* (beginning consonants, consonant blends, or consonant digraphs) and *rimes* (word families). Analogy is a technique in which words are taught in *rimes* as the following:

c-at
m-at
b-at
r-at
s-at
h-at
fl-at

Normally, the first word in a group of words is taught as the "header," and the children are then helped to generalize the identification of the remainder of the words in that group. Usually an onset composed of the initial consonant is attached to the remainder of the word (the "rime"). Consonant blends or consonant digraphs are included later. Here are several examples of rimes to which initial consonants, consonant blends, or consonant digraphs can be attached:

-et
-an
-ill
-ake
-oat
-ell
-en
-ad
-in
-ing
-it
-un
-ug

WHAT ARE SOME COMMON PHONIC ELEMENTS AND GENERALIZATIONS?

Since the area of phonics instruction and phonic analysis is very complex, this book provides only an introduction to the subject. The interested teacher should consult one or more of the resource books on this subject that are included in the next section of this chapter. Indeed, there are many books devoted solely to the subject of phonic elements and rules.

Phonemes can be defined as the sounds that occur in a language. There are forty-four or forty-five phonemes in English, depending on whom is consulted. A phoneme is conventionally written as a letter or more often as a phonetic symbol between slash marks: /g/. A *grapheme* is the written symbol for a phoneme or sound. A grapheme can be composed of one or more letters. For example, it takes the two letters *s* and *h* to represent the single phoneme /*sh*/. There are approximately 251 graphemes in written English. Therefore, it can be seen that English does not have a regular phoneme-grapheme relationship.

Consonants

A *consonant* is caused when the outgoing breath stream is obstructed by an organ of speech. The organs of speech are the hard palate, the larynx, the soft palate, the tongue, the teeth, the lips, and the vocal cords. When the obstruction is complete, the resulting sounds are known as *plosives* or *stops.* Those in which the obstruction is partial are called *continuants.* Consonants also are classified as voiceless or voiced, depending on whether or not the vocal cords vibrate while producing the sound. Here are examples of plosives:

p	*pill*	*b*	*boy*
t	*top*	*d*	*dog*
k	*kitten*	*g*	*goat*

The following nasal sounds are one type of continuant:

m	*mother*	*n*	*new*

Fricatives are continuants that are made when the outgoing breath stream escapes with audible friction:

f	*fish*	*v*	*violet*
s	*sail*	*z*	*zoo*
h	*her*		
th	*thin* (voiceless)	*th*	*then* (voiced)

ch   <u>ch</u>in   j   <u>j</u>am   u   t<u>u</u>rn

sh   <u>sh</u>ip   y   fl<u>y</u>   y   lad<u>y</u>   y   m<u>y</u>th

The *liquids* are the following: w   ho<u>w</u> (diphthong) (see explanation below)

r   <u>r</u>un   l   <u>l</u>unch   y   bo<u>y</u> (diphthong) (see explanation below)

The *glides* are as follows:

y   <u>y</u>ear   w   <u>w</u>ash

Consonant Blends (Consonant Clusters)

A *consonant blend* (or *consonant cluster*) consists of two or, less often, three consonant letters that appear together. Each consonant contains some element of its own sound while blending with that of the others. Although most consonant blends occur at the beginning of words, they also can be found at the end.

bl	<u>bl</u>ue	br	<u>br</u>own	cl	<u>cl</u>ean
cr	<u>cr</u>awl	dr	<u>dr</u>op	fl	<u>fl</u>ew
fr	<u>fr</u>iend	gl	<u>gl</u>ue	gr	<u>gr</u>eat
pl	<u>pl</u>ay	pr	<u>pr</u>etty	sc	<u>sc</u>are
sk	<u>sk</u>ate	sm	<u>sm</u>oke	sn	<u>sn</u>ow
sp	<u>sp</u>eak	spl	<u>spl</u>ash	spr	<u>spr</u>inkle
st	<u>st</u>op	str	<u>str</u>ike	sw	<u>sw</u>im
tr	<u>tr</u>uck	tw	<u>tw</u>ice		

Consonant Digraphs

A *consonant digraph* is composed of two consonant letters that record a single sound that is different from the sound that either letter would record separately. Here are some examples of consonant digraphs:

th (voiceless)	<u>th</u>ick	th (voiced)	<u>th</u>ose
sh	<u>sh</u>oe	ch	<u>ch</u>ur<u>ch</u>
wh	<u>wh</u>en	ph	<u>ph</u>ase
ng	si<u>ng</u>	gh	rou<u>gh</u>

Vowels

Vowels result when the organs of speech modify the resonance chamber without impeding the flow of the outgoing breath. All vowels are voiced, and there are no nasal vowels in English. One vowel is distinguished from another by the quality of its sound.

a	b<u>a</u>ke	a	<u>a</u>pple		
a	c<u>a</u>ll	a	c<u>a</u>r	a	<u>a</u>ir
a	f<u>a</u>ther				
e	h<u>e</u>	e	p<u>e</u>t	e	<u>e</u>arn
e	h<u>e</u>rd	e	w<u>e</u>ar	e	s<u>e</u>rgeant
i	<u>i</u>ce	i	<u>i</u>t	i	sh<u>i</u>rt
o	h<u>o</u>pe	o	t<u>o</u>p	o	<u>o</u>ften
o	<u>o</u>r	o	w<u>o</u>rm		
u	<u>u</u>se	u	j<u>u</u>ice	u	n<u>u</u>t

The Schwa Sound

The *schwa sound* ə is the unstressed vowel sound in a word of more than one syllable. Any one of the five vowel letters can be the schwa sound when it is found in an unaccented syllable. The schwa sound has a sound very much like that of the short *u*. Here are some words that contain a schwa sound:

a	comm<u>a</u>	e	lab<u>e</u>l	i	penc<u>i</u>l
o	li<u>o</u>n	u	min<u>u</u>s		

Diphthongs

A *diphthong* is composed of two vowel sounds that together record one sound that is different from the sound that either of the vowels would have recorded alone. Here are several examples of words that contain a diphthong:

ow	h<u>ow</u>	ou	h<u>ou</u>se	oy	t<u>oy</u>
oi	s<u>oi</u>l	ew	f<u>ew</u>		

Vowel Digraphs

A *vowel digraph* occurs when two adjacent vowels record one sound. Here are some examples of words that contain a vowel digraph:

ai	r<u>ai</u>n	ay	pl<u>ay</u>
ee	m<u>ee</u>t	ea	h<u>ea</u>t, br<u>ea</u>d, gr<u>ea</u>t
oa	g<u>oa</u>t	oe	h<u>oe</u>
oo	b<u>oo</u>k	oo	m<u>oo</u>se
ow	bl<u>ow</u>		
ui	j<u>ui</u>ce		

Rimes (Phonograms, Word Families, or Graphemic Bases)

A *rime (phonogram, word family,* or *graphemic base)* is a group of vowel and consonant letters that are often learned and pronounced as a unit. They are groups of letters to which *onsets* (initial consonants, initial consonant blends, or consonant digraphs) are attached. Here are several examples. An earlier section of this chapter also included some of them.

-ad	s<u>ad</u>	-am	h<u>am</u>	-an	v<u>an</u>	-at	h<u>at</u>
-ed	f<u>ed</u>	-ell	s<u>ell</u>	-en	h<u>en</u>	-et	l<u>et</u>
-id	d<u>id</u>	-ig	d<u>ig</u>	-ill	p<u>ill</u>	-in	w<u>in</u>
-ing	s<u>ing</u>	-it	s<u>it</u>				
-op	h<u>op</u>	-ot	h<u>ot</u>				
-ug	h<u>ug</u>	-un	r<u>un</u>	-up	c<u>up</u>	-us	b<u>us</u>

Homophones

A *homophone* is a word that is pronounced the same as another word but has a different spelling and meaning. Here are some examples:

bear	*bare*
beat	*beet*
blue	*blew*
brake	*break*
cheap	*cheep*
forth	*fourth*
lessen	*lesson*
made	*maid*
sail	*sale*
wood	*would*

Homographs

Homographs are words that are written the same but sound different. Here are several examples:

I will read the book.
I read the book yesterday.

The wind blew very hard on Tuesday.
Don't forget to wind the grandfather clock.

Jeremy received a birthday present yesterday.
My aunt will present a piano concert tomorrow evening.

The Phonic Generalizations that Clymer Found Consistent Enough to Teach

As you probably are aware, there are many phonic generalizations that sometimes are taught to young children. Clymer (1963) suggested that only eighteen phonic generalizations are consistent enough to warrant being taught to primary-grade children. He conducted a classic research study in which he attempted to determine the stability or consistency of forty-five commonly taught phonic generalizations. Clymer used sets of basal readers to determine the phonic generalizations that were presented in the primary grades at that time. Then he arbitrarily decided that a phonic generalization should be at least 75 percent consistent or stable to be presented to children. Out of the forty-five generalizations that were studied, Clymer found only eighteen that were at least 75 percent consistent and, therefore, should be presented to primary-grade children.

The eighteen generalizations that Clymer believed should be presented to children in the primary grades are as follows:

The *r* gives the preceding vowel a sound that is neither long nor short.

Words having the double *e* usually have the long *e* sound.

In *ay* the *y* is silent and gives *a* its long sound.

When *y* is the final letter in a word, it usually has a vowel sound.

When *c* and *h* are next to each other, they make only one sound.

Ch is usually pronounced as it is in *kitchen, catch,* and *chair,* not like *sh.*

When *c* is followed by *e* or *i,* the sound of *s* is likely to be heard.

When the letter *c* is followed by *o* or *a,* the sound of *k* is likely to be heard.

When *ght* is seen in a word, *gh* is silent.

When two of the same consonants are side by side, only one is heard.

When a word ends in *ck,* it has the same last sound as in *look.*

In most two-syllable words, the first syllable is accented.

If *a, in, he, ex, de,* or *be* is the first syllable in a word, it usually is unaccented.

In most two-syllable words that end in a consonant followed by *y,* the first syllable is accented and the last is unaccented.

If the last syllable of a word ends in *le,* the consonant preceding the *le* usually begins the last syllable.

When the first vowel element in a word is followed by *th, ch,* or *sh,* these symbols are not broken when the word is divided into syllables and may go with either the first or second syllable.

When there is one *e* in a word that ends with a consonant, the *e* usually has the short sound.

When the last syllable is the sound *r,* it is unaccented.

Since this book cannot include all of the information about phonic elements and generalizations and strategies for teaching phonics that the teacher of young children may want to have, you are encouraged to consult one or more of the following resources in the field, all of which this author has found very helpful.

Cunningham, P. (1995). *Phonics they use: Words for reading and writing.* NY: HarperCollins.

Fry, E., Kress, J., & Fountoukidis, D. (1993). *The reading teacher's book of lists.* Englewood Cliffs, NJ: Prentice Hall.

Gaskins, I., Cress, C., O'Hara, C., & Donnelly, K. (1986). *Benchmark word identification/vocabulary development program.* Media, PA: Benchmark School.

Goodman, K. (1993). *Phonics phacts.* Portsmouth, NH: Heinemann.

Heilman, A. (1998). *Phonics in proper perspective.* Upper Saddle River, NJ: Merrill.

Hull, M., & Fox, B. (1998). *Phonics for the teacher of reading.* Upper Saddle River, NJ: Merrill.

Rinsky, L. (1997). *Teaching word recognition skills.* Upper Saddle River, NJ: Gorsuch Scarisbrick Publishers.

Wilson, R., & Hall, M. (1997). *Programmed word attack for teachers.* Upper Saddle River, NJ: Merrill.

STRATEGIES FOR IMPROVING ABILITY IN PHONIC ANALYSIS

The next part of this chapter contains a number of strategies for improving competency in phonemic awareness and phonic analysis. Although they should prove useful in both whole language classrooms and traditional classrooms, any of them should be modified to best meet the needs and interests of your own pupils. This especially is the case in whole language programs.

Strategies for Improving Phonemic Awareness

A number of young children need instruction and/or reinforcement in improving the emergent literacy skill of *phonemic awareness.* This skill was called auditory discrimination ability in the past (see Chapter 1). Chapter 1 also summarized a number of the emergent literacy skills that are helpful in preparing young children for success in phonic analysis, whether this skill is taught in the context of integrated themes or in isolation.

Here are several strategies that can be used for this purpose:

- Read nursery rhymes to the child. Have the child listen for and repeat the rhyming patterns found in this material.
- Read predictable books such as those listed in Chapter 2 to the child and have him or her read along with you. This is an example of teaching phonemic awareness in a whole language context.
- Pronounce pairs of words orally or on cassette tape. Some word pairs should be alike, while others should be different. Have the child tell you or record on tape whether each word pair is the same or is different. Here are several word pairs that can be used for this purpose:

hat—hat	fill—fell
rub—tub	well—will
pick—pick	top—tip
pen—pan	cube—tube

- Show the child some objects. All but one of the objects should begin with the same sound. Have the child point out the object that begins with a different sound. Here are some objects for the phoneme /d/: doll, dish, duck, baby

- Obtain pictures that represent minimal pairs of words. Place each pair of pictures on a table and have the child point out the picture whose word you say. For example, from the pair *rat* and *cat* ask the child to point to the picture of the cat.
- Have the child practice rhyming words. Illustrate the concept of rhyming by modeling examples. A number of children at the emergent literacy stage can rhyme words but do not know what the term *rhyming* means.

Presenting Phonic Analysis in Integrated Themes

Chapter 2 explained how important it is to present and practice phonic skills in the context of the themes that are used in whole language instruction. Any of the themes that an early childhood teacher selects has innumerable opportunities for children to learn and practice the various elements of phonics. All of the strategies that are included in this section can easily be adapted to a thematic unit, and this will enable children to learn the phonic skills in a more meaningful and effective manner.

Cross-Checking Word Identification Strategies

It is very important for children to learn the value of *cross-checking* word identification by using more than one cueing system. Children can identify many words by thinking about what word would make sense in a sentence and noticing whether the consonants in that word match what he or she is thinking of. The ability to use the consonants in a word along with the context is a very important decoding strategy. The child should learn to do two things simultaneously—think about what would make sense and think about letters and sounds. Many children like to do one or the other but not both of these things. Thus, some children may guess at an unknown word with a word that makes fairly good sense in context, while others guess with a word that begins with the proper consonant or consonant blend but makes no sense in the sentence. In order to help children cross-check meaning with sound, first have them guess the word using no letters. Then reveal some of the letters, and finally show the entire word and help them to confirm which guess makes sense and contains the right letters.

For each cross-checking lesson using different cueing systems, you should write sentences on the chalkboard or an overhead transparency. Then cover the word to be guessed with two pieces of paper, one of which only covers the first letter. You can use magnets to hold the pieces of paper on the board. Here are some sample sentences. You can use the children's own names to make this activity more interesting for them.

Hope likes to go to the <u>zoo</u>.

Mike likes to see the <u>elephants</u>.

Maria likes to feed the <u>deer</u>.

Joey likes to watch the <u>monkeys</u> playing.

Pauli likes to see the tall <u>giraffes</u>.

Show the children the sentences, and tell them that they will read each sentence and try to guess what word you have covered up. Have the children read the first sentence and guess what the covered up word is. They may guess *park, circus, mall, toy store,* etc. Next to each sentence write each guess that makes sense. When you have received several guesses, take away the paper covering the first letter, *z.* Erase any guesses that do not begin with this letter and ask if there are any more guesses that make sense and begin with *z.* If there are any more such guesses, write them down. However, be certain that all the guesses both make sense and begin correctly. Some children may begin guessing anything that begins with *z* whether or not it makes sense. Respond with, "zero does begin with *z,* but I can't write the word *zero* because people don't like to go to the *zero.*"

When you have written all the guesses that make sense and begin with the correct letter, uncover the word. See if the word that you have uncovered is one that the children guessed. If it is, praise them, and if it is not, tell them that it was very difficult and you are sure that they will be able to do it correctly the next time. Continue with each sentence by going through these same steps.

- Read the sentence and write any guesses that make sense.
- Uncover the first letter and erase any guesses that do not begin with that letter.
- Have the children make more guesses and write only those that make sense and also begin with the correct letter.
- Uncover the entire word and determine whether any of their guesses was correct.

The Elkonin Strategy and Elkonin Boxes

The *Elkonin strategy* and Elkonin *boxes* are very useful if children have difficulty learning to phonetically segment words. Elkonin (1973) has developed this strategy which is used regularly and very successfully in the Reading Recovery Early Intervention Program for first-grade children with special needs. Elkonin attempted to make the abstract skill of *segmenting* more concrete by using drawings and markers. In this strategy the child is given a drawing of a short word block that corresponds to the number of sounds in the word. Below a drawing of the word *man,* for example, there would be three blocks. A token is placed in each block to represent the three sounds in *man.* Here is a brief summary of the exact steps involved in this strategy:

- Explain the task, model it, and guide the child through it.
- Give the child a drawing of a man. Remind the child to say the word that names the picture and to stretch the word out so that he or she can hear the separate sounds. If the child has difficulty hearing the sounds,

pronounce the word very carefully and deliberately. Although you should emphasize each sound, try not to distort the sounds more than necessary.

- Have the child place a marker in each square while saying each sound. The child should say /m/ and put a marker in the first block, then say /a/ and put a marker in the second block, and finally put a marker in the third block while saying /n/.
- Using the blocks tells the child how many separate sounds there are in a word. As the child becomes more adept at this strategy, he or she can tell you how many different sounds that there are in a word.
- Finally, the child can learn to segment words by drawing boxes such as these which clearly illustrate how many sounds are found in any particular word. These are called Elkonin boxes. Each square of a box should contain the grapheme(s) that represent the phoneme for which it (they) stands. Here is an example of two boxes that illustrate this concept. This aspect of the strategy is often used in Reading Recovery lessons.

- Notice that the word *cat* is composed of three sounds and three letters while the word *thin* is composed of three sounds but four letters since the consonant digraph *th* is only one phoneme but is represented by two letters.

Magnetic Letters

Magnetic letters and some sources from which to obtain them were mentioned earlier in this chapter. However, magnetic letters also are extremely useful in teaching graphophonic (phonic) skills of various kinds. Magnetic letters are very commonly used in the Reading Recovery Early Intervention Program.

Magnetic letters can easily be used as a very effective hands-on manipulative activity in which children put letters together to form words. It therefore provides excellent practice for word building using onsets and rimes. Children are able to assemble a dozen words or more beginning with two-letter words and extending to five-letter or even longer words (Cunningham & Cunningham, 1992). The last word that the children assemble should contain all of the letters that they were given. As an example, they are given the letters *a, c, d, n, s* and *t* and are asked to do the following:

- Take away a letter to make *an.*
- Add a letter to make *can.*
- Take away a letter to make *an.*

- Change a letter to make *at*.
- Add a letter to make *cat*.
- Take away a letter to make *at*.
- Add a letter to make *sat*.
- Take away a letter to make *at*.
- Change a letter to make *an*.
- Add a letter to make *tan*.
- Now break up your word and see what other words you can make with the letters.

Word Wall

A *word wall* is an excellent device for reinforcing both word patterns and high-frequency words. Words should be placed on the wall in alphabetic order, and the early childhood teacher should add about five new words each week to the wall. These words can be selected from language-experience charts and stories, basal readers, trade books, and real-world materials. They should be high-frequency words that the children will meet many times in their reading and writing. Since these words are on the wall, they can be used as a type of dictionary. For example, if a child wants to find out how to spell the words *laugh, have,* or *their,* he or she needs only to look at the proper place on the word wall. Difficult to remember words also can be reviewed by using the word wall on a regular basis.

As one example, after a rime such as *-all* has been introduced, put the pattern words on the wall. However, you should put them on a different place on the wall and arrange them alphabetically by rime. For example, the *-ab* pattern should be first, followed by the *-ack* and *-ad* pattern, etc. The first word in each rime should be the model word, accompanied by an illustration so that the children can refer to the illustration if they forget how to identify the model word. When children have difficulty with a pattern word and are not able to use a pronounceable word part to unlock the word's pronunciation, they should be referred to the word wall. Encourage them to identify the model word and then use the analogy strategy to help them identify the unknown word.

Have the children review the pattern words on the word wall on a regular basis by using strategies such as these:

- Pantomime an action (*walk, hop, dig*) or use gestures to indicate an object or other item (*pan, ball, hen*), and then have the children write the appropriate rime on an every-pupil response card (explained later in this section) and hold it up so that you can see. Have a volunteer point to that word on the word wall and identify it. Before pantomiming the word, tell students what the model word of the rime is.
- Use the "secret word" strategy (Cunningham & Allington, 1994). Choose a pattern word from the word wall and write it on a sheet of paper but do not tell the children what it is. Have children number a

piece of paper from 1 to 5, and then give a series of five clues about the identity of the word. After each clue, the children should write down their guess. The object of this activity is for a child to guess the secret word from the fewest clues. The clues may be the following:

1. The secret word is in the *-all* rime.
2. It has four letters.
3. It is something that a child can play with.
4. It can be made of rubber.
5. Jill threw the red _____.

- After giving the five clues, show the secret word (*ball*) and talk with the children about their responses. You can give either praise or a small token prize to the child who guessed the secret word first.

Mnemonic Devices

Mnemonic devices can be useful in teaching elements of graphophonic (phonic) analysis, especially to learning disabled children. A mnemonic device usually involves teaching the child a *key word* for each different consonant phoneme and vowel phoneme. Each key word also can be illustrated by using a picture of an object. As an example, these usually are the key words for the short vowel phonemes: *apple for /a/, Eskimo for /e/, igloo for /i/, ostrich for /o/,* and *umbrella for /u/.* One of my former graduate students, Kay Gillespie, who teaches young learning disabled pupils near Peoria, Illinois, has developed the following system which she says has proven very effective.

First, she sends the following letter home to parents:

Dear Parents,
We are working on beginning consonant sounds and short vowel sounds. In order to help each child, we are associating *one* picture symbol with each letter. The letter in the picture is part of the object. The initial (front) sound of the pictured object is the letter. This provides a cue that aids in the sound-symbol association. For instance, *B, b* has the picture symbol: boy kicking a ball. Attached is a sound-symbol worksheet. You can help your child: (1) find the picture symbol in magazines, (2) hunt for the letter in common words, and (3) listen for the sound.

Then she prepares worksheets (see the samples on the next two pages) and attaches a copy of each page to the letter sent home to parents.

Other reading specialists also have used mnemonics successfully in teaching beginning graphophonic analysis to children who have had difficulty learning symbol-sound correspondences. For example, Ehrid Robbins (1992) found that picture mnemonics, in which the letter to be learned was highlighted in a picture of a word, was very effective.

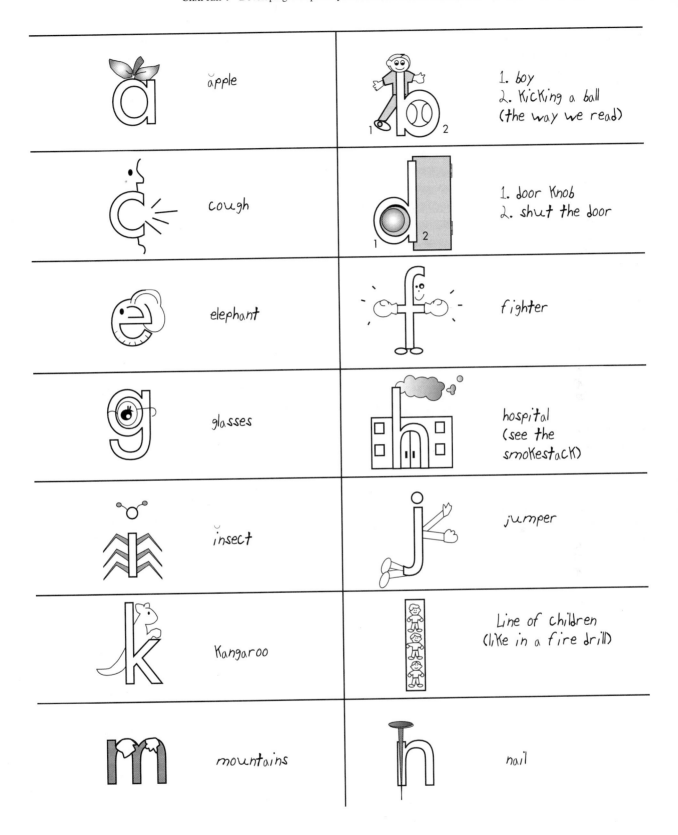

	ăpple		1. boy 2. Kicking a ball (the way we read)
	cough		1. door Knob 2. shut the door
	elephant		fighter
	glasses		hospital (see the smoKestack)
	insect		jumper
	Kangaroo		Line of children (liKe in a fire drill)
	mountains		nail

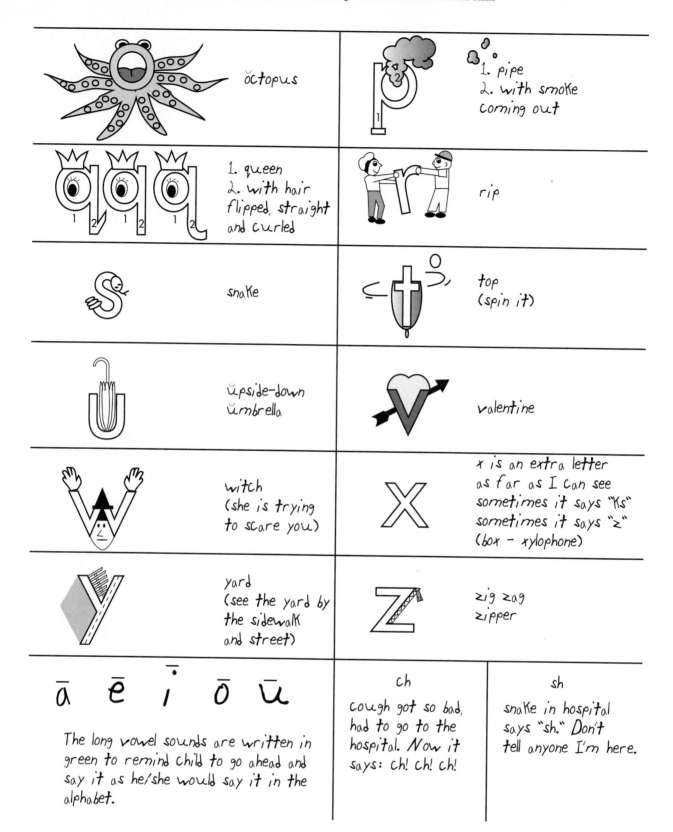

ŏctopus

1. pipe
2. with smoke coming out

1. queen
2. with hair flipped, straight and curled

rip

snake

top
(spin it)

ŭpside-down
ŭmbrella

valentine

witch
(she is trying to scare you)

x is an extra letter as far as I can see sometimes it says "Ks" sometimes it says "z" (box - xylophone)

yard
(see the yard by the sidewalk and street)

zig zag
zipper

ā ē ī ō ū

The long vowel sounds are written in green to remind child to go ahead and say it as he/she would say it in the alphabet.

ch
cough got so bad, had to go to the hospital. Now it says: ch! ch! ch!

sh
snake in hospital says "sh." Don't tell anyone I'm here.

Innovative Strategies to Practice Auditory Blending

There are several strategies that will help a child blend various sounds, often a very difficult skill, especially for a child with learning disabilities. Use analogies between auditory blending and other activities such as ice skating. Put large letters on the floor and have the child "skate" from one to another while saying the letter sounds out loud or have the child stretch a rubber band between words. You also can use letter tiles or other moveable letters that may be gradually moved apart while a word is sounded slowly and then brought back together as the entire word is pronounced. Teach the child to use his or her voice to "slide" through the sounds of unfamiliar words.

Every-Pupil Response Techniques

One *every-pupil response technique* that has relevance to phonic instruction involves giving each child three cards on which are printed the numbers *1, 2,* and *3,* or the words *beginning, middle,* and *end.* As you say the words, have each child respond by holding up the appropriate card. For example, "I am going to say some words that have the *n* sound in them. If you hear it at the beginning of the word, hold up your number 1 card; if you hear it in the middle of the word, hold up your number 2 card; and if you hear it at the end, hold up your number 3 card."

The every-pupil response technique provides each child the opportunity to respond to each question or task, which is different than typically is done either in whole-class or small-group instruction where the number of responses typically is small and limited to only a few children.

The Tape Recorder

A tape recorder can be used in a number of different ways to teach or review graphophonic elements. For example, tape record a number of words for the child in order to determine whether he or she hears a long or short vowel sound. The following can be recorded on tape: "Number your paper from 1 to 20. Turn the tape recorder off until you have done this. Then turn the tape recorder back on. Now you will hear some words pronounced. As you hear the sound, write *long* or *short* after the number of that word. Here are the words: number 1—*bat,* number 2—*cake,* number 3—*bed,*" etc. You should have the child mark each blank with a breve (˘) or macron (¯) if the child has learned that diacritical marking. This type of activity also can be done with initial consonants, consonant blends, consonant digraphs, and the hard and soft sounds of /c/ and /g/, among others.

Word Sort

Obtain a number of shoe boxes. Place an initial *s,* a consonant blend with an initial *s* such as *sl,* or a consonant digraph with an initial *s* such as *sh* on each shoe box. Then obtain a number of small objects that begin with these various sounds. Have a group of children sort the objects by placing each object into the correct box according to the initial sound.

Phonic Tree

Make a *phonic tree* by placing a small tree branch in a jar of sand. At the top of the tree attach a card with the letter or letters to be stressed. Have the children hang pictures of words beginning with the selected phonic element on the tree branches. Word cards may also be hung from the tree branches if desired.

Word Wheels

Word wheels can be used to practice the attachment of an initial consonant or later a consonant blend or digraph (onset) to various rimes (phonograms). A word wheel is made by cutting two circles of tagboard, one of which is slightly smaller than the other. The two disks can be fastened with a brass fastener. Print rimes on the large disk, while the initial consonant or consonant blend is printed on the smaller disk (see illustration). The smaller disk then is spun, and the child pronounces each of the newly formed words. For example, a word wheel using the consonant *b* can be used to form the words: *ball, bell, bet, bit, but, back, bad, bang,* etc. You may also purchase commercial word wheels.

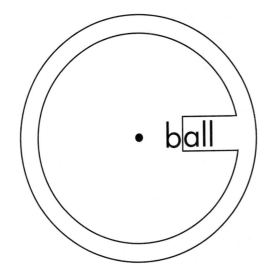

Make a Word from a Rime

Make a number of cards, each one containing eight rimes (phonograms). In addition, make a number of small cards of tagboard and print a consonant, consonant blend, or consonant digraph (onset) on each one. Each child participating in this activity selects a small card from the deck of cards and attempts to place it in front of a rime to form a word. The child must pronounce the formed word correctly. This activity works well as an independent activity in the literacy center.

Newspapers and Magazines

Have the child search for and circle a target graphophonic (phonic) element in a local newspaper, school newspaper, or magazine. Suitable graphophonic elements for this activity are as follows: consonant blends, consonant digraphs, diphthongs, vowel digraphs, rimes (phonograms), and r-controlled vowels.

If the child wishes, he or she can cut out each word containing the target graphophonic element that he or she has found and paste all of them onto a sheet of paper to form a collage.

Tongue Twisters

Tongue twisters are very useful for reviewing consonants because they give many word examples for the sound and are very enjoyable to say. First just say them and have children repeat them after you without letting the children see the words. Then have the children say them as rapidly as they can and as slowly as they can. When the children have said them enough times to memorize them, have them watch you write the tongue twisters on a piece of chart paper. Underline the first letter of each tongue twister with a different color marker. Then have the children read them several times. If you are making posters of the tongue twisters, you can have one or several children illustrate each of them.

Add one or two new tongue twisters every day. You should always say them first and write them only after the children have memorized them. After you write the new ones, review all of the old ones. Leave the charts or posters displayed, and refer the children to them if they forget or become confused about a sound.

Here are some tongue twisters that you can use as examples. You can make your own additional ones. It is motivating if you use your own pupils' names when they contain the correct letters and sounds.

Betsy's baby brother behaved badly.
Carl's Christmas cake certainly collapsed.
Davy's dog dug deeply.
Father's friend found French fries Friday.
George's grandfather gave Gina gold.
Harold had hot hamburgers.
Jimmy jumbled Julie's jacks.
Louie's lamb likes little lights.
My mother made me mittens.
New neighbors need nice nieces.
Patty's pal picked peppers.
Rita's red ribbon ripped.
Sally's sister's socks slipped.
Willie's wife was wonderful.

Some General Guidelines for Teaching Phonics

Rinsky (1997) has formulated the following guidelines for teaching phonics that early childhood teachers should carefully consider before using any of the strategies contained in this or any professional book:

- The purpose of teaching phonic skills in reading is to help children develop the ability to recognize *at sight* large numbers of words.
- Periodic evaluation of students' skill needs must be made through both informal and formal assessment.
- Students must, after the beginning stages, apply what they have learned through follow-up activities and lessons that involve actual reading.
- Students must be taught to rely on contextual and other visual clues, together with phonics.
- Individual differences must be considered. It is not unusual to find reading levels spanning six years in a single elementary classroom.
- A teacher must know the skills thoroughly so that what is taught is not only correct, but appropriate and necessary.

Computer Software

Since graphophonic analysis is a lower-level reading skill, it lends itself very well to reinforcement by using appropriate, motivating computer software. You can locate many useful programs by consulting an appropriate educational software catalog or by visiting computer software booths at local, state, regional, or national reading conventions or software conventions. For illustrative purposes, here are a few software programs:

Instant Zoo (ages 7–10) by Apple Computer. This is a set of four games plus a word list editor. Two of the games concern reading words. In *Quick Match,* pairs of words appear on the screen. The student decides if they match and presses a key to indicate a match. If the child answers incorrectly or too slowly, the computer gets a point. In *Scramble,* letters jog in animated tennis shoes and must be unscrambled before they jog to the bottom of the screen. Individual word lists to be used with *Scramble* may be created by the teacher.

Phonics for Grades 1–3 by SRA. The program includes nine levels and can be used along with any basal series. Tape cassettes with a human voice comprise the audio component.

Building Reading Skills by Jostens Learning System. K–3. The program features two disks that use graphics and a voice synthesizer to present and review initial consonant letters and sounds. Games for practice and rewards are provided. A third disk presents the short and long vowel sounds.

Word Spinner by Learning Company. K–4. Provides practice in recognizing three- and four-letter words with a consonant letter pattern. A computer-based dictionary for 500 three-letter and 1,000 four-letter words is included.

Sound-Sense Strategy

The *sound-sense strategy* (Houghton Mifflin, 1981) is a very helpful strategy that should be taught to all children as soon as they have progressed beyond the beginning stages of reading. When using this strategy, the child is taught to briefly pause at an unknown word and then follow these main steps:

1. Skip the unknown word, and read to the end of the sentence.
2. Return to the unknown word, and associate appropriate sounds for initial and final letters of the word.
3. Return to the beginning of the sentence and reread, attempting to identify the unknown word.

A Phonic Strategy Especially Designed for Children with Learning Disabilities

Harwell (1989) uses a strategy for teaching beginning graphophonic elements to children with learning disabilities that you may want to consider using in your early childhood class. She stated that if a child has acquired few or no phonic sounds from prior phonic instruction, the process usually takes about twenty consecutive days, with the longest time that it has ever taken being forty days. She further wrote that the teacher may work with one child at a time for 30 minutes daily, but that it was possible to work with up to four beginning readers at a time. Harwell also stated that it was necessary to give adequate blending and feedback time to each child. Very briefly, here is how the system is used. If you want more information about Harwell's system, you should consult her book, *Complete learning disabilities handbook* (West Nyack, NY: The Center for Applied Research in Education, 1989, pp. 119–123).

- Print each alphabet letter on the chalkboard or on a sheet of paper. Say: "The letter's name is *a*. Repeat please." Be sure that the children repeat "The letter's name is *a*," rather than just saying *"a."*
- Say: "The letter's sound is _____" (give the short *a* sound). Simultaneously, draw an *apple* on the

chalkboard, or if you are working with a group, the children each can draw his or her own apple. Do not allow them to say, "The letter's name is *apple.*"
- Say: "*Apple* is a word that starts with _____" (again pronounce the short *a* sound—really overemphasize it), "but it takes five letters to spell *apple.*" Write *apple,* point, and count to the five letters, and then repeat, "The letter's sound is _____."
- Harwell then continues this same procedure for each of the other symbol-sound relationships.

Hinks Pinks

Hinks pinks is a very motivating strategy to use in teaching and/or reviewing rhyming. These are rhyming pairs which children love to illustrate, make up, and then use to solve riddles. Teachers also like them because they emphasize the spelling pattern-rhyme relationships and provide children with a real purpose for looking for and manipulating rhyming words.

At the bottom of this page are several drawn illustrations made up for hinks pinks, followed by a number of hinks pinks you can use in your classroom. Of course, children will be eager to construct many of their own hinks pinks once they understand their purpose and have started doing so.

pink drink	loose goose	rub tub
stuff muff	tall ball	bump hump
slick Dick	fat cat	mess dress
far star	lap cap	bum gum
black sack	quick pick	stuck duck
crude dude	hot tot	lark park
sank bank	hunk junk	strong gong
fast blast	sick trick	king ring
drink sink	rat sat	meal deal
cake bake	rap cap	sup cup
cut hut	rub cub	goat boat

Picture Dictionary

A *picture dictionary* is a very effective strategy for helping beginning readers learn initial consonant sounds. To enable your pupils to construct a picture dictionary, collect a supply of pictures from discarded workbooks, magazines, and catalogues. The children should work with one letter at a time such as /B—b/.

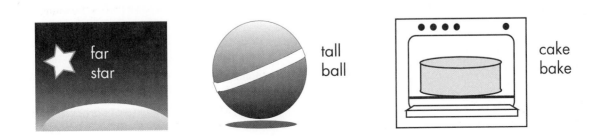

far
star

tall
ball

cake
bake

After teaching the initial sound of /B—b/ in words, have the children gather pictures whose naming words begin with that letter-sound. Children may work independently, with a partner, or in small groups. Then prepare a page (or several pages) for each letter-sound. Print a capital and lowercase letter at the top of the page and have the children fill the page with pictures whose naming words begin with that letter-sound.

If a child wishes, he or she can draw pictures for each letter-sound on the proper page of the picture dictionary instead of cutting out pictures.

List of Children's Books that Reinforce Vowel Patterns

Here is a partial list of children's books that reinforce various vowel patterns. Many of the books that reinforce initial consonant sounds were listed in an earlier section of this chapter that dealt with letter-name knowledge, and the reader should also refer to that section. Although using children's books for this purpose exemplifies the whole language philosophy, they also are very valuable in more traditional reading programs.

Long Vowel Patterns

Long /a/

Neasi, B. J. (1984). *Just like me.* Chicago: Children's Press.

Oppenheim, J. (1990). *Wake up, baby!* NY: Bantam.

Robart, R. (1986). *The cake that Mack ate.* Toronto: Kids Can Press.

Stader, J. (1984). *Hooray for Snail!* NY: Harper.

Long /e/

Bonsall, C. (1974). *And I mean it, Stanley.* NY: Harper.

Pigeen, S. (1985). *Eat your peas, Louise.* Chicago: Children's Press.

Shaw, N. (1986). *Sheep in a jeep.* Boston: Houghton Mifflin.

Ziefert, H. (1988). *Dark night, sleepy night.* NY: Puffin.

Long /i/

Hoff, S. (1988). *Mrs. Brice's mice.* NY: Harper.

Ziefert, H. (1984). *Sleepy dog.* NY: Random House.

Ziefert, H. (1987). *Jason's bus ride.* NY: Random House.

Ziefert, H. (1987). *A new house for Mole and Mouse.* NY: Puffin.

Long /o/

Hamsa, B. (1985). *Animal babies.* Chicago: Children's Press.

Kessler, L. (1976). *Ghosts and crows and things with O's.* NY: Scholastic.

Oppenheim, J. (1992). *The show-and-tell frog.* NY: Bantam.

Schade, S. (1992). *Toad on the road.* NY: Random House.

Short /a/

Antee, N. (1983). *The good bad cat.* Grand Haven, MI: School Zone.

Bayer, J. (1982). *My name is Alice.* NY: Dial Press.

Carle E. (1987). *Have you seen my cat?* NY: Scholastic.

Hawkins, C., and Hawkins, J. (1983). *Pat the cat.* NY: Putnam.

Moncure, J. (1984). *Short a and long a: Play a game.* Elgin, IL: Child's World Publishing.

Moncure, J. (1981). *Word bird makes words with cat.* Elgin, IL: Child's World Publishing.

Short /e/

Freschet, B. (1977). *Elephant and friends.* NY: Scribner's.

Gregorich, B. (1984). *Nine men chase a hen.* Grand Haven, MI: School Zone.

Hawkins, C., & Hawkins, J. (1985). *Jen the hen.* NY: Putnam.

Moncure, J. (1984). *Short e and long e: Play a game.* Elgin, IL: Child's World Publishing.

Short /i/

Fischer, A. (1965). *In the woods, in the meadow, in the sky.* NY: Scribner's.

Moncure, J. (1984). *Short i and long i: Play a game.* Elgin, IL: Child's World Publishing.

Moncure, J. (1984). *Word bird makes words with pig.* Elgin, IL: Child's World Publishing.

Wang, M. (1989). *The ant and the dove.* Chicago: Children's Press.

Short /o/

Allen, L. (1979). *Ottie and the star.* NY: Harper & Row.

Moncure, J. (1984). *Short o and long o: Play a game.* Elgin, IL: Child's World Publishing.

Short /u/

Gregorich, B. (1984). *The gum on the drum.* Grand Haven, MI: School Zone.

Lewison, W. (1992). *Buzz said the bee.* NY: Scholastic.

McKissack, P., and McKissack, F. (1988). *Bugs!* Chicago: Children's Press.

Moncure, J. (1984). *Short u and long u: Play a game.* Elgin, IL: Child's World Publishing.

Pinkwater, D. (1982). *Umbrellas and parasols.* NY: Dutton.

Yashima, T. (1969). *Umbrella.* NY: Viking.

/r/-controlled vowels

Hooks, W. (1992). *Feed me!* NY: Bantam.

Penner, R. (1991). *Dinosaur babies.* NY: Random House.

Wynne, P. (1986). *Hungry, hungry sharks.* NY: Random House.

/oo/ vowels

Blacksma, M. (1992). *Yoo hoo, moon!* NY: Bantam.

Brenner, B. (1990). *Moon boy.* NY: Bantam.

Wiseman, B. (1959). *Morris the moose.* NY: Harper & Row.

Word families

Brown, M. (1984). *Goodnight moon.* NY: Harper & Row.

Butler, A., & Neville, P. (1987). *May I stay home today?* Crystal Lake, IL: Rigby.

Cowley, J. (1990). *Dan the flying man.* Bothell, WA: Wright Group.

Patrick, G. (1974). *A bug in a jug.* NY: Scholastic.

Seuss, Dr. (1957). *The cat in the hat.* NY: Random House.

ACTIVITY

Games for Improving Ability in Graphophonic (Phonic) Skills

The chapter now includes several games that can be used to practice various elements of phonics. Such games are not in keeping with the whole language philosophy, but they may be motivating and effective with some children if they are not overused. They may be especially helpful with children who are difficult to motivate in any other way including by reading interesting materials.

Mystery Word Match

To Play the Game

This is a game in which children try to guess a *mystery word* which has letters in the same place as do three clue words. To play, divide the children into two groups. Each word is worth ten points. With each "No" answer to a question, the turn goes to the other team, and a point is subtracted.

Write each sentence and its clue words on the chalkboard. Then read the sentence, saying "blank" for the mystery word. Pronounce the clue words, and have the children pronounce them. Children can ask, "Does the mystery word begin like (one of the clue words)? Does it end like. . .?" Here is an example:

At the zoo my favorite animal is the _____.
    salmon
    popcorn
    healthy

Teacher: Listen while I read this sentence, and try to decide what word might fill in the blank. The clue words are *healthy, salmon,* and *popcorn.* Say them after me. Since Ellie's team won the toss, they can go first. The mystery word is worth ten points.

Ellie's team member: Does the word begin like *salmon?*

Teacher: No, it doesn't.

Jimmy's team member: Does the word end like *salmon?*

Teacher: Yes, it does. (Write an *s* on the board near the end of the blank line.) You now get another turn.

Jimmy's team member: Does the word begin like *healthy?*

Teacher: Yes, it does. (Write an *h* on the board near the beginning of the blank line.) Go again.

Jimmy's team member: Does the word have a letter in the middle of it that begins the same as *popcorn?*

Teacher: Yes, it does. (Write a *p* in about the middle of the blank line.) You now can get together with the rest of your team and try to figure out what the word is.

Jimmy's team confers and decides that the word probably is *hippopotamus,* since this animal name has an *h* at the beginning, a *p* about in the middle, and an *s* at the end. Jimmy's team receives nine points for this win, and the game continues with other mystery words and clue words.

Beach Ball Bounce

To Play the Game

Purchase a plastic beach ball that is divided into different colored sections. On each section print a consonant with a black permanent marker. The children may take turns bouncing the ball to each other. The person who catches the ball must say one word that begins with the consonant that his or her right thumb is on and one word that begins with the consonant that his or her left thumb is on.

ACTIVITY

Old McDonald

To Play the Game

Have the children sing the names of the five vowels in order in the song "Old McDonald Had a Farm." When they reach the "animal sound," they use the long sound of each vowel. For example:

Old McDonald had a farm.
a-e-i-o-u
And on his farm he had some letters,
a-e-i-o-u
With an a a here and an a a there
Here an a, there an a,
Everywhere an a a.
Old McDonald had a farm,
a-e-i-o-u

Continue through four more verses using another vowel sound each time.

Ring-a-Blend

To Construct the Game

Make a gameboard from a 4″ thick piece of Styrofoam that measures 30″ × 20″. Push nine large primary pencils (or similar objects) into the Styrofoam in three equally spaced rows. Next to each pencil attach to the Styrofoam small cards with consonant blends (consonant clusters) written on them. You can change the cards for this game when needed.

To Play the Game

From a distance of four to eight feet, a player tries to ring the pencils with plastic rings. (Rings can be cut from plastic lids.) A player scores five points for ringing a pencil. He or she scores an extra three points if he or she can give a word that begins with the consonant blend that is represented by that pencil.

Grocery Store

To Construct the Game

To construct this game, you need five large shopping bags labeled *a, e, i, o,* and *u,* and many empty containers (boxes, cartons, or cans) of foods whose names include the vowel sounds being studied.

To Play the Game

Have the children playing this game sort the food items into the correct shopping bag. Explain whether the children are to listen for and to sort by long or short vowel sounds. Here are some suggested foods that can be used in this game.

Long Vowels

potato	peach	beets	rice
yogurt	peas	seeds	raisins
beans	cheese	pie	cake

Short Vowels

apple	ham	butter	olives
jam	eggs	chips	popsicle
muffin	cabbage	pickle	fish

Continued

A C T I V I T Y

Continued

Treasure Hunt Game

To Construct the Game

Make forty word cards with one r-controlled vowel on each, a Treasure Hunt gameboard (see the illustration), and four cards to represent rafts. Here are some suggested words:

ur	**ir**	**er**	**ar**
burn	skirt	father	car
urge	shirt	mother	park
turn	bird	dresser	dark
purr	first	her	mark
fur	whirl	kernel	ark
hurt	third	other	large
plural	birth	brother	bark
blurt	thirsty	sister	star
urgent	dirty	herd	bar

Here is an example of a word card:

To Play the Game

Two to four players are needed to play the game. Cards are shuffled and placed at appropriate r-controlled vowel island points. The first player begins by proceeding to the first island. He or she selects one card, saying the r-sound at the top of the card and then the word. If the word is pronounced correctly, the child moves his or her raft to the next island. If the word is mispronounced the child leaves his or her raft where it is. Used cards are placed at the bottom of each pile. A recorder keeps track of the number of times a child visits an island. The child who has visited all islands three times wins the game.

Here is a sample gameboard:

Balloon Blends

To Construct the Game

You will need 2 pieces of 8″ × 11″ red posterboard and 2 pieces of 1½″ × 11″ red posterboard. You also will need a felt-tipped pen, scissors, and glue or tape.

You first print the following blends shown in the illustration on one of the posterboard strips. Put the drawings shown on the other posterboard strips.

Cut the 8″ × 11″ piece of posterboard into a balloon shape, as shown. Cut out two windows in one of the balloon pieces, about 1″ × ½″. Glue or dry mount the two balloon pieces together at the sides.

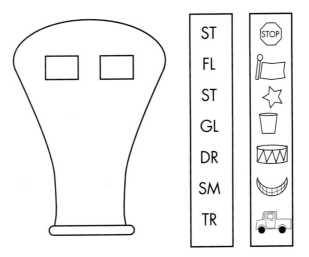

To Play the Game

The child should take the balloon out of the box and place the posterboard strips through the balloon. He or she should see the blends and the pictures in the windows. Then the child should match the blend with the picture of a word that begins with that blend. The child then moves the picture strip until he or she finds the correct word. If the child wishes, a partner can watch and help. The child also should say the words as he or she locates them.

Follow the Digraph Road

To Construct the Game

You will need the following materials:

12″ × 18″ posterboard
felt-tipped marking pens
different colors of construction paper
scissors
glue
4 large lima beans
clear self-stick vinyl

In constructing the game you should make a gameboard as shown in the illustration on the next page. Each square in the road should be a 1″ piece of construction paper cut from different colors and glued to the board. On each square in the road, write the letters that represent different consonant digraph sounds. On construction paper cards, write the numerals 1 through 5. Cover the cards and gameboard with clear self-stick vinyl or laminate them. Color the lima beans different colors such as blue, red, green, and purple with the marking pens.

Continued

ACTIVITY

Continued

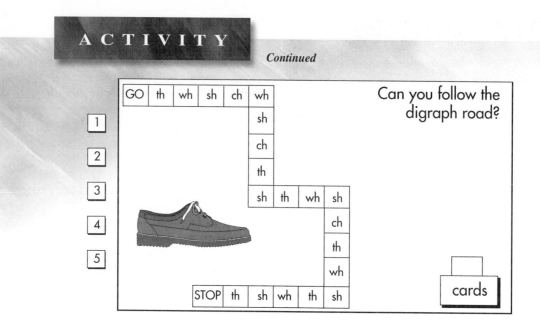

To Play the Game

The child draws a card for the number of the moves to be taken. At each landing, the child says a word that begins with the consonant digraph found in that square. If he or she is unable to give a word, the child loses the turn. A similar gameboard can be made for ending consonant digraph sounds.

Use a Clothespin

To Construct this Game

You will need the following materials:

8″ pizza boards (these can sometimes be obtained from local pizza restaurant)
clothespins
fine-line marking pens
old workbooks or catalogs
scissors
glue
clear self-stick vinyl

To construct the game around each pizza board, you glue pictures that represent the vowel combinations being reviewed. On the back side, write each word. Write words on the clothespins for these pictures. The vowel element should be written in red letters. Cover the pizza board with clear self-stick vinyl. Several illustrations that should help you to construct the board are shown on the next page.

ACTIVITY

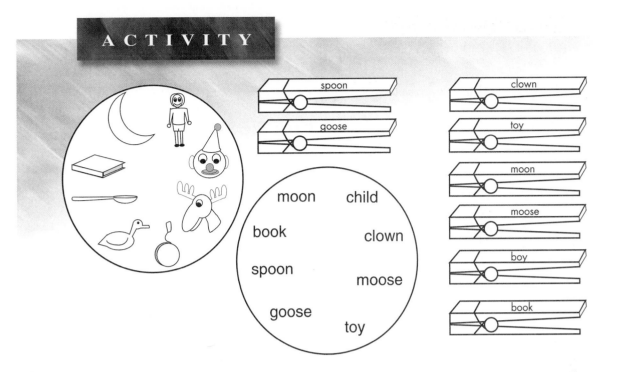

To Play the Game

Have the child clip the correct clothespins to each picture around the board and then read the word. The back of the wheel may be referred to for self-checking.

Reproducibles that Can Be Used to Improve Ability in Graphophonic (Phonic) Analysis

This chapter now includes several reproducibles that you may want to use for improving your pupils' ability in the various elements of graphophonic analysis. The use of such activity sheets is not in keeping with the true whole language philosophy, but they may be of use with some children if they are not overused.

Continued

A C T I V I T Y *Continued*

Name_____ Grade_____

Word Puzzles

First Grade, Second Semester, or Second Grade, First Semester

Read each question and print the right answer on the line.

The right answer will be <u>one of the underlined words.</u>

1. What is part of person's leg, a <u>knew</u> or a <u>knee</u>?

_____

2. What is a baby cow, a <u>calf</u> or a <u>half</u>?

_____

3. What can you eat for dinner, <u>born</u> or <u>corn</u>?

_____

4. What can a woman wear on her head, a <u>hat</u> or a <u>mat</u>?

_____

5. What can you ride in, a <u>duck</u> or a <u>truck</u>?

_____

6. What is part of a person's hand, a <u>thumb</u> or a <u>crumb</u>?

_____

7. What can you eat at a birthday party, a <u>rake</u> or a <u>cake</u>?

_____

ACTIVITY

8. What likes to eat cheese, <u>mice</u> or <u>lice</u>?

_____

9. What do you wear outside, a <u>goat</u> or a <u>coat</u>?

_____

10. What do you read at school, a <u>look</u> or a <u>book</u>?

_____

11. What can a child play in, <u>sand</u> or <u>hand</u>?

_____

12. What does a car have, <u>wheels</u> or <u>heels</u>?

_____

13. Which has wool on it, <u>sleep</u> or <u>sheep</u>?

_____

14. Where can you shop, a <u>mall</u> or a <u>wall</u>?

_____

15. Where can a child go to play ball, a <u>park</u> or a <u>dark</u>?

_____

A C T I V I T Y   *Continued*

Name _____   Grade _____

Can You Make New Words?
Second-Grade Level

Read each sentence and follow the directions.

1. **arm**   Add one letter to make a place in the country.

   _____

2. **pear**   Change one letter and get the name of an animal.

   _____

3. **came**   Add one letter and get the name of an animal.

   _____

4. **kitten**   Change one letter and get the name of something you wear.

   _____

5. **other**   Add two letters and get a member of your family.

   _____

6. **snail**   Take off one letter and get something that a carpenter uses.

   _____

7. **breeze**   Change one letter and get a word that means very cold.

   _____

8. **ring**   Add two letters and get a word for a season of the year.

ACTIVITY

9. **tall**   Change a letter to make something that a child can throw.

_____

10. **crab**   Change one letter to make something that a baby can sleep in.

_____

11. **big**   Change one letter to make a farm animal.

_____

12. **clown**   Change two letters to make a color word.

_____

13. **rate**   Take off a letter to make the name of an animal.

_____

14. **past**   Add a letter to make something you use in school.

_____

15. **beat**   Change one letter to make the name of a vegetable.

_____

Continued

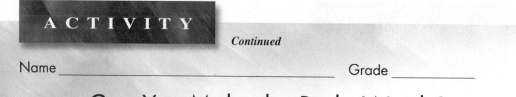

ACTIVITY *Continued*

Name _____ Grade _____

Can You Make the Right Words?
Third-Grade Level

Read the word at the beginning of the line. Then fill in the right words in the rest of that line. One word in each line has been done for you.

	ea	ee	or	oa
living things	eagle			
things to eat		beets		
things to buy at a store				coat
school words			work	
words in the home				oatmeal
vacation words	bear			
words related to a car		beep		
related to the out of doors			storm	

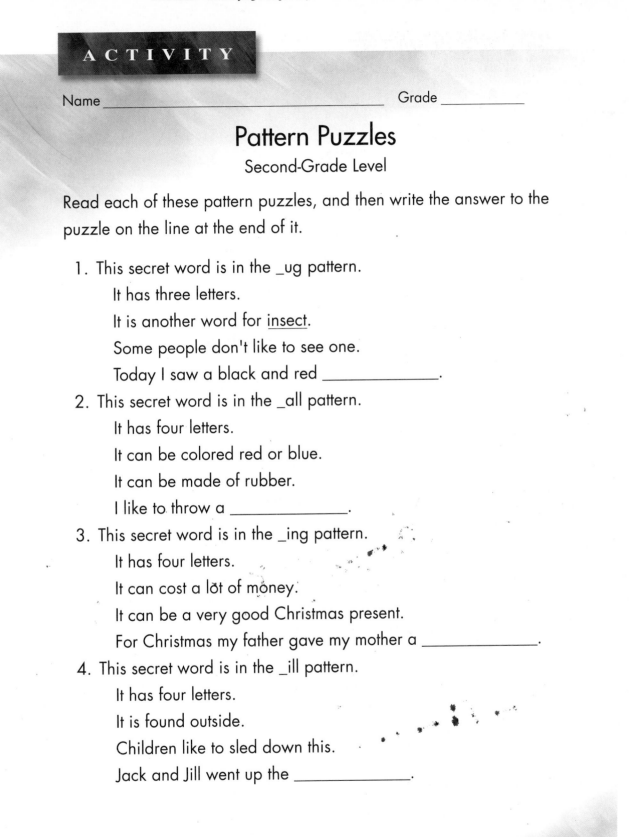

ACTIVITY

Name _____   Grade _____

Pattern Puzzles
Second-Grade Level

Read each of these pattern puzzles, and then write the answer to the puzzle on the line at the end of it.

1. This secret word is in the _ug pattern.

   It has three letters.

   It is another word for <u>insect</u>.

   Some people don't like to see one.

   Today I saw a black and red _____.

2. This secret word is in the _all pattern.

   It has four letters.

   It can be colored red or blue.

   It can be made of rubber.

   I like to throw a _____.

3. This secret word is in the _ing pattern.

   It has four letters.

   It can cost a lot of money.

   It can be a very good Christmas present.

   For Christmas my father gave my mother a _____.

4. This secret word is in the _ill pattern.

   It has four letters.

   It is found outside.

   Children like to sled down this.

   Jack and Jill went up the _____.

Continued

A C T I V I T Y

Continued

5. This secret word is in the _ed pattern.

   It has three letters.

   It is found in the house.

   It can be made of wood.

   I have a very good _____.

6. This secret word is in the _uck pattern.

   It has five letters.

   Many people own one.

   It costs a lot of money.

   My father would like to buy a new blue _____.

7. This secret word is in the _ell pattern.

   It has four letters.

   I like to hear the sound of one.

   It can be big or small.

   Did you hear the ringing of that _____?

8. This secret word is in the _at pattern.

   It has three letters.

   It can be a child s pet.

   It is an animal.

   I have a friendly yellow _____.

9. This secret word is in the _ack pattern.

   It has five letters.

   This sky looks like this at night.

   It is a color word.

   I like the color _____.

10. This secret word is in the _ib pattern.

    It has four letters.

    Corn can be stored in this.

    It also can be found in a bedroom.

    A baby can sleep in a _____.

ACTIVITY

Name _____   Grade _____

Make a Word that Goes with the Clue
Second-Grade Level

Read the clue on the left and then fill in the correct letter or letters to make a word.

1. frog   _____ oak
2. dog   _____ ark
3. boat   _____ ail
4. brush   _____ eeth
5. speak   _____ alk
6. play   _____ all
7. railroad   _____ ack
8. leaves   _____ ake
9. hole   _____ ig
10. money   _____ ank
11. tail   _____ ag
12. doctor   _____ ill
13. bird   _____ est
14. ring   _____ ell
15. father   _____ ad
16. throw   _____ ick
17. engine   _____ ain
18. airplane   _____ et
19. fly   _____ ag
20. horse   _____ arm

STRUCTURAL ANALYSIS

Structural or morphemic analysis is using word structure or word parts to determine the pronunciation and meaning of unknown words that are met while reading. This word identification technique can be helpful in improving a child's meaning vocabulary, especially if it is used along with semantic analysis and graphophonic analysis. Although it is more useful with older students, it can be somewhat helpful in the upper primary grades.

Structural or morphemic analysis is composed of a number of subskills. One subskill is attaching a *prefix* or *suffix (affix)* to a base or root word to form a *derivative.* Derivational suffixes change the part of speech of a word or its function in some way. Common derivational suffixes can form adjectives, as in the words *musical* and *worthless,* while others form nouns, as in the words *happiness* and *tolerance.* Still others change the function of a noun or verb so that it indicates a person rather than an action or inanimate object, as in the words *teacher* and *farmer.* Some of the most common suffixes presented in the primary grades are *-er, -able, -y, -al,* and *-ness.*

Inflectional suffixes indicate grammatical items and include plural *-s* as in *girls,* third-person singular *-s* as in *plays,* present participle *-ing* as in *working,* past tense *-ed* as in *walked,* past participle *-en* as in *loosen,* comparisons *-er* and *-est* as in *bigger* and *biggest,* and the adverbial *-ly* as in *quickly.* Young children learn some of the inflectional suffixes early in the primary grades. For example, *-s, ed,* and *-ing* are commonly found in beginning reading materials of all kinds and are presented in first grade. On the other hand, *-er, -est,* and *-ly* are taught in most basal reader systems in second grade (Harris & Jacobson, 1982).

Morphemic analysis also uses the term *morpheme,* which is the smallest unit of meaning in a language and can be either *free* or *bound.* A free morpheme is a group of letters that comprise any meaningful word such as the following: *house, lady, baby, father,* or *bicycle.* A *bound morpheme* is composed of one or more letters that have a meaning but cannot function in isolation as do real words. Several examples of bound morphemes are the suffix *-ing* in the word *playing,* the suffix *-ed* in the word *hunted,* and the prefix *un-* in the word *unhappy.*

Understanding the use of *compound words, syllabication, stress,* and *word origins* are also subskills of structural or morphemic analysis. Even though *contractions* usually are considered a part of structural analysis or word structure, they often should be learned as sight words, especially at the beginning stages of reading instruction. It normally is not very helpful for a child to determine what two or three letters are omitted when the contraction is formed. It is more useful to learn it as a sight word that is instantly recognized.

Discussing prefixes, suffixes, compounds, and root words may remind the reader of memorizing lists of word elements. However, learning morphemes is a constructive process that children begin as early as the age of two (Brown, 1973). For example, a young child around the age of four may make a statement such as this: "He goed to school yesterday." This is an example of a young child overgeneralizing a grammatical concept of which he or she is becoming aware. The child has constructed a rule for the past tense of the verb *go* that seems to make sense. Later he or she will refine the process and say *went.*

Clymer's list of phonic generalizations was included in the section about graphophonic analysis in this chapter. Since a number of these generalizations also deal with structural analysis, the reader is encouraged to refer to this list when necessary. Since a direct link exists between spelling generalizations about suffixes and the reader's ability to mentally separate suffixes from roots in order to identify the total derived or inflected word, it is useful to teach older primary-grade children the following generalizations:

- When adding a suffix beginning with a vowel to a word that ends with an *e,* the *e* usually is dropped; i.e., *believe + able* is *believable* and *secure + ity* is *security.* However, in a word such as *changeable,* the *e* is not dropped since to do so would give the *g* a hard sound.
- When adding a suffix beginning with a vowel to a word that ends in one single consonant with a short vowel before it, the last consonant is usually doubled; i.e., *hop + ing* is *hopping* and *run + er* is *runner.* In the first case this enables the person to discriminate between the words *hopping* and *hoping.*
- When adding a suffix to a word that ends with a *y* preceded by a consonant, the *y* is usually changed to an *i;* i.e., *lady + es* is *ladies* and *greedy + ness* is *greediness.* However, the letter *y* is not changed to an *i* when adding *ing* as in the words *cry/crying.* This is the case because English does not permit two *i's* together and without the *y* the word would be spelled *criing.*
- When adding a suffix to a word that ends with a *y* preceded by a vowel, the *y* is not changed; i.e., *turkey + s* is *turkeys* and *monkey + s* is *monkeys.*

This process of becoming aware of oral and written grammar continues through the elementary school as children refine their concepts of past tense and third-person plural. Structural or morphemic analysis as a word attack skill should build on these *constructive elements.* The instruction given to children should be generative and conceptual rather than mechanical and isolated. For example, even many primary-grade children can use their knowledge of the meaning of the prefix *-un,* which means *not,* to construct meanings for such words as *unhappy, unfold,* and *untie,* among others.

If a child always reads for meaning and uses grammatical (syntactical) clues as well as semantic clues, translating the letters into sounds happens automatically.

For example, a child's innate grammatical sense will tell him or her that a /z/ sound is used in the italicized word in the following sentences: Josh received many *toys* for Christmas. It also is not necessary to tell the child that the suffix *s* is represented by the /z/ sound in other common words such as *cars, boys, farmers,* and the like. As another example, children usually can pronounce the *-ed* suffix correctly in these words even though three different pronunciations are possible: *walked, called,* and *landed.* Therefore, it is not necessary to teach children to identify the pronunciations of /t/, /d/, or /id/ that *-ed* represents.

Compound words are one element of word structure that receives a great deal of emphasis in the primary grades, beginning in first grade. One way of generating or forming new words is to put two words together to form a new composite word. The English language has been enhanced with thousands of compound words. For example, according to Rinsky (1997, p. 87) about 60 percent of the new words that are presently coming into the English language are compound words, with some examples being *software, cyberspace,* and *spacecraft.*

Remember that even though compound words may appear simple to adults, they can be difficult for children. For example, a child who can easily identify both of the words *play* and *ground* may have a more difficult time in identifying the word *playground* because it looks both long and difficult. Children should learn to identify each word of which a compound word is composed separately and then simply pronounce them together. They also should learn that the meaning of the compound word most often is a composite meaning of the two words of which it is composed, although they also should understand that the meanings of the individual words that comprise a compound word do not always give a clue to the meaning of the compound word, as in, for example, the words *shortstop* and *into.*

Here are the titles of several children's trade books that can be used to reinforce compound words:

Berenstain, S., & Berenstain, B. (1969). *Inside, outside, upside down.* NY: Random House.

Freeman, P. (1986). *A home of my own.* NY: Viking.

Heller, R. (1990). *Merry-go-round.* NY: Grosset & Dunlap.

Moncure, J. (1988). *The biggest snowfall.* Chicago: Children's Press.

Rice, E. (1980). *Goodnight.* NY: Greenwillow.

However, another element of structural analysis is that some leading syllabication specialists do not believe that traditional syllabication is particularly useful in word identification or even spelling in light of the widespread use of computer word processing programs. One such reading specialist is Groff (1981), who believes that it usually is more helpful to divide a word into "chunks of meaning" rather than into traditional syllables that match those of a dictionary. For example, Groff probably would chunk the word *letter* as *lett/er* instead of the syllabic division *let/ter,* which is the more common one. I agree with Groff on this point.

It also is interesting to note that on the primer level only 15 percent of the words are polysyllabic, in first grade about 25 percent of the words have more than one syllable, by second grade 30 percent of the words are polysyllabic, and by sixth grade 80 percent of the words contain more than one syllable. Therefore, you can see that children in the primary grades should begin to understand simple syllabication. The next section of this chapter provides suggestions about how to do this.

As stated earlier, structural analysis often is the most useful when it is used along with semantic clues and graphophonic analysis. As an example, if a child attacks a polysyllabic word structurally, he or she first must be able to decode each of the syllables phonetically and then blend the syllables into a recognizable word that is in his or her meaning vocabulary. After the word has been analyzed both structurally and phonetically, the child must then use semantic analysis to determine whether or not it makes sense in sentence context.

In summary, children in the primary grades begin to learn structural or morphemic analysis skills, which then are continued and refined in the intermediate grades and above.

A C T I V I T Y

Strategies for Improving Ability in Structural or Morphemic Analysis

The next part of this chapter includes several strategies for improving ability in the various elements of structural or morphemic analysis. Although they should be useful in both whole language classrooms and traditional classrooms, any of them should be modified in response to the needs and interests of your own children.

The Language-Experience Approach (LEA)

The language-experience approach (LEA) is very useful for teaching and practicing various elements of word structure such as simple suffixes like *-s, -ing,* or *-ed.* Experience stories and charts can be used for this purpose as early as the kindergarten and first-grade level. A complete description about how to use LEA was provided in Chapter 2.

Playdough and Clay

Playdough and clay are very effective in providing children practice with inflectional endings at the beginning reading level. Have the child use clay or playdough to construct objects that indicate comparatives and superlatives. As an example, have the child use either medium to illustrate the following:

big, bigger, biggest
tall, taller, tallest
little, littler, littlest,
short, shorter, shortest
small, smaller, smallest
wide, wider, widest

The same concept can be illustrated by having the child fold a sheet of 12″ × 18″ newsprint or manila paper into thirds. Then have the child print words such as the following on the paper: *big, bigger, biggest; tall, taller, tallest; little, littler, littlest; short, shorter, shortest; small, smaller, smallest; wide, wider, widest.* Have the child draw pictures to illustrate each of these comparisons. Here is an illustration of the first comparison mentioned.

A C T I V I T Y

Tying Words Together

For this activity, you need a sheet of 8″ × 10″ posterboard, a felt-tipped pen, scissors, and ten pairs of 16″ shoestrings. Print the first half of appropriate compound words on the left of the posterboard and the second half of the words on the right side of the posterboard (in scrambled order). Punch holes by each of the word halves. Have the child thread a shoelace through the hole beside half of each compound word to its counterpart in order to form a complete compound word. Have the child continue until he or she has matched all of the words and formed compound words.

Magnetic Compound Words

To provide practice in forming compound words, print each part of a number of compound words on small word cards. Then attach a paper clip to each word card. Have the child pick up the two word cards that form a true compound word with a horseshoe magnet. Have the child then pronounce the word and write all of the formed compound words on a sheet of paper.

Here is an illustration of this activity.

Are These Real or Make-Believe Compound Words?

Write a number of compound words on the chalkboard or a transparency. Some of them should be actual compound words, while others should be make-believe compound words. Have the child then write all the words in two columns on a sheet of paper—those that are the true compound words and those that are not. This activity also can be placed on an activity sheet for a child to complete independently or with a partner(s).

Here are some words you might use in this activity.

Real Compound Words	Make-Believe Compound Words
doghouse	dogpaw
cowboy	horseboy
snowman	snowcat
blackberry	purpleberry
spaceship	spacehouse
bluebird	greenbird
playground	playdoll
railroad	carroad
bedroom	windowroom
treehouse	treebranch

Continued

Structural Graffiti

Cover an area of the classroom such as part of a bulletin board with butcher paper. Label the paper with some element of structural analysis such as compound words, contractions, suffixes, or prefixes. Throughout the week in their free time, have children write their contributions on the paper. Have the entire class discuss and evaluate their "graffiti" at the end of the week. This activity is the most appropriate for children in the upper primary grades.

Compound Pocket Words

To use this strategy for improving ability in compound words, you construct a folder with pockets. On one side write the first part of about ten to fifteen compound words. On the other side write the second part of these words. Then have the children combine these pieces to form compound words. If you want, you can write the answers on the back of the folder for self-checking.

Here is an illustration that should clarify this strategy.

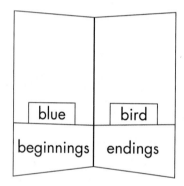

What Are These Compound Words?

To expand the children's knowledge of compound words, construct a large wall chart with five headings, such as *Types of Animals, People, Things, Places,* and *Time* written on the top. Then ask the children to locate compound words that fit under these and/or other appropriate headings. Here is a sample of such a list.

Types of Animals	People	Things	Places	Time
bloodhound	firefighter	doghouse	bedroom	
bluebird	policeman	baseball	farmhouse	birthday
blackbird	cowgirl	playhouse	barnyard	afternoon
starfish	milkman	fruitcake	sidewalk	bedtime
bulldog	grandfather	firewood	highway	playtime
dragonfly	grandmother	scarecrow	downtown	daylight
grasshopper	salesperson	nutcracker	uptown	weekend
goldfish	housewife	basketball	sidewalk	weekday
jellyfish		railroad	drugstore	
		flashlight	bathroom	

ACTIVITY

Games for Improving Ability in Structural (Morphemic) Analysis

The chapter now includes several games that can be used to practice various elements of structural or morphemic analysis. Such games are not in keeping with the whole language philosophy, but nevertheless they may be useful with some children.

Playing Cards with Word Endings

To Construct the Game

You will need construction paper, fine-line marking pens, scissors, and clear self-stick vinyl. Make two decks of playing cards. On one set write sentences with the verbs omitted. On the other set write the missing words. On the back side of the sentence cards write the missing word. Then cover both decks with clear self-stick vinyl.

Here is an illustration of this procedure.

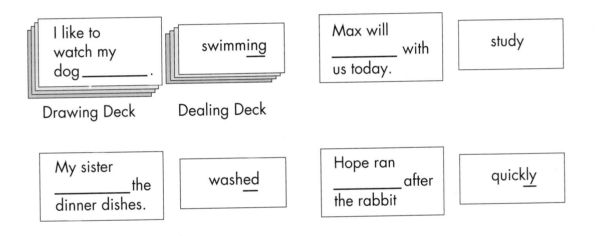

To Play the Game

Deal the word cards to 2 to 4 children. The sentence cards are laid face up as the drawing pile. Each child draws a sentence card, taking turns. The child who has a word card to complete the sentence lays down the card and then reads the completed sentence.

Contraction Pizza Board

To Construct the Game

To construct this game you need pizza boards, which often can be obtained inexpensively or for free from a local pizza restaurant. You also need wooden clothespins, fine-line marking pens, and clear self-stick vinyl.

With a marking pen, divide the pizza board into sections. Write two words that can comprise a contraction in each section of the pizza board. Then write on the clothespins the corresponding contractions. Cover the pizza board with clear self-stick vinyl. An illustration of this follows on the next page.

Continued

ACTIVITY

Continued

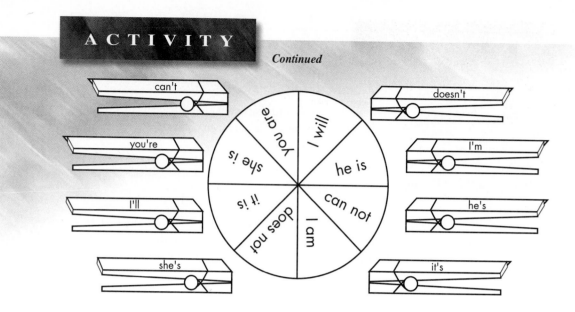

To Play the Game

Have the child match the contraction to each set of double words by clipping the corresponding clothespin to the correct section.

Do You Want to Do a Compound Puzzle?

To Construct the Game

You need 2 pieces of 8″ × 10″ posterboard, a felt-tipped pen, scissors, and ten pairs of 16″ shoestrings.

Write the following words on the 8″ × 10″ pieces of posterboard. Then punch holes next to each of the words.

• fire			• snow		• crow		• ground
	• after			• boat		• bird	
• craft		• light			• post		• cow
		• cracker				• ache	• basket
	• grand			• gold		• rail	
	• bath		• nut		• doll		• star
		• barn		• day		• dog	• time

	• fish		• house			• play	
• noon		• space			• man	• house	
	• sail		• fighter		• scare		• noon
	• day		• boy		• tooth		• ball
• father			• road		• light		• room
	• yard		• bull			• day	

To Play the Game

Have the child choose one of the words on the board and thread a shoelace through the hole to the left of that word. Then the child should look over the board and try to find another word that will combine with the first

word to make a compound word. Sometimes several words can be used with other words to make other combinations. When th child has found a compound word, he or she should thread the other head of that shoelace into the hole to the left of the second word. The game should continue until the child has matched all of the words to form actual compound words.

Reproducibles that Can Be Used to Improve Ability in Structural or Morphemic Analysis

The chapter now includes several reproducibles that you can use for improving your pupils' ability in various elements of structural or morphemic analysis.

Continued

A C T I V I T Y   *Continued*

Name _____ Grade _____

Making Compound Words
Third-Grade Level

There are two compound words under the blank in each sentence.
Write part of one word and part of the other word to make a compound word. The new compound word must make sense in the sentence.
The first one is done for you.

1. My father has always liked to pick _____blackberries_____ .
   blackbird/strawberries

2. A man that I know won a _____ as a prize in
   a contest.   greenhouse/bluebird

3. Sarah's father built her a _____ for her birthday.
   housefly/playground

4. Since I had a _____ , I had to go to the dentist.
   toothbrush/headache

5. My father landed a large _____ in the ocean
   off Florida.   jellyfish/sailboat

6. Our class once saw a cocoon turn into a beautiful black and gold
   _____.
   buttermilk/horsefly

7. My puppy Honey chewed a big hole in a _____ when
   she was left alone in the kitchen yesterday. dishpan/tablecloth

8. Eddie is my favorite _____ in third grade.
   playhouse/classmate

ACTIVITY

9. The _____ is a make-believe person who is supposed to help children go to sleep.

   postman/sandbox

10. A _____ is used to break the shells of nuts before eating them.

    peanut/firecracker

11. Betty never does her _____ in the evening but watches television instead.   homemade/workman

12. A _____ is a pretty yellow flower that grows in the woods.

    buttermilk/cupcake

Continued

ACTIVITY
Continued

Name _____ Grade _____

Syllable Circles
Third-Grade Level

Draw a small circle inside of each large circle for each syllable that is found in the word under the circle. The first one has been done for you.

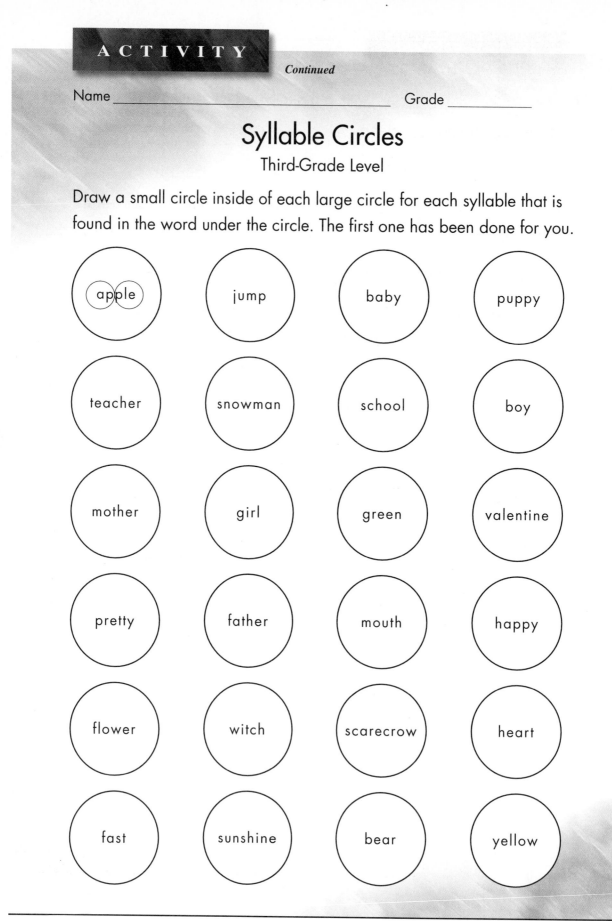

A C T I V I T Y

Name _____ Grade _____

The Contraction Path
Third-Grade Level

Write each contraction on the line under the two words it is composed of.
Begin at START and continue to FINISH. You may have a partner help you.

Start | can not | do not | I will | I am | he is | did not | was not | you are | it is | I have | has not | did not | will not | are not | have not | does not | I have | you will | she is | has not | let us | he would | Finish

DESCRIPTION OF SEMANTIC (CONTEXTUAL) ANALYSIS

Semantic analysis (contextual analysis or *context clues)* is a word-identification technique in which the reader determines the meaning and sometimes the pronunciation of unknown words by examining the context in which they are located. That context can be the sentence, the adjacent sentences, the paragraph, or the entire passage. It usually also involves syntactical or grammatical clues.

Sometimes semantic analysis is not very helpful (Schatz & Baldwin, 1986). Although context may determine the particular meaning of a word, it may not readily reveal it to the reader (Deighton, 1959). An informal survey of difficult words in children's periodicals, textbooks, and trade books indicates that usable semantic clues are provided only about one-third of the time (Gunning, 1990). Some reading specialists estimate that the average reader is able to use context successfully only between 5 and 20 percent of the time (Jenkins, Matlock, & Slocum, 1980; Nagy & Herman, 1987).

Even when context may be very helpful, some children do not take advantage of it. However, children become more proficient in its use as they progress through the elementary grades. They also must be given direct instruction and practice in the use of semantic analysis if they are to use it effectively. A teacher cannot simply tell children to use semantic or contextual clues without providing them with instruction and practice in their use. They also must be given feedback to let them know that they are correct (Carnine, Kameenui, & Coyle, 1984).

Reading specialists have determined that there are a number of different kinds of semantic clues. Although the categories of semantic clues differs somewhat, here is one classification that often has been used (Herber, 1967, p. 16).

- **Experience clues.** A reader uses prior knowledge to determine the meaning of the unknown word. That is why it is imperative for a child to have much appropriate prior knowledge to be an effective reader either of narrative or content material.
- **Association clues.** A reader attempts to associate the unknown word with known words. For example: That *loquacious* man certainly talks a great deal.
- **Synonym clues.** There is a synonym to the known word in the sentence to explain it. For example: Since my father needed to have a mole checked for possible skin cancer, he went to a *dermatologist,* or a doctor who specializes in skin diseases.
- **Summary clues.** Several sentences can be used to summarize the meaning of the unknown word.
- **Comparison or contrast clues.** There is a comparison or contrast to the unknown word in the sentence or paragraph which gives the word's meaning.
- **Previous contact clues.** The child can ascertain the meaning of the unknown word from previous contact with a similar word.

Other similar classification systems for semantic clues are found in Gunning, 1996, and Rinsky, 1997. You may want to consult one or both of them for additional information.

With the current emphasis on whole language and reading as a global, meaning-based process that stresses comprehension from the beginning, it is obvious that semantic analysis is the single most useful technique of word identification. However, it is the most effective when used in conjunction with structural and graphophonic analysis and when there are few unknown words in the reading material. Usually there should not be more than one in fifty unknown words in the material if semantic analysis is to be used effectively.

Semantic analysis can be presented as early as the emergent literacy level when the teacher orally provides a sentence with an omitted word. The teacher then asks the children to provide a word orally that makes sense in that sentence. This also is readiness for the cloze procedure. At the primary-grade level the importance of semantic clues should be explained to children, and they should be encouraged to use context to deduce the meaning of unknown words that they meet while reading. In addition, children at this level can be asked to read simple sentences silently and select the omitted word that makes sense in each sentence from the options that are provided. For example:

Rachel received many nice _____ for Hanukkah.

gates

gifts

gets

It is very important to ensure that children in the primary grades always are encouraged to supply words that make sense while reading, both silently and orally, even if the provided words are not the actual words found in the reading material. All primary-grade children should be taught that semantic analysis is not merely guessing at the meaning of unknown words. Rather it is a calculated estimate of the meaning of unknown words that demands interpretive thinking on the child's part.

Especially in the primary grades, children often are discouraged from risk-taking, which in turn may hinder their reading since too much stress then is placed on word-perfect oral reading. However, the practice of word substitution can be carried to an excess when children miscall up to half of the words in the reading material. Such children should continue to have instruction and/or reinforcement either in sight word identification, structural analysis, or graphophonic analysis, depending on their weaknesses.

Here are the advantages of using semantic clues:

- Most children can identify words in context that they cannot identify in isolation. A possible exception may be children with learning disabilities.

- Readers who can use context clues become independent decoders much more quickly. They learn to be good predictors of what a word might be. They then are able to confirm or reject their prediction, depending on whether or not it makes sense in the context of what they are reading. They then quickly read on.
- Words that do not have consistent sound-symbol relationship may be more easily generalized by using semantic clues.
- Children who have difficulty with phonic skills that require closer attention to visual features may identify unknown vocabulary more easily in this way.

Here are some of the limitations of using semantic clues:

- Since beginning readers have a very limited reading vocabulary, they often have difficulty in using semantic clues effectively.
- Since there are many synonyms in English that could make sense in different contexts, when semantic clues are used alone, this may not result in exact word identification. When the exact word is required, a child must also use other clues such as structural or graphophonic cues along with semantic clues.
- In a number of cases the surrounding context may not be enough to provide for accurate word identification or may provide misleading information about the word.

In summary, semantic (contextual) analysis is the one technique of word identification that best represents the concept of reading as a language-based process that emphasizes comprehension. It also best reflects the true whole language philosophy. Therefore, it undoubtedly should receive the most emphasis as a word identification technique, with the possible exception of children with learning disabilities who may need more emphasis placed on the other word identification techniques. However, these children also need to understand the importance of using semantic clues.

STRATEGIES AND MATERIALS FOR IMPROVING SEMANTIC (CONTEXTUAL) ANALYSIS

The chapter now includes several strategies that early childhood teachers can use to improve the semantic (contextual) analysis skills of their children. All of them have been used successfully by my teacher-trainees in various kinds of tutoring situations over the years. All of these strategies should fit in fairly well with the whole language philosophy, since they emphasize word identification in context.

Wide Reading of Interesting Materials

Wide reading of various kinds of materials undoubtedly is the single best way of improving ability in semantic

(contextual) analysis. This reading can take place in predictable books (see the list of predictable books in Chapter 2) and nursery rhymes in which the children participate. It also can be from dictated language-experience stories, trade books of various types including picture storybooks and simple informational books, simple children's newspapers and magazines, and child-written books.

As you know, reading is a skill that improves the most with motivated practice from material that the children can read easily. Therefore, it is obvious that the more a young child reads, even if it is from simple materials, the better the reader he or she should become. However, children who have difficulty with reading activities such as children with learning disabilities or other special needs children often do as little reading as possible and therefore do not make good reading progress. Although it may be hard to motivate such children, it should be possible to do so by using very interesting, easy, predictable materials that are especially chosen for them. You may be successful with such children by encouraging them to read self-selected interesting, easy materials. Predictable books including the various Dr. Seuss books usually have been very effective with various kinds of special needs children, including those with learning disabilities.

Listening for Reading Miscues

Children can be helped to become aware of *miscues* (errors) that interfere with comprehension by having them listen to material (either teacher-read or tape-recorded), indicate when disruptions occur, and state why the miscue is inappropriate. When a child meets an unknown word in context or is not aware that a disruptive miscue (one that interferes with comprehension) has occurred, he or she usually should finish reading the sentence because it may provide additional useful information. Usually the words *after the unknown word* provide more help than the words before it. A *place-holder* (a word that makes sense and is syntactically [grammatically] appropriate) can be used until new information makes it necessary to try another response. If neither strategy is effective, rereading the sentence containing the unknown word may help. However, before doing so, the child should examine the unknown word by using graphophonic (phonic) clues along with semantic clues—a powerful combination method of word identification. If none of these strategies is effective, it may be useful to read the sentence before or after the sentence containing the unknown word.

Dahl and Samuels (1977) have presented the following strategy for using semantic clues:

1. Use information from the passage, prior knowledge, and language clues.
2. Make a prediction as to which word is the most likely to occur.

3. Compare the printed and predicted words to see if they fit.
4. Accept or reject the prediction.

Taylor and Norbush (1983) also have recommended a four-step procedure for encouraging children to self-correct disruptive miscues. It contains the following steps:

1. One a one-to-one basis, the child reads a 100- to 300-word passage at the appropriate instructional level to the teacher who gives very little feedback.
2. The teacher praises the child for something well done in this oral reading, especially his or her self-correction.
3. One or two uncorrected miscues are shown to the child by reading his or her rendition to the child and having the child tell what word did not make sense or sound right.
4. The child is helped to recognize the miscued words by demonstrating how context and graphic clues could have been used.

Presenting the Concept that Semantic (Contextual) Clues Are Not Always Effective

It is important for children to learn that semantic (contextual) clues are not always effective in helping determine the meaning and/or pronunciation of an unknown word. The child should look at the following three groups of words with your help. He or she then should notice that some sentences provide very good clues, others provide limited help, and still others provide no help at all.

Group I (Context is effective for the child.)
1. On a clear day, the s _ _ is always shining.
2. When it rains, a child needs to take an u _ _ _ _ _ _ with him or her to school.
3. I like to make a snowman out of pretty white s _ _ _.

Group II (Context provides some clues for the child.)
1. I saw a bl_____ flying last night. (bluebird, blackbird)
2. Jenny would like to get a b_____ for her birthday. (bicycle, ball, bird)
3. I really like to eat a h_____. (hamburger, hot dog)

Group III (Context provides no help.)
1. The m_____ came yesterday.
2. That man is very h_____.
3. Today is a cl_____ day.

Magazine Pictures

An example of an emergent literacy strategy for semantic analysis is to provide the child with pictures from magazines or catalogs, and then read some sentences aloud or record them on tape, omitting one word in each sentence that can be completed by the use of one of the pictures. Have the child show the picture that can take the place of the omitted word.

Rebuses

Another emergent literacy activity is to have the child dictate (or the teacher formulate) a chart that uses *rebuses* (pictures) in place of some of the difficult but interesting vocabulary words. One of the most effective ways to use rebuses is by providing them in recipes for cooking or baking activities. The recipe is written on chart paper. Baking cookies, gingerbread figures, or bread, or making deviled eggs or butter, among other items, are all appropriate for this kind of activity.

Fill in the Blanks

Print a number of simple sentences on the chalkboard or on a transparency. Each sentence should contain an omitted word that could reasonably be replaced by a number of different alternatives. Have the child read a sentence aloud, completing it with one possible option. Other children in this group can suggest alternatives. Read each sentence aloud if your pupils cannot do so. In this case the children suggest possible words for each omitted word. Here are several examples:

My favorite food is _____.
Kay would like to receive a _____ for Christmas.
My favorite color is _____.

Variation

As a variation, divide a large piece of 12″ × 18″ manila paper or newsprint into fourths. Print four sentences on the chalkboard. In each sentence one word is omitted that can be illustrated by a primary-grade child. Have the child read each sentence silently and then draw the illustration of the omitted word on the proper place on the sheet of paper. Each sentence should allow for a creative response. Here are several sentences that can be used in this activity:

The animal that I would really like to have for a pet is _____.
Mario's favorite toy is _____.
My favorite person is _____.

Self-Monitoring

It is very important for children to learn to monitor their silent and oral reading. The concept of self-monitoring is explained very briefly in the next chapter; it is a mind-set in which a child consistently thinks about what he or she is reading. If he or she is not understanding the material effectively, the child must learn how to apply fix-up strategies, which also are explained briefly in the next chapter. Good readers of all ages monitor their comprehension much more effectively than do poor readers.

Simple Variations of the Cloze Procedure

The cloze procedure is one of the most useful ways of improving ability in semantic analysis since it involves using both semantic (meaning) and syntactic (grammatical) clues. The cloze procedure is most relevant with older students; a young child must have completed a number of readiness activities before being exposed to actual cloze experiences.

As one example, select sentences from experience stories and print each sentence on a strip of tagboard, omitting one word. Then print each omitted word on a word card. Have the child place the proper word card in each sentence strip. You can make slits in each sentence strip if you want. Then have the child read each sentence aloud. As another example, print a short passage of the appropriate reading level on a transparency and place masking tape over the words to be omitted. Do not omit more than one out of every ten words. Have a child or several children guess each omitted word. After each guess is made, remove the masking tape and have the children compare the actual word with their guesses. As one more example, *zipper cloze* involves printing some sentences on an overhead projector with one word covered by a small piece of tagboard. Place a piece of tape across the tagboard to fasten it to the transparency so that the tape serves as a *hinge*. Then when you want to show the word to the children after having them guess what it might be, lift the tagboard flap. In the upper primary grades, children should be able to discuss why various answers may or may not be possible in terms of semantic or syntactic clues.

REPRODUCIBLES FOR IMPROVING ABILITY IN SEMANTIC (CONTEXTUAL) ANALYSIS

This chapter concludes by including several ready-to-use reproducibles that any early childhood teacher can use to improve his or her pupils' ability in semantic analysis. Any of them can be used in their present form or modified in any way in which you wish. It is important that you make any of these reproducibles compatible with your reading program.

Name _____ Grade _____

These Words Don't Belong
Third-Grade Level

Read each sentence and cross out the one word that doesn't belong in that sentence.

1. When our class went to the bread zoo, my favorite animal was an elephant.

2. When a dog meets a lake porcupine, it can lead to real trouble.

3. Anita's favorite subject in hamburger school is reading.

4. In January my brother and I made a big hot snowman.

5. Swimming in a lake or pool in the hot winter weather is fun.

6. Josie has to feed her neighbor's raining cats and clean their litter box.

7. My father and mother bought a new fish car last weekend.

8. How many brothers and lion sisters do you have?

9. Bobbi had to go to the grocery store yesterday to buy some fast milk.

10. My mother won't let me have a skateboard for my month birthday.

11. Fanny really would like to learn how to use a baby computer.

12. What is your favorite holiday—Halloween or brown Thanksgiving?

Name _____ Grade _____

What is the Mystery Word?
Third-Grade Level

Read this entire story to yourself or with a partner. As you read it, try to figure out what one word has been omitted from the whole story. After you have read the entire story, write in the one mystery word in each blank in this story so that it will make sense.

Jennifer feels as though she is the only child in the world who has never visited _____. Jennifer is a pupil in Ms. Jackson's third-grade class at Fairview School. She is a very good pupil who really likes school. She lives with her parents and her two younger brothers in a small city in the Midwest.

Although Jennifer is usually very happy, she has been disappointed that her family has never visited _____. So many of the children in her class at school have been to _____. It is supposed to be so much fun there, and there are lots of things to do at _____. Jennifer also has heard that there are lots of things to eat at _____. Besides, there are many stores at _____ with lots of interesting souvenirs to buy.

Oh, how very much Jennifer wants to visit _____ during her next summer vacation. Do you think that she and her family will be able to visit _____ then? She and her family can even fly right from her city to Florida so that she can visit _____. Let's really hope that Jennifer will get her wish to see _____ next summer.

SUGGESTED ACTIVITIES

1. Read a predictable book three or four times to a four- or five-year-old child. Encourage the child to read the book along with you and later to read it aloud himself or herself. Did the child read the book accurately, or did he or she retell the story using only a few of the predictable language patterns? How effective do you think that predictable books are in encouraging beginning reading? Summarize your findings orally or in writing.

2. If possible, teach a four- or five-year-old child several difficult-to-learn letter names or sight words using one of the tactile strategies that was described. Summarize orally or in writing how effective this tactile strategy seemed to be and how much the child enjoyed it. Would you use this tactile strategy again? Why or why not? Discuss your results with your classmates.

3. If possible, attempt one of the cooking activities mentioned in this chapter with a young child. Summarize orally or in writing its effectiveness in teaching the target letter name. Can you think of more effective ways to accomplish the same purpose? What are your ideas, and why do you think that they might be more effective?

4. Construct one of the games for improving sight word identification that was mentioned in this chapter. If possible, play the game with one or several children who are attending first or second grade. Summarize orally or in writing your view about how successful this game was in improving sight word identification. Do you believe that its use encouraged undue competition for the children or instead was very motivating for them?

5. Take a commercially available phonics test for teachers. If you did not do well on this test, you should study the phonics elements and generalizations that were included in this chapter again. Every early literacy teacher needs to have a good mastery of phonics so he or she can teach them effectively. The following book includes a test that can be used for this purpose:

   G. Thomas Baer. (1999). *Self-paced phonics: A text for education.* Upper Saddle River, NJ: Prentice Hall.

6. Use Elkonin boxes with one or more children in first or second grade. Summarize orally or in writing how effective they were in teaching phoneme (sound)-grapheme (symbol) correspondence.

7. Construct some of your own hinks pinks and then share them with several children or with your classmates.

8. Construct a number of your own make-believe compound words, and then have several children in second or third grade determine whether or not they are real or make-believe compound words.

9. Construct your own Group I sentences (context is effective for the child), Group II sentences (context provides some clues for the child), and Group III sentences (context provides no help). Be prepared to turn these sentences in. You may want to have some children in second or third grade attempt to complete the sentences if this is possible.

SELECTED REFERENCES

Anselmo, S., Rollins, P., & Schuckman, R. (1986). *R is for rainbow.* Menlo Park, CA: Addison-Wesley Publishing Company.

Brown, R., & Carey, S. (1995). *Hands-on alphabet activities for young children.* West Nyack, NY: The Center for Applied Research in Education.

Cheek, E., Flippo, R., & Lindsey, J. (1997). *Reading for success in elementary schools* (pp. 115–136). Madison, WI: Brown & Benchmark Publishers.

Fry, E., & Perry, Leslie. (1987). *Fry's instant word puzzles and activities.* Englewood Cliffs, NJ: Prentice Hall.

Gipe, J. (1998). *Multiple paths to literacy* (pp. 168–205). Upper Saddle River, NJ: Merrill.

Graves, M., Juel, C., & Graves, B. (1998). *Teaching reading in the 21st century* (pp. 134–183). Boston: Allyn & Bacon.

Gunning, T. (1996). *Creating reading instruction for all children* (pp. 77–161). Needham Heights, MA: Allyn & Bacon.

Heilman, A., Blair, T., & Rupley, W. (1998). *Principles and practices of teaching reading* (pp. 146–200). Upper Saddle River, NJ: Prentice Hall.

Machado, J. (1995). *Early childhood experiences in language arts* (pp. 359–389). NY: Delmar Publishers.

Mallett, J. (1975). *Classroom reading activities kit.* NY: The Center for Applied Research in Education.

May, F. (1998). *Reading as communication* (pp. 141–203). Upper Saddle River, NJ: Merrill.

McAllister, E. (1987). *Primary reading skills activities kit* (pp. 123–203). West Nyack, NY: The Center for Applied Research in Education.

Morrow, L. (1997). *Literacy development in the early years* (pp. 228–255). Needham Heights, MA: Allyn & Bacon.

Muncy, P. (1995). *Complete book of illustrated reading and writing activities for the primary grades* (pp. 1–170). West Nyack, NY: The Center for Applied Research in Education.

Pavlak, S. (1985). *Classroom activities for correcting specific reading problems* (pp. 8–90). West Nyack, NY: Parker Publishing Company.

Rinsky, L. (1997). *Teaching word recognition skills* (pp. 37–119). Upper Saddle River, NJ: Gorsuch Scarisbrick Publishers.

Snow, C., Burns, M., & Griffin, P. (1998). *Preventing reading difficulties in young children.* Washington, DC: National Academy Press.

WORKS CITED IN CHAPTER 4

Adams, M. (1990). *Beginning to read: Thinking and learning about print.* Cambridge, MA: MIT Press.

Anbar, A. (1982). Reading acquisition of preschool children without systematic instruction. *Early Childhood Reading Quarterly, 1,* 69–83.

Anderson, R., Hiebert, E., Scott, J., & Wilkinson, I. (1985). *Becoming a nation of readers: The report of the commission on reading.* Washington, DC: National Institute of Education.

Baer, G. T. (1999). *Self-paced phonics: A text for education.* Upper Saddle River, NJ: Prentice Hall.

Baghban, M. (1984). *Our daughter learns to read.* Newark, DE: International Reading Association.

Bloomfeld, L. (1942). Linguistics and reading. *Elementary English Review, 19,* 125–130, 183–186.

Brown, R. (1973). *A first language: The early stages.* Cambridge, MA: Harvard University Press.

Carnine, D., Kameenui, E., & Coyle, G. (1984). Utilization of contextual information in determining the meaning of unfamiliar words. *Reading Research Quarterly, 19,* 188–204.

Chall, J. (1967 & 1983). *Learning to read: The great debate.* NY: Macmillan.

Clymer, T. (1963). The utility of phonic generalizations in the primary grades. *The Reading Teacher, 12,* 252–258.

Cunningham, Patricia. (1980). Teaching were, with, what, and other "four-letter" words. *The Reading Teacher, 34,* 160–163.

Cunningham, P., & Allington, R. (1994). *Classrooms that work: They all can read and write.* NY: HarperCollins.

Cunningham, P., & Cunningham, J. (1992). Making words: Enhancing the invented spelling-decoding connection. *The Reading Teacher, 46,* 106–115.

Dahl, P. R., and Samuels, S. J. (1974). A mastery based experimental program for teaching poor readers high speed word recognition skills. Unpublished paper, University of Minnesota.

Deighton, L. (1959). *Vocabulary development in the classroom.* NY: Columbia University Press.

Dickerson, D. (1982). A study of the use of games to reinforce sight vocabulary. *The Reading Teacher, 36,* 46–49.

Durrell, D. (1980). Letter-name value in reading and spelling. *Reading Research Quarterly, 16,* 159–163.

Dykstra, R. (1974). Phonics and beginning reading instruction. In C. Walcutt, J. Lampert, & G. McCracken (Eds.), *Teaching reading: A phonic/linguistic approach to developmental reading* (pp. 373–397). NY: Macmillan.

Ehri, L. (1991). Development of the ability to read words. In R. Barr, M. Kamil, P. Rosenthal, and P. D. Pearson (Eds.), *Handbook of reading research, volume II* (pp. 383–417). NY: Longman.

Ehri, L. & Robbins, C. (1992). Beginners need some decoding skill to read words by analogy. *Reading Research Quarterly, 27,* 13–26.

Elhert, L. (1996). *Eating the alphabet.* NY: Red Wagon.

Elkonin, D. (1973). Reading in the USSR. In J. Downing (Ed.), *Comparative reading* (pp. 551–579). NY: Macmillan.

Fry, E., Kress, J., & Fountoukidis, D. (1993). *The reading teacher's book of lists.* Englewood Cliffs, NJ: Prentice Hall.

Groff, P. (1986). The maturing of phonics instruction. *The Reading Teacher, 19,* 912–923.

Groff, P. (1981). Teaching reading by syllables. *The Reading Teacher, 14,* 659–664.

Guarino, D. (1989). *Is your mama a llama?* NY: Scholastic.

Gunning, T. (1996). *Creating reading instruction for all children.* Boston: Allyn & Bacon.

Gunning, T. (1990). *How useful is context?* Unpublished study. New Haven, CT: Southern Connecticut State University.

Harris, A., & Jacobson, M. (1982). *Basic reading and writing vocabularies.* NY: Macmillan.

Harwell, J. (1989). *Complete reading disabilities handbook.* West Nyack, NY: The Center for Applied Research in Education.

Herber, H. (1967). *Teaching reading in content areas.* Englewood Cliffs, NJ: Prentice Hall.

Hiebert, E. (1981). Developmental patterns and interrelationships of preschool children's print awareness. *Reading Research Quarterly, 16,* 230–260.

Hildreth, G. (1936). Developmental sequences in name writing. *Child Development, 7,* 291–302.

Houghton-Mifflin. (1981). *Sound-sense strategy.* Boston, MA: Houghton Mifflin.

Jenkins, J., Matlock, B., & Slocum, T. (1989). Approaches to vocabulary instruction. *Reading Research Quarterly, 24,* 215–235.

Lapp, E., & Flood, J. (1986). *Teaching students to read.* NY: Macmillan.

Lass, B. (1982). Portrait of my son as an early reader. *The Reading Teacher, 36,* 20–28.

Lomax, R., & McGee, L. (1987). Young children's concepts about print and reading: Toward a model of word reading acquisition. *Reading Research Quarterly, 22,* 219–256.

Martin, B., Jr. (1967). *Brown bear, brown bear, what do you see?* NY: Holt, Rinehart, & Winston.

May, F. (1994). *Reading as communication.* NY: Merrill/Macmillan.

McBroom, M., Sparrow, J., & Eckstein, C. (1944). *Scale for determining a child's reader level.* Iowa City, IA: Bureau of Publications, Extension Service, University of Iowa, p. 11.

Miller, W. (1998). First-grade children's perceptions of reading. *Arizona Reading Journal, 25,* 7–12.

Morgan, A. (1987). The development of written language awareness in Black preschool children. *Journal of Reading Behavior, 19,* 49–67.

Nagy, W. & Herman, P. (1987). Breadth and depth of vocabulary knowledge: Implications for acquisition and instruction. In M. McKeown & M. Curtis (Eds.), *The nature of vocabulary acquisition* (pp. 19–35). Hillsdale, NJ: Lawrence Erlbaum.

Richek, M. (1997–1998). Readiness skills that predict initial word learning using two different methods of instruction. *Reading Research Quarterly, 13,* 200–222.

Rinsky, M. (1997). *Teaching word recognition skills.* Upper Saddle River, NJ: Gorsuch Scarisbrick Publishers.

Samuels, J. (1967). Attentional processes in reading: The effect of pictures in the acquisition of reading responses. *Journal of Educational Research, 58,* 337–342.

Samuels, J. (1994). Toward a theory of automatic information processing in reading revisited. In R. Ruddell, M. Ruddell, & H. Singer (Eds.). *Theoretical models and processes of reading* (pp. 816–837). Newark, DE: International Reading Association.

Schatz, E., & Baldwin, R. (1986). Context clues are unreliable predictors of word meanings. *Reading Research Quarterly, 21,* 439–453.

Singer, H., Samuels, S., & Spiroff, J. (1973–1974). The effect of pictures and contextual conditions on learning responses to printed words. *Reading Research Quarterly, 9,* 555–567.

Snow, C., Burns, M., & Griffin, P. (1998). *Preventing reading difficulties in young children.* Washington, DC: National Academy Press.

Stahl, S., Osborne, J., & Lehr, F. (1990). *Beginning to read: Thinking and learning about print: A summary.* Urbana, IL: Center for the Study of Reading, University of Illinois at Urbana-Champaign.

Taylor, W. (1953). Cloze procedure: A new tool for measuring readability. *Journalism Quarterly, 30,* 415–433.

Taylor, B. M. & Norbush, L. (1983). Oral reading for meaning: A technique for improving word identification skills. *The Reading Teacher, 39,* 234–237.

DEVELOPING COMPETENCY IN VOCABULARY AND COMPREHENSION SKILLS

CONCEPTS THAT YOU SHOULD LEARN FROM READING THIS CHAPTER

After reading this chapter, you will be able to:

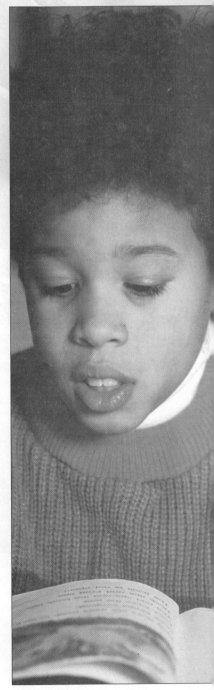

- **Explain the different types of conceptual (meaning) vocabularies and how children develop them**

- **Describe classroom-tested strategies and materials for improving conceptual (meaning) vocabularies in young children**

- **Define the following aspects of comprehension, and list and describe the various subskills that comprise them:**
  - literal (textually explicit or factual)—Right There or Reading the Lines
  - interpretive (textually implicit or inferential)—Think and Search or Reading Between the Lines

- critical (textually implicit or evaluative)—Reading Between the Lines
- creative (in script or schema, implicit or applied)—On My Own

- **Illustrate strategies and materials that can be used to improve the ability of young children in conceptual (meaning) vocabularies of various types**

- **Illustrate and explain strategies and materials that can be used to improve the ability of young children in all of the various aspects of comprehension**

There is a traditional story in reading instruction about a boy named Johnny, whose teacher asked him to read a paragraph of a story aloud. After he had read it flawlessly, his teacher said, "Now Johnny, will you please tell us what it was about?" Johnny is reported to have said "I don't know. I wasn't listening." This may be a true story or merely fiction. In any case, it serves to prove the point that without comprehension there is truly no reading, but merely pronouncing words.

After reading this chapter, you should be able to present and/or reinforce both conceptual knowledge and reading comprehension skills very effectively.

DIFFERENT KINDS OF CONCEPTUAL (MEANING) VOCABULARIES

It may be helpful to first define *conceptual (meaning) vocabularies.* This refers to the number of words to which an individual adult or child can attach one or more meanings. Literacy teachers also should understand that there are several different types of meaning vocabularies. As an example, the *listening vocabulary* is the first type of vocabulary that a young child must acquire. It is primarily learned in the home by hearing family members and others with whom the young child comes in contact speak. It is obvious that if a very young child attends any type of early childhood facility, the adults there also are very important in the acquisition of the listening vocabulary. Next, the young child learns the *speaking vocabulary* from the imitation and modeling of family members and other adults with whom he or she comes in contact. That is why it is important for the young child's speech models to use correct grammar and interesting, precise vocabulary. That is also the reason the child may learn a dialect such as the African-American dialect or the Latino dialect.

Next the child may learn the *reading vocabulary,* although he or she may learn the *writing vocabulary* first. Or, the reading vocabulary and the writing vocabulary may well develop simultaneously. The reading vocabulary is primarily developed in school unless the child is an early reader, in which case it can be learned in the home or in some kind of child-care facility. By the time the child is in the intermediate grades, his or her reading vocabulary usually much exceeds the speaking vocabulary unless the child is a disabled reader. The fourth type of vocabulary is the *writing vocabulary,* which also primarily is learned in school, although a start can be made before school entrance especially if the child is encouraged to use *invented spelling.* Normally the writing vocabulary is the smallest, because a person often does not use a number of words in his or her writing that are used in speaking or met while reading.

The fifth type of vocabulary is the *potential or marginal vocabulary.* This type of meaning vocabulary is composed of all the words that the child may be able to determine the meaning of by using semantic (contextual) clues; by examining prefixes, suffixes, or word roots; or by understanding derivatives of words. It usually is impossible to determine the size of a child's potential vocabulary, since the context in which a word is located may determine whether or not the child will know its meaning. It is important for each child in the primary grades to have a good understanding of context and know the meaning of many words so that he or she will have a large and useful potential vocabulary. However, the potential vocabulary is of fairly limited importance in the primary grades in comparison to its importance in the middle-upper grades.

Research studies have found that meaning vocabulary knowledge is related to reading comprehension.

However, this conclusion also can be drawn by logical analysis. In a very well-known study, Davis (1944) researched the reading process and found by factor analysis of reading comprehension that it was composed of two primary skills—word meanings (vocabulary) acquisition, and reasoning ability, which probably can be equated with reading comprehension (Davis, 1944).

Chall (1987) has estimated that the average child begins first grade with about 5000 to 6000 words in his or her meaning vocabulary and that during the twelve years of schooling, the typical child learns about 36,000 more words. However, other researchers have found different results than Chall's. For example, in 1897 Canton found that six-year-old children have a vocabulary of 2000 words while in 1941 Smith stated that children in first grade have a vocabulary of about 24,000 words! Still later another researcher named Shibles (1959) wrote that the vocabulary of first-grade children was about 26,363 words. Over the years other researchers have come up with different results. It is clear that young children today undoubtedly have a more extensive meaning vocabulary than they did in the past due to the influence of television, computer software, the World Wide Web, and radio, among many other things. However, it is important to remember that whether young children "know" a word or are just able to repeat it superficially in context is a matter that must be determined by each teacher (Dale, 1965).

It is fairly obvious that the size of a child's meaning vocabulary does correlate positively with success in school. Meaning vocabulary consists of such elements as knowledge of the multiple meanings of words, knowledge of synonyms and antonyms, knowledge of homonyms and homographs, and understanding the meaning of relational terms. While some of these elements are relevant with young children, some of them are not.

According to Dale and O'Rourke (1971), knowing a word is not an either/or proposition. For example, they wrote about four stages in word knowledge:

1. I never saw it before.
2. I've heard of it, but I don't know what it means.
3. I recognize it in context—it has something to do with . . .
4. I know it. (p. 3)

Graves (1987) expanded the stages in learning words to include:

Task 1: Learning to read known words.

Task 2: Learning new meanings for known words.

Task 3: Learning new words that represent known concepts.

Task 4: Learning new words that represent new concepts.

Task 5: Classifying and enriching the meanings of known words.

Task 6: Moving words from receptive to expressive vocabulary.

As can be seen from the six tasks that were just described, even when a vocabulary word is "known," it often is a question of degree. For example, a person who uses *hairweaving* to style her hair obviously has a better understanding of just what is involved in this process than a person who does not.

At any grade level, developing vocabulary is not just a process of listing some vocabulary word and having children look up the definition of each one. Instead it is truly a part of living. For example, young children learn the approximately 6000 words that they know on first-grade entrance by interacting with family members, other adults, and other children, gradually learning the labels for people, animals, objects, and concepts that are found in their environment. As children grow and continue to have many varied experiences, their vocabularies continue to develop. For example, they learn such terms as *touchdown, goal, quarterback, fullback,* and *fourth down,* among others by being involved in football either as a participant or a spectator.

It also is important to realize that a word is seldom "known" in isolation. Rather it is usually "known" in the context of a phrase, a sentence, a paragraph, or an entire passage. Thus, a case can be made for learning the meanings of new words in a whole language setting rather than in isolated lists of words. For example, the word *run* has many different meanings depending upon the context in which it is located. For example, the following sentences illustrate only a very few of the meanings for this abstract word:

> I can *run* faster than anyone else in my class.
>
> When you spill a glass of water on the kitchen floor, it may *run* under the refrigerator.
>
> My mother has a *run* in her black pantyhose today.
>
> Latasha hit a home *run* yesterday.
>
> That play had a wonderful *run* on Broadway.
>
> I wonder who will *run* the soccer team next year.
>
> The bingo winner had a great *run* of luck, didn't she?

In summary, development of meaning vocabularies obviously is a complex process that must continue over many years. However, young children can make a beginning in this most important aspect of literacy.

THE CONE OF EXPERIENCES

Dale has proposed a *cone of experiences* that is relevant for a teacher of young children. This cone of experiences demonstrates the importance of what are called "activities of action" through which a child learns vocabulary and concepts by direct experience whenever possible. However, when hands-on experiences are not possible, children need "activities of observation" such as school trips, scientific experiments, demonstrations, interactive computer software, models, graphics, and visuals. Dale stated that learning concepts and vocabulary by beginning with written language instead of some type of experience is very difficult for disabled readers and children with learning disabilities (1969).

Dale has constructed a very helpful visual representation of his beliefs that he has called the *cone of experiences model for vocabulary building.* The figure on the following page shows Dale's "Cone of Experiences," and it is reprinted with the permission of Holt Rinehart, & Winston.

STRATEGIES, READY-TO-USE ACTIVITY SHEETS, AND GAMES FOR IMPROVING COMPETENCY IN CONCEPTS AND MEANING KNOWLEDGE

Strategies, ready-to-use activity sheets, and games for improving competency in many of the items included in Dale's cone of experiences are contained in this chapter. As you remember from previous chapters, you are encouraged to modify any of these strategies and materials to suit the needs, abilities, and interests of your own pupils.

Direct Experiences

Direct experiences are probably the single best way of developing the meaning vocabulary and conceptual knowledge of young children in the home, in any preschool setting, and in kindergarten and the primary grades. When using direct experiences of any kind for vocabulary and concept building, parents, day-care providers, or early childhood teachers should be certain to attempt to build vocabulary and concepts prior to the experience, during the experience, and after the experience. For example, before a kindergarten class takes a trip to the local wildlife preserve, the teacher should discuss with the children the types of animals, birds, and reptiles that they are likely to see there. He or she also should write some of the important vocabulary terms on the chalkboard or on a piece of large chart paper. During the experience the teacher can point out the wildlife they discussed in school. After the class returns to school, the children as a large group, a small group, or individually if there is a teacher's aide or volunteer available can again discuss the vocabulary. Sometimes the children can dictate a language-experience chart or story about the experience, gearing it toward emphasis of the vocabulary and concepts (see Chapter 2).

Each community has its own unique sites for direct experience excursions. Several examples of places that are interesting to young children for family or school trips include the zoo, wildlife preserve, forest preserve, pet shop, veterinarian's office, hospital, nursing home,

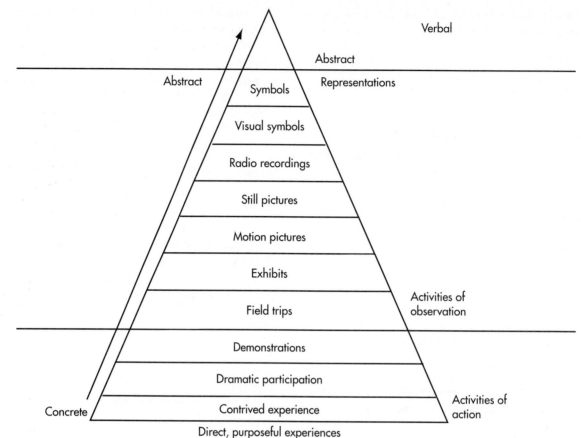

Figure from *Audio-Visual Methods In Teaching,* Third Edition by Edgar Dale, Copyright © 1969 by Holt, Rinehart and Winston, reproduced by permission of the publisher.

greenhouse, dairy, post office, police station, fire station, airport, train station or train trip, grain farm, dairy farm, pig farm, park, playground, and candy making facility.

Second-Hand or Vicarious Experiences

It is obvious that not all experiences for children can be direct experiences. Some must be second-hand or vicarious experiences. Although such experiences are not really a substitute for direct experiences for vocabulary and concept building, they often are more practical than are direct experiences. For example, when a third-grade class is studying about the solar system in a whole language thematic unit, they obviously cannot take a trip in a spaceship to see the planets. However, researching and constructing a model of the solar system which then is placed in their classroom should teach them a great deal about it.

There are a myriad of second-hand experiences which can be used for vocabulary and concept development, including using the World Wide Web, watching a videotape, watching films, looking at slides, using interactive computer software, using other computer software, watching scientific experiments or demonstrations, examining models and realia, looking at pictures, looking at dioramas, listening to cassette recordings, and listening to CDs. As in the case of direct experiences, the early

childhood teacher must pay particular attention to the conceptual and vocabulary development while using any type of second-hand experience if the children are going to gain as much as possible from it.

Wide Reading

Wide reading both to children and by children is one of the best ways of developing concepts and vocabulary. Think about all the concepts and vocabulary that a young child can learn by having a family member, early childhood provider, kindergarten teacher, or primary-grade teacher read aloud any type of trade book to him or her. This may be the case especially with simple informational books which most young children very much enjoy hearing. It is essential that young children hear all types of material read aloud to them on a daily basis.

According to research, children who are identified as voluntary or wide readers demonstrate high levels of reading achievement in both vocabulary and reading comprehension (Anderson, Wilson, & Fielding, 1985; Greaney, 1980; Taylor, Frye, & Marayama, 1990). In addition, Nagy and Herman (1987) have demonstrated that the number of words children learn through context during periods of sustained silent reading far outnumbers the words they learn from direct instruction. In another study, Anderson, Wilson, & Fielding (1988) found that the amount of "free reading" done by a child was the best predictor of vocabulary growth between grades two and five. Thus, you can see that encouraging young children to read for pleasure and information is very important even in the primary grades for vocabulary and conceptual development.

Books to Promote the Enjoyment of Words

In school, words can be used to create enjoyment and pleasure. Recite appropriate limericks, riddles, puns, fingerplays, and jokes to your children, and encourage them to share their favorites also. Here are some books that can be used to encourage word play and word enjoyment. There also are many others in your school library and local public library.

Berenstein, J., & Cohen, P. (1988). *Grand-slam riddles*. NY: Whitman. This book presents baseball riddles.

Burns, D. (1988). *Snakes alive!* Minneapolis: Lerner. This book includes a number of riddles about snakes.

Clark, E. (1991). *I never saw a purple cow and other nonsense rhymes*. Boston: Little, Brown. This collection contains about 120 rhymes about animals.

Cole, W. (1981). *Poem stew*. NY: Lippincott. This books contains a number of poems with interesting vocabulary for young children.

Corbett, P. (1990). *Playtime nursery*. NY: Doubleday. This is an illustrated collection of games, rhymes, and songs involving guessing, pretending, counting, clapping, and acting.

Defty, J. (1992). *Creative fingerplays and action rhymes*. Phoenix, AZ: Oryx Press. This is an index of fingerplays and action rhymes. It also includes a useful teacher's guide.

Degen, B. (1983). *Jamberry*. NY: Harper & Row. This is a book with highly motivating vocabulary.

Eichenberg, F. (1992). *Ape in a cape: An alphabet of odd animals*. NY: Harcourt Brace Jovanovich. This is a book with interesting words about animals.

Heller, R. (1991). *A cache of jewels and other collective nouns*. NY: Grossett & Dunlap. This book has rhyming text and illustrations that introduce a variety of collective nouns. Other books by the same author are *Many luscious lollipops* (adjectives) and *Up, up, and away* (adverbs).

Langstaff, J. (1974). *Oh, a' hunting we will go*. NY: Atheneum. Much interesting language is used in this traditional book.

Lear, E. (1991). *The owl and the pussycat*. NY: Putnam. In this traditional book, after a courtship of a year and a day, Owl and Pussycat buy a ring from Piggy and are married.

Martin, W., Jr., & Archambault, J. (1989). *Chicka chicka boom boom*. NY: Simon & Schuster. This interesting book contains creative language and is very appealing to young children.

Meddaugh, S. (1992). *Martha speaks*. Boston: Houghton Mifflin. This book is about the family dog who is named Martha and how she learns to speak after eating alphabet soup. It is a very humorous book for young children.

Pearson, T. (1984). *Old McDonald had a farm*. NY: Dial. This is a traditional tale which usually is sung.

Rosenbloom, J. (1988). *The world's best sports riddles and jokes*. NY: Sterling. This book features riddles and jokes from different sports.

Spier, P. (1967). *To market, to market*. NY: Doubleday. This is a traditional book for young children that uses creative, interesting language.

Watson, C. (1971). *Father fox's pennyrhymes*. NY: Harper & Row. This is an interesting book of rhymes for young children.

Zelinsky, P. (1990) *The wheels on the bus*. NY: Dutton. This traditional book is usually sung as a rhyming song.

Zuromskis, D. (1978). *The farmer in the dell*. Boston: Little, Brown & Company. This traditional book is usually sung as a rhyming song.

Word Play

Word play is a very interesting strategy for young children to use in motivating vocabulary development. It can provide multiple exposures to words in different contexts that are important to children for word meaning mastery. For example, Gale (1982) stated:

> Children who play with words show a stronger grasp of meaning than those who do not. To create or comprehend a pun, one needs to be aware of a word (p. 220).

Here are some ways to motivate young children to engage in word play:

- Use hinks pinks (see Chapter 4).
- Have children in the upper primary grades write words in ways that demonstrate their meanings. As an example, they may write *around* in a circle, *backward* as *drawcab*, *up* slanting upward, and *down* slanting downward.
- Ask children silly questions about the new words they have been learning. As an example: "Would you find a dolphin in a grocery store?"
- Explain to children what *puns* are, and provide some examples. Then ask children to make up puns or find

puns to bring to school. Let them explain the play on words to their peers who do not understand them. For example: What is black and white and red all over? The answer is the newspaper.

- Have children use what Ruddiman (1993) calls the "Vocab Game" to develop their word knowledge. For this game, have each child bring in a word from their reading each week. Have the children try to stump you with their words. In addition, other children can try to figure out their classmates' words. While this is being done, a simplified dictionary can be used, and children can use their knowledge of synonyms and antonyms. The class can earn points by stumping you or by figuring out another student's word. Have a child who acts as recorder keep a record of the information about the words which you can then duplicate for the class. This activity is the most applicable in the upper primary grades.
- Riddles can be very motivating to children. To use riddles, children must interact with others. To construct riddles, children must organize information and decide how this information can be presented in the form of a riddle. Riddles can be helpful in moving children from the literal to the interpretive level of understanding (Gale, 1982). Tyson and Mountain (1982) have written that riddles encourage children to use both semantic (meaning) clues and high-interest material, both of which can encourage vocabulary learning.
- Older children in the primary grades usually very much enjoy completing crossword puzzles and hidden-word puzzles. These also can be used to improve sight word recognition.

Scaffolding

Scaffolding also can be effective with young children in encouraging the development of concepts and vocabulary. Scaffolding in literacy is based loosely on the technique that house painters or carpenters use in their work. For example, typical house painters do not merely stand on a ladder. Instead they construct a scaffold by placing a wooden plank between two sawhorses or something similar. Then the house painters stand on the scaffold. This is both safer and more convenient for them.

In the same way, scaffolding provides help to young children instead of requiring them to complete a task on their own. For example, in scaffolding an adult provides a verbal response for a baby who is not yet able to make that response him/herself. When a baby says *dog,* the adult can say: "Do you see that dog walking with its owner? It is a big, brown, furry dog, and it looks very friendly, doesn't it?" In addition to expanding the child's vocabulary knowledge, the adult can ask the child to do something that extends his or her knowledge and demonstrates his or her understanding. Questions that consist of more than one word are preferable, such as, "What does that dog look like?" or "What does the dog's owner look like?" Questions beginning with *what, who, when,* and *where* usually elicit only one-word answers, while *why* questions are likely to elicit more complete answers that have required thought. As a child's vocabulary develops, the adults needs to provide much less scaffolding.

Key Word of the Day

An early childhood teacher can use the *key word of the day* as one strategy to improve the meaning and conceptual knowledge of young children. In this strategy, select a word that could be used in daily conversation. Then attach the key word to a word mobile that is hanging at some location in the classroom. Also write the word on the "Interesting Word Chart" that is found in the classroom. Then use the word over and over again in different contexts and have the children do the same.

Many of the children will try to guess the meaning of the word before the group time which takes place at the end of the school day. The key word of the day always is discussed near the end of the day. Predicting the meaning of the key word of the day becomes a game for the children. After the first week of school they understand that their teacher will use a new word each day or at least three times during the week.

Using words in meaningful situations builds word knowledge. Using words over and over helps children to remember them. When children begin to use words in their oral and written language, the words really belong to them.

Semantic Mapping (Webbing)

Semantic maps are a very helpful strategy for young children to use in improving meaning vocabulary knowledge, in improving reading comprehension, and in motivating writing. Semantic maps or webs for vocabulary or conceptual development can be used both before and after reading. Semantic maps can be called *semantic webs, story webs, advance organizers,* and *think-links,* among others. Although there may be slight variations among all of these strategies, they are very similar. Children often prefer to use semantic maps rather than semantic webs because with the latter they have to write the vocabulary terms inside the circles on the web, which often is difficult to do.

In formulating a map or web, you should first display a complete map on the chalkboard or a transparency using the vocabulary you wish to emphasize. With young children the map obviously should be a simple one. Illustrate to the children how the map shows the relationship among the selected vocabulary terms. Then place a partially completed map on the chalkboard or transparency and help the children complete it.

Only after they have had much experience with completing semantic maps or webs should young children be asked to complete a map, even with a partner(s). If semantic mapping is not presented very carefully and with much preparation, a child will likely experience much frustration and never wish to use this strategy again.

Here is an example of a simple semantic map for young children that has been constructed about deer.

Invented Spelling

Using *invented spelling* can help improve the vocabulary knowledge of young children. As is explained in Chapter 6, using invented spelling while writing for any purposes frees young children from the task of having to ask their teacher or a peer how to spell an unknown word. When invented spelling is used, the child is simply encouraged to spell any unknown words phonetically. In many cases, this invented spelling is understandable both to adults and to other children and allows children to explore new vocabulary.

Computer Software

Computer software lends itself very well to improving both conceptual and vocabulary knowledge. Simple computer crossword puzzles are very effective with young children for improving vocabulary knowledge. Crossword puzzles may be most valuable if they are based on a theme that is part of a whole language unit. With young children, begin with crossword puzzles that have only five to ten words and expand them as children develop proficiency in this technique. *Crossword Matic* (L & S Computerware) or a similar piece of software can easily be used to create crossword puzzle grids. All you have to do is supply the words and the word definitions.

To obtain a complete listing of computer software for improving vocabulary knowledge in young children, consult *The Educational Software Selector* (TESS) from the EPIE Institute (Hampton Bays, NY). This resource describes more than sixteen thousand pieces of software and videodisks. TESS is available on CD-ROM. Computer software is reviewed on a regular basis in the journals *Electronic Learning and Technology and Learning.*

GAME FOR IMPROVING ABILITY IN MEANING VOCABULARY

The chapter now includes one game for improving ability in meaning vocabulary. Although not in keeping with the whole language philosophy, a game can be motivating and useful with young children.

REPRODUCIBLES THAT CAN BE USED TO IMPROVE ABILITY IN MEANING VOCABULARY

The chapter now includes three reproducibles that you may want to consider using. You should modify any of these activity sheets in any way that seems relevant.

READING COMPREHENSION

Since reading comprehension is a very complex process that is related to the thinking process, it is difficult to explain it succinctly. Briefly, comprehension is constructing meaning from the printed material. It is an interactive process that requires using prior knowledge in combination with the printed material. When this definition is used, it is important to consider the characteristics of both the reader and the printed material. In the case of the reader, his or her prior knowledge of the material, interest in reading the material, purpose for reading the material, and ability to pronounce the words found in the material must be considered. In the case of the printed material, the number of difficult words, the syntax or sentence structure, the length of the sentences, and the format must be taken into account.

Although both prior knowledge and features of the print material are important, in most cases the reader's prior knowledge is most important. In addition, the more prior knowledge a reader possesses, the less use that he or she has to make of the printed material. That is the reason a specialist in a particular area (history, zoology, geology, etc.) usually reads material in that area much more rapidly and with better comprehension than does a person with less prior knowledge.

Another definition of comprehension describes it as a process of building a connection between what the reader knows and what he or she does not know, between the new and the old (Searfoss & Readence, 1994). On the other hand, Shanklin and Rhodes (1989) have written that comprehension is an evolving process, often beginning before a book is opened, changing as the material is read, and continuing to change even after the book is completed. The developmental nature of comprehension is enhanced when the child interacts with others about aspects of the material after it has been read. Therefore, classroom interaction about reading materials is important to comprehension development and should be planned carefully.

The Classification Game

To Construct the Game

Construct category sheets like the one shown for each group of children. You can divide the entire class into groups of three or four.

To Play the Game

When you give a signal, have the children begin writing as many words as they can think of that fit in each category. When you signal that the time is up, a child from each group should read the group's words to the class. Have the children compare their lists and discuss why they placed particular words in particular categories.

TV cartoons	Other TV shows	Movies

Other sample categories are mammals, vegetables, fruits, sports of various types, insects, and reptiles, among many others.

Name _____ Grade _____

Vocabulary Word Puzzles
Third-Grade Level

Here are some vocabulary words about transportation that you should know. Fill in the missing letters of each word. When you are finished, check each word to be sure that it is correct. You can work with a partner(s) if you want to.

1. au/_ _ /m_ /b_ _ _

2. h_ / _ _ /c_ _/_ _

3. t r _ _ _

4. i _ _

5. t _ _ cks

6. _ _ _ r/p_ _ _ _

7. _ _ _ p

8. e _ /g_ _ _

9. b_ _

10. s _ _ p

11. b_ /c_ _ /c_ _

12. v_ _

13. c_ _ _

14. mo/t_ _ _/b_ _ _

15. sno_ /mo/b_ _ _

Name _____   Grade _____

Hinks Pinks
Third-Grade Level

Make up your own hinks pinks. A hinks pink is a rhyming definition for a word of one syllable. The first one has been done for you. You may work with a partner(s) if you want, and you may use your dictionary.

1. tricky insect   _sly_____   _fly_____

2. useful material   _____   _____

3. prepare dessert   _____   _____

4. overweight feline   _____   _____

5. slight wind   _____   _____

6. uncontrollable youngster _____   _____

7. room divider   _____   _____

8. aquatic meal   _____   _____

9. black boat   _____   _____

10. ill boy   _____   _____

*Answers should be placed on another sheet. They are sly fly, good wood, bake cake, fat cat, slow blow, wild child, hall wall, fish dish, dark ark, sick Dick.

Name _____ Grade _____

Figurative Language
Third-Grade Level

Draw the literal meaning of each of the underlined figurative expressions on a separate sheet of paper. You should number each of your pictures. You may work with a partner(s) if you want to.

1. I hope that Joe and Jeff will <u>bury the hatchet</u> real soon.

2. Ashley always is as <u>slow as a turtle</u>.

3. I am as <u>hungry as a bear</u> today.

4. Mr. French is like <u>an ostrich with its head in the sand</u>.

5. Mrs. Levy <u>flew the coop</u> last week when she made a mistake at work.

6. There are days when my father feels <u>as old as the hills</u>.

7. Eve always acts as <u>sly as a fox</u>.

Contemporary research in reading comprehension also focuses on *schema theory*. Schema theory attempts to explain how a person stores information or knowledge in his or her mind, how the knowledge that is possessed is used, and how new knowledge is acquired. For example, Anderson wrote that comprehension involves activating or constructing a schema that accounts for the elements in a text, similar to constructing the outline of a script. As an example, a script outline for reading about a Civil War battle might include the following categories (also called *slots*): *battlefield, general, Union, Confederacy, amputation, victory,* and *defeat,* among others (Rumelhart, 1980). Comprehending the material then involves filling these slots with particular examples or instances.

Although activating a schema is necessary, reading is more complex than simply filling in slots. As they transact with printed material, competent readers constantly relate what they are reading to other experiences they have had and other information they have read. In addition, their interest in the material plays a very important role in the web of linkages they construct (Hartman, 1994).

Another recent focus of comprehension is *metacognition,* which is concerned with a reader's awareness of his or her own thinking as he or she is attempting to understand the printed material. It also is very important that a student learn how to *monitor* his or her own reading comprehension. Research has consistently found that good readers are much better at monitoring their comprehension than are poor readers. Later this chapter suggests several strategies for helping young children learn to monitor their comprehension.

Research also has shown close relationships between comprehension and decoding (word pronunciation) (Adams, 1991). Thus, developing decoding strategies to the automatic stage is important. However, you should remember that use of decoding strategies is only a means of accessing the meaning of the printed material. When good decoders have problems with comprehension, they need help in developing language proficiency and listening comprehension.

THE DIFFERENT LEVELS OF COMPREHENSION

In the past, comprehension skills usually have been divided into four major categories: literal, interpretive, critical, and creative. Today, comprehension is considered by most researchers to be a language-based process that cannot really be divided into arbitrary categories. Instead, they state that there are only two major categories of comprehension: vocabulary knowledge (word meaning) and the understanding of the reading material.

Some contemporary reading specialists have stated that since comprehension cannot be accurately divided into subskills in research studies, the various levels of comprehension therefore should not be taught to students.

I believe it is important to try to teach the most important aspects of comprehension separately, at least to most students, perhaps especially to disabled readers and children with learning disabilities. Students sometimes need to focus on a specific subskill of comprehension in order to understand and master it.

Here are the various levels of comprehension and the more important subskills that comprise them (Miller, 1999).

Textually Explicit (Literal or Factual—"Right There") Comprehension

- answering "Right There" questions found in the reading material
- locating directly stated main ideas
- locating significant and irrelevant details
- placing items in correct sequence or order
- reading and carrying out directions

Textually Implicit (Interpretive or Inferential—"Think and Search") Comprehension

- answering "Think and Search" questions (the reader has to deduce the answers from reading the materials)
- answering questions that call for interpretation (the answer is not found directly in the material)
- drawing conclusions and generalizations
- predicting the outcomes
- summarizing what was read
- sensing the author's mood and purpose
- locating implied main ideas

Critical (Textually Implicit or Evaluative—"Think and Search") Comprehension

- responding to questions in which the reader must evaluate the reading material
- discriminating between fact and fantasy (real and make-believe)
- evaluating the accuracy or truthfulness of the reading material
- sensing an author's biases
- recognizing propaganda techniques such as the bandwagon technique, testimonials, emotionally toned words, and cardstacking

Script Implicit (Schema Implicit, Creative, or Applied—"Reading Beyond the Lines") Comprehension

- answering "On My Own" questions (the reader has to combine his or her prior knowledge with the printed material to arrive at new knowledge or actions)
- applying knowledge gained from reading to one's own problem solving

- bibliotherapy (solving a problem through reading about a similar problem)
- cooking and baking after reading simplified recipes
- participating in art activities as a follow-up to reading
- creative writing of prose and poetry (including using invented spelling if necessary)
- participating in construction activities as a follow-up to reading
- participating in rhythm activities as a follow-up to reading
- putting on creative dramatics and socio-dramas
- puppetry
- conducting scientific experiments (demonstrations)
- writing creative book reports
- reading material that appeals to the emotions (the affective aspect of reading)

It is obvious that a number of these subskills of reading comprehension are not applicable with young children. Indeed, some of them are relevant only for older students in the middle school and beyond. However, all young children can make a beginning in all four levels of reading comprehension that were mentioned and should be provided with the opportunities to do so. The remainder of the chapter includes many classroom-tested strategies, reproducibles, and games that can be used to improve the ability of young children in the various elements of comprehension.

STRATEGIES AND MATERIALS THAT CAN BE USED TO IMPROVE ABILITY IN THE VARIOUS ELEMENTS OF READING COMPREHENSION

The chapter now includes a number of practical strategies and reproducible materials that can be used to improve children's abilities in the various aspects of reading comprehension. You are encouraged to modify any of these strategies or materials to suit your class's needs.

The Whole Language Approach, Thematic Unit Teaching, and Wide Reading

The whole language approach, thematic unit teaching, and wide reading probably are the single most effective ways to improve overall comprehension ability (see Chapter 2). In the whole language approach and thematic unit teaching, children read trade books of various types, including informational books, both for pleasure and information. These books usually are self-selected and are related to the theme of the unit that the child's class is studying. Skills are taught as needed either individually or in small groups. Since the reading material is self-selected and related to the theme of the unit, theoretically comprehension of what is read should not pose a problem for most children. In addition, the shared book experience

and the language-experience approach (LEA) are incorporated into whole language teaching. Both of these also greatly enhance a young child's reading comprehension.

Without a doubt, however, wide reading of interesting, motivating, relevant, easy material is the single best way to improve the reading comprehension of young children. The major purpose of such reading should be to understand what is read. Comprehension improves the most if the child has purposes for the reading. Such reading can take place in trade books of various types including predictable books, simple children's magazines and newspapers, simple informational books, and easy, relevant computer software. The child always should have purposes for the reading, monitor his or her comprehension as the reading is being done, and be prepared in some way to show that he or she has understood the material.

Prediction Strategies

There are a number of prediction strategies that can greatly improve a young child's comprehension skills. For example, encouraging children to use prediction both before and during reading is undoubtedly a highly effective way of improving reading comprehension. This simple strategy requires no special materials but merely a mind-set on the part of the young reader. If children make predictions about the content of the material before and during reading, their comprehension greatly improves. Prediction can begin as early as the preschool level when children are asked to make simple predictions about story content from hearing the title of a book read to them and during the reading aloud of the material. Before listening to a trade book being read aloud or reading it for themselves, children can answer the teacher's questions such as these:

What do you think this book (story) will be about?

What do you think will happen in this book (story)?

What would you like to have happen in this book (story)?

During the reading of the material, such questions as the following can be asked:

What do you think will happen next in this book (story)?

What would you like to have happen next in this book (story)?

What do you think that (story character) will do next in the book (story)?

What do you think that (story character) should do next in this book (story)?

Two other very effective prediction strategies that are applicable for use in the primary grades are the *Directed Listening-Thinking Activity (DL-TA)* (see Chapter 2) and

Directed Reading-Thinking Activity (DR-TA). These two prediction strategies follow basically the same format, except in the former the children listen to the material, while in the latter they read it for themselves. Both were developed in some form by the late Russell G. Stauffer of the University of Delaware (1980, 1975). Both are useful strategies, since they involve prediction and listening (reading) with specifically formulated purposes. Briefly, both DL-TA and DR-TA encourage active involvement with the reading material by having children generate hypotheses about the material and then checking the accuracy of their predictions. That is why either strategy can improve understanding and remembering so effectively.

Here are the basic steps of DL-TA and DR-TA. Of course, in the former the child listens to the material, while in the latter he or she reads the material.

1. Have the children listen to (read) the title of the trade book and then on the basis of this title and their own prior knowledge formulate predictions about the content of the book. If you wish, in the DR-TA the child can dictate (or write if he or she is able) the predictions.
2. Tell the children that they should listen to (read) the trade book to see if the material confirms or disconfirms the predictions they made. Then have the child listen to (read) the book a section at a time.
3. After the trade book is completed, have the children discuss each of their predictions, indicating which ones were confirmed and which ones were not. Help the children to determine what criteria should be used in deciding whether or not the predictions were confirmed. This portion of the DR-TA also can be written if you wish.
4. If the trade book was not read at one time, alternate periods of silent reading and discussion until the entire book has been read. In each case, emphasize the validity of the children's reasoning rather than the correctness of the original hypotheses.

The *Anticipation Guide,* which was developed by Readence, Bean, and Baldwin (1981, 1992), is another interesting strategy that can be used with children in the upper primary grades to improve their prediction abilities and thus the comprehension of what they are going to read. This prereading strategy helps children to activate their prior knowledge before reading and uses statements instead of questions as an initial way to get children more involved in their learning. Very briefly, here are the steps in this prediction strategy:

1. *Identify the major concepts.* The teacher first identifies the major concepts in the reading selection (either a trade book or a simple informational book) by careful reading of the material and the teacher's manual if one is available.
2. *Determine children's knowledge of these concepts.* The teacher should try to determine how the main concepts in the reading material support or refute what the children already know about the material.
3. *Create statements.* The teacher then creates three to five statements about the material. The children have enough knowledge to understand what the statements say, but not enough to make any of them completely known.
4. *Decide statement order and presentation.* The order of the statements should follow the order of the statements presented in the material. The Anticipation Guide can be presented on the chalkboard, a transparency, or a reproducible activity sheet.
5. *Present guide.* When giving the guide to children, the reading teacher usually should read the directions and statements orally. Children also should be told that they will later share their thoughts and opinions about each statement by defending their agreement or disagreement with the statement. Children can work individually or with a partner(s) while making the responses.
6. *Discuss each statement briefly.* The teacher should first ask for a show of hands from children to indicate their agreement or disagreement with each statement.
7. *Have the children read the material.* The children then read the material with the purpose of deciding what the author may say about each statement.
8. *Conduct follow-up discussions.* After they have read the material, the children can respond again to the material. The anticipation guide serves as the basis for a very important post-reading discussion in which children can share the new information gained from the reading and talk about how their previous thoughts may have been modified by what they believe the author said.

This chapter includes a reproducible anticipation guide at about the third-grade reading level in the next section.

Questioning Strategies and QARs

Questioning strategies or *QARs* can be both an assessment strategy and a teaching strategy for comprehension in young children. In several research studies, Raphael (1986) taught students three kinds of *question-answer relationships* (*QARs*) or *questioning strategies*. QAR instruction encourages children to consider both their prior knowledge and the reading material when answering questions. The relationship for questions with answers directly stated in the material in one sentence was called "Right There." The researchers encouraged the children to look for words in the questions and read the sentence containing the answer.

The relationship between questions with their answers in the material that required information from a number of sentences or paragraphs was called "Think and Search." The relationship of questions for which the answer had to come from the student's own prior knowledge was called "On My Own."

It is very important that teachers ask young children a majority of "Think and Search" (interpretive or critical) and "On My Own" (creative) questions if they are to be able to respond at higher levels of comprehension rather than solely at the literal or factual level. For example, in a research study Guszak (1967) found that teachers asked mainly explicit or lower-level questions. Although this study is not recent, the results undoubtedly would be about the same today, since lower-level questions are easy for teachers to both formulate and to evaluate. If children have not been asked many "Think and Search" and "On My Own" questions about the material that they have heard read aloud to them or read for themselves, it is not logical to assume that they ever will become competent in answering this very important type of questions. Even young children must make a beginning in responding to questions that test higher levels of comprehension.

In the research studies about QARs, the researchers found the *modeling the decision* about the kind of QAR that questions constituted was an important part of teaching the students about the concept of QARs. *Supervised practice* following the teacher's modeling also was very important. It is interesting to note that average and below-average students made the greatest improvement after training in the use of QARs.

Later, Raphael (1986) modified QAR instruction to include four categories, clustered under two different headings. In the modified plan, the "On My Own" category is divided into questions that involve both the reader's prior knowledge ("Author and You") and the text information and those that can be discovered from the reader's experience without any information from the material ("On My Own"). Below is a diagram designed by Raphael that illustrates the recent and useful QARs.

Reciprocal Questioning: the ReQuest Procedure

Reciprocal questioning (the ReQuest procedure) is an extremely useful strategy for helping children in third and perhaps second grade to become active questioners at the implicit (higher) levels of comprehension. The original ReQuest procedure was developed by Manzo (1969) and has been used and revised by many different reading specialists. It remains one of the most useful strategies for improving interpretive and critical comprehension.

One of my teacher-trainees used reciprocal questioning in tutoring a fourth-grade student named Matt several years ago. Matt's major reading problem was interpretive comprehension. Although a tutor had tried using mainly activity sheets to improve Matt's interpretive comprehension in the fall, she had been largely unsuccessful. The following semester another tutor used reciprocal questioning as the major strategy to help improve Matt's interpretive comprehension skills, and this strategy proved very successful. Matt truly enjoyed reading material at his grade level very carefully so that he could ask his tutor higher-level questions about the material that she really was unable to answer! He found "tricking" her to be very motivating, and she really was unable to answer all of the detailed higher-level questions that he asked her.

Here are the basic steps in this strategy:

1. The teacher first asks the children to ask some higher-level questions about each *sentence* in a selection that they think the teacher might ask.
2. The teacher then answers each question as fairly and completely as possible and tells the children that they must subsequently do the same.
3. Then the teacher and the students both silently read the first sentence.
4. The teacher closes the book, and a child asks questions about that sentence that the teacher is to answer.

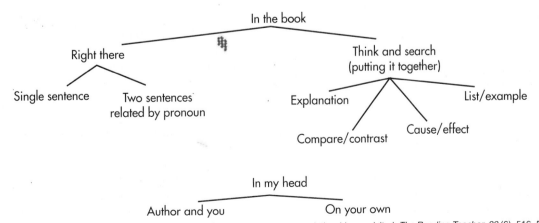

QAR Diagram from Raphael, Taffy E. (1986, February). Teaching question answer relationships, revisited. *The Reading Teacher, 39* (6), 516–522.

5. Next, the child closes the book, and the teacher asks questions about the material. The teacher should provide an excellent model for the child's questions. The questions should always be interpretive, critical, or creative.
6. After a number of additional sentences, the procedure can be modified to use an entire paragraph instead of individual sentences if the children seem able to do so.

Every-Pupil Response Techniques

The *every-pupil response technique* provides each child with multiple opportunities to respond to explicit (literal) comprehension questions in either a whole-class or small-group setting. One variation of this technique is to have the child make two small cards of posterboard and then print the word *yes* on one card and *no* on the other card. Then the teacher asks lower-level (explicit) comprehension questions about a story or trade book that the children have read. Each child answers each question by holding up a *yes* or *no* card.

Other variations of every-pupil response techniques may consist of cards with faces, stick figures, letters, sight words, homonyms, or numbers printed on them. After the teacher asks a question, each child must select the appropriate answer and hold up the correct response card for the teacher to see. By looking at all the raised cards, the teacher can easily determine which children have mastered the skill and which have not. Such a technique enables all children to actively participate in the lesson and also helps the more reluctant children to respond also, which may not be the case with traditional questioning.

Text Lookbacks

Text lookbacks are a very obvious but often overlooked way of improving children's comprehension after they have read any type trade book, basal reader story, or simple content textbook. Obviously, a child should look back in the reading material for an answer when he or she is uncertain about it, but children who do not comprehend well also are not as adept in using text lookbacks to answer questions as are children who are more effective comprehenders.

Although it may seem obvious to teachers, some children may not realize that they can look back in a reading selection when they cannot recall a specific piece of information or do not understand the material well (Garner, Hare, Alexander, Haynes, & Winograd, 1984). If a child's overall comprehension of the material is not good, he or she may have to reread the entire passage. However, if the child has misunderstood or forgotten a detail, he or she may use the text lookback strategy, which is skimming back over the material and locating the part that contains the information that is needed.

Retelling

Retelling is one of the oldest strategies that teachers have used both to assess and to teach comprehension. It was widely used in the 1920s on the first standardized tests to assess reading ability. Although it was effective for this purpose, it was later abandoned, since retelling does not lend itself well to mechanized scoring, and retelling was not widely used for many years. Due to the recent popularity of the whole language approach, it has again been in favor because it is a global approach for either assessing or improving comprehension. However, the retelling technique needs to be introduced gradually with much scaffolding (modeling) of the procedure. It is not an easy skill for young children to master. In addition, the literacy teacher should use either retelling or asking a few comprehension questions about the material that was read. These strategies should not be used simultaneously with young children, as this is overwhelming for them.

Allowing a listener or reader to retell a book or story offers active participation in a literacy experience that helps a young child develop language structure, comprehension ability, and a sense of story structure. It also engages the child in holistic comprehension and organization of thought. In addition, it allows the child to include his or her own prior knowledge into the retelling. With practice in retelling, children are able to assimilate the concept of story structure and learn to introduce a book or story with its beginning and setting. In retelling, children also can demonstrate their comprehension of story details and sequence.

Since retelling is not an easy task for young children to master, they should be told before they listen to or read a book or story that they will be asked to retell it. Further help depends on the teacher's purpose in the retelling. If the purpose is to teach or assess sequence, the children should be asked to focus on what happened first, second, third, and so on. If the purpose is to teach or assess the ability to make inferences from the material, children can be asked to think about things that have happened to them that are similar. Props such as flannelboard characters or the pictures in the material can be used to help children feel more comfortable in the retelling. Before and after discussion of the book or story also helps children to improve their retelling ability.

If you want, you can assess the child's retelling in terms of setting, theme, plot episodes, and resolution. To do this you must first parse the material or divide it into these categories. I have included a parsed story with the directions for scoring it in the following book:

Miller, W. H. (1995) *Alternative assessment techniques for reading and writing.* West Nyack, NY: The Center for Applied Research in Education, pp. 113–115 and 117.

I believe that in most cases simple observation of the child's retelling ability and providing help to him or her in improving this ability is much more important than is evaluating the retelling with this formula.

ACTIVITY

The Herringbone Technique

The *herringbone technique* is very effective in improving reading comprehension ability in both second and third grades. This strategy helps children to locate important information in either narrative or simple content material by asking variations of the following six basic comprehension questions—Who? What? When? Where? How? and Why? Prepare a fish outline and place it on posterboard. If you laminate it, it can be used again and again with different narrative and content materials. The child writes (dictates) the main idea on the horizontal line and the appropriate details on the slanted lines of the fish. These are the details that answer the six questions mentioned earlier (Tierney, Readence, & Dishner, 1990).

To present the herringbone technique, show the fish diagram variation of the strategy on the chalkboard or a transparency. Children should not be asked to use this strategy until it has been thoroughly explained and demonstrated. They also need directed practice with it before they are asked to complete it independently. Even then it may be helpful to have them work with a partner(s) in completing it. Depending on the material, they can complete the herringbone form either as they are reading or when they have finished reading. It often is more effective to have them complete the form during their reading.

After the children have completed this technique, a follow-up large- or small-group discussion often is helpful. Children can be helped to notice that the material does not always provide all of the information that is required to complete the herringbone diagram or that some of the information required on the outline is not particularly helpful to the comprehension of the material. If a few children think that some of the missing information is important, they may be encouraged to locate it by using other simple resources.

This part of the chapter now includes a reproducible herringbone diagram in the form of the fish outline. You can duplicate it and have your pupils use it with any appropriate reading materials. You probably should laminate it after cutting it out so that it can be used many times.

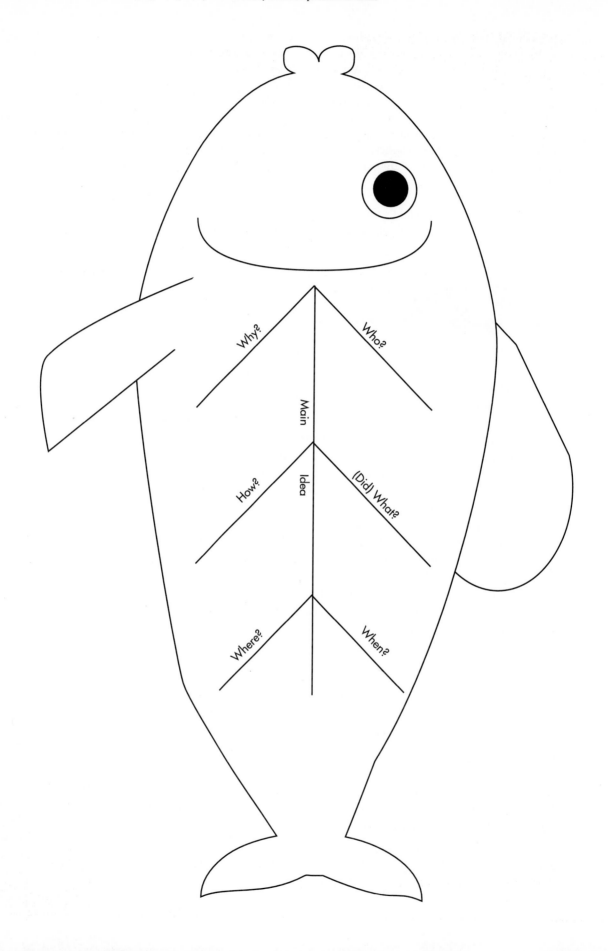

ACTIVITY

Story Impressions

The use of *story impressions* is a very helpful strategy for improving comprehension of narrative material such as narrative trade books. Story impressions can be used effectively with children in second and third grades. This strategy consists of the following easy-to-implement steps (McGinley & Denner, 1987):

- Select an interesting trade book at the appropriate grade level with a clearly defined plot and clearly defined characters.

- As you read this trade book, select about seven key words from the book that will serve as the story impression clues. These clues should be about story characters or important story events.

- Place these clues on the chalkboard or a transparency in the following way. Each clue should be placed in the order in which it is found in the trade book.

Story Clue

Story Clue

Story Clue

Story Clue

Story Clue

Story Clue

Story Clue

- Have the children formulate a prediction about the reading material from each of the story clues. You should write each prediction on the chalkboard opposite the numbers *1, 2, 3,* and so on. Encourage the children to make predictions that can be drawn logically.

- Have each child who is participating in the story impressions activity read the material, focusing on determining whether or not the predictions were correct. Thus, this strategy encourages purposeful, motivated reading which should lead to improved comprehension.

Continued

ACTIVITY

Continued

- After the children have finished reading the entire trade book, they again should look at their predictions. Each prediction that proved to be accurate is allowed to remain written with nothing else being written opposite it. However, each prediction that proved to be inaccurate should be corrected by having the children dictate the correct story summary statement opposite the inaccurate prediction.

The strategy of story impressions has these unique advantages:

- It gives children purposes for reading, and therefore their comprehension is often improved significantly.
- It helps children learn to make valid and logical predictions.
- It motivates children to read relevant, appropriate materials.

This author has selected the children's picture storybook *The Christmas witch* by S. Kellogg (NY: Dial, 1992) to illustrate the story impression technique. This book is about a student witch who wanted to be a good Christmas witch. In the book she is successful in ending the long-standing feud between the peoples of Valdoon and Pepperwill. At the end of the book it becomes the land of Pepperdoon. Here are the story impression clues for this picture storybook:

Story Impression Clues

Student witch, Gloria

↓

Christmas wish

↓

lands of Valdoon and Pepperwill

↓

Christmas celebration

↓

elves

↓

castle

↓

Christmas cake

↓

Pepperdoon

If you wish, you can write your own predictions in the **Predictive Summary** portion of the following reproducible activity sheet. Then locate this trade book from your university library or a local public library and read it. After you have read it, do not add anything to the correct predictions, but you should write the correct story summary opposite any incorrect predictions. You may find that this activity is fairly challenging for you even as an adult. If you make multiple copies of the story impressions activity sheet, use only one of them at this time and use the others later for the children with whom you may work.

ACTIVITY

Name _____ Grade _____

Story Impressions Activity Sheet
Primary-Grade Level

Predictive Story Summary	Actual Story Summary

K-W-L and K-W-H-L

The story strategies of *K-W-L* and *K-W-H-L* may be of value in the second and third grades when the teacher has modeled them and provided sufficient scaffolding. They are study strategies that can be used only with content material such as social studies and science. However, able readers in the primary grades may well profit from exposure to them, and then their use can be refined in the intermediate grades. These are excellent strategies to use in improving comprehension of content material.

K-W-L is an acronym for *What do I know—What do I want to know—What have I learned?* Developed by Ogle (1986, 1989), K-W-L stresses a child's prior knowledge, encourages him or her to formulate questions to read to answer, directs him or her to look for answers to these questions, and enables him or her to effectively summarize what was read. The strategy is helpful primarily because it helps children use their prior knowledge while reading and gives them purposes for reading.

The strategy should be presented in a group setting to those readers who seem able to profit from using it. First identify the most important concepts in the material, and then ask the children to state what they already know about these concepts. Write these concepts on the chalkboard under a heading titled "What Do I Know?" In the second step, provide motivation by focusing on what the children want to learn about these concepts that they do not now know. Write these questions under a column labeled "What Do I Want to Find Out?" Once the children have determined their purposes for reading, they should read the material to locate the answers to their questions.

In the final part of K-W-L have the children orally summarize what they have learned from reading the material. They can dictate this portion of the activity sheet to you, and you write it down under the column headed "What Have I Learned?" or "What I Have Learned." Have them do this without referring to the material that they read.

K-W-H-L adds a step before the final step called "How Can I Find Out?" In this step, with your help the children brainstorm for resources that they can use to locate needed information. In addition to simple content textbooks, other resources that may be used are as follows: informational trade books, simple children's newspapers and magazines, the World Wide Web, computer software, videotapes, films, or classroom visitors.

For illustration, the chapter now includes a short sample K-W-L activity sheet that can be used as a model for such a sheet that you may want to construct for your own pupils.

What do I know?	What do I want to find out?	What have I learned?

Visual Imagery

Formulating *visual imagery*, sometimes called *mental imagery*, is a very good way of improving reading comprehension. It is especially effective if children are given material that lends itself well to formulating mental images of what is read. Many children do not use this strategy unless they have had specific instruction and practice in how to do it. Creating mental images promotes the use of prior knowledge and improves the ability to make predictions and draw inferences. In addition to improving comprehension, imaging can help retention.

One reason that visual imaging is effective is that it is an active, generative process. In a research study comparing fourth-grade students who read a story without illustrations and created their own images with fourth-grade students who made use of textbook illustrations, the group that constructed their own images remembered more of the story (Gambrell & Javitz, 1993). Evidently creating one's own images is more effective than using someone else's creations. Imaging is a fairly easy strategy to teach. Gambrell & Bales (1986) found that students' comprehension increased somewhat after just thirty minutes of instruction.

One way of enhancing mental imaging ability is to read high-imagery selections to children and ask them to try to picture the main character, the setting, or a specific scene. Some trade books that can be used for this purpose with young children are as follows:

Burton, V. (1942). *The little house.* Boston: Houghton Mifflin.

Eastman, P. (1960). *Are you my mother?* NY: Random House.

Hoban, F. (1960). *Bedtime for Frances.* NY: Harper & Row.

Johnson, C. (1955). *Harold and the purple crayon.* NY: Harper & Row.

Mahy, M. (1987). *17 kings and 42 elephants.* NY: Dial.

Mayer, M. (1969). *There's a nightmare in my closet.* NY: Dial.

Rathmann, P. (1991). *Ruby the copycat.* NY: Scholastic.

Sendak, M. (1963). *Where the wild things are.* NY: Harper & Row.

Stevenson, J. (1980). *That terrible Halloween night.* NY: Greenwillow.

Williams, M. (1922). *The velveteen rabbit.* NY: Holt.

When teaching children to use imagery, begin with single sentences and then move on to short paragraphs and later to longer selections. Have children read the sentence or paragraph first and then ask them to create a picture of it. Creating images serves the purposes of improving understanding, improving retention, and monitoring comprehension. If children are unable to form an image or they form an incorrect or incomplete one, encourage them to read the selection and then add to the picture in their minds or create a new one.

If you wish, primary-grade children can draw one or several of the mental images they have created as they read a trade book or story. If they want, they can compare their drawing with an illustration in the material and also with the material itself to be sure they have included all the important components.

Like all comprehension strategies, visual imagery should be taught directly. The teacher first should explain and model the strategy; discuss when, where, and under what conditions it can best be used; and provide much guided practice and application. The teacher should review the strategy on a regular basis and encourage children to apply it.

When used with either fiction or nonfiction material, visual imagery should follow these general guidelines (Fredericks, 1986):

- Teachers must realize that since children will create their own images based on their own prior knowledge and comprehension of the material, the mental images or drawings will be different.
- Children must be given enough time to formulate either mental or drawn images.
- Although teachers should not criticize a child's mental images or illustrations, they may suggest that children reread a selection to decide if they want to change their mental images or illustrations.

Later this chapter includes a reproducible activity sheet at the second-grade level that contains a short high-interest reading selection and provides the opportunity for children to formulate an illustration about this selection.

Discriminating Between Real and Make-Believe and Between Fact and Opinion

Discriminating between real and make-believe and between fact and fantasy are both elements of critical or evaluative reading which is, of course, a higher-level comprehension skill. Since critical reading is a very important skill in a democratic society, it is important that young children be provided with opportunities to make a beginning in this most important literacy skill.

Although only a few children in first grade may be able to discriminate between real and make-believe, most children in second grade should be able to learn this reading skill. One good way of doing this is simply to ask young children if they think that a trade book or story that they have listened to or read for themselves is real or make-believe and to provide reasons why they believe as they do. Young children, for example, are able to determine that books and stories in which animals talk or behave human in other ways could not be real, since animals are not able to behave that way in real life.

In third grade children can be given a series of statements orally by the teacher and asked to determine if they are *fact* or *opinion*. This is a fairly difficult literacy skill for young children to master, and it should be presented thoroughly. Later, children can be given activity sheets that are devoted to this reading skill so they can practice. Here are several sample items from such a sheet:

Fact or Opinion

A turtle draws its head, feet, and tail inside its shell when it is afraid.

A golden retriever is the best breed of dog to own.

A porcupine can use its quills to protect itself from its enemies.

Wolves usually live in groups or packs.

A snake can bite with its forked tongue.

A cat has nine lives.

An ostrich often buries its head in the sand.

Later this chapter contains a reproducible activity sheet at about the third-grade level that is designed to provide practice for children in discriminating between fact and opinion.

Some key phrases can alert children to the fact that they are reading a make-believe book or story. They can be taught such key phrases as *once upon a time, in a far-away land, in the make-believe land of . . .* or *the animals in this book are talking to each other.*

Activities to Develop Ability in Sequencing

There are several simple activities that can be used with young children to help them develop the ability to place a number of items in correct sequence. You should realize that sequencing ability is a complex reading skill that takes children quite a bit of time and practice to master. Therefore, you must begin by having children put only two or three items in correct sequence in the early primary grades and then progress to having them put perhaps five to eight (the maximum) items in correct sequence by the time that they are in third grade. Even at that grade level, there are a number of children who will find this to be a very difficult task. This reading skill can be practiced using both actual objects and activity sheets.

Here are several ways of providing instruction and/or practice in placing items in the correct sequence:

- Obtain a simple comic strip that has five or fewer frames. Cut the comic strip apart by frames and then laminate the frames to make them more durable and long-lasting. Have children try to reassemble the comic strip by placing it in correct sequence. If you want, each comic strip that is to be used for this purpose can be placed in a large envelope. This is a good activity to use in a literacy center as an independent activity. If you want to make this a self-checking activity, you can place the correct sequence number on the back of each comic strip frame before laminating it.

- There are many commercially available sets of cards that are designed to help young children learn sequential ability. They usually can be checked out of an elementary school's media center or purchased in a school supply store. In each case the child simply places the cards in correct sequential order. If you want, the child also can describe the action that is taking place in each of the cards after he or she has put them in correct order. In this way these cards also can improve oral language ability.
- You can construct your own activity sheets or purchase commercial activity sheets that emphasize placing items in correct sequence. Such an activity sheet usually is constructed in about this way:

> Place the items on this activity sheet in the correct order.
>
> _____ The rain started to pour yesterday afternoon.
>
> _____ It got cloudy right after I ate lunch yesterday.
>
> _____ All of a sudden it began to thunder and lightning.
>
> _____ All my clothes got soaked when I walked home.
>
> _____ I changed into dry clothes as soon as I got home.

Later the chapter contains a simple reproducible activity sheet at about the third-grade level that is designed to provide practice in placing items in correct order.

Videotaped Stories

To provide independent practice in comprehension for young children, teachers can videotape stories, providing an introduction to each story and the story structure to be studied. The children should receive directions for follow-up activities such as drawing pictures of characters, the setting, and the plot resolution. Children also can select pictures related to the story theme from several that are presented by the teacher. In addition, children can place pictures that are related to the plot in correct sequence. To be sure that the procedures are clear to children, the entire class or group should do the activity under the teacher's direction the first few times this activity is used (McGee & Tompkins, 1981).

Circle Stories

To help children understand that some books and stories start and end at the same place with a series of events in between, the *circle story* can be effective (Jett-Simpson, 1981; Smith & Bean, 1983). In this strategy the teacher

draws a circle on a large sheet of paper and divides it into a number of pie-shaped sections corresponding to the number of events in a trade book or story. Then the teacher reads the book or story to the children, who decide which events should be pictured in each section of the circle. Circle story completion can be done in small groups or individually. I prefer that it be done in small groups, with each child responsible for illustrating a different event. If the paper is large enough, all of the children can work at the same time.

Discussion Webs

Alvermann (1991) has developed a simple but useful graphic device called the *discussion web* for helping all children participate in discussions about books to improve comprehension. Here is the problem that discussion webs is designed to correct:

> A problem with most discussion is the tendency for teachers and a few highly verbal students to monopolize classroom talk. When this happens . . . other students soon become inhibited, self-conscious, and unwilling to voice their opinions. One way to counteract [this tendency] . . . is to provide all children with the opportunity to assume their own voices in these discussions. The Discussion Web gives students this opportunity (1991, pp. 92–93).

This strategy probably is the most appropriate for children in the third grade and beyond.

Alvermann has explained using the comprehension strategy of discussion webs. Suppose that a group is just about to read the book *Stone soup* (by M. Brown, NY: Macmillan, 1942). The teacher might say, "This book is about three soldiers who propose to make soup out of three stones, but who are able to get the villagers to add enough vegetables, meat, and milk that they all have a feast on the soup that theoretically is made out of three stones. You might think that the soldiers were not honest and tricked the villagers into providing all of the ingredients for the soup, which they would not have done otherwise. Now who do you admire in this book—the soldiers or the villagers?"

The teacher would continue: "Now look at the format for the discussion web. When you are finished, we will complete the discussion web together, and you will all contribute." Here are the steps for using the discussion web:

> *Step one.* Develop the children's schemas. In the case of *Stone soup* these schemas are concerned with fooling people, eating good soup at a feast, and the willingness of the villagers to go along with the soldiers who came to their village.
>
> *Step two.* Help the children establish purposes for reading, such as to discover whether the people in the village will actually make soup.

Step three. Have the children read the book to satisfy their purposes.

Step four. Introduce the discussion web question. In the case of *Stone soup* the question might be, "Did the soldiers treat the people in the village honestly?"

Step five. Have the children work in teams of two, taking turns writing approximately the same number of responses in the **YES** and **NO** columns. Here are sample responses for this book:

Yes	No
The soup did have three stones in it.	The villagers would not have provided the ingredients otherwise.

Step six. Before the partners have enough time to fill up all the blanks, have two pairs form a new group of four and compare their reasons. Encourage each group to stay open-minded and try to reach agreement, if possible.

Step seven. Select a child from each group who will do the talking for the group. This child should explain the group's best idea to the rest of the class or large group. Before the total class meeting, give the small groups about five minutes or less to decide on their best idea.

Step eight. Let the spokespersons for the group compare their best ideas (and also mention any dissenting ideas from their group).

Step nine. Have the children each write a sentence or two explaining their individual opinion on the discussion web question. Invented spelling can be used in the sentence(s).

Step ten. If you want, you can post all of the individual sentences for the other children to read. Do not do so, however, if you believe that it would embarrass any child. (Alvermann, 1991).

The discussion web strategy may have these advantages:

- Children are working in cooperative learning groups, which promotes purposeful practice in listening, speaking, reading, and writing.
- Children receive practice in critical thinking.
- The active involvement of every member of the class is promoted.

Discussion Web

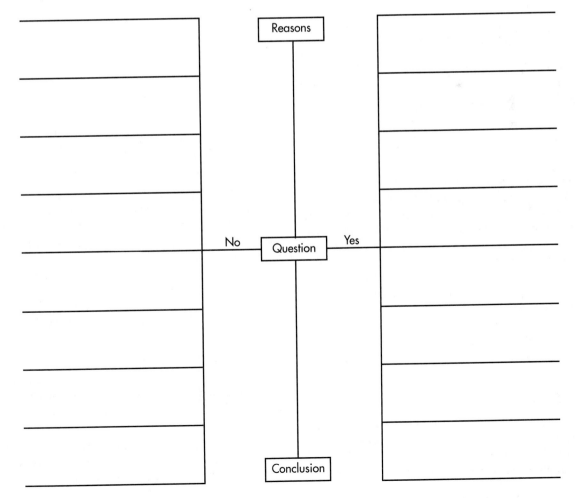

Poetry

Exploring children's poetry is a very enjoyable way of improving both comprehension and listening skills. Poetry has a condensed quality that makes every word important. It also encourages visual imagery through its sensory descriptions and can introduce enchanting stories. Poetry also provides an opportunity for a child to learn new words, ideas, and attitudes and to experience life through the eyes of a poet. It has form and order and is dependable and easy to learn.

In summary, poetry can be used for the following reasons:

- training children to experience the pleasure of hearing sounds
- providing enjoyment through the use of poems with silly words and humor
- stimulating children's imaginations
- increasing children's vocabulary and knowledge
- improving children's self-worth and self-confidence
- encouraging the understanding of rhyming

Here are some types of poetry:

- *Lyric.* This is melodic, descriptive poetry that often has a song quality.
- *Narrative.* This is poetry that tells a story or describes an event or happening.
- *Limerick.* This is poetry with five lines of verse set in a specific rhyming pattern that is usually humorous.
- *Free verse.* This is poetry that does not rhyme.
- *Nonsense.* This is poetry that is often ridiculous and whimsical.
- *Haiku.* This is an ancient but currently popular Japanese verse that contains three lines consisting of seventeen syllables and often dealing with the topic of nature.

Placing poems in prominent places in the classroom may help to create interest in poems, especially if pictures or illustrations are placed by the poems. For example, a *poetry tree* made by placing a smooth tree limb in plaster of paris can have paper leaves with poems on the back that can be chosen at group times. Sharing a "poem of the day" has worked well in a number of classrooms. Pictures and flannel boards can be used in presenting poetry in an interesting way. A poem can be enjoyed either indoors or outdoors as a valuable learning resource at the end of a lesson or when the teacher or children are waiting in line.

You also can create your own personalized poems for your class. The following suggestions for writing poems for young children may be helpful to you:

- Use frequent rhyming.
- Use themes and ideas that are familiar to young children.
- Vary the rhythm.

- Use definite rhythms that stimulate an urge to chant, move, or sing.
- Use words that children are able to understand easily.
- Make each line an independent thought.
- Use many action verbs.
- Try to include mental images in each line.

Here are a few books of poetry that you may want to use. There are, of course, many others that are equally worthwhile.

Adoff, A. (1991). *In for winter, out for spring.* NY: Harcourt.

Ciardi, J. (1985). *Doodle soup.* Boston: Houghton Mifflin.

Cole, J., & Calemnson, S. (1990). *Miss Mary Mack and other children's street rhymes.* NY: Morrow/Beech Tree.

dePaola, T. (1981). *The friendly beasts.* NY: Putnam.

Hoban, R. (1972). *Egg thoughts and other Frances songs.* NY: Harper.

Lear, E. (1946). *The complete book of nonsense.* NY: Dodd, Mead.

O'Neil, M. (1969). *My fingers are always bringing news.* NY: Doubleday.

Prelutsky, J. (1983). *The Random House book of poetry for children.* NY: Random House.

Prelutsky, J. (1986). *Ride a purple pelican.* NY: Greenwillow.

Schwartz, A. (1992). *And the green grass grew all around: Folk poetry for children.* NY: HarperCollins.

Silvermann, J. (1986). *Some time to grow.* Menlo Park, CA: Addison-Wesley.

Silverstein, S. (1974). *Where the sidewalk ends.* NY: HarperCollins.

Temple, C. (1996). *Train.* Boston: Houghton Mifflin.

Watson, C. (1987). *Father fox's pennyrhymes.* NY: HarperCollins.

Using Puppets to Improve Comprehension

Puppets are an extremely useful tool to use in literacy instruction with young children. As an example, a tutor working with a first-grade girl several years ago was having a very difficult time encouraging her to say anything. No matter what strategies the tutor used, this little girl wouldn't respond. One day the tutor brought a honeybee puppet, and the little girl pretended that she was a honeybee. She responded well to the reading instruction, including answering comprehensive questions. After a while she was talking easily. When she was tutored the next year in second grade, the first time I met her again she said, "Do you remember me from last year? I didn't talk at all then, and now I talk all the time!" This indeed was true. A puppet had performed a miracle with her. This is an example of the effect that puppets can have with a young child.

Koons (1986) stated the following about puppets:

> Imagine a lifeless puppet lying on a table. Suddenly, a child slips his hand into the puppet and it awakens to a life and personality of its own. Magic happens, and the world of make-believe begins. Children love to pretend, and puppetry allows them to create their own magic.

Using puppets is an example of creative or applied reading—the highest level of reading process. Here are some ways that you can use puppets in your classroom:

- Present puppet plays and skits. Some of these plays and skits can be follow-ups to a trade book or story that the child has heard or read.
- Provide props and puppet theaters.
- Find community resources for puppet presentations: puppeteer groups, high school and elementary classes, and skilled individuals.
- Have children use puppets when reading the parts orally in a trade book or story.

Puppets can be divided into two general categories—those worked with the hands and fingers and those that dangle on a string. Hand puppets are popular with young children because they are so practical. Moving arms and pliable faces on puppets increase the possibilities for characterization and action. Rubber, plastic, and papier-mâché puppet heads are durable, and cloth faces permit a wide variety of facial expressions.

Following are ways to construct some common puppets.

Sock Puppets

Materials Needed:

an old sock, felt, and a sewing machine

Construction Procedure:

1. Use an old wool sock or other thick sock. Turn it inside out and spread it out with the heel on top.

2. Cut around the edge of the toe (about three inches on each side).

3. Fold the mouth material (red felt) inside the open part of the sock and draw the shape. Cut the mouthpiece out and sew into place.

Papier-Mâché Puppet Heads

Materials Needed:

Styrofoam egg or ball (a little smaller than the size you want for the completed head) and soft enough to have a holder inserted into it

neck tube (made from cardboard—about one and a half inches wide and five inches long, rolled into a 1½″ tube and taped closed, or a plastic hair roller)

bottle (to put the head in while it is being created and to hold it during drying)

instant papier-mâché (purchased from a craft store)

poster paints

gloss coat spray (optional)

white glue

Construction Procedure:

1. Mix instant papier-mâché with water (a little at a time) until it is like clay—moist, but neither wet nor dry.

2. Place Syrofoam egg (or ball) on neck tube (or roller) securely. Then place egg (or ball) on bottle so it is steady.

3. Put papier-mâché all over head and halfway down the neck tube. Coating should be about a half inch thick.

ACTIVITY

4. Begin making the facial features, starting with the cheeks, eyebrows, and chin. Then add eyes, nose, mouth, and ears.

5. When you are done with the head, allow it to dry at least 24 hours in an airy place.

6. When the head is dry, paint the face with poster paint. When that is dry, coat it with spray gloss finish to seal paint.

7. Glue is useful for adding yarn hair if you want.

Paper Bag Puppets

Materials Needed:

paper bags, scissors, crayons, or marking pens, paste, yarn or paper scraps, and paint (optional)

Construction Procedure:

1. Paper bag puppets are easy to make. Give each child a small paper sack.

2. As shown in the illustration, the mouth is made in the fold at the bottom of the sack. Then show them how the mouth works and let them color or paste features on the sack.

3. You may want to have them paste a circle on for the face. Paste it on the flap part of the bag, and then cut the circle on the flap portion so that the mouth can move again.

4. Many children will want to add special features to their paper bag puppets.

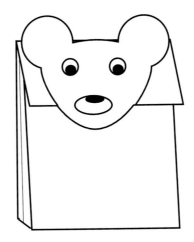

Stick Puppets

Materials Needed:

paper, glue, scissors, tongue depressors or popsicle sticks

Construction Procedure:

1. Children can draw characters and scenery. Depending on the age of the children, the characters and scenery can be simply colored or colored and cut out.

2. Older children can create their own figures.

Continued

Other types of puppets that can be made are as follows: cloth hand puppets, pop-ups, jumping jack puppets, box puppets, and frog and bird finger puppets. Many teacher resource books contain directions for constructing these types of puppets.

Other Strategies for Improving Comprehension

There are a number of other strategies that can be used to improve the various levels of comprehension. Due to space limitations, only a few more are mentioned here. You are encouraged to consult the professional books in the Selected References at the end of this chapter for many ideas about how to implement these strategies successfully with young children. Over the years my teacher-trainees have used all of them successfully while tutoring young children.

Here are some of these strategies:

- semantic maps or webs (see an earlier part of this chapter)
- readiness for the cloze procedure and simplified cloze procedures
- observing punctuation marks
- locating the directed stated main idea (only for competent readers at the third-grade level)
- locating important and irrelevant details (only for competent readers at the third-grade level)
- placing a number of items or later placing words into the correct category (categorization or classification activities)
- writing dialogue on comic strips in which the words in the balloons have been whited out
- creative writing of prose and poetry
- writing an ending to an incomplete story
- writing an alternative ending to a book or story
- participating in creative dramatics
- writing in the text for wordless (textless) books

ACTIVITY

Game for Improving Ability in Comprehension

Games are not a particularly good way of improving comprehension; however, this game *may* be interesting and useful to children at the upper-primary-grade level. In addition, other useful games can be found in resource books of various types.

Finish the Story

Constructing the Game

To construct this game you need old basal readers, a stapler or glue, construction paper, and a marker. Break the binding of the basals and tear out the beginning of several stories that are appropriate for your pupils. Turn the edges and staple or glue the pages into a booklet using the construction paper as a cover. Put the ability level in the lower right-hand corner if you want.

To Play the Game

Have the child take a booklet out of the box, open it, and read the beginning of the story. He or she should then finish the story by writing it on a piece of paper.

Reproducibles for Improving Ability in Comprehension

The chapter now includes four reproducibles that you can use as is or modify to improve elements of comprehension.

Name _____ Grade _____

Anticipation Guide
Second-or Third-Grade Level

Here are some statements about twin black bear cubs climbing a tree in northern Wisconsin. Read each statement to yourself or with a friend and put an X next to each statement that you agree with. Be sure you are ready to defend your ideas when we talk about the statements later.

_____ Three dogs are very likely to try to run after two black bear cubs.

_____ Twin bear cubs are likely to attack three dogs that are walking with their owners.

_____ Bears like dogs and never would hurt them.

_____ Dogs always are aware of bears because of their scent.

Now read the story to yourself. Remember what you should look for as you read the story so we can discuss later what you learned from reading the story.

Three Dogs and Twin Bear Cubs

Last summer my neighbors and I were walking our dogs down an asphalt road in northern Wisconsin one morning. The husband and wife were walking a springer spaniel and a cocker spaniel, and I was walking my golden retriever.

All of a sudden the man said, "Look, there are twin black bear cubs climbing up that tree over there." Sure enough, I saw the two cute cubs climbing a big tree as quickly as they could.

I said, "I hope that we don't meet the mother bear, since bears don't like dogs at all," and the man and woman agreed with me.

Strangely enough, none of our three dogs ever smelled or saw the bear cubs and apparently didn't even know they were there. The three dogs just walked as usual.

Finally the couple turned around to go home with their dogs, and I went on toward my house down the road. Fortunately, my dog and I never saw the mother bear. Later, however, my neighbors told me that they saw the mother bear after they turned around. Luckily, she just walked the other way and didn't bother those two dogs who apparently didn't even know that she was there.

Aren't you surprised that three dogs never were aware of the bear cubs and their mother? I sure was!

Name _____   Grade _____

Riddles
Second-Grade Level

Read each of these riddles to yourself. Then write the correct answer on the line below the riddle.

1. I have a big screen.
   Children like to look at me.
   Your home probably has at least one.
   What am I? _____

2. I can be a child's pet.
   I can jump very well.
   My name rhymes with hat.
   What am I? _____

3. I can grow very tall.
   Children like to climb me.
   I change colors in the fall.
   What am I? _____

4. I can be blue.
   Children swim in me in the summer.
   People also fish in me.
   What am I? _____

5. I am a very small animal.
   I may be gray.
   I like to eat cheese and bread crumbs.
   What am I? _____

6. I am a farm animal.

    I like to eat grass and hay.

    I rhyme with how.

    What am I? _____

7. Children eat me at birthday parties.

    I usually have frosting on me.

    I may have candles on me.

    What am I? _____

8. I am very cute and cuddly.

    I am warm and furry.

    When I grow up, I am called "man's best friend."

    What am I? _____

9. I like boys and girls

    I work in a school.

    My name rhymes with bleacher.

    What am I? _____

Name _____   Grade _____

Activity Sheet for Determining Fact and Opinion
Third-Grade Level

Read each of these sentences to yourself. In the blank before each
sentence write the letter T if the sentence is a statement of fact.
Write the letter O if the sentence is a statement of opinion.
You can work with a friend if you want.

All About Animals

_____ 1. A porcupine can use its sharp quills to protect itself.

_____ 2. A dog is the best pet that a kid can have.

_____ 3. A bat can use its ears as well as its eyes to find its way
when it is dark outside.

_____ 4. Some snakes are very useful.

_____ 5. The queen bee is bigger than the rest of the bees in the hive.

_____ 6. The animals in the circus that are the most fun to watch
are the elephants.

_____ 7. Cats can jump very well.

_____ 8. Pigs are very dirty animals.

_____ 9. Every farm should have some horses.

_____ 10. No one should have a snake for a pet.

_____ 11. Some foxes have red fur.

_____ 12. Bears are very scary animals.

_____ 13. Some dogs look almost like wolves.

_____ 14. Goats will eat almost anything.

_____ 15. A small dog is a better pet for a girl than a big dog is.

Name _____   Grade _____

Activity Sheet for Putting Items in Correct Order
Third-Grade Level

In each set of five sentences, put the sentences in correct order by putting the number 1, 2, 3, 4, or 5 in front of the right sentence. When you are finished with each set of sentences, read them again to be sure that they are all correct. The first one has been completed for you.

The Circus

_3_   The clowns were the first thing that they saw at the circus.

_5_   When the circus was over, Jenny was tired but happy.

_4_   During the circus there were three rings to watch at once.

_1_   On Saturday afternoon Jenny and her family went to the circus.

_2_   As soon as they got to the circus, Jenny's mother bought the tickets.

Planting a Garden

_____   Eric spaded and raked the soil to get ready to plant a garden.

_____   When the plants were all planted, Eric watered them carefully.

_____   After the soil was ready, Eric planted the tiny plants.

_____   In the fall Eric was able to harvest the vegetables.

_____   Eric had to keep his garden watered and weeded all summer.

Going Swimming at the Lake

_____   The drive to the nearby lake took only a little while, but Tony thought that they would never get there.

_____   Tony and his father packed their van before they drove to the lake which was near their home.

_____ Since Tony had taken swimming lessons at the pool by his house, he had a lot of fun swimming in the lake.

_____ As soon as his family arrived at the lake, Tony put on his swimming trunks.

_____ After five hours of swimming, Tony was ready to head for home.

Making a Snowman

_____ First, the girls rolled three big snowballs for the body of the snowman.

_____ As soon as it stopped snowing, Sarah and Amy decided to make a giant snowman.

_____ Last, Sarah and Amy took a picture of their snowman with Jay's camera.

_____ After the girls had made the three big balls of snow, they put the biggest one on the bottom, the next-biggest one in the middle, and the smallest one on the top.

_____ Then the girls made eyes, a nose, and a mouth on the snowman.

Buying a Puppy

_____ Joanie just loved playing with all of the puppies at the animal shelter.

_____ Joanie and her mother went to look at the puppies in the animal shelter in late February.

_____ Joanie's mother planned to get her a puppy at the animal shelter for her ninth birthday, which is March 8.

_____ After watching how all of the puppies at the animal shelter acted, Joanie finally chose a female black puppy.

_____ On March 8 Joanie was able to bring her new puppy, whom she named "Holly," home with her!

SUGGESTED ACTIVITIES

1. If possible, take an older preschool child, kindergarten child, or primary-grade child on an excursion. If this is not possible, use one of the second-hand experiences mentioned in this chapter. Prepare the child for the experience by stressing the vocabulary terms that he or she can learn during the experience. After the experience, review these vocabulary terms and perhaps have the child participate in LEA dictation or in process writing (see Chapter 2 or Chapter 6).

2. Try constructing hinks pinks (see the chapter under "Word Play"). You can work with a partner(s) if you want. Be prepared to share these with your classmates.

3. Select a primary-grade children's narrative or informational trade book. Then write three questions at each of the four levels of comprehension: literal (explicit), interpretive (implicit), critical (implicit), and applied (creative). Be prepared to share these questions with your classmates.

4. Make a copy of the herringbone technique fish outline and laminate it so that it can be used with primary-grade children.

5. If possible, videotape a children's story, providing an introduction to the story and story structure. In addition, videotape directions for follow-up activities such as drawing pictures of the characters, the setting, and the plot resolution.

6. Construct one or more of the different kinds of puppets described in this chapter so that it (they) can be used by young children.

SELECTED REFERENCES

Burns, P., Roe, B., & Ross, E. (1996). *Teaching reading in today's elementary schools* (pp. 161–309). Boston: Houghton Mifflin.

Carnine, D., Silbert, J., & Kameenui, E. (1997). *Direct reading instruction* (pp. 228–281). Upper Saddle River, NJ: Prentice Hall.

Cheek, E., Flippo, R., & Lindsey, J. (1997). *Reading for success in elementary schools* (pp. 95–176). Madison, WI: Brown & Benchmark Publishers.

Gipe, J. (1998). *Multiple paths to literacy* (pp. 207–240). Upper Saddle River, NJ: Merrill.

Graves, M., Juel, C., & Graves, B. (1998). *Teaching reading in the 21st century* (pp. 184–289). Needham Heights, MA: Allyn & Bacon.

Gunning, T. (1986). *Creating reading instruction for all children* (pp. 162–276). Needham Heights, MA: Allyn & Bacon.

Hall, K. (1997). *Reading stories for comprehension success.* West Nyack, NY: The Center for Applied Research in Education.

Heilman, A., Blair, T., & Rupley, W. (1998). *Principles and practices of teaching reading* (pp. 202–296). Upper Saddle River, NJ: Merrill.

Miller, W. (1999). *Ready-to-Use Activities & Materials for Improving Current Reading Skills.* West Nyack, NY: The Center for Applied Research in Education.

Miller, W. (1990). *Reading comprehension activities kit.* West Nyack, NY: The Center for Applied Research in Education.

Morrow, L. (1997). *Literacy development in the early years* (pp. 196–227). Needham Heights, MA: Allyn & Bacon.

Sampson, M., Sampson., M. B., & Allen, R. (1995). *Pathways to literacy* (pp. 350–383). Fort Worth, TX: Harcourt Brace College Publishers.

Savage, J. (1998). *Teaching reading and writing: Combining skills, strategies, and literature* (pp. 157–248). Boston: McGraw-Hill.

Savage, J. (1994). *Teaching reading using literature* (pp. 135–211). Madison, WI: Brown & Benchmark.

Vacca, J., Vacca, R., & Gove, M. (1995). *Reading and learning to read* (pp. 184–260). NY: HarperCollins.

WORKS CITED IN CHAPTER 5

Adams, M. (1991). *Beginning to read: Thinking and learning about print.* Urbana-Champaign, IL: Center for the Study of Reading.

Alvermann, D. (1991). The discussion web: A graphic aid for learning about the curriculum. *The Reading Teacher, 45,* 92–99.

Anderson, R., Wilson, P., & Fielding, L. (December 1985). A new focus on free reading. Paper presented at the National Reading Conference, San Diego, CA.

Anderson, R., Wilson, P., & Fielding, L. (1988). Growth in reading and how children spend their time outside of school. *Reading Research Quarterly, 23,* 285–303.

Chall, J. (1987). Two vocabularies for recognition and meaning. In M. G. McKeown & M. E. Curtis (Eds.).

The nature of vocabulary acquisition (pp. 7–17). Hillsdale, NJ: Erlbaum.

Dale, E. (1965). Vocabulary measurement: Techniques and major findings. *Elementary English, 42,* 895–901.

Dale, E. (1969). Audio visual methods in teaching. Orlando, FL: Holt, Rinehart & Winston.

Dale, E., & O'Rourke, J. (1971). *Techniques of teaching reading.* Chicago: Field.

Davis, F. (1944). Fundamental factors in comprehension in reading. *Psychometrika, 9,* 185–197.

Fredericks, A. (1986). Mental imagery activities to improve comprehension. *The Reading Teacher, 40,* 78–81.

Gale, D. (1982). Why word play? *The Reading Teacher, 36,* 220–222.

Gambrell, L., & Bales, R. (1986). Mental imagery and the comprehension monitoring performance of fourth- and fifth-grade poor readers. *Reading Research Quarterly, 21,* 454–464.

Gambrell, L., & Javitz, P. (1993). Mental imaging text, illustrations, and children's story comprehension. *The Reading Teacher, 28,* 264–276.

Garner, R., Hare, V., Alexander, P., & Winograd, P. (1984). Inducing use of a test lookback strategy among unsuccessful readers. *American Educational Research Journal, 21,* 789–798.

Graves, M. (1987). Roles of instruction in fostering vocabulary development. In M. G. McKeown & M. E. Curtis (Eds.). *The nature of vocabulary acquisition* (pp. 165–184). Hillsdale, NJ: Lawrence Erlbaum.

Greaney, V. (1980). Factors related to amount and types of leisure reading. *Reading Research Quarterly, 15,* 337–357.

Guszak, F. (1967). Teaching questioning and reading. *The Reading Teacher, 21,* 227–234.

Hartman, D. (1994). The intertextual links of readers using multiple passages: A postmodern semiotic/cognitive view of meaning making. In R. B. Ruddell, M. R. Ruddell, & H. Singer (Eds.). *Theoretical models and processes of reading.* Newark, DE: International Reading Association.

Jett-Simpson, M. (1981). Writing stories using model strategies. *Language Arts, 58,* 293–300.

Koons, K. (1986). Puppet plays. *First Teacher, 7.5,* 56–64.

Manzo, A. (1969). The ReQuest Procedure. *Journal of Reading, 13,* 123–126.

McGee, L., & Tompkins, G. (1981). The videotape answer to independent reading comprehension. *The Reading Teacher, 34,* 427–433.

McGinley, W., & Denner, P. (1987). Story impressions: A prereading/writing strategy. *Journal of Reading, 31,* 248–253.

Miller, W. (1999). *Ready-to-Use Activities & Materials for Improving Content Reading Skills.* West Nyack, NY: The Center for Applied Research in Education.

Nagy, W., & Herman, P. (1987). Breadth and depth of vocabulary knowledge. In M. G. McKeown and M. E. Curtis (Eds.). *The nature of vocabulary acquisition* (pp. 19–35). Hillsdale, NJ: Lawrence Erlbaum.

Ogle, D. (1986). K-W-L: A teaching model that develops active reading of expository text. *The Reading Teacher, 39,* 564–570.

Ogle, D. (1989). The know, want to know, learn strategy. In D. Muth (Ed.). *Children's comprehension of text* (pp. 205–223). Newardk, DE: International Reading Association.

Raphael, T. (1986). Teaching question-answer relationships, revisited. *The Reading Teacher, 39,* 516–522.

Readence, J., Beans, T., & Baldwin, R. (1981). *Content area reading: An integrated approach.* Dubuque, IA: Kendall/Hunt.

Readence, J., Beans, T., & Baldwin, R. (1992). *Content area literacy: An integrated approach.* Dubuque, IA: Kendall/Hunt.

Ruddiman, J. (1993). The vocab game: Empowering students through word awareness. *Journal of Reading, 36,* 400–401.

Rumelhart, D. (1980). Schemata: The building blocks of cognition. In R. J. Spira, B. C. Bruce, & W. F. Bruner (Eds.). *Theoretical issues for reading comprehension* (pp. 33–58). Hillsdale, NJ: Lawrence Erlbaum.

Searfoss, L., & Readence, J. (1994). *Helping children learn to read.* Boston: Allyn & Bacon.

Shanklin, N., & Rhodes, L. (1989). Comprehension instruction as sharing and extending. *The Reading Teacher, 42,* 496–500.

Shibles, E. (1959). Vocabulary of first-grade children. *Elementary School Journal, 30,* 216–221.

Smith, M., & Bean, T. (1983). Four strategies that develop children's story comprehension and writing. *The Reading Teacher, 37,* 295–301.

Stauffer, R. (1975). *Directing the reading-thinking process.* NY: Harper & Row.

Stauffer, R. (1980). *The language-experience approach to the teaching of reading.* NY: Harper & Row.

Taylor, B., Frye, B., & Marayama, M. (1990). Time spent reading and reading growth. *American Educational Research Journal, 27,* 351–362.

Tierney, R., Readence, J., & Dishner, E. (1990). Reading strategies and practices: A compendium (pp. 312–316). Boston: Allyn & Bacon.

Tyson, E., & Mountain, L. (1982). A riddle or pun makes learning words fun. *The Reading Teacher, 36,* 170–173.

ASSESSING AND DEVELOPING WRITING AND SPELLING SKILLS

CONCEPTS THAT YOU SHOULD LEARN FROM READING THIS CHAPTER

After reading this chapter, you will be able to:

- *Describe the importance of learning writing skills in the home, preschool, kindergarten, and primary grades*

- *Briefly describe the major goals of primary-grade writing instruction*

- *Describe some of the strategies and materials that can be used to assess the writing skills of young children*

- *Explain some strategies and materials that can be used to improve the writing skills of young children*

- *Explain the importance of process writing in the primary grades and its steps*

- *Describe the elements that the typical writing workshop consists of when it is used with young children*

- *Briefly describe the main stages of acquiring spelling ability that young children progress through on their way to traditional (conventional) spelling*

- *Discuss the reasons why early childhood teachers must explain the stages of developmental spelling to parents, administrators, and perhaps other teachers*

- *Explain the Developmental Spelling Test and its use as a spelling skills assessment device*

- *Describe some of the most useful strategies for teaching spelling skills in the primary grades*

© PhotoDisc/Education

217

One of the most important and useful emphases of the 1980s and 1990s was the attempt to integrate the teaching of all the elements of literacy—listening, speaking, reading, and writing. For too long, for example, reading and writing have been taught in most elementary schools as separate entities with by far the most emphasis being placed on reading instruction. Perhaps two statements by the noted writing researcher Graves best points out the importance of writing and the little attention that schools typically have given it. Graves wrote, "for every $3000 spent on children's ability to receive information, $1.00 was spent on their power to send it in writing" (1980). In addition, he wrote the following:

> Children want to write. They want to write the first day they attend school. This is no accident. Before they went to school they marked up walls, pavements, newspapers with crayons, chalk, pens, or pencils . . . anything that makes a mark. The child's marks say, "I am" (1983, p. 1).

Calkins has written the following about children's writing which illustrates its great importance:

> For me, it is essential that children are deeply involved in writing, that they share their texts with others, and that they perceive themselves as authors. I believe these three things are interconnected. A sense of authorship comes from the struggle to put something big and vital into print, and from seeing one's own printed words reach the hearts and minds of others (1986, p. 9).

Thus, you can see that the teaching of writing is vitally important in the education of young children. The same also can be said of the stages of spelling which begins early in a child's life when he or she scribbles on a chalkboard in the home or in an early childhood classroom. Both are important skills for young children to master. After reading and studying this chapter, you should feel very confident about teaching writing and spelling skills to the young children with whom you will work in many different types of early educational settings.

AN OVERVIEW OF CHILDREN'S WRITING

In the past, writing instruction largely has been de-emphasized in elementary literacy instruction. However, today it is receiving considerably more emphasis. Both children and adults will very likely need to use writing skills more extensively in the future than they do at present. For example, it is quite clear that over the next decade or so American workers in most settings will probably write more than they have before. The prevalence of electronic communications in everyday life will ensure that this happens. For example, a large portion of many workdays is now spent composing or answering E-mail, which is computerized communication that comprises everything from business memoranda to friendly letters, gossip, medical information, recipes, want ads, directions, or information about government budgets and tax reform. E-mail is the tip of the iceberg in a communications revolution that is likely to change not only the way in which people communicate but also the way they shop, bank, invest, learn, and entertain. Levy wrote that "Getting in touch with each other is more fun than the coolest computer game, or the hottest information" (1995–1996, p. 27).

It is important to note that society allows young children to learn to speak by trial and error or experimentation. However, in the case of reading and writing, adults expect them to be right the first time. This view does not allow young children to experiment with either reading or writing in the way in which they need to. For example, children must experiment with invented (temporary) spelling. Children teach themselves to write primarily by experimentation with writing materials of various types. This writing begins in early childhood with scribbling and subsequently progresses to letter-like forms, random letters or letter strings, invented spelling, and finally conventional spelling (see a later section of this chapter).

According to Dyson (1989) and Graves (1994), children's writing develops through constant invention and reinvention of the forms of written language. For example, children invent ways of making letters, words, and texts, moving from primitive forms through successively closer approximations of conventional forms. As they reconstruct their abilities to produce messages and texts, they simultaneously reconstruct their knowledge about written language (Bissex, 1985; Graves, 1994). Parents of preschool children who are interested in writing typically accept and support their children's production of primitive written forms and do not offer criticism nor rejections of those forms. Morrow (1997) has called such writing *proto-writing*. Although no one teaches young children proto-writing, they just invent it from their observation of environmental print and through observation, modeling, and interacting with more literate adults and children.

Birnbaum and Emig (1983) stated that readers and writers transform their experiences through verbal symbols. Writers reconstruct meanings by constructing texts while readers reconstruct texts by anticipating meanings. Therefore, the parallels between reading and writing are more obvious for young children than for older students and adults. As stated earlier, young children teach themselves to write in much the same way in which they teach themselves to read, by personally motivated and directed trial and error. They invent and decorate letters, symbols, and words and mix drawings and writing. Young children often continue to use invented forms of writing even after they have begun to master more conventional types. Therefore, to learn writing, children need active models, supportive conversation and writing, and praise for what they have written and how they wrote it. It also is important to remember that *what looks like writing to children is writing,* whether it is drawing, scribbling, letterlike forms, or a type of writing that is nearer to conventional writing.

In the future, writing instruction must not be teacher dominated. Instead, children must be allowed to devise their own personal writing process. It also is important that young children have teachers who themselves are writers and demonstrate this.

Young children learn the function of writing earlier than they do the forms of writing. For example, most young children are well acquainted with the function of grocery lists, lists of things to do, thank-you letters and cards, birthday greetings, letters, and probably E-mail before they are aware of written forms.

Here are some of the goals for primary-grade writers:

- to experience pleasure in writing
- to want to write often
- to like the sound of words
- to create for oneself and for others
- to be part of an audience for other writers
- to like literature and to like being a listener who creates word pictures, selects favorite words to use in writing, and thinks about his or her writing vocabulary
- to find favorite books and authors
- to write for more than one kind of audience
- to try writing in many forms, such as dictation, process writing with published books, or research writing
- to try to use readable (not necessarily completely correct) spelling which can easily be read by other children as well as adults

Burrows (Burrows, Jackson, & Saunders, 1984), who often is considered a pioneer in the writing movement, has categorized writing into two kinds of experiences: *practical writing* and *personal writing.* It is important to remember that sometimes the terms *content writing* and *creative writing* are used instead of practical writing and personal writing. However, they essentially are the same. Practical writing performs a service and usually requires an audience. For example, letters, memos, captions, reports, and lists are practical ways to share writing. Sharing with an audience of classmates, parents, grandparents, or pen pals is very important. Personal writing, on the other hand, is spontaneous, as children write for themselves. The audience is the writer herself or himself. The purpose is to use writing for relaxation and as a way to sincerely communicate ideas, feelings, emotions, triumphs, and hardships. A good example of this is a book that this author recently read entitled *The Diary of Mattie Spenser* (by S. Dallas, NY: St. Martin's Press, 1997). This book is a reprint of the actual personal diary of a woman who homesteaded in the Colorado Territory in the 1860s.

In summary, the writing of young children usually is self-initiated and learned by experimentation and should be valued in whatever form it takes. It develops over time, and young children should be encouraged and supported as it develops, no matter what form it takes at any particular time.

ASSESSING WRITING SKILLS

Emergent and beginning writing skills can be evaluated in a number of primarily informal ways. One of these assessment strategies is simply to have the young child write all the words that he can. As part of the assessment program for entrance into the contemporary Reading Recovery Program, each child is given a sheet of paper and asked to write all of the words he or she is able to write on the paper.

Normally when a teacher asks a child at the emergent literacy level to write all of the words that he or she can, invented (temporary) spelling should be considered correct if it is decipherable. The following book will provide you with precise instructions about how to evaluate this part of the assessment:

Clay, M. (1993). *A classroom survey of early literacy achievement.* Portsmouth, NH: Heinemann.

For the purposes of the typical literacy teacher, an informal assessment with simple examination and ranking of the children's responses in his or her classroom should be sufficient. An early childhood teacher can learn a great deal about a child's sight word identification ability, phonic analysis ability, and spelling ability by this very simple quick assessment technique.

One of the best measures of sophistication competency in either oral or written language is the number of words used per T-unit. A *T-unit* is defined as any independent clause with all of its subordinate clauses and modifiers. Not only is this technique for determining sophistication of language supported by research, it also is logical, as can be seen from the following two eleven-word sentences, containing about the same basic idea:

My dog was hot yesterday, and she waded in the lake.
Since it was hot yesterday, my dog waded in the lake.

The first sentence is a compound sentence and consists of two T-units: *My dog was hot yesterday,* and *and she waded in the lake.* Thus, this writer used an average of 5.5 words per T-unit. However, in the second sentence, which is a complex sentence containing a subordinate clause, there is only *one independent clause* which contains a T-unit of eleven words. It requires a higher degree of language sophistication to subordinate ideas within the same sentence, and more sophisticated thinking tends to be expressed in more complex sentences.

Evaluation by the use of T-units is not appropriate for atypical pieces of writing such as poetry or some types of prose. However, the T-unit measure is objective and reliable for individuals or groups of children if the goal is to determine relative status of writing ability or writing growth over time. Loban (1976) found that third-grade children used an average of 7.60 T-units per written sentences. Apparently, the research about the use of T-units done prior to that grade level is very limited.

Using Checklists to Assess Writing Skills

Checklists are a very effective way for early childhood teachers to evaluate the writing skills of young children.

Checklists are especially good because their use does not require any special materials or teaching strategies. They can be used as part of the regular curriculum. Some examples of these kinds of checklists are as follows: checklist of emergent writing behaviors, checklist of primary-grade writing behaviors, checklist of editing behaviors, and an individual writing survey. The chapter now includes a reproducible checklist of primary-grade writing behaviors and a reproducible individual writing survey for the second- and third-grade levels. You can duplicate and use these two assessment devices in their present form or modify them in any way you want.

ACTIVITY

Name _____ Grade _____

Checklist of Primary-Grade Writing Behaviors

	Usually	Sometimes	Not Yet
1. Is able to print his or her own first and last names correctly.	☐	☐	☐
2. Holds the writing implement correctly.	☐	☐	☐
3. Enjoys exploring with writing materials such as unlined and lined paper, pencils, markers, and materials for making books.	☐	☐	☐
4. Dictates words, phrases, sentences, and stories that he or she wants recorded.	☐	☐	☐
5. Uses invented spelling when necessary instead of asking the teacher or classmates for help.	☐	☐	☐
6. Uses conventional spelling when writing most words.	☐	☐	☐
7. Seems to enjoy most writing activities.	☐	☐	☐
8. Is able to use correct segmentation between words, sentences, lines, and the end of the page while writing.	☐	☐	☐
9. Is able to write attentively for 15–20 minutes.	☐	☐	☐
10. Writes to some extent in varied genres such as creative expression, narration, exposition, persuasion, and description.	☐	☐	☐

Continued

ACTIVITY

Continued

	Usually	Sometimes	Not Yet
11. Is able to brainstorm to select a topic for writing.	☐	☐	☐
12. Is able to write an acceptable rough (first) draft.	☐	☐	☐
13. Is able to effectively edit his or her rough (first) draft, making additions, deletions, and reorganizations.	☐	☐	☐
14. Understands and uses correct mechanics such as complete sentences, capital letters, periods, commas, question marks, and exclamation points.	☐	☐	☐
15. Demonstrates some organization in story form (beginning, middle, and ending).	☐	☐	☐
16. Is able to publish his or her writing in an acceptable form when appropriate.	☐	☐	☐
17. Is willing to receive and give advice to his or her classmates about writing in writing conferences.	☐	☐	☐
18. Is able to reread his or her own writing effectively.	☐	☐	☐
19. Is able to share his or her writing with classmates.	☐	☐	☐
20. Listens attentively to the writing of his or her classmates.	☐	☐	☐
21. Is able to use a computer for word processing when it is appropriate and available.	☐	☐	☐
22. Is willing to enter his or her writing in some type of informal competition such as the "Young Authors" contest when he or she has the opportunity to do so.	☐	☐	☐

A C T I V I T Y

Name _____   Grade _____

Individual Writing Inventory
Second-and-Third-Grade Level

I. Have the child write his or her own first and last names (if able).

	below average	average	above average
1. accuracy	☐	☐	☐
2. legibility	☐	☐	☐
3. spelling	☐	☐	☐

4. Teacher comments _____

II. Have the child write a description of what is pictured.

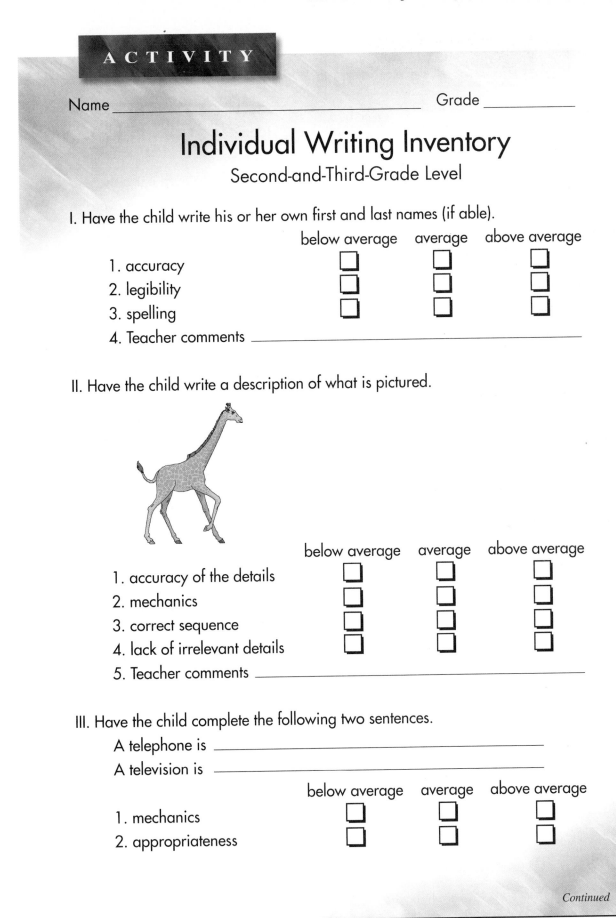

	below average	average	above average
1. accuracy of the details	☐	☐	☐
2. mechanics	☐	☐	☐
3. correct sequence	☐	☐	☐
4. lack of irrelevant details	☐	☐	☐

5. Teacher comments _____

III. Have the child complete the following two sentences.

A telephone is _____

A television is _____

	below average	average	above average
1. mechanics	☐	☐	☐
2. appropriateness	☐	☐	☐

Continued

Continued

IV. Have the child fill in an omitted word from each of three sentences.

It is a cloudy, damp, _____ today.

My cat had four cute _____ last week.

My brother cuts _____ in the summer to earn extra money.

	below average	average	above average
1. accuracy	☐	☐	☐
2. semantic acceptability	☐	☐	☐
3. syntactic acceptability	☐	☐	☐
4. prior knowledge	☐	☐	☐
5. Teacher comments			

_____

V. Dictate three sentences, repeating each sentence three times. Rate the child's transcription for:

	below average	average	above average
1. accuracy	☐	☐	☐
2. mechanics*	☐	☐	☐
3. penmanship	☐	☐	☐
4. Teacher comments			

_____

*Mechanics in this Individual Writing Inventory refers to spelling, capitalization, grammatical usage, and punctuation.

Using Holistic Scoring to Assess Writing

Holistic scoring can be used in the second and third grades to assess children's writing. It is not relevant to use in first grade, and even at the second- and third-grade levels the results from using it must be interpreted very cautiously. There are a number of different classification schemes for scoring children's writing holistically. Usually writing is scored using a 1–4, 1–5, 1–6, or 1–8 rating. This author has written a book that describes holistic scoring in detail. This book uses a 1–5 rating and evaluates writing using these five criteria: clarity, support, organization, mechanics, and overall rating.

Since holistic scoring has limited value in evaluating early childhood writing, detailed information about how to implement this type of scoring has not been included in this book. You may consult the following teacher's resource book if you want to know exactly how to do this:

> Miller, W. (1995). *Alternative assessment techniques for reading & writing* (pp. 389–421). West Nyack, NY: The Center for Applied Research in Education.

STRATEGIES AND MATERIALS FOR IMPROVING WRITING SKILLS

This chapter now includes a number of practical ideas and materials for improving ability in writing skills, any of which can be modified for your own use.

Writing Center

It is important for any early childhood classroom to have a *writing center* to provide opportunities for young children to engage in writing as well as to motivate them to do so. The writing center in any early childhood classroom should be placed in a location that provides a degree of privacy but also encourages cooperation when appropriate. A good writing center should contain the following:

- unlined and lined paper
- markers
- crayons
- pencils
- a portable chalkboard
- a computer or typewriter if the children are able to use one
- blank (bare) books
- construction paper for making books
- hole punch, yarn, staples, etc. for constructing books
- index cards for recording "my very own words"
- magnetic letters
- alphabet chart

Within the writing center, children should be encouraged to write for real purposes, such as composing birthday cards, thank-you cards and letters, letters and notes, grocery lists, lists of other types, dialogue journals, journals, and reading response journals (the last three are explained in a later part of this section). Materials written to other students can be delivered to the classroom mailbox (the mailboxes can be made of brown envelopes, shoeboxes, file folders, etc.).

Process Writing

Process writing is an excellent strategy to use with children in the second and third grades. Its usefulness is limited in first grade, and it should not be used very often at that level. In process writing the child writes a "published" book which can be shared with other children while sitting in the "author's chair," read by other children in the class, entered in a young author's contest, or taken home and read to family members. However, with young children the process writing always should be of more importance than the product. Therefore, young children's writing should rarely go through the steps of process writing, but mainly be only first or rough drafts.

Here is a description of the steps that are involved in process writing:

- *Prewriting (brainstorming).* Before a young child attempts to write a rough draft, he or she should brainstorm to try to decide on a topic for the writing. In most instances, the child should be allowed complete freedom in deciding on a writing topic. However, on rare occasions it is acceptable to provide the child with a choice of several topics (ideas) that he or she can choose to write about. Rarely, if ever, should the teacher insist that the child write on an assigned topic without giving him or her the opportunity to provide input. If you want, the child can have some type of experience to provide him or her with a topic to write about. Some experiences that can be used for this purpose are a class field trip, an art experience, a rhythm experience, a cooking or baking experience, a class pet, classroom visitors, or the use of puppetry (see Chapter 5). The prewriting experience on occasion also may consist of introducing children to different types of writing and ways of effectively organizing their writing.
- *Rough draft ("sloppy copy").* The child writes a rough or first draft of the story. This may be called a "sloppy copy." In this draft the child should be told not to be concerned about mechanics such as spelling, grammar, punctuation, or handwriting but rather concentrate on the content of the writing. The rough draft can be as extensive or as brief as the child would like. If the child wants, the rough draft can be written on the computer. If the rough draft is written on every other line, there will be space available to make revisions without rewriting the entire copy.

- *Conferencing.* Next the child should have a conference with either the teacher or one or more classmates to determine in what ways the writing can be improved. This conference should focus on the positive aspects of the writing while also helping the child to improve the structure and mechanics of the writing so that it can later be written in a finished form. During the conference the teacher or a classmate can mark the child's mechanical errors so that they can be corrected. It is usually better to mark a child's errors with a pen or pencil which is any color except red. At the primary-grade level content always should receive more emphasis than does mechanics. If children are going to act as peer conferees, they need to have some training and need to be aware that the tone of all conferences should be positive. A child also can confer with himself or herself about the writing if this is what he or she really wants to do.
- *Final draft.* The child writes the final draft of the material, being sure to incorporate all of the suggestions that were made and agreed upon during the conference. If the child has written the rough draft on the computer, it is a simple process to write the final draft, entering only the changes needed on the first draft.
- *Editing.* During the editing phase of the writing, the child should make sure that he or she has incorporated all of the agreed-upon changes. In addition, the child must check that the final draft is as correct and as professional appearing as possible.
- *Publishing.* The child should prepare to "publish" the writing. When children publish, they make reading-writing connections. The final product can be bound in a child-made or teacher-made book (see Chapter 2 for suggestions about how to construct professional appearing books). In addition, the entire final draft can be written in a blank (bare) book if the child wants. These are available at a nominal cost from many teacher stores. They also can be ordered from the following address:

  Treetop Publishing
  220 Virginia Street
  Racine, WI 53405

Bare books are available in several different sizes including "big book size." One way to publish children's books is to simply fold a piece of brightly colored binding tape around the outer edges of the page. The result is an eloquent frame. However, the methods of publication should be as authentic as possible. Occasionally the child's written product can be in some other form.

- *Author's chair (author's spot).* The final step in processing writing is to have the child share the finished book with the entire class or with a group of children. Before sharing his or her book, the child should practice reading it several times. When the book is being shared, all of the listeners should pay attention, including the teacher.

Writing Workshop

The *writing workshop* is the cornerstone of the writing process as it typically is presented in contemporary primary-grade classrooms. Although it is difficult to describe a writing workshop briefly, it generally consists of several or all of the following elements:

- a predictable, sometimes daily, time for writing
- as much time for writing as is feasible
- a simple structure for writing that can be easily implemented
- mini-lessons in writing (see the next part of this section)
- celebrating the writing process much more than the product of writing, although the product of writing also can be celebrated occasionally. This is why a young child usually should write only rough or first drafts and rarely go through the entire process writing procedure that was just described.
- In the primary-grade classroom the children should be encouraged to write in any way in which they can, including scribbling (at the very beginning stages), letterlike forms, random letters (letter strings), invented (temporary) spellings, or conventional (traditional) spelling.
- In the writing workshop writing can be motivated by relating it to other areas of the curriculum such as the dramatic play center or the block center.

If you want much more detail on the writing workshop, the following book is an excellent source to consult:

Calkins, L. (1994). *The art of writing* (pp. 188–345). Portsmouth, NH: Heinemann.

Mini-Lessons

Mini-lessons are the cornerstone of the writing workshop. They are short lessons that focus on one or several writing skills in which a child or several children need assistance. They often are informal and somewhat unstructured. Mini-lessons are very different from traditional writing lessons of the past. Here are some components that can be included in mini-lessons:

- They can begin or end a writing lesson.
- They offer motivation or instruction in one or several aspects of writing such as story content, story structure, or mechanics.
- They can be work time for beginning writing projects, working on ongoing writing projects, having teacher-pupil writing conferences, or writing response groups.

- They can be celebrations of publishing writings.
- They can be sharing sessions in which children share the process of writing or share the products of writing.
- They can be brief whole-class meetings, small-group meetings, or one-to-one sessions.
- They can occur in the first five minutes of the writing workshop, in the middle, or at the end.
- They are designed for demonstrating writing strategies to children.
- They are designed to initiate conversations about writing with children.
- They teach to children's own contexts in writing.

Helpful Mini-Lessons for Young Writers

Here are some helpful mini-lessons for young writers:

- to teach the function of environmental print
- to brainstorm the kind of writing that a child might want to do
- to encourage children to spell words in their writing in the way in which they think is correct. You can encourage them to "stretch out a word like a rubber band" in order to spell it.
- to motivate writing by reading books to children
- to teach peer conferencing to children
- to learn the writing workshop procedures
- to learn writing revision strategies
- to take risks as young writers
- to have children bring favorite books as a motivator for their own writing
- to have a child tell how he or she began writing a story

Writing Notebooks

Writing notebooks also are useful in motivating the writing process. Writing notebooks can be useful in the second and third grades to help young children extend their writing. Children can make entries in their notebooks that can encourage writing. This writing then can be shaped into specific genres of writing which can be published. However, notebooks should not be used like journals or for dead-end collections of first-draft writing. Instead, children should write first drafts from different genres and then revise them for publication.

Keeping a notebook has several advantages. Usually children in the second and third grades write a little, then take a rest, and (one hopes) then continue writing. Since the medium is the message in the primary grades, materials should encourage young writers to stay with and continue writing about a particular subject. If they make themselves small subject-specific notebooks (comprised of five or six sheets of paper stapled together), the shape of the pages and the number of pages should encourage them to gather more information about their topic.

Notebooks also can be helpful in the primary grades when young children collect related material as they try to "write more" about a subject. The material will be divided into separate entries rather than run altogether on one chaotic page. In addition, notebooks are helpful at this age because they encourage children to deal constructively with their emerging ability to anticipate an audience's response to their writing.

It is interesting to note that informal "notebooks" for writing in first grade can be found in children's pockets by observing the collection of objects that are found there, such as rocks, small toys, and baseball cards. Children in first grade may well be excellent writers except for the written part. This means that if they are allowed to use any form of writing with which they are comfortable, they can write very well.

Story Starters and Story Topics

Although not acceptable to proponents of the whole language approach, story starters may be somewhat useful in motivating young children to write if they are used only rarely and if children are not required to engage in this activity unless they want to do so. Story starters are partially complete stories which the child is to finish. Each story starter should have a number of possible endings so that the child can use his or her creativity in finishing it. Invented (temporary) spelling is perfectly acceptable to use in completing the story. The last section of this chapter contains a reproducible story starter for use in the second or third grade.

Occasionally the teacher can suggest several topics and allow the child to select one to write about. The teacher should never require a child to write on a single predetermined topic for he or she may not want to do so. Here are several topics that may be used with children in the second and third grades to motivate their writing.

Once Upon a Time There Was . . .

If I Were a Dog

Fun in the Snow

If I Were a Mouse

My Toy that Came Alive

Everything Went Wrong Yesterday

If I Were One Inch Tall

Why My Pet Would Choose Me!

The Book Character I'd Like to Meet

I Was Scared

My Mom (Dad/Grandma/Grandpa)

The Best Pet in the World Is . . .

The Best Sport Is . . .

DESCRIPTION OF SPELLING IN THE PRIMARY GRADES

There are several stages of spelling that the typical young child progresses through. Each of these stages is considered to be correct spelling in terms of the child's development at that time. Here is a brief description of each of these stages:

- *Writing (spelling) via drawing.* The child uses drawing to stand for writing. Actually the child is working on the relationship between writing and drawing and not truly confusing the two of them. The child believes that drawing/writing is a communication of a specific and purposeful message. Children who participate in writing via drawing read their drawings as if there is writing on them. Here is an illustration of this stage.

- *Writing (spelling) via scribbling.* The child scribbles but intends it as writing. The child may appear to be writing as he or she scribbles from left to right. The child moves the pencil just like an adult does, and the pencil makes sounds like those of writing. The scribbling resembles writing in some ways. Here is an illustration of this stage:

- *Writing (spelling) via making letterlike forms.* At this stage the shapes in the child's writing actually resemble letters. Careful observation, however, reveals that they only look like letters, but are not actually letters. In addition, they are not just poorly formed letters, but are actually unique creations made by the child. Here is an illustration of this stage:

- *Writing (spelling) via making random letters or letter strings.* At this stage the child uses letter sequences learned from such sources as his or her own first name. The child sometimes changes the order of the letters, writing the same letters in a number of

different ways, or reproduces letters in long strings or in random order. Here is an illustration of this stage:

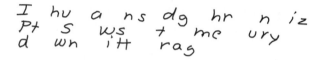

- *Writing (spelling) via invented (temporary) spellings.* Children demonstrate many varieties and levels of invented spelling. Usually a child creates his or her own spelling for words when he or she does not know the conventional spelling. In invented spelling one letter may represent an entire syllable, and words may overlap and not be properly spaced. As the child's writing matures, the words look more like conventional spelling, with perhaps only one or two letters invented or omitted. Here is an illustration of this stage:

- *Writing (spelling) via conventional (traditional) spelling.* At this stage, the child's writing resembles adult writing in most instances. Here is an example of this stage:

ASSESSING SPELLING IN THE PRIMARY GRADES

Perhaps spelling can be assessed most efficiently by teacher observation while the child is writing all types of material. A structured checklist can often assist in this observation. Weekly spelling tests often are not an effective way of evaluating a child's true spelling ability, since a number of instances the child simply memorizes the spelling words for the week and does not apply the correct spelling of these words to his or her writing. Correct spelling always should be modeled and stressed for children in all types of writing activities. A word wall composed of commonly spelled words also can be helpful in motivating correct spelling (see Chapter 4).

The Developmental Spelling Test

The *Developmental Spelling Test* is a very useful informal assessment device for the beginning stages of literacy. By studying the relation between the letters written and the letters that are expected, you can make some tentative inferences about what a child understands about letter-sound relationships. You also can infer the developmental stage that the child has achieved in understanding conventional English spelling. While this device is especially useful near the beginning of the school year, it also can be used during the school year to assess the development of a child's knowledge.

The Developmental Spelling Test may be especially useful because it includes words that differ in complexity and because it allows the teacher to be sensitive to changes that occur in the beginning stages of spelling. This spelling test has been used successfully with both kindergartners and first-graders. In a research study Morris and Perney (1984) found it to be a good predictor of later first-grade reading achievement.

The spelling test is composed of twelve words. Before giving it, prepare the children through a simple demonstration of spelling. First ask them to list the letter names that they hear in a few sample words not on the list, such as *hat* and *pet*. Then write these letters on the chalkboard, supplying any unknown letter if necessary. As an example, if the children hear only the /h/ and /t/ in *hat,* you could say "Fine" and write h_t on the chalkboard and then say, "There also is an *a* in the middle of the word *hat.*" After such a demonstration, the child should be asked to write each word the best that he or she can. The child writes all the letter names that he or she is able to hear as you pronounce the twelve words on the list. Pronounce each word several times and allow the children enough time to think and to write what they hear. The early spelling responses of children can be classified developmentally according to several stages. In the first stage, words are represented by letters and numbers, and the spellings do not resemble correct spellings. Such answers indicate that children understand that words are represented by a series of characters, but they have not yet learned that the elements within spoken words are represented by letters.

The second stage is alphabetic writing, in which children represent some sounds of words in a systematic way, mainly those at the beginning of words. The second stage can be divided into the following two substages: the stage in which only the initial consonants are represented and the stage in which both the initial and final consonants are represented, which is sometimes called the *consonant frame.*

In the third stage, children represent within-word patterns more completely. At this stage letters representing vowels are included. Next, in the transitional stage, the correct vowels and letters marking the pronunciation of words are represented. However, the spellings still differ in systematic ways from standard spelling for some words. Finally, children learn to spell words the conventional way.

From a child's responses to the Developmental Spelling Test, you can ascertain whether most of the child's responses are *preliterate, initial consonant, consonant frame, phonetic, transitional,* or *standard.* After making

this assessment, you then can direct the child's instruction in letter-sound relationships to his or her stage of development. As an example, in the preliterate stage, you can determine which, if any, of the letter names the child still needs to learn, while in the phonetic stage, you can determine which long and short vowels that the child still needs to learn.

The following table will provide you with some guidelines for evaluating the results of the Developmental Spelling Test.

DEVELOPMENTAL SPELLING TEST

Teacher Directions

Pronounce each of these words slowly and carefully, allowing the children enough time to write it the best that they can.

1. BACK
2. SINK
3. MAIL
4. DRESS
5. LAKE
6. PEEKED
7. LIGHT
8. DRAGON
9. STICK
10. SIDE
11. FEET
12. TEST

Children's responses at the various spelling stages are found in the following table:

Developmental Spelling Test Items and Illustrative Spellings at Each Stage

Correct	Preliterate	Initial Consonant	Consonant Frame	Phonetic	Transitional
BACK	RE	BET	BC	BAK	*
SINK	E	C	SE	SEK	SINCK
MAIL	A	MM	MOL	MAL	MAEL
DRESS	S	DN	JS	GAS	DRES
LAKE	AH	L	LAE	LAK	LACE
PEEKED	TTT	PF	PT	PECT	PEKED
LIGHT	IEIX	LSIE	LAT	LIT	LIET
DRAGON	ATJA	JK	GAN	DAGN	DRAGIN
STICK	F	S	TC	SED	STIK
SIDE	TC	ST	CI	SID	CIDE
FEET	V	F	FT	FET	*
TEST	ABT	TS	TST	TAST	TEEST

*No transitional spellings were produced by the subject for these words.

Source: Ferroli, L., & Shanahan, T. (1987). Kindergarten spelling: Explaining its relationship to first-grade reading. In J. E. Readence & R. S. Baldwin (Eds.). *Research in literacy: Merging perspectives.* Thirty-sixth yearbook of the National Reading Conference. Rochester, NY: National Reading Conference, 93–99. Based on Morris, D., & Perney, J. (1984). Developmental spelling as a predictor of first-grade reading achievement. *Elementary School Journal, 84,* 441–457. Copyright 1984 by The University of Chicago Press.

EXPLAINING THE STAGES OF INVENTED (TEMPORARY) SPELLINGS TO PARENTS, ADMINISTRATORS, AND OTHER TEACHERS

Before an early childhood teacher implements invented (temporary) spellings in his or her classroom, it is very important for him or her to explain this concept to parents, administrators and even to other teachers if they are not familiar with it. If this is not done, parents, for example, may be chagrined when their child brings home a written story with many invented (temporary) mis-spellings on it that have not been corrected. Parents may wonder what is happening at the school and may well contact the principal or other teachers.

Invented (temporary) spellings should be explained to parents, administrators, and if necessary, other teachers as a developmental stage through which young children progress on their way to traditional or conventional spelling. It should be explained as a preliminary stage in the same way in which young children first spoke in single words, then two-word sentences, later more complete sentences, and finally complete sentences.

The teacher can explain invented (temporary) spellings at a parent-teacher meeting near the beginning of the school year, in a newsletter to parents, or by any other acceptable means. It is very important that it be explained carefully to ensure that this program is not subject to undue criticism.

STRATEGIES FOR IMPROVING SPELLING IN THE PRIMARY GRADES

This part of the chapter contains classroom-tested strategies for teaching spelling in the primary grades. These strategies and materials are suggestions for you to work with.

Graphophonic (Phonic) Analysis Skills

Graphophonic (phonic) analysis skills may be very useful in helping young children develop spelling skills. The basic knowledge of the consonant sounds, consonant blends, consonant digraphs, long and short vowels, and some other simple vowel elements such as vowel digraphs, diphthongs, and r-controlled vowels may help young children to spell many words that they otherwise could not spell.

When children are writing, they should be encouraged to spell words in the way that they sound as much as possible. Of course, this suggestion does not apply for words that are not phonetically regular such as *rough, though, right,* and *aisle,* among many others. All logical attempts to spell words correctly should be praised. It is very helpful to tell young children the following about the words that they spell:

That is a good way to spell the word. [For invented (temporary) spellings such as the word *snoin* (snowing)]

This is the grown-up way to spell the word. (snowing)

In summary, invented spelling is an excellent way for children to learn both spelling and graphophonic skills.

Principles about Teaching Spelling

Kasten (1993) has stated the following principles about spelling instruction:

1. Children learn to spell words they need to know how to write in everyday writing.
2. Learners forget how to spell words that they have little occasion to use.
3. Spelling is a developmental process. It develops along the same lines as oral language, and children have a natural desire to spell like grown-ups (as they also want to talk like grown-ups).
4. Having children work out their own invented (temporary) spellings of low-frequency words reinforces their knowledge of phonics and English orthography and enables them to make and test hypotheses about how language works.
5. Always giving children the spelling of words that they ask for takes away valuable learning opportunities from them.
6. Expectations about spelling should be realistic. Expectations should be consistent with the child's development and experience. Spelling should be a low priority when children are new or emerging writers.
7. Spelling skills will develop thorough consistent writing, such as keeping journals, with no direct instruction.
8. Spelling is a subset of writing. It should never be presented as more important than writing, used as a prerequisite to writing, or taught in place of the teaching of writing.
9. Some people are naturally good spellers; some are not. There is no relationships between ability to spell and intelligence. A perfect speller is extremely rare. There often is, however, a relationship between good reading skills and good spelling skills, and the disabled reader may well also be a disabled speller (this author's observation).
10. The most important aspect of spelling after one is a fluent writer is learning what one knows and what one doesn't know. This enables one to develop strategies to spell difficult words and utilize available resources.

One additional principle about the teaching of spelling can be added, which is that it is important to develop a positive attitude toward spelling. A child with a good attitude toward spelling is interested in spelling new words, wants to spell words correctly, accepts responsibility for learning to spell correctly, and studies word spellings carefully.

Several Useful Spelling Strategies

Young children need to learn a useful spelling strategy. This is *not* the strategy of requiring them to write the weekly spelling words ten times each. When I was a child, my teachers required that I do this, and I simply wrote the first letter of each word ten times, the second letter ten times, the third letter ten times, etc. This obviously was meaningless.

Here is a spelling strategy that many children have found effective:

1. Look at the word, and say it to yourself.
2. Say each letter in the word to yourself.
3. Close your eyes, and spell the word to yourself.
4. Write the word, and check that you have spelled it correctly.
5. Write the word again, and check that you spelled it correctly.

According to Galda, Cullinan, & Strickland (1993), the visual recreation of target words is a powerful tool for learning to spell. Careful attention to sound, quite helpful and necessary for invented (temporary) spellings, becomes less helpful as children develop conventional spelling.

Tompkins (1997) has proposed a repertoire of strategies in order to spell unfamiliar words. Some of these spelling strategies may be useful to young children and are as follows:

- inventing spellings for words based on children's phonological, semantic, and historical knowledge of words
- proofreading to locate and correct spelling errors
- locating words on word walls and other charts
- predicting the spelling of a word by generating possible spellings and selecting the best alternative
- applying affixes to root (base) words
- spelling unknown words by analogy to known words
- locating the spelling of unfamiliar words in a simplified dictionary
- writing a letter or two as a placeholder for a word they do not know how to spell when they are writing rough drafts and sloppy copies
- asking the teacher or another person how to spell a word

Test-Study-Test Sequence

According to Galda, Cullinan, & Strickland (1993), the *test-study-test sequence* with self-correction of mistakes

is the most effective way of teaching spelling. Very briefly, this study sequence for spelling words involves the following steps:

1. Take a pretest on the words that have to be learned. Often this should be an individual, not a group, spelling list.
2. Study only those words that were spelled incorrectly on the pretest. This study can include using the spelling strategy that was mentioned earlier. The spelling words also should be used as much as possible by the child in his or her everyday writing activities.
3. At the end of the week, take a test only on the words that were missed earlier. The teacher reads the master list, and the children write only those words that they have missed earlier in the week. To make it easy to administer the test, have the children first list the number of the words that they practiced from their study lists on their test papers. Any words that are misspelled should be included on their lists the next week.

This approach is recommended instead of the textbook (study-test) approach. Usually textbooks are arranged in week-long units with lists and practice activities that often require up to thirty minutes per day. It also is important to note that researchers have found that only 60 to 70 minutes per week should be spent on spelling instructions, as greater periods of time do not result in increased spelling ability (Johnson, Langford, & Quorm, (1981). The study-test spelling procedure is time-wasting in that the child may well study words during the week that he or she already could spell, which would be avoided if a pretest were given.

Selecting Spelling Words to Study

Many specialists in this area recommend the use of individualized spelling lists, with some of a young child's spelling words coming from his or her own writing needs. There usually should be a balance of spelling words that the entire class studies because of their usefulness and spelling words that only the child studies because they are relevant to him or her. In addition, in choosing spelling words there should be a balance between those words that follow spelling generations and those that do not. For example, if the young child has learned to spell the word *fast,* he or she also should be able to spell the words *cast, last, mast,* and *past.* In addition, there should be a balance in teaching spelling words using a procedure such as the test-study-test strategy, with children discovering spelling generations for themselves.

Tompkins (1997) has proposed a slightly different method for selecting spelling words for the child to study. She recommends the individualized approach to spelling instruction in which children choose which words that they are going to study. Many of the words they select are words that they need in their writing projects. Students then study 5 to 10 specific words during the week using a study strategy. This approach places more responsibility on children for their own learning. Teachers also could develop a weekly word list of 20 to 50 words of varying difficulty from which children select words to study. Words for the master list are high-frequency words, words from the word wall related to literature units and theme studies, and words children need for their writing projects begun during the previous week. Words from spelling textbooks can be added to the list.

Several Other Strategies to Use in Early Childhood Spelling

Here are several other strategies that can be useful in presenting spelling to young children.

- crossword puzzles constructed of relevant spelling words
- word-step puzzles constructed of appropriate spelling words
- homonym games

- words-that-begin-alike games
- card games using selected spelling words
- riddles that are related to selected spelling words
- rhyming poetry that is related to the chosen spelling words
- Here are three spelling lists that can be provided on an individual basis or on charts in the writing/publishing center of the early childhood classroom:

  1. A List of Words for Spelling and Editing
  2. Words Often Spelled and Pronounced Incorrectly
  3. The "Yucky" List of Spelling words (Clark, 1989). The "yucky" list is a list the early childhood teacher creates for each class. The list is composed of words that the teacher notices children consistently misspell. This list will change during the school year as children progress as spellers.

REPRODUCIBLES FOR IMPROVING WRITING SKILLS WITH YOUNG CHILDREN

The chapter now includes a reproducible self-assessment checklist of the primary grades and a story starter that you can use to motivate writing in second or third grade.

ACTIVITY

Name _____   Grade _____

Self-Assessment Checklist about Writing
Second- or-Third-Grade Level

Read each of these sentences to yourself.
Then put an X in the box under Yes or No.

	Yes	No
1. I really like to do different kinds of writing.	☐	☐
2. I want to write often at both school and home.	☐	☐
3. I like the sound of words.	☐	☐
4. I like to write stories for other people to listen to and for me to read for myself.	☐	☐
5. I like to listen to the writing of other children.	☐	☐
6. I like to write for more than one kind of audience.	☐	☐
7. I like to try different types of writing, such as story writing, journal writing, dictation, and different types of lists.	☐	☐
8. I try to spell the words in my writing correctly or at least spell words so that other people can read them.	☐	☐
9. I try to remember to use capital letters when they are necessary.	☐	☐
10. I try to use marks of punctuation correctly, such as periods, commas, question marks, apostrophes, and exclamation points.	☐	☐

Continued

A C T I V I T Y *Continued*

Name _____ Grade _____

A Story Starter
Second-or-Third-Grade Level

Read this story beginning to yourself. Then write your own ending to the story. You can end it in any way that you want. You should try to spell the words the best that you can or look at the word wall for help.

What Happened to Honey?

Eddie is an eight-year-old boy with red hair and freckles. He has a golden retriever named Honey who is about two years old. Honey is really pretty and very smart too. Honey is Eddie's best friend.

Eddie always lets Honey outside in his family's big fenced backyard. She likes to play ball with Eddie there. One day while Eddie and Honey were playing ball, Eddie's mother called him into the house to talk on the telephone to his friend Matt who had called.

When Eddie went back to the yard to play some more ball with Honey, he was shocked to find her gone. The gate in the fence was standing open, and Honey was nowhere to be seen!

Now finish this story by writing what you think happened to Honey.

SUGGESTED ACTIVITIES

1. If possible, collect a brief writing sample from a three-year-old, a four-year-old, a five-year-old, and a six-year-old child. In what ways do the writing of these children reflect the stages of writing (spelling) that were explained in this chapter?

2. If possible, have a seven-year-old child or an eight-year-old child engage in a sample of practical writing, such as a letter, some type of list, or a card to a relative or friend. Then examine the spelling of this example of practical writing to determine if it is at the stage of invented (temporary) spellings, conventional spelling, or a combination of both.

3. If feasible, have a seven-year-old child or an eight-year-old child provide you with a brief sample of his or her writing. Then analyze this sample in terms of words per T-unit as described in this chapter.

4. If possible, have a child in second or third grade work with you in making a published book by using the process writing approach. When the child is finished, he or she will have a published "book" to read to his or her family or friends.

5. If you are able, administer the Developmental Spelling Test to a young child. Attempt to evaluate this test using the information contained in this chapter.

6. Consult a dictionary and select several difficult words that you do not know how to spell. Try to learn how to spell these words using the five-step spelling strategy explained in this chapter. Was this a successful spelling strategy for you? Why or why not?

SELECTED REFERENCES

Calkins, L. (1994). *The art of teaching writing* (pp. 3–137). Portsmouth, NH: Heinemann.

Cheek, E., Flippo, R., & Lindsey, J. (1997). *Reading for success in elementary schools* (pp. 268–306). Madison, WI: Brown & Benchmark.

Clarke, L. (1988). Invented versus traditional spelling in first graders' writings: Effects on learning to spell and read. *Research in the Teaching of English, 22,* 281–309.

Fields, M., & Spangler, M. (1995). *Let's begin reading right* (pp. 139–216). Englewood Cliffs, NJ: Prentice Hall.

Galda, L., Cullinan, B., & Strickland, D. (1993). *Language, literacy and the child* (pp. 180–245). Fort Worth, TX: Harcourt Brace Jovanovich College Publishers.

Glazer, S. (1994). *An integrated approach to early literacy* (pp. 244–252). Boston: Allyn & Bacon.

Graves, M., Juel, C., & Graves, B. (1998). *Teaching reading in the 21st century* (pp. 384–431). Boston: Allyn & Bacon.

Gunning, T. (1996). *Creating reading instruction for all children* (pp. 45–54). Needham Heights, MA: Allyn & Bacon.

Hillerich, R. (1985). *Teaching children to write.* Englewood Cliffs, NJ: Prentice Hall.

Morrow, L. (1997). *Literacy development for the early years* (pp. 257–297). Needham Heights, MA: Allyn & Bacon.

Richgels, D. (1995). Invented spelling ability and printed words, learning in kindergarten. *Reading Research Quarterly, 30,* 96–109.

Sampson, M., Sampson, M., & Allen, R. (1995). *Pathways to literacy* (pp. 124–261). Fort Worth, TX: Harcourt Brace Jovanovich College Publishers.

Spandel, V., & Stiggins, R. (1997). *Creating writers.* NY: Longman.

Tompkins, G. (1997). *Literacy for the 21st century* (pp. 111–120). Upper Saddle River, NJ: Prentice-Hall.

Tompkins, G., & McGee, L. (1993). *Teaching reading with literature* (pp. 21–27). NY: Macmillan.

WORKS CITED IN CHAPTER 6

Birnbaum, J., & Emig, J. (1983). Creating minds: Creating texts. In R. Parker & F. Davis (Eds.). *Developing literacy: Young children's use of language.* Newark, DE: International Reading Association.

Bissex, G. (1985). Watching young writers. In A. Jaggar & M. Smith-Burke (Eds.). *Observing the language learner.* Urbana, IL: National Council of Teachers of English.

Burrows, A., Jackson, D., & Saunders, D. (1984). *They all want to write.* Hamden, CT: Library of Professional Publications.

Calkins, L. (1986). *The art of teaching writing.* Portsmouth, NH: Heinemann.

Clark, R. (1989). *Free to write.* Portsmouth, NH: Heinemann.

Dyson, A. (1989). *The multiple worlds of child writers: Friends learning to write.* NY: Teachers College Press.

Galda, L., Cullinan, B., & Strickland, D. (1993). *Language, literacy and the child.* Fort Worth, TX: Harcourt Brace Jovanovich College Publishers.

Graves, D. (1980). A new look at writing research. *Language Arts, 57,* 914–918.

Graves, D. (1983). *Writing: Teachers and children at work.* Portsmouth, NH: Heinemann.

Graves, D. (1994). *A fresh look at writing.* Portsmouth, NH: Heinemann.

WORKS CITED IN CHAPTER 6—*Continued*

Johnson, T., Langford, K., & Quorn, K. (1981). Characteristics of an effective spelling program. *Language Arts, 58,* 581–588.

Levy, S. (1995–1996). The year of the Internet. *Newsweek,* 12/25/95–1/1/96, 21–30.

Loban, W. (1976). *Language development: Kindergarten through grade twelve.* Urbana, IL: National Council of Teachers of English.

Morris, D., & Perney, J. (1984). Developmental spelling as a predictor of first-grade reading achievement. *Elementary School Journal, 84,* 441–457.

Morrow, L. (1997). *Literacy development in the early years.* Needham Heights, MA: Allyn & Bacon.

Tompkins, G. (1997). *Literacy for the 21st century.* Upper Saddle River, NJ: Prentice-Hall.

ASSESSMENT DEVICES AND STRATEGIES THAT CAN BE USED IN AN EARLY LITERACY PROGRAM

CONCEPTS THAT YOU SHOULD LEARN FROM READING THIS CHAPTER

After reading this chapter, you will be able to:

- *Explain evaluation, assessment, and authentic assessment*

- *Describe the advantages and limitations of using standardized assessment devices in an early literacy program*

- *Explain the advantages and limitations of using various kinds of informal assessment devices and strategies in an early literacy program*

- *Explain the basic characteristics of standardized reading tests and explain their relevance in an early literacy program*

- *Describe the basic characteristics of criterion-referenced assessment using benchmarks and illustrate their relevance in an early literacy program*

- *Explain how basal reader tests can be used in reading analysis*

- *Explain "kid-watching" and discuss its usefulness in any early literacy program*

- *Describe how checklists can be used in an early literacy program*

- *Explain in detail how to use a running record in reading analysis*

- *Explain the relevance of using miscue analysis*

- *Briefly describe the basic characteristics of the Individual Reading Inventory*

- *Describe the El Paso Phonics Survey*

- *Explain how retelling can be used in assessing reading skills*

- *Explain how portfolio assessment is used and why it is relevant in all types of literacy programs, especially whole language programs*

© PhotoDisc/Education

This author has presented a speech entitled "Alternative Assessment Techniques in Reading and Writing" at several reading conventions. She always reads the children's book entitled *First grade takes a test* (by M. Cohen, NY: Greenwillow Books, 1980) aloud at the beginning of this presentation. Very briefly, the book describes how a first-grade class took a standardized reading achievement test. It clearly shows how the children found both the test and its results disturbing, how the activity was not connected in any substantive way with classroom reading instruction, and how many of the questions were subject to misinterpretation. You are encouraged to obtain a copy of this simple book from a library. You will find yourself much enlightened about children's views of standardized testing from reading it.

After completing this chapter, you should be well aware of the many components that comprise standardized and informal assessment of reading skills and be better able to select those devices and strategies that are the most relevant for the children with whom you work.

AN INTRODUCTION TO ASSESSMENT IN AN EARLY CHILDHOOD READING PROGRAM

It may first be useful to define the terms *evaluation, assessment,* and *authentic assessment* as they are used in this book. *Evaluation* is judging or evaluating the information that is gathered by assessment. It is evaluating the responses that the child gave, and it usually is more formal than is assessment. For example, *standardized tests* are an example of evaluating a child for the purpose of making a diagnosis of his or her reading skills strengths and weaknesses. Having a child respond to a standardized criterion-referenced test with its *benchmarks* is an example of evaluation. *Summative evaluation,* which occurs near the end of a predetermined period, evaluates the impact of instruction. The final exam that a college student takes at the end of a course is an example of summative evaluation. When teachers evaluate children summatively, the evaluation is often in the form of a grade. On the other hand, *formative evaluation* is ongoing and is used to improve instruction (Bertrand, 1991). I believe that virtually all of the evaluation done with young children should be of the formative type for reasons that are explained later in this chapter.

Evaluation has three main perspectives, those of the *self, collaborative others,* and *society* (Short, 1990). The self obviously is the child. The collaborative others are all those who work with the child, including the teacher, peer editor, learning team, and discussion groups. Society includes parents, the community at large, and officials of the school and school district. Each group may have a different purpose for evaluating and may require a different type of evidence. For example, the school board may want to examine norm-referenced, multiple-choice, standardized test scores to see how the skills of children in their schools compare with skills of children elsewhere; children in first grade may already know that they are not doing well in reading and may need test results to help them know what to focus on; a teacher may observe that a child is weak in such graphophonic skills as discriminating between the short vowel sounds and want to evaluate progress after focused practice. Because children, teachers, parents, and school boards all have different perspectives, they all need different kinds of information (Farr, 1992). This is one reason standardized reading tests will continue to be mandated in the future even for young children with whom they are not very relevant.

Assessment can be defined as gathering information to meet the particular reading needs of a child. It involves looking at what children can and cannot achieve. Although assessment usually is informal, it still can be very useful. Since assessment usually is informal it often is called *authentic assessment.* The word *authentic* is used because these assessment procedures "reflect the actual learning and instructional activities of the classroom and out of school worlds" (general society) (Hiebert, Valencia, & Afflerbach, 1994, p. 10). In authentic assessment, for example, children may retell or summarize a children's trade book as opposed to objective testing in which they answer multiple-choice questions about short paragraphs. Authentic assessment also can include "kid-watching," teacher observation using checklists, and anecdotal records. Although authentic assessment currently is most closely identified with whole language instruction, it is equally useful in more traditional early childhood reading programs.

Authentic assessment programs also strongly emphasize the process of literacy, while standardized reading tests mainly evaluate the product aspect of reading. Assessment also should resemble real reading and writing activities as much as possible. The five main purposes of authentic assessment are as follows:

- to document mileposts in children's development as readers and writers
- to identify children's strengths in order to plan for instruction
- to document children's reading and writing activities
- to determine grades
- to help teachers to learn more about how children became strategic readers and writers

Assessment is more than testing—it is an integral part of teaching and learning (Goodman, Goodman, & Hood, 1989). The main purpose of assessment should be to inform and influence classroom instruction. Through authentic assessment, teachers learn about their students, about themselves as teachers, and about the impact of the instructional program. Similarly when children reflect on their learning and use self-assessment, they learn about themselves as learners and also about their learning.

ADVANTAGES AND LIMITATIONS OF USING STANDARDIZED READING TESTS AND OF USING INFORMAL (AUTHENTIC) ASSESSMENT DEVICES

Both standardized reading tests and authentic (informal) assessment devices have a number of unique advantages and limitations of which you should be aware. That is why both types of tools may have some uses in an early childhood reading program. However, the value of standardized evaluation devices is fairly limited with young children.

Here are some of the advantages of using any type of standardized reading test. Note that not all of the advantages are applicable with young children.

- They are very easy for all teachers, including novice teachers, both to give and to evaluate. Many are now evaluated by computer.
- They generally are not time-consuming for children to take.
- They are *norm-referenced,* which means that the teacher can compare the results achieved by his or her class with those of a standardization group of children who are similar in sex, age, grade level, geographic location, socioeconomic class, and so on.
- They are reliable and valid. *Test reliability* means that a test provides consistent results in that a child who takes equivalent forms of the test usually will receive very similar results. Test validity means that the test measures what it is supposed to measure or is truthful and accurate. Standardized reading tests have been formulated by test experts which theoretically makes them both reliable and valid.

Here are the major limitations of standardized reading tests:

- Although they theoretically are objective, they may not be completely objective in reality.
- They often overestimate a child's actual instructional reading level due to the guessing factor. For example, I had a child named Marty in my second-grade class during my first year of teaching. Although he was a (second grade, fifth month) nonreader near the end of the school year, Marty received a score of **2.5** on the *Stanford Achievement Test.* This occurred because he went through the entire test guessing at all of the items, while none of the children who actually read the test was able to finish it! This example indicates how truly misleading standardized test scores can be, especially when they are used as the only criterion for reading achievement.
- They are not *culture-fair.* This means that they evaluate a child's prior knowledge and experiences. Usually these are middle-class experiences and culture, and therefore a child who does not possess

this culture is greatly penalized. The score that such a child earns on a standardized test is very likely to be significantly lower than his or her actual reading level.

- Especially with young children, the taking of the test may be much more difficult for the child than the material that is included in the test. For example, a child may well know the answer to a test item but be unable to locate the proper space on the test on which to mark the answer. Filling in answer bubbles is an extremely difficult task for some young children who can easily comprehend the material on the test.
- Although standardized tests are improving in this regard, most of the test items remain at the lower levels of comprehension. Although lower-level (literal or factual) questions are easy for the teacher to both formulate and score, they usually are not nearly so relevant as are questions at the higher levels of comprehension.
- The grade equivalent score is subject to misinterpretation, although it is very commonly used in reporting the results of standardized tests to parents. The grade equivalent score represents the grade level for which a raw score is the median score. For example, if the median raw score of all the students in the norm sample who were in the third month of the second grade was 41, any child getting 41 correct answers has earned a grade equivalent score of 2.3. Bauman and Stevenson (1982) have written an informative article on how standardized reading test scores are used by test publishers in determining grade equivalent scores. They wrote that the processes of interpolation and extrapolation (estimating) involves some guesswork and makes scores prime for misinterpretation. They wrote that this is particularly the case in the use of extrapolated scores that are very high or very low. Thus, grade equivalent scores may be the most accurate with average readers and the least accurate with very good or very poor readers. It is important to understand that a child cannot be expected to read material on the grade level that is indicated by a grade equivalent score, as it often represents his or her frustration reading level rather than instructional reading level. Usually a child does not possess the prior knowledge, interests, or vocabulary to be able to read up to that level.
- Although standardized reading tests are improving in this area, the early childhood teacher must be certain that the items on a test are passage dependent. Some test items can be answered merely on the basis of a child's prior knowledge without his or her having read the material. Sometimes a child can answer the majority of the items on a test solely on the basis of his or her prior knowledge.
- The teacher must be certain that the child is given the proper level of a standardized reading test. This concept is called *out-of-level testing.* For example, if a

child with reading problems is given a test that is too difficult, the score is likely to be inaccurate. Therefore, a standardized reading test usually is most accurate with average readers and less accurate with either above average or below average readers.

In summary, standardized reading tests have both advantages and limitations. The limitations often far outweigh the advantages with young children. However, an early childhood teacher usually must give such tests due to the requirements of administrators, school boards, and parents. In any case, it is important that these tests comprise only a small component of evaluating young children's reading skills, as there are many other ways in which reading evaluation is done more accurately. Standardized reading tests always must be thought of only as a tentative indicator of a child's actual instructional reading level and his or her reading needs. Their use always should be supplemented by using many informal assessment devices such as those mentioned later in this chapter.

Informal reading assessment devices are much more relevant with young children. Here are the main advantages of using them in an early childhood reading program:

- They generally are authentic in evaluating reading skills.
- They usually are relevant to the information that is being taught in the classroom or special reading program.
- They better reflect the whole language approach than do standardized reading tests.
- They emphasize the process aspects of reading rather than the product aspects, in contrast to standardized tests.
- They are able to assess the affective (attitudinal) aspects of reading fairly effectively.
- They usually reflect more accurately the accomplishments and attitudes of children with special needs than do standardized tests. Standardized tests may well discriminate against all types of children with special needs.
- They usually reflect different styles of teaching and learning more effectively than do standardized tests.
- They do not have the prescribed directions and time limits that typically are found on standardized tests. Such tests often penalize the slow, but accurate, reader.

Here are the major limitations of informal assessment devices:

- Their results often do not meet the requirements of administrators, school boards, state boards of education, or parents, since they do not appear to be "scientific."
- They usually are neither statistically reliable nor valid. However, this does not mean that they are not useful. They simply do not meet the statistical requirements for reliability and validity.

- They can be time-consuming to construct and to evaluate.
- They may make it difficult to evaluate children by predetermined criteria such as traditional report cards and grades. This is why holistic report cards and teacher-parent conferences must be used in conjunction with informal assessment if it is to be successful.
- They are not always easy to locate commercially.

In conclusion, in spite of their limitations, I believe that informal assessment devices are much more developmentally appropriate for young children than are standardized tests. However, most often some standardized devices must also be used in an early childhood literacy program.

A BRIEF DESCRIPTION OF STANDARDIZED TESTS

Standardized tests are not developmentally appropriate for young children, since pencil and paper tests are very difficult for them. Standardized tests do not evaluate emergent or beginning reading skills very well. However, you may be required to administer one or more of them in an early childhood reading program. According to Neill & Medina (1989), an estimated 105 million standardized tests are administered during every school year—an average of 2½ tests per pupil per year, and this may be a conservative estimate. In addition, the amount of testing that is done in schools seems to be increasing (Haney & Madaus, 1989). Schools have a heavy philosophical and financial investment in formal testing.

Of all the curriculum areas, testing seems to impact reading most of all. Because success in reading is so important to success in all school activities, everyone seems to be interested in reading tests. Reports on local performance on achievement tests make the front page of the newspaper. According to Valencia & Pearson (1987, p. 727), "the influence of (reading) testing is greater now than at any time in our history."

Most standardized reading tests are norm-referenced. A norm-referenced test is designed to enable a teacher to compare his or her pupils' scores with a standardized sample that is similar in age, grade level, sex, geographic location, and socioeconomic status. These norms are typically reported in all of the following ways:

- *Raw score.* The total number of correct answers. This score has no meaning until it is changed into a percentile rank, stanine, or some other type of score.
- *Percentile rank.* The point on a scale of 1 to 99 that indicates what percentage of pupils obtained an equal or lower score. For example, a percentile rank of 65 means that 65 percent of those who took the test received an equal or lower score.

- *Grade equivalent score.* The score that an average pupil at a certain level achieved (see the earlier description). For more detail see page 239.
- *Stanine.* The point on a nine-point scale with 5 being the average stanine. The word *stanine* is a combination of the words *standard* and *nine*. The nine-point scale is used because stanines are based on a bell-shaped curve of performance. Most children's scores fall in the middle stanines.

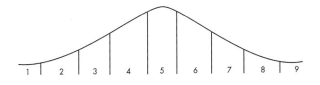

- *Scaled score.* A continuous ranking from 000 to 999 of a series of norm-referenced tests, from the lowest to the highest test. These tests may be useful for tracking long-term reading development through the grades.

Children often are given standardized survey reading or achievement tests to determine their overall reading progress. This type of test is a screening device that evaluates a child's word meaning (vocabulary), sentence comprehension, paragraph comprehension, and perhaps word-study skills. It is mainly given to locate those children who need additional testing. These tests are often given in September to determine a child's current overall reading level or in April or May to determine how much progress the child has made during the school year. Such tests usually are very easy to administer and often can be scored by computer. They are not particularly relevant in an early childhood reading program for the reasons mentioned in the previous section; however, they may well be mandated by a school district. The results from such a test much be interpreted with great caution, especially when the test is given to a young child.

In the primary grades a few children may be given a standardized diagnostic reading test. Such a test is mainly given to a child who did poorly on the survey reading or achievement test. This test attempts to evaluate a child's reading in terms of his or her exact weaknesses in sight word identification, graphophonic (phonic) analysis, word structure, explicit (literal) comprehension, implicit (higher-level) comprehension, and study strategies (usually not in the primary grades). This type of test does not purport to locate the causes for a child's reading difficulties but it does attempt to locate the exact difficulties with as much precision as possible. The results usually are reported by norms.

CRITERION-REFERENCED ASSESSMENT

Criterion-referenced assessment is another way of assessing the reading progress of young children. In some cases this is a type of authentic assessment. The results of such a test are reported in terms of a standard or criterion: for example, the child answered *80 percent* of the comprehension questions correctly. Two types of standards now being used in criterion-referenced measures are the *benchmark* and the *rubric.*

The *benchmark* is a written description of a key task that children are expected to perform. For instance, a benchmark for word identification might be "Uses both phonics and context to identify unknown words in print." Benchmarks are useful because they provide a concrete description of what pupils are expected to do. Therefore, they provide children, teachers, parents, and administrators with an observable framework for assessing reading accomplishments and needs. Using benchmarks the teacher can assess when a pupil has mastered key skill strategies and is ready to move ahead.

Contexts for observing benchmark behaviors include standardized criterion-referenced tests, observing reading skills during shared reading, retelling, drama, and teacher-pupil conferences. Allowing children a variety of ways to demonstrate benchmark behaviors seems more natural and is preferred by some teachers. However, other teachers choose to use standard tests and standard materials so that the tasks are the same for all children. Weaver (1992) established a series of tasks and observational guidelines that can be used to assess primary pupils' progress. Her benchmarks include activities such as "Can use various cueing strategies while reading." For most benchmarks the teacher uses one of a series of texts that gradually progress in difficulty. For example, on the emergent literacy level, the teacher can use *Cat on the mat* (Wildsmith, 1982) and suggestions contained in the *Benchmark assessment guide* to assess children's reading performance. The advantages of using designated books for the assessment of benchmark behaviors is that they provide material at the appropriate level of difficulty. If children are given material that is too difficult, they cannot effectively demonstrate various strategies.

Basal reader series may be accompanied by an extensive assessment and placement system. Basal tests often are one type of criterion-referenced tests. Such a test focuses on a pupil's ability to reach a certain level of performance in areas that the test is designed to measure. Most often, this is the 80 percent level of competency. Both group and individual inventories are usually available in basal reader assessment. Assessment devices may include periodic tests to be administered at the end of a unit, a section, or a book (which may be criterion-referenced). Current basal series may feature holistic tests in which children read a fairly lengthy selection and write essay-type responses. Checklists, observation guides, and portfolios may also be an important part of the basal assessment system.

Another type of standard is the rubric. A *rubric* is a written description of what is expected in order to meet a certain level of performance and is accompanied by samples of typical performance. Although rubrics are most typically used in assessing writing tasks, they also can be used to assess reading tasks, portfolios, and other literacy elements. The main advantage of a rubric is that it provides criteria for task assessment.

USING "KID-WATCHING" AND OTHER OBSERVATIONAL STRATEGIES WITH YOUNG CHILDREN

It is very important for early childhood reading teachers to be consistent and expert observers of children's reading behaviors. I believe that if reading teachers observed children's reading behaviors regularly and acted upon those observations, many cases of reading disabilities could effectively be prevented. In addition, children would enjoy reading much more.

The term "kid-watching" was introduced by Yetta Goodman (1978) of the University of Arizona, a proponent of the whole language philosophy. She stated that "kid-watching" is direct or informal observation of a child in various classroom settings. It is based on the premise that literacy development is a natural process. "Kid-watching" allows teachers to explore these two questions:

1. What evidence exists that literacy development is occurring?
2. What does a child's unexpected production of literacy behaviors say about each child's knowledge of literacy?

"Kid-watching," or *informal teacher assessment,* consists of these three aspects:

- *Observation.* Carefully observing activities of a single child's, a group of children's, or the entire class's literacy use and social behavior.
- *Interaction.* This takes place when the teacher raises questions, responds to journal writing, and conferences with children in order to stimulate further literacy and cognitive growth.
- *Analysis.* The teacher obtains information by listening to a child read and discuss and by considering a child's written work. The teacher then applies knowledge of learning principles to analyze the child's literacy abilities.

Expert "kid-watchers" demonstrate the following behaviors:

- They understand the reading and writing processes thoroughly. They also have excellent knowledge of children's and adolescent's literature. Since trained Reading Recovery teachers have a very extensive knowledge of the literacy processes, the Reading Recovery Program, an early intervention program for first-grade children with special needs, has been very successful.
- They recognize important patterns of behavior differences in competencies exhibited by different children.
- They listen attentively and perceptively to children.
- They continuously evaluate while teaching.
- They accept responsibility for curriculum development, and they do not place undue emphasis on standardized test scores.
- They keep detailed records of a child's literacy competencies, weaknesses, and progress. This also is an important reason for the success of Reading Recovery (running records and simple miscue analysis are explained in a later section of this chapter). Some teachers keep records by jotting dated notes on self-stick tags while meeting with children and later placing them in the child's files. Teachers also can use class sheets with a square for each name as in the form of a calendar. As a teacher writes notes, he or she sticks them on the child's name. Other teachers carry clipboards on which they have class lists with space for important comments. These comments later are placed in the child's file but must first be transcribed or cut apart and glued on each child's record sheet. Here is a sample of this kind of recordkeeping:

Observational Checklist for Class

Activity

_____ Date _____

Name	Comment
Jim Carlson	_____
Saul Kasidowski	_____
Linda Gettys	_____
Mary Ann Krenz	_____
Ralph Swanson	_____

Anecdotal records and teacher-completed observational checklists can also be part of the recordkeeping that is required for effective "kid-watching." On the other hand, standardized test scores provide little help in "kid-watching," which involves moment-to-moment decision making in literacy teaching. Based on effective "kid-watching" (informal observations and hunches), literacy teachers can modify teaching strategies, clarify explanations, give extra help, and provide appropriate reinforcement (teacher-made and commercial games, teacher-made and commercial activity sheets, and computer software, among others).

Effective "kid-watching" is crucial to successful whole language programs for the following main reasons:

- Whole language programs are unstructured in comparison to traditional basal reader or phonic approaches.
- The teacher, not a prescribed program, must determine in which precise literacy skills a child needs instruction and reinforcement and also how to effectively teach or reinforce those particular reading skills.

- There is no real guide that tells a literacy teacher what skills to teach or how to teach them.

"Kid-watching" also is extremely helpful in all reading programs, and every early childhood teacher should use it on a daily basis. Although "kid-watching" is a difficult, demanding task, it can be made easier by using checklists such as the two reproducible checklists that are included next in this chapter.

TWO REPRODUCIBLE CHECKLISTS TO AID "KID-WATCHING" OR TEACHER OBSERVATION

The chapter now includes a Concepts About Books checklist at the emergent reading level and a Concepts About Print checklist at the primary-grade reading level. You can duplicate and use each of these checklists in their present form or create your own similar checklists.

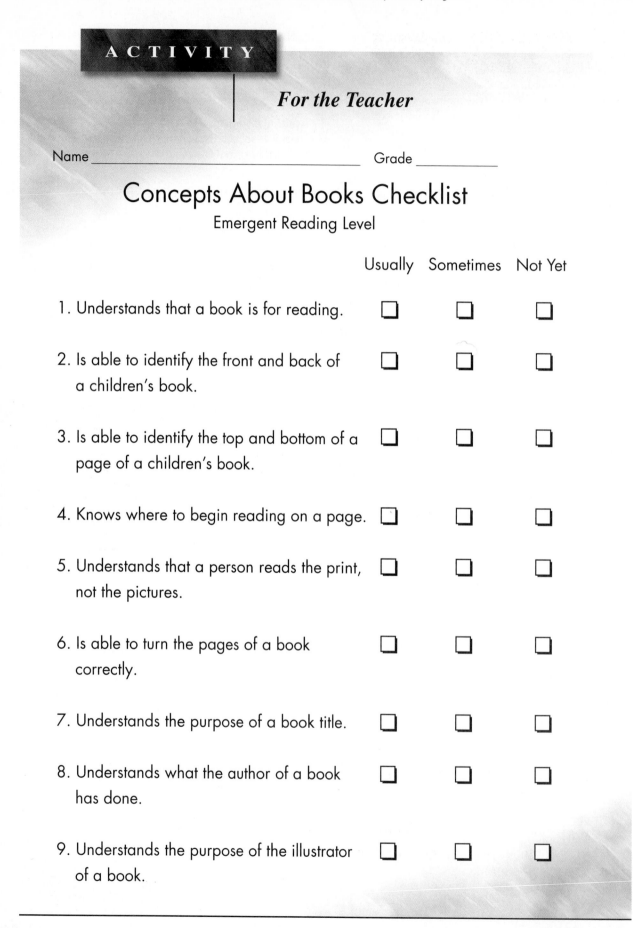

A C T I V I T Y

For the Teacher

Name _____ Grade _____

Concepts About Books Checklist
Emergent Reading Level

	Usually	Sometimes	Not Yet
1. Understands that a book is for reading.	☐	☐	☐
2. Is able to identify the front and back of a children's book.	☐	☐	☐
3. Is able to identify the top and bottom of a page of a children's book.	☐	☐	☐
4. Knows where to begin reading on a page.	☐	☐	☐
5. Understands that a person reads the print, not the pictures.	☐	☐	☐
6. Is able to turn the pages of a book correctly.	☐	☐	☐
7. Understands the purpose of a book title.	☐	☐	☐
8. Understands what the author of a book has done.	☐	☐	☐
9. Understands the purpose of the illustrator of a book.	☐	☐	☐

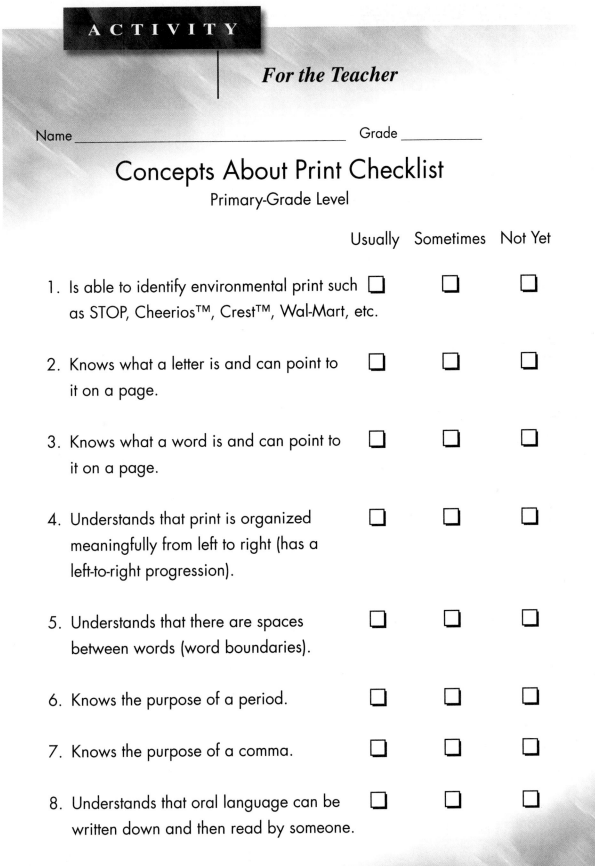

ACTIVITY

For the Teacher

Name_____ Grade_____

Concepts About Print Checklist
Primary-Grade Level

	Usually	Sometimes	Not Yet
1. Is able to identify environmental print such as STOP, Cheerios™, Crest™, Wal-Mart, etc.	☐	☐	☐
2. Knows what a letter is and can point to it on a page.	☐	☐	☐
3. Knows what a word is and can point to it on a page.	☐	☐	☐
4. Understands that print is organized meaningfully from left to right (has a left-to-right progression).	☐	☐	☐
5. Understands that there are spaces between words (word boundaries).	☐	☐	☐
6. Knows the purpose of a period.	☐	☐	☐
7. Knows the purpose of a comma.	☐	☐	☐
8. Understands that oral language can be written down and then read by someone.	☐	☐	☐

Continued

A C T I V I T Y

Continued

For the Teacher

	Usually	Sometimes	Not Yet
9. Can identify simple sight words such as *dog*, *cat*, *mother*, *ice cream*, and *school*.	☐	☐	☐
10. Can provide a rhyming word to a word that is supplied (*ball*, *call*, *hall*, *tall*, and *wall*).	☐	☐	☐
11. Can identify all of the capital letter names.	☐	☐	☐
12. Can identify all of the lowercase letter names.	☐	☐	☐
13. Associates consonants with their beginning and final sounds.	☐	☐	☐
14. Associates consonant blends with their sounds (*bl*, *cl*, *fl*, *gl*, etc.).	☐	☐	☐
15. Associates vowels with their matching long and short vowel sounds (/a/—apron, apple; /e/—eat, egg; /i/—ice, igloo; /o/—oatmeal, ostrich; /u/—use, umbrella).	☐	☐	☐
16. Can blend phonemes (sounds) into words.	☐	☐	☐

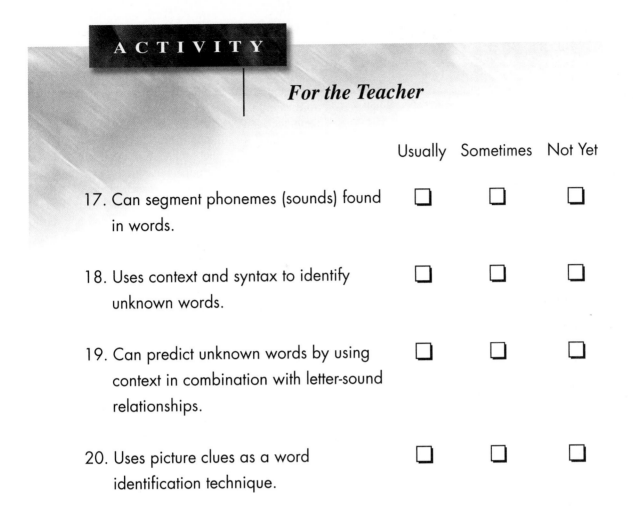

ACTIVITY

For the Teacher

	Usually	Sometimes	Not Yet
17. Can segment phonemes (sounds) found in words.	☐	☐	☐
18. Uses context and syntax to identify unknown words.	☐	☐	☐
19. Can predict unknown words by using context in combination with letter-sound relationships.	☐	☐	☐
20. Uses picture clues as a word identification technique.	☐	☐	☐

USING THE RUNNING RECORD TO ASSESS READING SKILLS

Running records are an excellent way to assess a young child's reading progress. The running record is administered individually and does not require any special materials except the child's own copy of the material that he or she is going to read aloud and a sheet of paper and a pencil or pen for the teacher. A pen is preferable because it makes less noise while the child is reading. An oral reading sample is obtained, and comprehension is not evaluated. That is why many reading specialists believe that a running record should sometimes be followed up by having the child briefly retell the material.

The running record has two major purposes: to determine whether a child's reading materials are on the proper level and to obtain information about the word identification processes that he or she is using. Although running records actually are desirable with older children also, they are most often used to assess the performance of young children, especially in first grade. They also can be used in second and third grades.

As used in the Reading Recovery early intervention program and described in Clay's (1993) *An observational survey of early literacy achievement,* running records are administered according to a standardized format in which pupils' errors and corrections are recorded on a separate sheet of paper. As adapted for use for early childhood classroom teachers, running records may be recorded (as long as the fair-use provision of the copyright laws is adhered to or permission is obtained from the publisher) on a photocopy of the reading material that the child is reading or on a blank sheet of paper (this is more common) (Learning Media, 1991).

To assess whether materials are on a suitable level of difficulty and to determine whether a child makes good use of the cueing strategies (meaning, visual, syntactic [grammar]) previously learned, take a running record on a child's trade book or textbook that he or she recently has read. To assess a child's ability to read more difficult materials and apply cueing strategies independently, take a running record on material that the child has not previously read. If the book is quite short, take a running record on the entire book. However, if the book is fairly long, take the running record from a 100- to 200-word sample. As the child reads the material aloud, record his or her performance using symbols such as those found on the next page. You will find that it takes a good deal of practice to be competent in taking running records. Therefore, you may want to tape record the child's oral reading until you become competent in this assessment strategy, even though a true proponent of running records does not recommend this. Instead of the running record symbols shown on the next page, you can use the traditional Individual Reading Inventory symbols if you are more familiar with them. After taking the running record,

record the number of words in the selection, the number of errors made, the error rate, the number of self-corrections made (a desirable reading strategy), and the accuracy rate.

Although Clay (1993) accepts 90 percent as adequate oral reading accuracy, 95 percent is more desirable. Since word identification is emphasized in the running record, comprehension is not evaluated, as stated earlier. You can use retelling as a comprehension check if you wish.

It is important that you analyze the child's reading errors in order to determine what strategies he or she is using. Some young children use such incorrect reading strategies that they are greatly hindering their reading progress. These strategies must be corrected before the children can make significant reading progress. As you examine the child's errors, you can consider the following questions:

- Do the student's errors usually make sense? Does the child usually read for meaning?
- Is the child using visual or sound-symbol (graphophonic) cues? Are the child's errors similar in appearance and sound to the target word?
- Is the child using picture cues?
- Is the child using grammar (syntactic) cues?
- Is the child integrating cues? Does he or she balance the use of meaning and sound-symbol cues?
- Is the child self-correcting errors, especially those that interfere with the meaning of the sentence? Is the child using meaning cues?
- Based on the child's performance, what reading strategies does he or she need to master?

You can also notice whether or not young children read from left to right and from top to bottom and whether there is one-to-one correspondence (voice-print match). For detailed information on analyzing and interpreting running records you should consult Clay's book (1993).

USING MISCUE ANALYSIS TO DETERMINE READING SKILLS

Miscue analysis is another strategy that can be used to assess a young child's reading skills. Some early childhood teachers think that this strategy is not quite as helpful as is the running record, but you may find it useful, so this book provides a very brief description of this strategy. For more information, you are encouraged to consult one of the professional books included in the Selected References. I have excerpted much of the information contained here from the following teacher's resource:

> Miller, W. H. (1995). *Alternative assessment techniques for reading and writing.* West Nyack, NY: The Center for Applied Research in Education.

A useful, fairly simple system for coding reading miscues (errors) was developed by Argyle (1989). Very

Running Record Symbols

Symbol	Text	Example
Each word read correctly is marked with a check mark.	Jim ran home very fast.	✓ ✓ ✓ ✓
Substitutions are written above the line.	Sammy saw a red fox.	✓ ✓ ✓ ✓ *fix* / *fox*
Self-corrections are marked SC.	Sammy saw a red fox.	✓ ✓ ✓ ✓ *fix* | *SC* / *fox*
A dash is used to indicate no response.	The old man walked slowly.	✓ ✓ ✓ — —
A dash is used to indicate an insertion of a word. The dash is placed beneath the inserted word.	I have a big tan dog.	✓ ✓ ✓ *pretty* / — ✓ ✓
A *T* is used to indicate that the child has been told a word.	My neighbor lost her cat yesterday.	✓ *T* ✓ ✓ ✓ / *neighbor*
The letter *A* indicates that the child has asked for help.	It is sunny and warm today.	✓ ✓ *A* ✓ ✓ ✓ / *sunny*
At times the child becomes so confused that it is suggested that he or she "try that again" (coded TTA). Brackets are put around the section that has been misread, the whole misreading is counted as one error, and the child reads it again for a second time.	[I saw a baby deer running after its mother last week.] *TTA*	✓ ✓ ✓ ✓ *did* ✓ ✓ ✓ ✓ *list* ✓ / *deer* / *last*
A repetition is indicated with a *R*. Although not counted as errors, repetitions are often part of an attempt to puzzle out a difficult item. The point to which the child returns in the repetition is indicated with an arrow.	I saw a baby deer running after its mother last week. *R*	✓ ✓ ✓ *SC did* ✓ ✓ ✓ ✓ *list* ✓ / *deer* / *last*

simply, this coding system attempts to determine if the miscue caused a meaning change or a graphic change or was a self-correction. If the child's miscues resulted in few meaning changes, they usually are not very significant, since they probably would not interfere with comprehension. If the child made a number of miscues that resulted in graphic changes, he or she may need additional instruction and/or reinforcement in graphophonic (phonic) analysis and structural analysis, depending upon the miscue frequency and whether or not the miscues interfered significantly with comprehension. If the child made a number of self-corrections, he or she probably does not have a very significant reading problem as compared with a child who does not recognize his or her miscues and therefore does not attempt to correct them.

In general, Argyle recommends the following steps for using this system of miscue analysis:

1. Select reading material that is unfamiliar to your pupils. This may be part of a basal reader story, a trade book, or a passage from a simple content textbook. Usually even adept readers make some miscues with totally unfamiliar material.
2. Copy the reading selection.
3. If you want to administer the material on an individual basis, tell the child that it is not a test in order to reduce his or her anxiety about it.
4. Have the child read the passage orally without any preparation. Tape recording helps you to code all of the miscues but may not be completely practical in a noisy setting. It is possible to code the miscues while the child is reading, but it is quite difficult.
5. Place the miscues on a summary sheet so that they can be analyzed.

Here is a very brief example of how Argyle's system may work.

Omission	met a (porcupine)
Addition	met a ˄ porcupine *baby*
Pause	met a // porcupine
Substitution	met a ~~porcupine~~ *pig*
Repetition	met a porcupine (underlined)
Reversal	met a porcupine (reversal mark)
Self-Correction	met a porcupine (underlined)
Word Supplied by Teacher	met a porcupine (T marked)

Argyle, Susan, Miscue analysis for classroom use, reprinted from *Reading Horizons*, 29, © 1989.

Illustration of the Miscue Analysis Coding System

An oral reading passage entitled "Ben and the Porcupine" was written at the second-grade level and was taken from the book *Alternative assessment techniques for reading & writing* (by W. Miller, West Nyack, NY: The Center for Applied Research in Education, 1995, p. 168). It was given to Ryan, a second-grade child who had exhibited reading problems. The passage was tape recorded, and Ryan's teacher coded his miscues using the system just described. The coded copy of this reading passage is included on page 251.

Ryan's teacher transferred his miscues to a brief summary sheet that she had constructed. For each miscue the correct word is written first. Then as close a representation of the child's response as possible is written in each sentence. If the miscue resulted in a complete meaning change, the word *yes* is written, and if only a partial meaning change occurred, the word *partial* is written. If no meaning change resulted from the miscue, the word *no* is written. Next, each miscue is analyzed in terms of whether the child made a graphic change in either the *beginning, middle,* or *end* of the word. In either case, a √ normally is written for a miscue in that part of the word, while a — is written for a correct response in that part of the word. If the child self-corrects a miscue, the self-correction also is coded.

After coding Ryan's responses on the summary sheet, his teacher attempts to analyze some of his reading strengths and weaknesses mainly in terms of patterns that can be detected. You will find that it takes considerable time and effort to become adept in the interpretation of oral reading miscues and to develop an in-depth understanding of the reading process.

You will notice that Ryan made thirty-four miscues that interfered with comprehension and two miscues that partially interfered with comprehension. In addition, he made three miscues that did not seem to interfere significantly with comprehension.

The percentages of graphic miscues that Ryan made also were coded by his teacher. From this analysis Ryan's teacher tried to notice if Ryan appeared to be more competent in identifying beginnings, middles, or endings of the miscued words. His teacher noticed that he had the most difficulty with word endings, only a little less difficulty with word middles, and the least difficulty with word beginnings. This is a somewhat common pattern of graphic miscues for a disabled reader. Most children are competent with word beginnings, which was the case with Ryan. Ryan's teacher noticed that he made no self-corrections, also indicative of a child with significant oral reading miscues who does not monitor his or her reading comprehension to see if the reading makes sense.

You will notice that Ryan made a total of thirty-nine oral reading miscues on this passage out of a total of 173 words. This indicates that he mispronounced about 22 percent of the words and correctly pronounced about 78 percent of them. Thus, this passage is definitely on Ryan's frustration reading level. It is much too hard for him to read.

Since the slash marks in the coding of Ryan's reading behavior indicate pauses in his oral reading, it appears that although he may not have good oral reading fluency, there are not as many pauses as are typical of children who truly read in a word-by-word manner. This type of reading often hinders comprehension, especially in the upper primary grades and beyond. In addition, Ryan did not have an excessive number of repetitions.

In summary, here are some of Ryan's reading strengths:

- fair, but not good, oral reading fluency
- fairly good knowledge of word beginnings

Here are some of his reading weaknesses:

- comprehension skills
- making meaning changes that have semantic acceptability (make sense in sentence context)
- ability to identify word endings
- ability to identify word middles
- the use of self-correction while reading

Based on these observations, it is clear that Ryan's program of reading improvement should include a number of different elements to ensure his optimum reading progress. He must be given reading materials that are on his own instructional (teacher support needed) or independent (no teacher support needed) reading level, even if that is well below the second-grade level. Additional analysis may be necessary to determine those levels with some degree of accuracy. The running record that was mentioned earlier may be very helpful for this purpose, as would an Individual Reading Inventory. (See the teacher's resource book cited earlier in this section among other professional books.)

Ryan also must receive extensive instruction and practice in the importance of using semantic (meaning) cues to identify the meaning of unknown words and of monitoring his own reading carefully by making self-corrections when necessary. In addition, he needs instruction and reinforcement in graphophonic (phonic) skills, especially to determine word endings and middles. The important vowel elements should receive some stress in Ryan's reading program. He must have extensive instruction and reinforcement in the various elements of reading comprehension and metacognition (monitoring his own reading to ensure that he is understanding).

In summary, the preceding is just one example of how a variation of oral reading miscue analysis can be used to determine a child's reading strengths and weaknesses. You will notice that although this is a fairly simple system to implement—as it is an informal assessment device—it does require considerable experience and expertise in the reading process to administer. This technique, therefore, should be used judiciously by an inexperienced reading teacher. In most instances, you may want to use a running record and certainly teacher observation as a supplement to this system of miscue analysis.

Sample Oral Reading Passage and Summary Sheets

The chapter now contains the sample oral reading passage and the completed summary sheet of oral reading miscues that was described in the previous section. You are encouraged to read and study them carefully so that you can develop an understanding of how to implement this system of oral reading miscue analysis. In addition, a reproducible example of the summary sheet for this type of miscue analysis is included. You can duplicate and use this example if you wish.

Name Ryan Grigalunas   Date March 24, 1999

Summary Sheet of Oral Reading Miscues

Text	Miscue	Meaning Change	Graphic B	M	E	Self-Corr.
1. brown	black	yes	—	—	—	
2. lives	_____	yes	—	—	—	
3. North	_____	yes	—	—	—	
4. Woods	_____	yes	—	—	—	
5. family	_____	yes	—	—	—	
6. woods	_____	yes	—	—	—	
7. whenever	when	no	✓	✓	—	
8. summer	sun	yes	✓	—	—	
9. porcupine	_____	yes	—	—	—	
10. woods	_____	yes	—	—	—	
11. friendly	from	yes	✓	—	—	
12. want	like	no	—	—	—	
13. trouble	_____	yes	—	—	—	
14. porcupine	pork	yes	✓	—	—	
15. just	jump	yes	✓	✓	—	
16. wanted	_____	yes	—	—	—	
17. porcupine	_____	yes	—	—	—	
18. touched	toot	yes	✓	—	—	
19. nose	nice	yes	✓	—	—	
20. porcupine	_____	yes	—	—	—	
21. understand	know	no	—	—	—	
22. just	jump	yes	✓	✓	—	
23. wanted	went	yes	✓	—	—	
24. afraid	_____	yes	—	—	—	
25 raised	ride	yes	✓	—	—	

ACTIVITY

Text	Miscue	Meaning Change	Graphic B M E	Self Corr.
26. sharp	short	yes	✓ — —	
27. quills	_____	yes	— — —	
28. howling	_____	partial	— — —	
29. porcupine	porcupin	yes	✓ ✓ —	
30. quills	_____	yes	— — —	
31. body	_____	yes	— — —	
32. owners	oars	yes	✓ — —	
33. quills	_____	yes	— — —	
34. vet	vat	yes	✓ — —	
35. quills	quilts	yes	✓ ✓ —	
36. eighty	eight	yes	✓ ✓ —	
37. body	_____	yes	— — —	
38. even	every	yes	✓ — —	
39. fine	fun	yes	✓ — —	

Total 100%/46%/15%/0%

Continued

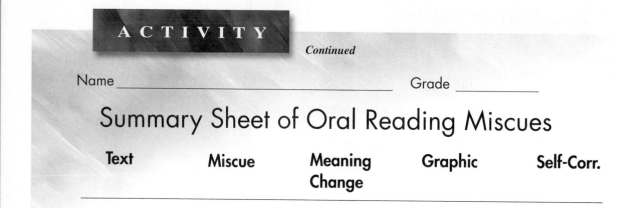

ACTIVITY *Continued*

Name _____ Grade _____

Summary Sheet of Oral Reading Miscues

Text	Miscue	Meaning Change	Graphic	Self-Corr.

THE INDIVIDUAL READING INVENTORY

Although the *Individual Reading Inventory* (IRI) is another informal device for assessing reading strengths and weaknesses, it is described only very briefly in this book. I believe that the running record and the miscue analysis strategies that were just explained are more effective informal means of assessment than is the IRI.

An IRI consists of graded word lists and graded oral reading passages similar to the passage "Ben and the Porcupine" that was just included. In developing the inventory, the child begins orally reading a graded word list that is about two grades below his or her present grade level and continues until he or she reaches the frustration reading level. Then the child begins orally reading a passage that also is about two grade levels below his or her current grade level. Again, the child continues reading until the frustration level is reached. Then the child answers both explicit (lower-level) and implicit (higher-level) comprehension questions about the passage.

After evaluating a child's performance on the graded word lists and graded passages, an IRI provides precise, detailed instructions about how to determine the child's independent (easy), instructional (with teacher support), and frustration (too difficult) reading levels. Thus, the reading teacher is able to match the child's actual independent or instructional reading levels with material chosen for him or her that he or she is able to read effectively.

Using an IRI with young children cannot be recommended, primarily because in a typical IRI the child must begin reading about two grade levels below his or her present grade level. Therefore, a child in first grade and even second grade will find that much of the material included in an IRI is too difficult. Although an IRI may be appropriate for children in third grade, the running record or miscue analysis often is more useful for that grade level also.

If you want to examine an Individual Reading Inventory and learn more about administering and evaluating one, you can consult the following source along with some of the professional books listed in the "Selected References" at the end of this chapter:

> Miller, W. (1995). *Alternative assessment techniques for reading and writing*. West Nyack, NY: The Center for Applied Research in Education, pp. 141–217.

THE EL PASO PHONICS SURVEY**

The *El Paso Phonics Survey* (Ekwall, 1986) is an excellent informal device for assessing the various elements of phonics. Although it is fairly time-consuming to administer and evaluate, it may well be worth your time and effort if you want precise information about just which phonic skills to present to a young child who seems very weak in this important skill. Although the survey may be somewhat useful with first-grade children, it probably is considerably more useful with children in the second and third grades. It was constructed by the late Eldon E. Ekwall of the University of Texas at El Paso. He used it many times with young children at the reading clinic that he directed for many years.

To construct the El Paso Phonics Survey, reproduce pages 257 and 258 and glue the survey on 5″ X 8″ cards, and then laminate them for durability. You also should make multiple copies of the answer sheet so that you can mark each child's responses on a separate copy. There are both general directions and specific directions for administering this survey which should be followed carefully.

General Directions for Administering the El Paso Phonics Survey

1. Before beginning the test, make sure that the child has instant recognition of the test words (**in, up, am**) that appear in the box at the top of the first page of the survey. If the words are not immediately recognized, the test should be given later when the child has been taught and has mastered them.
2. Give the child a copy of the El Paso Phonics Survey.
3. Point to the letter in the first column and have the child say the name of that letter (not the sound that it represents). Then point to the word in the middle column and have the child pronounce it. Point next to the nonsense word in the third column and have the child pronounce it.
4. If the child can give the name of the letter, the word in the middle column, and the nonsense word in the third column, mark the answer sheet with a **plus** (+).
5. If the child cannot pronounce the nonsense word after giving the name of the letter and the word in the middle column, mark the answer sheet with a **minus** (−); or you may wish to write the word phonetically as the child pronounces it. If the child can tell you the name of the letter and the small word in the middle column but cannot pronounce the nonsense word, you may wish to have him or her give the letter sound in isolation. If the child can give the sound in isolation, either the child is unable to blend or does not know the letter well enough to give its sound and blend it at the same time.
6. Whenever an asterisk appears on the answer sheet, refer to the Special Directions sheet.
7. To the right of each blank on the answer sheet is a grade-level designation. This number represents the point by which most basal reader series have taught that sound. As an example, the designation **2.2** means that by the second month of the second grade that sound should be known.

8. When the child comes to two- or three-letter consonant digraphs or blends, as with the **qu** in item 22, she is to say **"q-u"** as with single letters. The child is never to give the letter sounds in isolation while doing actual reading.

9. When the child comes to the vowels (item 59), he is to say **"short a"** and so forth and then explain what this means. The same is to be done with the long vowels.

10. All vowels and vowel combinations are put with only one or two of the first eight consonants. If any of the first eight consonants are not known, they should be taught before you attempt to test for vowel knowledge. You will probably find that a child who does not know the first eight consonant sounds rarely knows the vowel sounds anyway.

11. You will notice that words appear to the right of some of the blends on the answer sheet. These words illustrate the correct consonant or vowel sounds that should be heard when the child answers.

12. Included are phonic elements that Ekwall thought were worthwhile to teach to most young children. For example, the vowel pair **ui** is very rare, and when it does appear, it may stand for the short **i** sound in **build** or the long **oo** sound in **fruit.** Therefore, there is no reason to teach it as a sound. However, some letters such as **oe** may represent several different sounds but most often represent one particular sound. In the case of **oe** the long **o** sound should be used. In such cases, the most common sound is illustrated by a word to the right of the blank on the answer sheet. If the child gives another correct sound for the letter(s), you can say, "Yes, that's right, but what is another way you could pronounce this nonsense word?" The child must then say it as illustrated in the small word to the right of the blank on the answer sheet. Otherwise, the answer must be counted as wrong.

13. Discontinue the test after **five consecutive misses** or if the child appears frustrated from missing a number of items even though he or she has not missed five consecutive items.

Specific Directions for Administering and Evaluating the El Paso Phonics Survey

3. If the child uses another **s** sound as in **sugar** (**sh**) in saying the nonsense word **sup,** ask, "What is another sound?" The child must use the **s** as in the word **soap.**

15. If the child uses the **soft c** sound as in **city** in saying the nonsense word **cam,** ask, "What is another **c** sound?" The child must use the **hard c** as in the word **cup.**

16. If the child uses the **soft g** sound as in **gem** in saying the nonsense word **gup,** ask, "What is another **g** sound?" The child must use the **hard g** as in the word **gate.**

17. Ask, "What is the **y** sound when it comes at the beginning of a word?"

23. The child must use the **ks** sound of **x,** and the nonsense word **mox** must rhyme with **fox.**

35. If the child uses the **th** sound heard in **that,** ask, "What is another **th** sound?" The child must use the **th** sound as in the word **thin.**

44. If the child uses the **hoo** sound of **wh** in saying the nonsense word **whup,** ask, "What is another **wh** sound?" The child must use the **wh** sound as in the word **white.**

72. The child may either give the **ea** sound heard in **head** or the **ea** sound heard in **meat.** Be sure to indicate on the answer sheet which one the child said.

73. If the same **ea** sound is given this time as was given in item 72, say, "Yes, that's right, but what is another way you could pronounce this nonsense word?" Whichever sound was **not** used in item 72 must be used here. Otherwise, this item should be recorded as incorrect.

81. The child may give either the **ow** sound heard in the word **now** or the **ow** sound heard in the word **blow.** Be sure to indicate on the answer sheet which sound used.

82. If the same **ow** sound is given this time as was given for item 81, say, "Yes, that's right, but what is another way you could pronounce this nonsense word?" Whichever sound was not used in item 81 must be used here. Otherwise, this item should be recorded as incorrect.

88. The child may give either the **oo** sound heard in **book** or the **oo** sound heard in **goose.** Be sure to indicate on the answer sheet which sound was used.

89. If the same **oo** sound is given this time as was given for item 88, say, "Yes, that's right, but what is another way you could pronounce this nonsense word?" Whichever sound was not used in item 88 must be used here. Otherwise, this item should be recorded as incorrect.

ACTIVITY

El Paso Phonics Survey

in	up	am

1. p	am	pam	22. qu	am	quam
2. n	up	nup	23. m	ox	mox
3. s	up	sup	24. pr	am	pram
4. r	in	rin	25. sl	in	slin
5. t	up	tup	26. pl	up	plup
6. m	up	mup	27. fl	in	flin
7. b	up	bup	28. st	am	stam
8. d	up	dup	29. fr	in	frin
9. w	am	wam	30. bl	am	blam
10. h	up	hup	31. gr	up	grup
11. f	am	fam	32. br	in	brin
12. j	up	jup	33. tr	am	tram
13. k	am	kam	34. sh	up	shup
14. l	in	lin	35. th	up	thup
15. c	am	cam	36. ch	am	cham
16. g	up	gup	37. dr	up	drup
17. y	in	yin	38. cl	in	clin
18. v	am	vam	39. gl	am	glam
19. z	up	zup	40. sk	up	skup
20. c	in	cin	41. cr	in	crin
21. g	in	gin	42. sw	up	swup

Continued

A C T I V I T Y

Continued

43. sm	in	smin	67. ē		rete
44. wh	up	whup	68. ū		pune
45. sp	up	spup	69. ee	eem	
46. sc	up	scup	70. oa	oan	
47. str	am	stram	71. ai	ait	
48. thr	up	thrup	72. ea	eam	
49. scr	in	scrin	73. ea	eap	
50. spr	am	spram	74. ay	tay	
51. spl	in	splin	75. oi	doi	
52. squ	am	squam	76. ou	tou	
53. sn	up	snup	77. ar	arb	
54. tw	am	twam	78. er	ert	
55. wr	in	wrin	79. ir	irt	
56. shr	up	shrup	80. oe	poe	
57. dw	in	dwin	81. ow	owd	
58. sch	am	scham	82. ow	fow	
59. ă		tam	83. or	orm	
60. ĭ		rin	84. ur	urd	
61. ĕ		nep	85. oy	moy	
62. ŏ		sot	86. ew	bew	
63. ŭ		tun	87. aw	awp	
64. ā		sape	88. oo	oot	
65. ō		pote	89. oo	oop	
66. ī		tipe	90. au	dau	

EL PASO PHONICS SURVEY

Answer Sheet

Mark answers as follows:

Pass +

Fail − (or write word as pronounced)

PEK = point at which

              element is expected

              to be known

PEK

Initial Consonants _____

1. p   pam _____ 1.3

2. n   nup _____ 1.3

*3. s   sup _____ 1.3

4. r   rin _____ 1.3

5. t   tup _____ 1.3

6. m   mup _____ 1.3

7. b   bup _____ 1.3

8. d   dup _____ 1.3

9. w   wam _____ 1.3

10. h   hup _____ 1.3

11. f   fam _____ 1.3

12. j   jup _____ 1.3

Continued

A C T I V I T Y   *Continued*

PEK

13. k   kam _____ 1.3

14. l   lin _____ 1.3

*15. c   cam _____ 1.3

*16. g   gup _____ 1.3

*17. y   yin _____ 1.3

18. v   vam _____ 1.3

19. z   zup _____ 1.3

20. c   cin _____ 1.3

21. g   gin _____ 1.3

22. qu   quam _____ 1.3

Ending Consonant _____

*23. m   mox _____ 1.3

Initial Consonant Clusters (Blends)

24. pr   pram _____ 1.3

25. sl   slin _____ 1.6

26. pl   plup _____ 1.6

27. fl   flin _____ 1.6

28. st   stam _____ 1.6

29. fr   frin _____ 1.6

30. bl   blam _____ 1.6

31. gr   grup _____ 1.6

32. br   brin _____ 1.9

A C T I V I T Y

PEK

33. tr   tram _____ 1.9

34. sh   shup _____ 1.9

*35. th   thup _____ 1.9

         thin

36. ch   cham _____ 1.9

         chin

37. dr   drup _____ 1.9

38. cl   clin _____ 1.9

39. gl   glam _____ 1.9

40. sk   skup _____ 1.9

41. cr   crin _____ 1.9

42. sw   swup _____ 1.9

43. sm   smin _____ 2.5

*44. wh   whup _____ 2.5

45. sp   spup _____ 2.5

46. sc   scup _____ 2.5

47. str   stram _____ 2.5

48. thr   thrup _____ 2.5

49. scr   scrin _____ 2.5

50. spr   spram _____ 2.5

51. spl   splin _____ 2.5

52. squ   squam _____ 2.9

Continued

A C T I V I T Y   *Continued*

PEK

53. sn   snup _____ 2.9

54. tw   twam _____ 2.9

55. wr   wrin _____ 2.9

56. shr   shrup _____ 3.5

57. dw   dwin _____ 3.5

58. sch   scham _____ 3.9

Vowels, Vowel Teams, and Special Letter Combinations

59. ă   tam _____ 1.6

60. ĭ   rin _____ 1.6

61. ě   nep _____ 1.6

62. ŏ   sot _____ 1.6

63. ŭ   tun _____ 1.6

64. ā   sape _____ 1.6

65. ō   pote _____ 1.6

66. ī   tipe _____ 1.9

67. ē   rete _____ 1.9

68. ū   pune _____ 1.9

69. ee   eem _____ 1.9 (heed)

70. oa   oan _____ 1.9 (soap)

71. ai   ait _____ 1.9 (ape)

*72. ea   eam _____ 1.9 (meat)

ACTIVITY

PEK

*73. ea   eap _____ 2.5 (head)

74. ay   tay _____ 2.5 (hay)

75. oi   doi _____ 2.5 (boy)

76. ou   tou _____ 2.5 (cow)

77. ar   arb _____ 2.5 (harp)

78. er   ert _____ 2.5 (her)

79. ir   irt _____ 2.5 (hurt)

80. oe   poe _____ 2.9 (hoe)

*81. ow   owd _____ 2.9 (blow or now)

*82. ow   fow _____ 2.9 (blow or now)

83. or   orm _____ 2.9 (corn)

84. ur   urd _____ 2.9 (hurt)

85. oy   moy _____ 2.9 (boy)

86. ew   bew _____ 2.9 (few)

87. aw   awp _____ 2.9 (paw)

*88. oo   oot _____ 2.9 (book or goose)

*89. oo   oop _____ 3.5 (book or goose)

90. au   dau _____ 3.5 (paw)

USING RETELLING AS AN ASSESSMENT TECHNIQUE WITH YOUNG CHILDREN

The *retelling technique* also can be called the *tell-back strategy*. This strategy first was used around 1920 as the major way of testing reading comprehension. Retelling was discontinued after a time due to the difficulty of testing comprehension on a standardized test by this means. Instead, such tests used multiple-choice items to evaluate comprehension skills because they were easier to evaluate. Today retelling is used quite commonly because it assesses holistic comprehension in an informal way. It is an example of what is called *process comprehension*. Retelling contrasts with the traditional piecemeal approach of teacher-formulated questions that require a child to recall bits of information (Gambrell, Pfeiffer, & Wilson, 1985).

Allowing a listener or reader to retell a story or book offers active participation in a literacy experience that helps the child develop reading comprehension and a sense of story structure. Retelling in either an oral or written form engages the child in holistic comprehension and organization of thought. It encourages personalization of thinking as children merge their own life experiences into the retelling. In addition, they learn to recall book or story theme, plot episodes, and resolution as well as demonstrate understanding of story details and sequence.

Improving Ability in the Retelling Technique

To use this simple but valuable technique, it is important to tell the child before he or she listens to or reads a book or story that the book must later be retold (Morrow, 1985). Even then it is a difficult task for many young children, but with practice they make good improvement. Further guidance depends upon the teacher's purpose for the retelling. If the goal is to teach or assess sequential ability, the child should be told to concentrate on what happened first, second, and so forth. If the goal is to teach or assess the ability to integrate information and make inferences from the text, a child should be told to think of things that have happened to him or her like those that happened to characters in the book (story). Props such as puppets, felt-board characters, or the pictures in the material can be used to help a child retell a book (story).

After the child has heard or read a story or book, you can ask questions such as these:

- What was this book (story) about?
- Can you tell me all that you remember about this book (story)?
- What do you remember about the book (story) that you have just read?

You also can ask the child to retell the book (story) in this way:

"A little while ago I read the book (story) _____ _____ to you. Would you retell the book (story) as if you were telling it to a friend who has never heard it?"

You can use prompts such as these if they seem necessary:

- "Once upon a time"
- Who was this book (story) about?
- When did this book (story) happen?
- Where did this book (story) take place?
- Who was the main character in this book (story), and what problem did he or she have?
- How did (the main character) in this book (story) try to solve the problem?
- How was the problem finally solved?
- How did the book (story) end?

Evaluating a Book or Story Retelling

If you plan to evaluate book (story) retelling using the reproducible assessment device included in this book, during the introduction of the book (story) tell the child that he or she will be asked to retell it after listening to it or reading it. During evaluative retelling, do not give prompts beyond general ones such as:

- What happened next?
- Can you think of anything else about the story?

To assess the child's retelling for sense of story structure, you first should divide the events of the story into the four categories of setting, theme, plot episodes, and resolution. The retelling assessment device and the outline of the divided material then are used to record the number of ideas and details that the child includes within each category in the retelling. This device indicates which elements the teacher should stress in teaching about the setting, theme, plot episodes, and resolution. Comparing analyses of several retellings over a year indicates a child's progress in understanding story structure.

Here is an outline of a picture storybook, *Thunder cake* by Patricia Polaco (NY: Philomel Books, 1990). This book is the true story about how the author Patricia Polacco overcame her fear of thunder. When she was a young child, she spent the summers with her grandmother Babushka in Michigan. The author was so terrified of thunderstorms that she would hide under the bed when a thunderstorm approached and stay there until it was over. To help her overcome this fear, her grandma told her that they would together bake a "thunder cake" that they could eat during the storm. To gather the ingredients that they needed for this cake, her grandma told the author to do such things as gather eggs from mean old Nellie Peck Hen and pick overripe tomatoes and strawberries. Then they baked the thunder cake, and it was done just as the storm came roaring in. The author and her grandma then sat down and ate the thunder cake during the fierce thunderstorm. The author wrote that she never has been afraid of thunderstorms since. The book concludes with a recipe for thunder cake that children can make with a family member or family friend.

Here is a divided outline that can be used to help analyze a child's retelling of this book. It is included here for illustrative purposes.

DIVIDED STORY

Polacco, P. (1990). *Thunder cake.* NY: Philomel Books.

Setting

This book is set on the author's grandma's farm in Michigan during one sultry summer day when a thunderstorm is threatening.

Characters

The author Patricia Polacco when she was a little girl and her grandma Babushka

Plot Episodes

First Episode:

Grandma says that because a thunderstorm is coming, it is thunder cake baking weather, and she calls the author out from hiding under the bed.

Second Episode:

Grandma gets out the recipe for baking thunder cake, and she tells the author to get the eggs for the cake from old mean Nellie Peck Hen's nest.

Third Episode:

The author and her grandma get the milk, chocolate, sugar, and flour for the thunder cake.

Fourth Episode:

The author and her grandma get the secret ingredient for the thunder cake, which is three overripe tomatoes and some strawberries.

Fifth Episode:

By the time the thunder cake is done, the thunderstorm has arrived, and the author and her grandma each have a piece of thunder cake and a cup of tea.

Resolution

Since the author had been brave enough to help her grandma gather the ingredients for the thunder cake, she never was afraid of thunderstorms again.

VERBATIM TRANSCRIPTION

Here is a verbatim transcription of Salli's (aged six) retelling of *Thunder cake:*

> *The little girl was with her grandma on a farm and she was really scared of thunder just like I am. Her grandma made a special cake and she wasn't ever afraid any more.*

Salli's Book-Retelling Ability Checklist

Here is a "retelling ability checklist" that has been completed for Salli's retelling of the picture storybook *Thunder cake* (see pages 266–267). By examining it, you should easily be able to complete the reproducible model of this assessment device for any child's retelling of a book or story.

NOTE: In many instances, an early childhood teacher simply can complete the reproducible model of this checklist by using checkmarks instead of numbers. These checkmarks can easily be used to gain a general impression of the elements of the book or story that a child includes and of his or her progress over a period of time.

REPRODUCIBLE STORY (BOOK) RETELLING ABILITY CHECKLIST

The book now contains a reproducible book (story) retelling checklist. You can use it in its present form or modify it in any way in which you want. A quantitative analysis is optional.

A C T I V I T Y

Name _____   Grade _____

Book (Story) Retelling Ability Checklist
Primary-Grade Level

Title of Book (Story) Read   Thunder Cake

Directions for the Teacher: Score 1 point for each element the child included. Give 1 point for each character named as well as for generic words such as *boy*, *girl*, *dog*, or *cat*. Credit plurals (for example, the word *friends*) with 2 points under characters.

Sense of Story Structure

Setting

    1. Begins book (story) with an introduction   _1_

    2. Names main character   _1_

    3. Number of other characters named   1___

    4. Actual number of other characters   1___

    5. Scores for other characters (3/4)   _1_

    6. Includes statement about time and place   _1_

Theme

    Refers to main character's primary goal or problem to be solved   _1_

Plot Episodes

    1. Number of episodes recalled   1___

    2. Number of episodes in the book (story)   .5___

    3. Score for plot episodes (1 ÷ 2)   _.2_

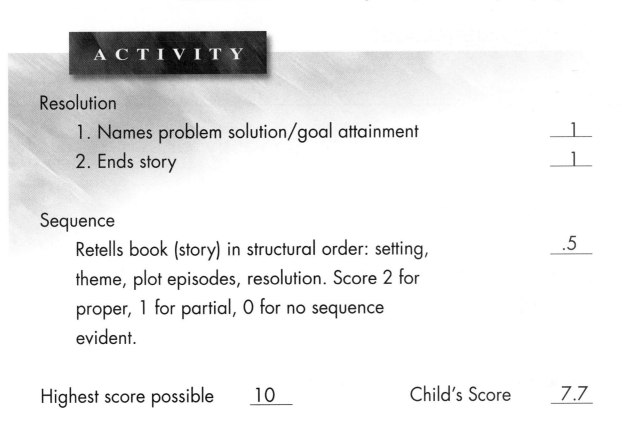

ACTIVITY

Resolution

    1. Names problem solution/goal attainment   <u> 1 </u>

    2. Ends story   <u> 1 </u>

Sequence

Retells book (story) in structural order: setting,   <u> .5 </u>
theme, plot episodes, resolution. Score 2 for
proper, 1 for partial, 0 for no sequence
evident.

Highest score possible   <u> 10 </u>   Child's Score   <u> 7.7 </u>

Continued

Continued

Name _____   Grade _____

Book (Story) Retelling Ability Checklist
Primary-Grade Level

Title of Book (Story) Read _____

Directions for the Teacher: Score 1 point for each element the child included. Give 1 point for each character named as well as for generic words such as *boy*, *girl*, *dog*, or *cat*. Credit plurals (for example, the word *friends*) with 2 points under characters.

Sense of Story Structure

Setting

    1. Begins book (story) with an introduction   _____

    2. Names main character   _____

    3. Number of other characters named   _____

    4. Actual number of other characters   _____

    5. Scores for other characters (3/4)   _____

    6. Includes statement about time and place   _____

Theme

    Refers to main character's primary goal or   _____
problem to be solved

Plot Episodes

    1. Number of episodes recalled   _____

    2. Number of episodes in the book (story)   _____

    3. Score for plot episodes (1 ÷ 2)   _____

ACTIVITY

Resolution

1. Names problem solution/goal attainment   _____
2. Ends story   _____

Sequence

Retells book (story) in structural order: setting,   _____
theme, plot episodes, resolution. Score 2 for
proper, 1 for partial, 0 for no sequence
evident.

Highest score possible   _____   Child's Score   _____

USING PORTFOLIO ASSESSMENT IN AN EARLY CHILDHOOD LITERACY PROGRAM

A *literacy portfolio* is a collection of a child's work in areas such as reading and writing. Using a literacy portfolio is an authentic assessment technique. The use of portfolios cannot completely replace traditional assessment such as standardized and informal tests of various types. Instead, portfolios should be an important part of a comprehensive assessment program.

A literacy portfolio, which is a record of a child's progress and self-assessment over time, is usually kept in some type of holder. Perhaps the most common type of holder for a portfolio is an accordion-type device with compartments and sections. The holder also can be a folder, a box, or even a paper bag. The holder should be large enough to keep numerous papers, tapes, and drawings, and the child also can design and illustrate its cover. The folders, boxes, or containers should be easily accessible to the children in any classroom in which portfolios play a major role. It is essential that children be able to take their portfolios out, look through them, organize them, and add or delete material when they need or want to do so.

Although the use of portfolios in instruction and assessment is not new, portfolios are now being used more often because they are very compatible with the increased understanding of how language develops and the more widespread use of the whole language philosophy in early childhood programs. Whole language emphasizes instruction that stresses the use of "real" reading materials, the integration of literacy skills, and constructing and reconstructing of meaning, all of which are promoted through portfolio use.

The idea of using portfolios in instruction and assessment in education probably stems from their use by other professionals such as artists, photographers, and models. When portfolios are used by professionals such as these, they usually are *show portfolios,* which display a range of the very best work done by that professional. However, many of these professionals also have a *working portfolio* from which the materials for the show portfolio were derived.

Both working and show portfolios can be used in literacy instruction and assessment; however, working portfolios are much more relevant for young children. A working portfolio contains all of the materials with which the child currently is engaged. On the other hand, a show portfolio can be made by selecting certain materials from the working portfolio, preferably by the child himself or herself but occasionally by the teacher, to be shown at parent-teacher conferences, to administrators, to school board members, or to various parent groups. A teacher can learn a great deal about a child's abilities and interests by carefully examining his or her portfolio on a regular basis and by having regularly scheduled short conferences with the child about the portfolio. At least four conferences should be held each year.

As stated, working portfolios are much more relevant and useful for children in an early childhood classroom. Very briefly, here are some of the elements that can comprise a working portfolio:

- a statement of the child's goals for the portfolio
- a table of contents to show the organization of the portfolio
- a reading/writing log
- various drafts of all types of writing that the child has done
- reading response journals
- dialogue journals
- writing done outside of class
- checklists and surveys of various types
- tape-recorded oral reading protocols (samples)
- audiotapes
- videotapes
- teacher-pupil conference notes
- various types of self-assessment devices
- teacher anecdotes and observations
- graphs of progress

You should remember that the major purpose of using a portfolio is the opportunity for a young child to self-assess his or her work as much as is feasible. If there is not ample opportunity and time to make such self-assessments, portfolios may have very little meaning, making them merely a collection of children's work. It is important for both the child and the teacher to have input into selecting what is going to be placed in the child's working portfolio, with the child having as much input into the process as possible. Each child should understand that his or her portfolio is going to be available for the teacher, his or her classmates, his or her parents, and others to look at on occasion. Sometimes materials from a child's working portfolio can be gathered and sent home after he or she has decided—with or without teacher input—that it is not relevant for inclusion in the portfolio.

Of course, family members must be thoroughly informed before a teacher uses portfolio assessment in a classroom. Such information can be shared by using a letter to family members, newsletters, a back-to-school meeting at the beginning of the school year, or some other means. It is crucial that family members understand the purpose and content of portfolios before a teacher attempts to implement them in any early childhood literacy program.

In summary, portfolios can be an integral part of a total assessment program. Their use has unique advantages that are summarized later in this section. You are encouraged to consider implementing portfolios as one important component of your assessment of literacy skills.

Should Standardized and Informal Test Scores Be Included in a Child's Portfolio?

Early childhood teachers disagree on whether or not standardized and informal test scores of various types should be included in a child's working portfolio or show portfolio. Some teachers recommend including all of a child's test scores, including achievement test scores, criterion-referenced test scores, and basal reader scores in portfolios. In addition, they recommend including all informal test scores such as running records, the results of miscue analysis, and results from all other informal assessment devices.

There are several valid reasons that may support this view. For example, it can be argued that a child has a right to know how well or poorly he or she performed on any type of standardized assessment device that he or she is required to take. All of these scores are then available in the child's portfolio to be shown to parents during parent-teacher conferences. It also can be said that all such test scores are part of an entire assessment program and should be included in a portfolio, since it also is devoted to being a record of a child's performance.

However, there are equally compelling reasons why test scores should *not* be included in a young child's portfolio. For example, a child's test scores may detract from his or her reactions to his or her reading or writing. The inclusion of test scores in a portfolio really is a contradiction to the major purpose of using portfolios—that of self-assessment. In addition, a child's test scores should *not* be made available to everyone who theoretically may have access to the portfolio.

In summary, each early childhood teacher should personally make the decision about whether or not to include standardized and informal test scores in the portfolios of his or her pupils. Especially with young children it may well not be desirable at all to do so, and therefore it is not recommended in this book.

The Advantages and Limitations of Using Portfolios in an Early Childhood Classroom

A literacy portfolio has many unique advantages. Briefly, here are some of them:

- It helps the child develop a positive attitude toward reading and writing activities.
- It improves a child's ability in self-assessment, an important skill.
- It supports child ownership for his or her reading and writing improvement.
- It can provide much helpful information about a child for his or her teacher.
- It can be used in teacher-parent conferences and in enlisting parent support for the child's instruction.
- It can be useful in conferences about children with principals, supervisors, and consultants.
- It shows the child his or her progress in reading, writing, and spelling in a concrete way.
- It is an example of authentic assessment, since it keeps the focus on genuine, child-oriented purposes for reading and writing.
- It promotes teacher-pupil interaction and collaboration among children.
- It emphasizes reading and writing activities that reflect each child's unique background and interests.
- It promotes writing with audience awareness.

Portfolio assessment does have a few limitations that you should be aware of before implementing it in an early childhood literacy program, as follows:

- It takes a great deal of time and effort to implement portfolio assessment in any type of literacy program. Therefore, it is best to begin portfolio assessment gradually.
- It takes considerable time for a child to compile, self-assess, and prepare his or her portfolios for teacher-pupil conferences.
- It is very time-consuming for a teacher to conduct twenty to thirty 10- to 15-minute teacher-pupil conferences at least four times a year.
- It must be thoroughly explained both to family members and school administrators before it is selected for use in any type of literacy program.
- It is fairly difficult to grade a literacy portfolio if this is required by a teacher's school system. It is to be hoped that this will not occur in any early childhood classroom.

I believe the many advantages of portfolio assessment far outweigh its limitations and recommend that you use it as *one means of assessment* in any early childhood classroom. You also should use other informal assessment devices of various types, and you most likely will be required to give some standardized tests to meet the requirements of your school district.

The Importance of Using Portfolio Assessment in a Whole Language Program

Portfolio assessment has a number of unique advantages that make it very well suited in a whole language classroom. Traditional assessment does not reflect the whole language philosophy well for a number of reasons. Following are some of the main reasons why standardized tests of various types are *not* reflective of a whole language program:

- Tests usually employ sentences or short passages, while a whole language program uses entire passages from different genres of children's literature.
- Tests usually evaluate isolated reading skills such as sight word identification, graphophonic analysis, word structure, and discrete elements of comprehension such as sentences or short paragraphs.
- Tests usually separate reading and writing skills, while a whole language program stresses all literacy skills including listening, speaking, reading, and writing.
- Tests usually do not stress a child's decision-making ability, while a whole language program emphasizes each child's decision-making skills a great deal.
- Tests usually do not evaluate a child's ability to apply knowledge but rather just to recall it, while a whole language philosophy stresses the application of knowledge, often using thematic units in social studies and science.
- Many tests do not allow children to use prior knowledge or construct meaning, both of which are stressed in most whole language programs.
- Some tests may use "artificial language" (language that does not appear natural to children), while a whole language program uses the language that is found in quality children's literature of various narrative and expository (content) genres.
- Many tests stress explicit (literal) thinking, since an explicit question has only one correct answer. A whole language program requires that children do much implicit (interpretive) thinking in planning and executing the thematic units that comprise a large portion of the program.
- A test may not be normed using children that entirely represent the particular balance of children in a school

or district. However, the children's scores will nevertheless be compared to those of the norming sample.

In summary, most standardized tests do not emphasize the authentic assessment that is necessary to teach within the whole language philosophy.

Portfolio assessment is, on the other hand, very well suited for assessing a whole language program for the following main reasons:

- It emphasizes authentic assessment.
- It stresses a child's self-assessment and decision-making abilities.
- It encourages the reading of actual children's literature of various genres.
- It stresses the integration of reading and writing skills.
- It emphasizes the use of the child's own prior knowledge.
- It stresses the application of the child's learning.
- It encourages various higher-level thinking processes.
- It compares the child's performance only with himself or herself instead of with a norm group that may not be comparable to the child.

Portfolio assessment is extremely well suited for use in any whole language program. It seems to meet the special requirements of such a program and therefore should be included in whole language classrooms. However, portfolio assessment is very useful in any traditional classroom as well. It should be an important part of the assessment that takes place in any early childhood program.

SUGGESTED ACTIVITIES

1. Carefully examine a standardized test for the primary grades. If possible, administer the test to a child for whom it is designed. What is your opinion of this test after giving it? What do you believe are its main advantages and limitations?

2. If possible, use either Concepts About Books or the Concepts About Print Checklist contained in this chapter as a guide in observing the reading skills of a young child. Do you believe the checklists are valid devices for this purpose? Why or why not?

3. Select an appropriate children's book of either the narrative or expository type. Learn the marking system of the running record technique and have either a primary-grade student (preferred) or a friend read a 100- to 200-word passage aloud from it while you mark his or her miscues. How valuable do you believe that the running record is as an assessment device?

4. Select an appropriate children's book of either the narrative or expository type. Learn Argyle's system of oral reading miscue analysis and have either a primary-grade child (preferred) or a friend read a 100- to 200-word passage aloud from it while you mark his or her miscues. How valuable an assessment tool do you believe this system of miscue analysis is?

5. Study the El Paso Phonics Survey carefully. If possible, administer it to either a second- or third-grade child. How difficult do you believe that this phonics survey is for a young child? Would you ever use it with a child in second or third grade who has difficulty with graphophonic (phonic) analysis? Why or why not?

6. Select an appropriate primary-grade children's book. Read it aloud to a child or have the child read it aloud himself. After that, have the child retell the book to you while you tape record the retelling. While you play the tape back,

complete the retelling book (story) ability checklist. What score did the child receive on this checklist?

7. Construct a portfolio that contains much of the material that you have been able to collect during all of your

literacy courses. What do you believe were the main advantages and limitations of constructing this portfolio?

SELECTED REFERENCES

Calfee, R. (1998). Classroom assessment. In M. Graves, C. Juel, & B. Graves. (Eds.). *Teaching reading in the 21st century* (pp. 476–531). Needham Heights, MA: Allyn & Bacon.

Cheek, E., Flippo, R., & Lindsey, J. (1997). *Reading for success in elementary school* (pp. 408–438). Madison, WI: Brown & Benchmark.

Farr, R., & Tone, B. (1994). *Portfolio performance assessment.* Fort Worth, TX: Harcourt Brace Jovanovich College Publishers.

Galda, G., Cullinan, B., & Strickland, D. (1993). *Language, literacy and the child* (pp. 321–363). Fort Worth, TX: Harcourt Brace Jovanovich College Publishers.

Gunning, T. (1996). *Creating reading instruction for all children* (pp. 486–523). Needham Heights, MA: Allyn & Bacon.

Heilman, A., Blair, T., & Rupley, W. (1998). *Principles and practices of teaching reading* (pp. 452–496). Upper Saddle River, NJ: Simon & Schuster.

Johnston, P. (1997). *Constructive evaluation of literate activity.* White Plains, NY: Longman.

Miller, W. (1995). *Alternative assessment techniques for reading and writing.* West Nyack, NY: The Center for Applied Research in Education.

Miller, W. (1986). *Reading diagnosis kit.* West Nyack, NY: The Center for Applied Research in Education.

Pavlak, S. (1985). *Informal tests for diagnosing specific reading problems.* West Nyack, NY: Parker Publishing Company.

Sampson, M., Sampson, M., & Allen, R. (1995). *Pathways to literacy* (pp. 288–324). Fort Worth, TX: Harcourt Brace Jovanovich College Publishers.

Savage, J. (1994). *Teaching reading through literature* (pp. 381–418). Madison, WI: Brown & Benchmark.

Shepherd, L. (1994). The challenges of assessing young children appropriately. *Phi Delta Kappan, 76,* 206–213.

Tompkins, G. (1997). *Literacy for the 21st century* (pp. 432–468). Upper Saddle River, NJ: Simon & Schuster.

Wiener, R., & Cohen, J. (1997). *Literacy portfolios: Using assessment to guide instruction.* Upper Saddle River, NJ: Prentice-Hall.

WORKS CITED IN CHAPTER 7

Argyle, S. (1989). Miscue analysis for classroom use. *Reading Horizons, 29,* 93–102.

Bauman, J., & Stevenson, J. (1982). Understanding standardized reading achievement test scores. *The Reading Teacher, 30,* 648–654.

Bertrand, J. (1991). Student assessment and evaluation. In B. Harp (Ed.). *Assessment and evaluation in whole language programs* (pp. 17–33). Norwood, MA: Christopher-Gordon.

Clay, M. (1993). *An observational survey of early literacy achievement.* Portsmouth, NH: Heinemann.

Ekwall, E. (1986). *Teacher's handbook on diagnosis and remediation in reading.* Boston: Allyn & Bacon.

Farr, R. (1992). Putting it all together: Solving the assessment puzzle. *The Reading Teacher, 46,* 26–37.

Gambrell, L., Pfeiffer, W., & Wilson, R. (1985). The effect of retelling upon comprehension and recall of text information. *Journal of Educational Research, 78,* 216–220.

Goodman, K., Goodman, Y., & Hood, W. (1989). *The whole language evaluation book.* Portsmouth, NH: Heinemann.

Goodman, Y. (1978). Kid watching: An alternative to testing. *National Elementary Principal, 57,* 41–45.

Haney, W., & Madaus, G. (1989). Searching for alternatives to standardized tests: Why, whats, and whithers. *Phi Delta Kappan, 70,* 683–687.

Hiebert, E., Valencia, S., & Afflerbach, P. (1994). Definitions and perspectives. In S. Valencia, E. Hiebert, & P. Afflerback (Eds.). *Authentic reading assessment: Practices and possibilities* (pp. 6–25). Newark, DE: International Reading Association.

Learning Media. (1991). *Dancing with the pen: The learner as a writer.* Wellington, New Zealand: Ministry of Education.

Morrow, L. (1985). Retelling stories: A strategy for improving children's comprehension, story structure and oral language complexity. *Elementary School Journal, 85,* 647–661.

Neill, D., & Medina, N. (1989). Standardized testing: Harmful to educational health. *Phi Delta Kappan, 70,* 688–697.

Short, K. (1990, March). Using evaluation to support learning in process-centered classroom. Paper presented at the spring conference of the National Council of Teachers of English, Colorado Springs, CO.

Valencia, S., & Pearson, D. (1987). Reading assessment: Time for a change. *The Reading Teacher, 41,* 726–732.

Weaver, B. (1992). *Defining literacy levels.* Charlottesville, NY: Story House.

Wildsmith, B. (1982). *Cat on the mat.* NY: Oxford University Press.

8

TEACHING LITERACY TO CHILDREN WITH SPECIAL NEEDS

CONCEPTS THAT YOU SHOULD LEARN FROM READING THIS CHAPTER

After reading this chapter, you will be able to:

■ *Explain how many children with cultural or language diversity will be attending North American schools in the near future*

■ *Summarize the advantages and limitations of "labeling" a child using one of the terms that schools commonly use at this time*

■ *Explain the main characteristics and learning styles of the following children:*
  • children with learning disabilities (LD children)
  • children with attention deficit disorders (ADD children) or children with attention deficit/hyperactivity disorders (AD/HD)
  • children who speak English as a second language (ESL), children with limited English proficiency (LEP), or bilingual children
  • children who are culturally or linguistically diverse
  • children with mild mental handicaps (EMH children)
  • children with visual impairments
  • children with hearing impairments
  • children with speech and language disorders

■ *Discuss the inclusion philosophy, and summarize your views of the main advantages and limitations of using this approach with children who have special needs.*

■ *Explain some general guidelines for teaching literacy to children with special needs and some principles for working with children from urban areas*

■ *Discuss some of the guidelines and strategies that can be used when teaching ESL, LEP, and bilingual children*

■ *Explain some of the strategies that early childhood teachers can use in teaching young children with special needs such as the whole language philosophy, the language-experience approach (LEA), scaffolding, cooperative learning groups, mnemonic devices, behavior management, multisensory approaches, technology, and family members' participation*

■ *List some trade books that may be especially beneficial to children who have special needs, including that of cultural and linguistic diversity*

Did you know that today's North American schools are becoming more and more a multicultural mosaic? Currently the percentage of children in schools who are culturally and linguistically diverse is rising. Shortly after the year 2000, pupils who are African American, Hispanic, Asian, or Native American will constitute one-third or more of the school population. In many schools today, such children already make up a majority of the population. In addition, more and more pupils are currently being designated as either learning disabled (LD), attention deficit disordered (ADD), or attention deficit/hyperactivity disordered (AD/HD). School administrators are not sure if the population of such children is really increasing or if they are being identified more frequently than before. In any case, it is imperative that each early childhood teacher be as well prepared as possible to teach all children with special needs including those with physical disabilities.

After carefully reading this chapter, you should be better able to present the various literacy skills to the young children with whom you will work. Certainly every child in our schools must be helped to achieve his or her optimum level of literacy success no matter what special needs that he or she may have.

AN INTRODUCTION TO CHILDREN WITH SPECIAL NEEDS

It is important at the outset to remember that the children who are labeled "at-risk" are actually—like all children—children of promise. In many ways it does them a disservice to call them "at-risk." To verify that they indeed are children of promise, early childhood teachers must have a deep belief in the worth of each child, have an accepting attitude toward them and their unique characteristics, and give them unqualified support. A teacher of young children must celebrate their differences and their culture. Most of the children who are labeled as having special needs can succeed very well with appropriate instruction and proper support. Many years ago this author's doctoral adviser told her that almost all children can learn to read, no matter what environmental, emotional, or physical limitations they have. After working with thousands of children over the years, I agree that this is the case.

Savage (1994) has coined an interesting acronym for early childhood teachers of the twenty-first century. It is *AHANA,* which is an acronym for African American, Hispanic, Asian, and Native American. He prefers to use it because this term does not have the pejorative connotations that often surround the word *minority.* Bill Cosby has written, "The word *minority* has connotations of weaknesses, lesser value, self-doubt, tentativeness, and powerlessness" (1990, p. 61). AHANA pupils bring prior knowledge to schools that is not usually well reflected in the curriculum. Such children need to see their own world

reflected in trade books and other reading materials. In the words of a white middle-class mother who has adopted a young Asian child, "I would like my child to read books that have children that look like him." This often is not now the case.

North American schools today have an increasing tendency to label children who have special needs. Some of the labels that are given them are children with learning disabilities (LD), children who have attention deficit disorders (ADD), children who have attention deficit/hyperactivity disorders (AD/HD), educable mentally handicapped children (EMH), children with mild disabilities, children who speak English as a second language (ESL), children with limited English proficiency (LEP), bilingual children, children who are culturally or linguistically diverse, children with visual impairments, children with hearing impairments, and children with speech and language disorders.

Using such labels for children has both advantages and disadvantages. In fact the disadvantages may outweigh the advantages, at least in some instances. Here are the major strengths of using such labels:

- Children who are identified as having some type of special need may get the specially trained teachers and the special materials that they need to expedite their learning as much as possible.
- Such children may receive the individually prescribed instruction that can enhance their potential to achieve at as high a level as possible.
- Such children may be grouped—at least for part of the school day—with children who have similar literacy needs and abilities.
- These children may experience more success than otherwise would be the case if their special needs had not been identified and met.
- Without the use of a label, some teachers might otherwise be unaware of the special needs of a certain child.

Labeling a child also has several limitations of which an early childhood teacher should be aware. They are as follows:

- There may be a self-fulfilling prophecy both for the teacher and the child. This is a construct that states that a child performs in about the same way in which his or her teacher expects him or her to perform. For example, the self-fulfilling prophecy is the main reason why children in the inner city so often achieve significantly below their potential level. Some teachers teach in inner-city schools without being either willing or properly trained to do so. They then may expect limited achievement from their so-called "at-risk" pupils and receive equally little in return. One of this author's teacher-trainees tutored an African-American sixth-grade boy several years ago who had just moved to central Illinois from inner-city Chicago. He was reading on the third-grade level. However, he was both intelligent and motivated, and when he received appropriate instruction, he was able to read up to grade level in a markedly short time. I am certain that Donald was the victim of a self-fulfilling prophecy.

- A child may well be incorrectly labeled, since some of the labels that currently are being used in schools are very hard to clearly define. For example, a child who is said to be ADD or AD/HD as well as LD may not really be labeled correctly. Some of the children who are labeled as LD, ADD, or AD/HD simply may have behavior problems that the teacher cannot deal with very easily. In some cases it may be easier to give a child a label and provide him or her with a behavior-altering drug such as Ritalin than to have a disruptive child in the classroom. In one Midwestern city the school board stated publicly that this was happening in their school system. Of course, the teachers in that school system were very upset about this statement, and they asked for a retraction from the board. Both sides compromised, and the matter was settled. However, it is likely that there was some truth to the board's statement.
- The use of a label may be very detrimental to a child's self-esteem. For example, how would you feel if you were said to be learning disabled, mildly disabled, attention deficit disordered, or attention deficit/hyperactivity disordered? Wouldn't you view yourself in a little different way than if you were called a good student or even a fairly good student?
- Unfortunately, not all teachers enjoy teaching a class made up of children with special needs or having even one child who has special needs. As stated before, only teachers who are prepared to and who desire to teach special needs children should ever do so.

In summary, before a special needs child should ever be labeled in any way, the teacher should be absolutely certain that the label is correct and that its use will help the child receive more effective instruction.

Description of Various Kinds of Children with Special Needs

The chapter now very briefly provides some of the characteristics of children with special needs. The material contained in this section is general, and there are significant differences among children who are given any of these labels.

Pellicano defined "at-risk" pupils as "uncommitted to deferred gratification and to school training that correlates with competition, and its reward, achieved status" (1987, p. 47). In general, the following is a brief comparison of expected and exhibited school behaviors of some children with special needs, especially those who have learning disabilities, attention deficit disorders, attention

deficit/hyperactivity disorders, or perhaps are culturally or linguistically diverse. Of course, not all children with a specific type of special needs necessarily have any of the exhibited behaviors mentioned here.

Expected Behavior	Exhibited Behavior
good listeners	inattentive listeners
good readers	reading below grade level
good writers	disinterested in writing and often exhibiting poor writing mechanics
self-controlled	impulsive
initiators	low motivation
independent	dependent or disinterested
organized	disorganized
high self-esteem	low self-esteem
able to delay immediate for long-term rewards	desire immediate gratification
good social skills	poor social skills

Children with Learning Disabilities (LD)

The term *learning disability (LD)* was first used by Kirk (1963) to refer to children who, despite apparently average or above average intelligence, had great difficulty with school learning. Since then the most common definitions of learning disability include the following features:

- a significant gap between expected achievement levels based on intelligence test scores and actual performance in at least one area (reading [most common], mathematics, spelling, writing, etc.)
- an uneven profile in achievement, with achievement in some areas being very high and in others very low
- poor achievement apparently not due to environmental factors
- poor achievement not due to low intelligence or emotional maladjustment

The federal government's definition of learning disability states the following:

"Specific learning disability" means a disorder in one or more of the basic psychological processes involved in understanding or in using language, spoken or written, which may manifest itself in an imperfect ability to listen, speak, read, write, or spell or do mathematical calculations (Federal Register, 1977).

In addition, a learning disabled child may exhibit some or most of the following behavioral characteristics that may be used in making the identification: hyperactivity to a moderate degree, distractibility to a moderate degree, perceptual problems, attention problems of a mild nature, and ineffective learning or problem-solving strategies. You should be aware that not all of the children who have learning disabilities are identified in kindergarten, first grade, or even second grade. Thus, they go undiagnosed until most of the basic reading skills are presented, almost ensuring that they will have reading problems later on.

Children with Attention Deficit Disorders (ADD) or Attention Deficit/Hyperactivity Disorders (AD/HD)

The number of children who are identified as attention deficit disordered (ADD) and attention deficit/hyperactivity disordered (AD/HD) recently has increased significantly. Shaywitz and Shaywitz (1992) stated that "attention deficit disorder (ADD) currently represents one of the most frequently diagnosed neurobehavioral disorders in childhood, affecting perhaps as much as 20 percent of the school-aged population" (p. ix). Although the 20 percent figure may be much too high, millions of children have been identified as ADD and represent one of the three subgroups: ADD without hyperactivity, ADD with hyperactivity, and ADD with aggression. According to the American Psychiatric Association's (1994) *Diagnostic and statistical manual of mental disorders (DSM-IV),* AD/HD is the diagnostic classification they use and define as "a persistent pattern of inattention and/or hyperactivity that is more frequent and severe than is typically observed in individuals at a comparable level of development" (p. 78). According to this manual, children with AD/HD represent about 3 to 5 percent of the school-aged children, and they can be classified as one of three subtypes: AD/HD predominantly inattentive, AD/HD predominantly hyperactive/impulsive, and AD/HD combined inattentive and hyperactive/impulsive. The American Psychiatric Association notes that AD/HD in its severe form is very impairing and affects social, familial, and scholastic achievement.

Children with AD/HD often demonstrate inattention, hyperactivity, and/or impulsivity. These children usually tend to exhibit normal sensory acuity, and intellectual, perceptual, and social-emotional abilities ranging from average to above average. Such children's reading, spelling, and arithmetic achievement often is significantly below that of their classmates. About 50 percent of children with AD/HD have difficulty in reading (Dykman & Ackerman, 1992).

In addition, the American Psychiatric Association (1994) has stated that in order for a child to be diagnosed with AD/HD, he or she must display for six months or more at least eight of the following fourteen characteristics before the age of seven:

1. fidgets, squirms, or seems restless
2. has difficulty remaining seated
3. is easily distracted
4. has difficulty awaiting turn
5. blurts out answers
6. has difficulty following instruction
7. has difficulty sustaining attention
8. shifts from one uncompleted task to another
9. has difficulty playing quietly
10. talks excessively
11. interrupts or intrudes on others
12. does not seem to listen
13. often loses things necessary for tasks
14. frequently engages in dangerous activities

These children often are treated with prescription medication, the most common of which are Ritalin, Cylert, and Dexedrine. All of these medications are amphetamines that apparently curtail an AD/HD child's inattention and disruptive behavior. Ritalin can be very effective with some young children, enabling them to concentrate better so that they can learn to read. The theory behind the use of medication is that as children mature, they will eventually outgrow the AD/HD and thus their need for medication. This may or may not happen.

ESL, LEP, or Bilingual Children

ESL pupils are those children who speak English as a second language. They make up the most rapidly expanding population in North American schools. Children who are labeled *bilingual* are very different in their language and literacy abilities. Some of them may be fluent orally in their home language only, but not able to read and write it. A few may have had strong background of knowledge and skills in their home country. Other children may have had few educational opportunities in their home country (or in their home, where English is not spoken). Others may have a fair mastery of oral English but will continue to have serious difficulties in written English. Therefore, there are great differences among children who have the designation bilingual, a term that must be defined more precisely to be useful. Children who are acquiring English as a second language may possess strong potential for fluency and literacy in two languages. However, the extent to which this potential may be realized depends upon their educational opportunities at home, in their community, and—perhaps most important—in school.

It is important to understand that more than 6 percent of the children in the public and private schools in the United States now are classified as limited English proficient (LEP) (Scarcella, 1990). According to data collected by the National Clearinghouse on Bilingual Education (1995), 66 percent of these children are in the elementary grades, 18 percent are in the middle school, and 14 percent are in the high school. The vast majority of these children—75 percent of them—speak Spanish at home. The rest of them speak Hmong, Vietnamese, Korean, Cambodian, Cantonese, and other languages. Research shows that it takes nonnative speakers of English between six and eight years to reach the oral skill level of their English-speaking classmates (Collier, 1987). This indicates that it is not an easy task for such children to become proficient in English, and early childhood teachers should be aware of this.

Within the category of bilingual children, the following four main categories sometimes are recognized:

- *English-dominant pupils with a home language other than English.* These pupils may need to improve their academic achievement in English-speaking schools while continuing to develop the home language skills and cultural ties that their parents want them to maintain.
- *Bilingual, bicultural pupils who are generally fluent in both languages.* Bilingual education enhances these pupils' academic experiences while reinforcing the cultural and linguistic identity of their families.
- *Limited English-proficient (LEP).* These children probably are the most typical of those receiving bilingual and ESL instruction. They do not have sufficient English language skills to achieve in the regular classroom and need specific instruction for developing linguistic and academic skills.
- *English speaking monolingual pupils with no minority language background.* Since the law requires classes to be integrated, English-speaking pupils who have no knowledge of other languages also may be in bilingual classes. This may help to socialize minority pupils and also help them to benefit from exposure to a second language such as Spanish.

Note: As of summer 1998, all classes in the state of California now must be totally conducted in English, since English is the official state language. This is not in keeping with the principles of much of bilingual instruction as it occurred in the past.

The early childhood teacher usually can easily identify ESL or LEP pupils by listening to them speak. However, the teacher must make this evaluation over a period of time, since the young child simply may be reserved or shy and not want to talk much at first.

Culturally or Linguistically Diverse Children

Almost every major language has a number of different *dialects.* Dialects are alternative language forms often used by regional, social, or cultural groups. Although dialects are usually understandable by speakers of the same main language group, they are different in several ways, including sounds (*aks* for *ask*), vocabulary (*gringo* for Caucasian*)*, and syntax (*He no here* for *He isn't here*). All dialects are equally logical and precise, and they are governed by rules. However, usually only one dialect becomes the standard language form in a society, because it is used by the educationally, socially, and economically advantaged members of that society. In the United States the standard language is called *Standard American English (SAE).* It usually is thought to be the form of English spoken by newscasters in most parts of the country. It normally is the

goal of schools to teach SAE to all children, because they must compete in a society that recognizes this as the standard form of speech. However, each child's diverse dialect always should be respected while attempting to add standard English on a gradual, tactful, accepting basis.

A common nonstandard dialect in the United States is *Black English.* However, people in Appalachia, the Northeast, and the South also each have a clearly definable dialect. Although the speakers of each of these dialects share certain language conventions, there may be some degree of variation within the dialect. Here are the more common characteristics of Black English.

Language Element	Standard American English	Black English
Phonological Differences		
INITIAL		
th—t	thin	tin
th—d	this	dis
str—skr	stream	scream
thre—tr	three	tree
FINAL		
r—no sound	door	doe
l—no sound	pool	poo
sk—ks	ask	aks
GENERAL		
Simplify final	talked	talk
consonant	looks	look
blends	best	bess
i—e before nasals	pin	pen
Syntactic Differences		
Dropping *to be* verbs	Shun is working.	Shun working.
Using *be* for extended time	Monique is always late.	Monique be always late.
Subject-predicate agreement *to be* verbs	I am working. There were five dogs.	I is working. There was five dogs.
Third-person singular verbs	Yetti lives in Chicago.	Yetti live in Chicago.
Irregular verbs	Latasha flew in a jet.	Latasha flied in a jet.
Double negatives	My mother doesn't want any cake.	My mother don't want no cake.
Omission of indefinite article	Sing me a happy song.	Sing me happy song.
Use of more for comparatives	My sister is younger than me.	My sister is more younger than me.

Here are the major differences between standard American English and Spanish.

Language Trait	Standard American English	Spanish
Phonological Differences		
a—e	sat	set
a—e	gate	get
i—e	big	beeg
b—p	bar	par
z—s	buzz	bus
j—ch or y	June	chun or yun
th—d	thin	din
th—s	think	sink
Syntactic Differences		
Negatives	My father is not at home.	My father is no at home.
	The men don't go to work.	The men no go to work.
	Please don't go to school.	Please no go to school.
Tense	The man will see you now.	The man see you now.
	Julio learned many things yesterday.	Julio learn many things yesterday.
Use of *be*	My grandfather is seventy.	My grandfather have seventy years.
	I am hungry.	I have hunger.
Omission of determiner	My mother is a teacher.	My mother is teacher.
Omission of pronoun		
in questions	Is it three o'clock?	Is three o'clock?
in statements	It is dark now.	Is dark now.

Culturally or linguistically diverse pupils are children who belong to an ethnic or minority group that differs from that of white Anglo-Saxon Americans. In addition to African-American (black) and Hispanic children, Native Americans and Asian Americans are considered to be culturally or linguistically diverse. In addition to having a dialect that is different from that of standard American English, some children may differ in their values and orientation toward and interest in school.

The term *multicultural education* refers to developing an understanding and appreciation of various racial and ethnic groups. This awareness should permeate the entire curriculum, and pupils should be taught with consideration for their cultural heritage, their language preferences, and their individual lifestyles.

Mildly Mentally Handicapped

The American Association on Mental Deficiency (AAMD) has defined *mental retardation* in the following way:

Mental retardation refers to significantly subaverage general intellectual functioning existing concurrently with deficits in adaptive behavior and manifested during the developmental period (1973).

According to this definition, two elements must be present for a child to be categorized as mentally retarded, mentally handicapped, or mildly mentally disabled: intellectual functioning that is significantly below average *and* inadequate adaptive behavior. According to the AAMD, "subaverage general intellectual functioning" indicates that a child must have an IQ score on the most commonly used individual intelligence test (WISC-R) of 69 or below. Children who have IQs between 70 and 85 are sometimes called *slow learners,* and literacy instruction also must be adapted for them. However, they normally are not called mentally retarded or handicapped. In evaluating adaptive behavior, the AAMD indicates that the educator should consider the age of the child in making this judgment. In early childhood, sensorimotor, communication, self-help, and socialization skills are evaluated.

Usually both mentally handicapped children and slow learners possess some of the same learning characteristics to a greater or lesser degree. Although they normally progress through the same developmental stages as do all other children, they usually do so at a slower rate. These children may have difficulty in perceiving, thinking, learning, socializing, and handling emotions. This is especially true in the academic tasks of literacy such as reading, writing, and spelling. They usually also have the following other characteristics that must be considered when planning a literacy program for them:

- delayed language development with a higher frequency of speech and language problems
- short attention span with possible distractibility
- poor short-term memory, especially of words, ideas, and numbers (long-term memory tends to be somewhat better.)
- difficulty in grasping abstract concepts but less difficulty in grasping concrete ideas
- deficiency in oral and silent reading, locating main ideas and significant details, using context clues, and implicit comprehension
- ability to learn sight words and graphophonic (phonic) analysis with appropriate instruction that has sufficient meaningful repetition

Children with Visual Impairments

Visually impaired children include the legally blind and partially sighted. A person who is considered legally blind has visual acuity that is less than 20/200. This means that with the better eye, a legally blind person can see at least 20 feet (or less) what a normally sighted person can see at 200 feet, even with the best possible correction. A partially sighted person has visual acuity that is between 20/200 and 20/70 with his or her better eye.

Legally blind persons are not necessarily entirely blind. Eighty-two percent of the legally blind have sufficient vision to be able to read print with the assistance of large print books or magnifying glasses. Twenty-one percent of the legally blind use only Braille for reading. Over one-half (52 percent) use large- or regular-print books for most or all of their reading. About one-tenth of one percent of school-aged children in the United States are believed to be visually impaired (United States Department of Education, 1984).

Visual impairment usually does not greatly change a child's language development as hearing impairment may do. The intelligence (IQ) scores of children with visual impairments are not significantly different from those of their normally sighted classmates. It appears that visual impairment has little direct effect on either linguistic or cognitive functioning (Hallahan & Kauffman, 1982).

Visually impaired persons may compensate for their limitations by improved listening skills, greater attention, and heightened tactile sensations. Teachers should be able to recognize behaviors that may indicate a student's possible visual problems. Although visual screening takes places in most, if not all, primary grades, once in a while undetected vision problems may occur. This happens occasionally with children who are being tutored for reading problems. The following symptoms may indicate a child who needs additional visual testing by a medical specialist:

- squinting
- rubbing eyes often
- holding reading materials very close or very far away from the eyes
- having red or watery eyes
- covering one eye while reading
- having crusty material around eyes and lashes

With proper instruction, the majority of children with visual impairments can make very good progress in literacy.

Children with Hearing Impairments

Hearing impaired children have reduced sensitivity to sounds in their environment because of genetic factors, illness, or some type of trauma. Usually hearing impaired children are not sensitive to sounds softer than about 26 decibels (dB, a unit of measure for the relative loudness of sounds). A classification system used by the Conference of Executives for American Schools for the Deaf defines degree of hearing impairment as follows:

Category of Hearing Impairment	Amount of Hearing Loss
mild	26–54 dB
moderate	55–60 dB
severe	70–89 dB
profound	more than 90 dB

Persons with hearing losses greater than 90 dB usually are considered *deaf,* while those with less severe hearing losses usually are thought to be *hard of hearing.*

In addition to knowing the degree of hearing loss, it also is useful to know when the hearing loss took place. It is obvious that the earlier the hearing loss occurred, the less likely that the child will have adequately developed language ability. The child with a hearing loss that occurred at an early age may experience considerable difficulty with reading comprehension, perhaps especially with implicit comprehension. This may be especially true if the hearing loss has gone undetected for a long period of time. About two-tenths of one percent of school-aged children are thought to be deaf or hard of hearing (United States Department of Education, 1984).

Some children with a hearing impairment compensate by using amplifying devices, speechreading (lip reading), sign language, finger spelling, or some combination of these. Some children with hearing impairments receive an oral communication program dependent upon amplification and speechreading, while others receive a manual communication program dependent upon sign language and finger spelling.

Recently, children with hearing impairments began receiving a total communication program that incorporates both oral and manual aspects. Such children are dependent upon the visual information in a classroom for obtaining information, including the literacy or content teacher's facial expression, lip movements, and written information around the classroom.

Although the vast majority of, if not all, schools today screen children for hearing impairments, some children with mild or moderate hearing losses may go undetected. You may request additional auditory testing using an audiometer for any child who has the following symptoms:

- has frequent earaches, head colds, or sinus infections
- has difficulty following oral directions
- often asks to have directions and explanations repeated
- is easily distracted by external noises
- has poor oral language development
- mispronounces words
- may have great difficulty with graphophonic (phonic) analysis
- gets tired easily during listening tasks
- is thought to be learning disabled, mentally handicapped, or emotionally disturbed

Children with Speech and Language Disorders

Children who have *speech disorders* produce oral language abnormally in terms of how it is said, not in what is said. There are several classifications of speech disorders:

- phonological disorders (substituting *w* for *r*)
- voice disorders (unusual pitch, loudness, or voice quality)
- disorders associated with abnormalities of the mouth and nose (for example, an orofacial cleft)
- disorders of speech flow (stuttering)
- disorders associated with the muscles used for speech production

In contrast, children who have *language disorders* have difficulty expressing their ideas in oral language or have difficulty understanding the ideas expressed by other people. Children who have language disorders may not have developed verbal language, may use words in abnormal ways such as echoing words spoken to them, may have delayed language development, or may have interrupted language development.

According to the federal government (1975), about 3 percent of school-aged children have speech disorders and about one-half of one percent have language disorders. Some students with speech disorders may do fairly well with literacy activities, while children with language disorders may have a difficult time developing proficiency in comprehension, since literacy is very dependent upon adequate language proficiency.

A literacy or content teacher may want to look for the following characteristics before referring a child to a speech pathologist:

- substantially less mature oral language than that of peers
- inability to tell a story with all of its elements
- making substitutions or omissions of sounds such as /w/ for /r/ or /l/, /b/ for /v/, /f/ for voiceless /th/, /t/ for /k/, voiceless th/ for /s/, /d/ for voiced /th/, and voiced /th/ for /z/
- difficulty being understood by other students
- speaking much more rapidly than other children, thus causing difficulty in being understood
- pitch, loudness, and quality very different from those of other children
- particular difficulty in understanding and following directions

UNDERSTANDING THE PHILOSOPHY OF INCLUSION WHEN TEACHING CHILDREN WITH SPECIAL NEEDS

Inclusion means that children with special needs are assigned to regular classrooms for the entire instructional day and are allowed to participate in all school activities and functions. This type of inclusive system obviously requires very good support systems. Classrooms must be made physically accessible to accommodate the needs of all children. In addition to the physical setting, provisions must be made for additional well-trained personnel, staff development, and technical assistance. This may mean that in addition to the regular classroom teacher, a special

education teacher will be made available to co-teach the entire class. It is important that the special education teacher be involved in the instruction of the entire class so that as much as possible children do not become overly aware of the children with special needs (Friend & Cook, 1992).

In most elementary schools, inclusion has replaced mainstreaming as the way of organizing instruction for children with special needs. In mainstreaming a child received part of his or her instruction in a regular classroom but normally not all of it. Inclusion is the ultimate result of The Education for All Handicapped Children Act, or Public Law 94-142. The most important part of PL 94-142 states that

> . . . in order to receive funds under the Act every school system in the nation must make provision for a free, appropriate public education for every child . . . regardless of how, or how seriously, he may be handicapped.

In addition to requiring schools to provide a free public education for all children with special needs, two other provisions of this legislation affect early childhood education teachers: *individual educational plans (IEPs)* and the concept of the *least restrictive environment.*

Individual Educational Plans

Public Law 94-142 mandates that a multidisciplinary team consisting of trained educational specialists evaluate each child who has special needs. This team submits a report at a case conference meeting at which a representative of the schools, the child's teacher, the parent(s), and other appropriate people responsible for developing an IEP for the child are present. According to federal guidelines (1975, p. 3), an IEP must include these elements:

- a statement of the present levels of performance
- a statement of the annual goals including short-term instructional objectives
- a statement of the specific educational services to be performed
- the extent to which each child will be able to participate in regular educational programs
- the projected date for the beginning and anticipated duration of the services
- appropriate objective evaluation procedures
- a schedule for determining at least annually whether or not the instructional objectives are being achieved

The Least Restrictive Environment

One of the most important decisions made at the group conference, in addition to whether or not to place the child in any type of special education program, concerns the recommended instructional environment. The IEP must state the extent to which the child will be placed in the regular classroom.

The *inclusion philosophy* states that as much as possible of the child's learning be done in a regular classroom setting with his or her own teacher doing much of the teaching. Any special education teacher usually then becomes a consultant to the regular classroom teacher, providing him or her with appropriate instructional strategies and materials. In addition, the special education teacher may come into the child's classroom and work with the child on an individual basis or even teach a group of children or the entire class. The concept behind inclusion is to avoid singling out a child with any type of special need(s). Inclusion also assumes that the child's own teacher can best present much of the required material to him or her with the unqualified support of the special educator without a pull-out program. Unfortunately, according to research, pull-out programs often have not resulted in long-term gains for the children.

The following are some of the main advantages of inclusion:

- It enables children to participate in the regular classroom and school activities as much as possible.
- It may avoid stigmatizing children, since in a pull-out program they are otherwise separated from their classmates and may feel stigmatized.
- It should teach all children to be tolerant of children who are different from them.
- Since the regular classroom teacher and the special education teacher work cooperatively in planning each child's program, the child should have the best learning experiences possible.

Here are the main limitations of inclusion:

- Regular classroom teachers must receive true support from special educators if inclusion is to be successful. Regular classroom teachers cannot be expected to know how to teach all types of children with special needs without appropriate, long-term support from special education teachers.
- Children with special needs must be actively welcomed into a regular classroom by both the early childhood teacher and the rest of the children so that they do not feel stigmatized or different. This may not happen unless the teacher makes a concerted effort to ensure that this is the case.
- The educational opportunities for the other children in the classroom must not be neglected by the need to help children with special needs. All children need to be provided with the best possible appropriate educational experiences.
- The parents of children with special needs must have the inclusion philosophy explained to them in detail before the school begins to implement it to be sure that they understand and support it.

STRATEGIES FOR TEACHING LITERACY TO CHILDREN WITH SPECIAL NEEDS

The next part of this chapter presents guidelines and strategies that should help early childhood teachers present literacy skills to children with special needs.

General Guidelines

Here are some general guidelines which were adapted from Mohr (1995) that you should consider when teaching literacy to children with special needs:

- Observe the child in authentic settings. Assess the child's learning strengths, styles, and differences and the conditions of any disability or difference that may interfere with learning.
- Teach to a child's strengths while remediating weaknesses and developing compensation skills.
- Restructure a task when a child cannot master it. Change the way in which the task is presented or change the method of response.
- Check understanding of the material or directions by following up with a specific question. Avoid asking, "Are you sure that you understand?"
- Repeat or rephrase what is being said in the classroom by varying the vocabulary and the mode of presentation or method of instruction.
- Give both oral and written directions in the classroom, and provide both visual and auditory cues for directions and instructions.
- Be aware of auditory and visual distractions in the classroom. Even subtle ones can be very distracting to some children, such as a pencil sharpener or sitting near a window or door.
- Provide help through peer tutoring or the "buddy system." Provide reinforcement for nearly learned or previously learned skills by allowing a child with special needs to become a peer tutor to another child who is just beginning to learn a skill.
- Include all children in classroom activities and projects. Minimize the differences and maximize the similarities of class members during classroom participation.
- Match a child's learning style with appropriate selection of methods and materials. Use learning styles and strengths of all learners in the classroom as tools for planning instruction.
- Evaluate children by their individual performance *without lowering the standards for the class.* Investigate evaluation alternatives to ensure success, not failure.
- Manage behavior positively, consistently, and assertively. Set limits, structure consequences, and follow through! The use of logical consequences, natural reinforcers, contingency contracting, praise, encouragement, and recognition will help structure

success for all children. Some children with disabilities and learning differences may need different discipline considerations.

General Principles for Working with Children Who Are Economically Disadvantaged

Delpit (1993) has presented ten principles for working with children who are economically disadvantaged. While some children who do not speak English as a native language are both urban and economically disadvantaged, a number are not; however, most of what Delpit has written also applies to children who are learning a second language. In fact, I believe all of these principles apply to all children, with or without special needs.

- Do not teach content, but recognize children's strengths and, if anything, teach more, not less, than the regular curriculum.
- Whatever methodology or instructional program you use, demand critical thinking from the children.
- Ensure access to the basic skills, conventions, and strategies necessary for success in education in the United States.
- Empower children to challenge racist views of their competence and worthiness.
- Build on strengths.
- Use familiar metaphors and experiences from the children's own world.
- Create a sense of family and caring.
- Monitor and assess needs, and then address them with a wealth of diverse ideas.
- Honor and respect children's home cultures.
- Foster a sense of children's connection to community—to something greater than themselves.

Beaty (1997) has provided the following suggestions for showing your acceptance for any child with special needs. They also are useful with all young children. She wrote that in order for children to know that they are accepted, you must show them that they are by the way you look at them, talk to them, and interact with them. She has given the four following points for developing self-esteem through acceptance:

1. Accept yourself personally.
2. Accept each child as a worthy person.
3. Show your acceptance by:
   - Calling each child by his or her accurate name
   - Making eye contact with the child and smiling at him or her
   - Greeting each child daily
   - Having a personal conversation with each child daily
4. Promote children's acceptance of themselves and of other children through picture book stories and activities.

General Guidelines for Working with ESL, LEP, and Bilingual Children

A number of strategies have been designed to help early childhood teachers promote both multicultural awareness and linguistic diversity. Some of these strategies are equally valuable with other types of children who have special needs. Here are the main instructional approaches for limited English-speaking children that are being used at this time:

- *Immersion approaches.* These approaches make no special provisions for LEP children. As teachers instruct all children in oral and written skills in English, limited English-speaking children are expected to pick up as much as they can from immersion in English. This has been the traditional form of instruction to LEP children in our country, although it is not necessarily the most effective.
- *ESL approaches.* These approaches teach limited English-speaking children oral English skills first before any reading instruction begins. Usually ESL approaches require that children leave the classroom for this instruction. Special ESL teachers work with children in structured oral drills to develop fluency in oral English. After children have begun to establish fluency in oral English, reading instruction is started.
- *Bilingual approaches.* These approaches promote the development of reading and writing skills in the children's native language concurrently with either formal or informal instruction in English. After children have learned to read and write in their own language and acquired proficiency in oral English, reading instruction in English begins. Bilingual approaches require special teachers who are fluent in the native language of the children with whom they work.

Here are some general guidelines for teaching culturally diverse children:

- Learn about their culture
- Participate in their community
- Value their unique contributions
- Share your ideas with other teachers
- Discuss universal concerns
- Provide a supportive classroom environment
- Develop background knowledge
- Use multicultural literature as much as possible

Here are several other effective ideas for working with limited English-speaking children:

- Seat the child near the front of the room so that he or she can see and hear better and have fewer distractions.
- Speak somewhat more slowly and distinctly than normal but not in an artificial manner.

- Use shorter sentences and few long words, and simplify concepts as much as possible.
- Use manipulative materials and concrete demonstrations as much as possible, especially in science and mathematics.
- Use visual materials such as pictures, videotapes, diagrams, dioramas, and the like as much as possible.
- Allow children to respond with only one or two words if necessary.
- Do not correct errors of vocabulary, comprehension, accent, or structure.
- Do not expect perfection in English in too short a time period.
- Assign a compatible "buddy" to work with the child whenever it is required.
- Provide a supportive classroom environment.

General Strategies for Presenting Literacy Skills to Young Children Who Have Special Needs

The chapter now presents several strategies that research has found to be especially useful with young children who have special needs of various kinds. Of course, all of these strategies must be modified somewhat to be appropriate for the different types of children with whom you are working. Since many of these strategies have been discussed in detail in other parts of this book, they are only very briefly mentioned here.

- *The whole language philosophy.* This type of early childhood literacy program is especially useful with children who have special needs because each child can read and write on his or her own level. The themes of the unit also can be selected to reflect the unique experiences of the children in your class. In addition, multicultural literature of various types can be used in the whole language units.
- *The language-experience approach (LEA).* This approach probably is the most single useful approach for teaching beginning literacy skills to all types of children with special needs. LEA uses the child's own language patterns and prior knowledge. In addition, it is highly motivational and allows children to experience immediate success. LEA can be successful with all these types of children: ESL, LEP, bilingual, LD, ADD, AD/HD, EMH, severely mentally disabled, and children with hearing impairments.
- *Learning centers.* Well-organized and well-equipped learning centers make it possible for children with special needs to learn a great deal on their own through playful interaction with materials while teachers provide attention to individuals or small groups.
- *Scaffolding.* Scaffolding strategies are a change in delivery systems which is especially helpful to children of all kinds of diverse backgrounds.

Scaffolded instruction allows teachers to mediate learning experiences for children—a teacher who mediates serves as an intermediary in helping diverse learners to negotiate meaning. The most important element in scaffolding is providing support to the child.

- *Cooperative learning groups.* In a cooperative learning group, the teacher usually gives heterogeneous groups of two to four children a topic to look up and report on later. This type of group is most useful at the upper primary-grade level.
- *Mnemonic devices.* This is a formal scheme designed to improve a child's memory. When used carefully, a mnemonic device can be very helpful in enabling a child with learning disabilities, attention deficit disorder, or attention deficit/hyperactivity disorder to remember important material. Here are several mnemonic devices that may be helpful in the upper primary grades: acronyms, acronymic sentences, rhymes, or abbreviations.
- *Behavior management.* Behavior management strategies may be very useful with children who have special needs who do not respond to ordinary classroom management procedures or who are unable to control their behaviors with self-monitoring methods. Some behavior modification strategies are as follows: counseling, modeling, reality therapy (having the child and teacher construct a contract outlining acceptable behavior that the teacher and child both sign), and behavior modification with primary (manipulative or object) and secondary (praise) reinforcers. Note that contracts can often be used very successfully with children who have special needs.
- *Multisensory approaches.* This concept is based on two premises: children learn through their senses, and the more senses tapped during the teaching-learning process, the greater are the chances that learning will take place. Having children use more than one sense at a time in a lesson (for example, having them see, hear, and touch a lamb) is thought to be more effective than having them use one or both of the traditional senses used in school (seeing and/or hearing a lamb). Here are some multisensory approaches for young children with special needs: Gillingham and Stillman's VAK Strategy (1970), Fernald's VAKT Strategy (1943), Dwyer and Flippo's Multisensory Spelling and Sight-Word Strategy (1983), and the Analytical-Tutorial Word Identification Strategy (Lindsey, Beck, & Bursor, 1981).
- *Media approaches.* Using videotapes, filmstrips, films, pictures, experiments, demonstrations, and story boards may be especially useful with children who have special needs, since they enable children to more clearly understand the concepts that are being presented orally.

- *Technology.* A variety of technological devices have been designed to help meet the needs of children with various kinds of disabilities. As an example, in the future overhead transparency projectors may well be replaced by a video camera called an ELMO. This device displays text material, graphics, and almost any image that is placed on its glass top on a video monitor. It is more adaptable than the overhead projector when presenting visual images.

    Many devices that are based on closed-captioning will help hearing-impaired children's learning. A machine known as an Optacon translates images to tactile Braille-like print or synthesized speech. Print-to-speech translators are being refined, and a variety of them will eventually be available. The Kurzweil Reading Machine reads aloud printed material placed on a glass desk. A child can pause it, rewind it to hear a word, and control volume, pitch, and speech rate.

- *Art and craft activities.* All types of art and craft activities easily can be adapted to encourage young children to tap into their cultural heritage. If you wish, family members also can be involved in these activities, making their own unique contributions.

- *Family members' participation.* It is vitally important to involve the family members of young children with special needs as much as possible in the early childhood literacy program. To do so greatly enhances the chances that the child will be successful in school. Some of the ways in which an early childhood teacher can involve the family of children who have special needs in the school program are as paid or volunteer literacy tutors, lunchroom and playground supervisors, and classroom visitors who share elements of their cultural heritage. Teachers can give workshops for parents about how literacy skills currently are taught and provide packets of materials that parents can use at home with children to promote literacy skills (books, children's magazines, reading games, and simple activity sheets).

- *Choral reading.* Norton (1995) states that books that include repetitive language are excellent for oral reading. The teacher reads the book to the group, and then the teacher and children chorally read it in unison. Everyone discusses the book, and they read it once again. In this approach the teacher selects individual words and phrases and emphasizes choral reading (with all or several children reading in unison). Research has found significant improvement in comprehension and word identification for LEP children who were taught with this method.

BOOKS FOR DIVERSE LEARNERS

The chapter now includes a sampling of the trade books for diverse learners that you can use with all young children. These books can be used as springboards to activi-
ties about children from different cultures and with other special needs. In the past, trade books for children with special needs were quite scarce. However, recently a large number of such books have come on the market. Many of these books have gained attention because of the quality of the writing by new authors in the field. A number of these authors are themselves multicultural writers whose books come from their own prior knowledge. In addition, new technology breakthroughs in reproducing book art have encouraged outstanding artists to enter the field of book illustration. The children in such trade books can become "super-characters" in young children's lives. Teachers now can introduce children to book heroes from every culture and with every disability and then follow up with valuable extension activities.

The importance of books to children's awareness of people from different cultures and with special needs cannot be overestimated. For example, Ramsey (1991) wrote:

> Children's books are a primary vehicle for this kind of teaching. By engaging children in stories, we enable our young readers and listeners to empathize with different experiences and points of view and experience a wide range of social dilemmas . . . When children role play situations and characters in a book, they learn how to perceive situations from a variety of perspectives and literally be "in another person's shoes" (pp. 168–169).

The following are trade books you may want to use with your students to help create a culturally diverse, inclusive atmosphere:

Aardema, V. (1991). *Pedro and the padre.* NY: Dial.

Aardema, V. (1982). *What's so funny, Ketu?* NY: Dial.

Aardema, V. (1977). *Who's in Rabbit's house? A Masai tale.* NY: Dial.

Adoff, A. (1973). *Black is brown is tan.* NY: Harper & Row.

Ashley, B. (1991). *Cleversticks.* NY: Crown.

Bardot, D. (1991). *A bicycle for Rosaura.* Brooklyn: Kane/Miller.

Begaye, L. (1993). *Building a bridge.* Flagstaff, AZ: Northland.

Binch, C. (1994). *Gregory Cool.* NY: Dial.

Bishop, C. (1938). *The five Chinese brothers.* NY: Coward-McCann.

Booth, B. (1991). *Mandy.* NY: Lothrop, Lee & Shephard.

Brown, T. (1982). *Someone special just like you.* NY: Holt.

Bryan, A. (1993). *The story of lightning and thunder.* NY: Atheneum.

Caines, J. (1977). *Daddy.* NY: Harper & Row.

Cohen, M. (1983). *See you tomorrow.* NY: Greenwillow.

Cowen-Fletcher, J. (1994). *It takes a village.* NY: Scholastic.

Crews, D. (1991). *Big momma.* NY: Greenwillow.

Dale, P. (1987). *Bet you can't.* NY: Lippincott.

Daly, N. (1985). *Not so fast Songololo.* NY: Viking Penguin.

Davol, M. (1993). *Black, white, just right!* Morton Grove, IL: Whitman.

Dooley, N. (1991). *Everybody cooks rice.* Minneapolis, MN: Carolrhoda.

Dorros, A. (1991). *Abuela.* NY: Dutton.

Fanshawe, E. (1975). *Rachel.* NY: Bradbury.

Fleming, V. (1993). *Be good to Eddie Lee.* NY: Philomel.

Flournoy, V. (1978). *The best time of day.* NY: Random House.

Flournoy, V. (1985). *The patchwork quilt.* NY: Dial.

Fox, M. (1989). *Sophie.* NY: Harcourt Brace.

Franklin, K. (1994). *The shepherd boy.* NY: Merrill/Macmillan.

Giovanni, N. (1994). *Knoxville, Tennessee.* NY: Scholastic.

Goble, P. (1988). *Iktomi and the boulder.* NY: Orchard Books.

Goble, P. (1989). *Iktomi and the berries.* NY: Orchard Books.

Goble, P. (1994). *Iktomi and the buzzard.* NY: Orchard Books.

Greenfield, E. (1988). *Grandpa's face.* NY: Philomel.

Greenfield, E. (1973). *Rosa Parks.* NY: Harper.

Greenfield, E. (1974). *She came bringing me that little baby girl.* Philadelphia, PA: Lippincott.

Greenfield, E. (1977). *Africa dreams.* NY: Harper.

Grifalconi, A. (1993). *Kinda blue.* Boston: Little Brown.

Havill, J. (1986). *Jamaica's find.* Boston: Houghton Mifflin.

Havill, J. (1989). *Jamaica tag-along.* Boston: Houghton Mifflin.

Heide, F. (1990). *The day of Amed's secret.* NY: Lothrop, Lee & Shephard.

Hirschi, R. (1993). *Seya's song.* Seattle, WA: Sasquatch Books.

Isadora, R. (1991). *At the crossroads.* NY: Greenwillow.

Johnson, A. (1990). *Do like Kyla.* NY: Orchard.

Johnston, T. (1990). *The badger and the magic fan.* NY: Putnam.

Joseph, L. (1990). *Coconut kind of day.* NY: Lothrop, Lee, & Shephard.

Keats, E. (1972). *The snowy day.* NY: Orchard.

Keats, E. (1969). *Goggles!* NY: Collier.

Kusugak, M. (1993). *Northern lights, soccer trails.* Toronto, Ontario, Canada: Annack Press.

Lautaure, D. (1992). *Father and son.* NY: Philomel.

Lee, J. (1985). *Toad is the uncle of heaven.* NY: Holt.

Levenson, R. (1988). *Our home is the sea.* NY: Dutton.

Loewen, I. *My kokum called today.* Winnipeg, Manitoba, Canada: Pemmican Publications.

Long, J. (1996). *The bee and the dream.* NY: Dutton.

Mahy, M. (1990). *The seven Chinese brothers.* The NY: Scholastic.

Maris, R. (1986). *I wish I could fly.* NY: Greenwillow.

Marzolo, J. (1993). *Happy birthday, Martin Luther King.* NY: Scholastic.

McDermott, G. (1994). *Coyote: A trickster tale from the American Southwest.* San Diego, CA: Harcourt Brace.

McKissack, P. (1988). *Mirandy and Brother Wind.* NY: Alfred A. Knopf.

McLellan, J. (1994). *Nanahbosho: How the turtle got its shell.* Winnipeg, Manitoba, Canada: Pemmican Publications.

Miller, M., & Ancona, G. (1991). *Handtalk.* NY: Four Winds.

Mitchell, R. (1993). *Hue boy.* NY: Dial.

Mora, P. (1992). *A birthday basket for Tia.* NY: Macmillan.

Namioka, L. (1995). *The loyal cat.* San Diego, CA: Harcourt.

Nodar, C. (1992). *Abuelita's paradise.* Morton Grove, IL: Whitman.

Palacios, A. (1993). *A Christmas surprise for Chabelita.* NY: Troll Associates.

Paulsen, G. (1995). *The tortilla factory.* San Diego, CA: Harcourt Brace.

Pennington, D. (1994). *Itse Selu, the Cherokee harvest festival.* Watertown, MA: Charlesbridge.

Rankin, L. (1991). *The handmade alphabet.* NY: Dial.

Rattigan, J. (1993). *Dumpling soup.* Boston: Little Brown.

Rhee, N. (1993). *Magic spring.* NY: Putnam.

Ringgold, F. (1991). *Tar beach.* NY: Crown.

Rodanas, K. (1991). *Dragonfly's tale.* NY: Clarion.

Roe, E. (1991). *Con mi hermano/With my brother.* NY: Bradbury.

Rosenberg, M. (1988). *Finding a way: Living with exceptional brothers and sisters.* NY: Lothrop, Lee & Shephard.

Sloat, T., & Hoffman, B. (1990). *The eye of the needle.* NY: Penguin.

Smalls-Hector, R. (1992). *Jonathan and his mommy.* Boston: Little, Brown.

Soto, G. (1993). *Too many tamales.* NY: Putnam.

Surat, M. (1983). *Angel child, dragon child.* NY: Scholastic.

Sun, C. (1994). *Mama Bear.* Boston: Houghton Mifflin.

Thomas, I. (1991). *Mermaid Janine.* NY: Scholastic Publications.

Wolkstein, D. (1981). *The banza.* NY: Dial.

Xiong, B. (1989). *Nine-in-one grr! grr!* San Francisco: Children's Book Press.

Zolotow, C. (1972). *William's doll.* NY: Harper.

SOURCES FOR MULTICULTURAL TEACHING AIDS

The following is a good source for multicultural dolls and puppets:

Constructive Playthings
1227 East 119th Street
Grandview, MO 64030

Here is a good source for multicultural speaking and music tapes:

Claudia's Caravan
Multicultural/Multilingual Materials
PO Box 1582
Alameda, CA 94501

This is a good source for Asian and Hispanic cooking sets:

Childcraft
20 Kilmer Road
PO Box 3081
Edison, NJ 08818

BIBLIOGRAPHIES FOR CULTURALLY AND LINGUISTICALLY BASED SPANISH READING MATERIALS

Several bibliographies for culturally and linguistically based Spanish reading materials follow:

Dale, D. (1985). *Bilingual books in Spanish and English for children.* Littleton, CO: Libraries Unlimited.

Schon, I. (1983, 1985, 1987). *Books in Spanish for children and young adults, Series II, III, IV.* Metuchen, NJ: Scarecrow Press.

Schon, I. (1986). *Basic collection of children's books in Spanish.* Metuchen, NJ: Scarecrow Press.

PROFESSIONAL RESOURCE BOOKS FOR EARLY CHILDHOOD TEACHERS OF CHILDREN WITH DISABILITIES

Here is a partial list of some of the professional resource books that teachers of children with various kinds of special needs may find helpful. They are all available from:

Prentice-Hall/The Center for Applied Research in Education
PO Box 11071
Des Moines, IA 50336
Telephone Number 1-800-288-4745
FAX 515-284-2607

Barnes, D. & Barnes, C. (1989). *Special educator's survival guide.*

Bernstein, R. (1993). *Ready-to-use phonic activities for special children.*

Elman, N. (1984). *The special educator's almanac.*

Harwell, J. (1987). *Complete learning disabilities handbook.*

Harwell, J. (1996). *Complete learning disabilities handbook, I and II.*

Kreplin, E. (1996). *Sound & articulation activities for children with speech and language problems.*

Mannix, D. (1992). *Life skills activities for special children.*

Mauer, R. (1994). *Special educator's discipline handbook.*

Pierangelo, R. (1994). *A survival kit for the special education teacher.*

Pierangelo, R. (1995). *The special education teacher's book of lists.*

Rief, S. (1993). *How to reach & teach ADD/AD/HD children.*

Waring, C. (1995). *Developing independent readers: Strategy-oriented reading activities for learners with special needs.*

Another very useful professional book is the following:

Blaska, J. (1996). *Using children's literature to learn about disabilities and illness.* NY: Practical Press.

SUGGESTED ACTIVITIES

1. If possible, observe a classroom that has one or more children who have special needs of various types. How do these children exemplify the behavioral characteristics that were mentioned in this chapter? In what ways is their behavior different from the information that was mentioned in this chapter?

2. If possible, listen to one or more children who speak a nonstandard dialect or listen to a tape recording of their speech. Summarize orally or in writing in what ways their speech is like or is different from the characteristics of that dialect mentioned in this chapter.

3. If possible, examine a simple Individual Education Plan (IEP). What do you think are the advantages and limitations of this kind of plan for a child with special needs?

4. If possible, learn to finger spell or sign enough words so that you can have a simple conversation with a young child who has a hearing impairment.

5. Select several concepts that a young child might want to remember and formulate a mnemonic device for each of these concepts. What do you believe are the main advantages and limitations of using a mnemonic device?

6. Read some of the trade books for diverse learners that are mentioned in this chapter then construct an annotated bibliography for these trade books. Which ones do you think that children with special needs would like the best? Why do you feel that way?

SELECTED REFERENCES

Beaty, J. (1997). *Building bridges with multicultural books.* Upper Saddle River, NJ: Prentice Hall.

Barnett, W. (1995). Long-term effects of early childhood programs on cognitive and school outcomes. *The Future of Children, 5,* 25–50.

Cheek, E., Flippo, R., & Lindsey, J. (1997). *Reading for success in elementary schools* (pp. 309–360). Madison, WI: Brown & Benchmark.

Cox, C., & Boyd-Batstone. (1997). *Crossroads: Literature and language in linguistically diverse classrooms.* Upper Saddle River, NJ: Merrill.

Division for Early Childhood Task Force on Recommended Practices (1993). *DEC recommended practices: Indicators of quality in programs for infants and young children with special needs and their families.* Reston, VA: Council for Exceptional Children.

Graves, M., Juel, C., & Graves, B. (1998). *Teaching reading in the 21st century* (pp. 432–475). Boston: Allyn & Bacon.

Hannon, P. (1995). *Literacy, home and school.* London: Falmer.

Heilman, A., Blair, T., & Rupley, W. (1998). *Principles and practices of teaching reading.* (pp. 532–568). Upper Saddle River, NJ: Simon & Schuster.

Miller, W. (1999). *Ready-to-Use Activities & Materials for Improving Content Reading Skills* (pp. 463–487). West Nyack, NY: The Center for Applied Research in Education.

National Association for the Education of Young Children. (1996). NAEYC position statement: Responding to linguistic and cultural diversity—Recommendations for effective early childhood education. *Young Children, 51,* 4–12.

Neuman, S., & Roskos, K. (1993). Access to print for children of poverty: Differential effects of adult mediation and literacy-enriched play settings on environmental and functional print tasks. *American Educational Research Journal, 30,* 95–122.

Sampson, M., Sampson, M. B., & Allen, R. (1995). *Pathways to literacy* (pp. 476–508). Fort Worth, TX: Harcourt Brace Jovanovich College Publishers.

Savage, J. (1994). *Teaching reading through literature* (pp. 324–380). Madison, WI: Brown & Benchmark.

Strickland, D. (1994). Educating African-American learners at risk: Finding a better way. *Language Arts, 71,* 328–336.

Temple, C., Martinez, M., Yokota, J., & Naylor, A. (1998). *Children's books in children's hands* (pp. 81–133). Boston: Allyn & Bacon.

WORKS CITED IN CHAPTER 8

American Psychiatric Association. (1994). *Diagnostic and statistical manual of mental disorders.* Washington, DC: American Psychiatric Association.

Beaty, J. (1997). *Building bridges with multicultural literature.* Upper Saddle River, NJ: Prentice Hall.

Collier, V. (1987). Age and rate of acquisition of second language for academic purposes. *TESOL Quarterly, 21,* 617–641.

Cosby, B. (1990). 45 years from today. *Ebony, 46,* 61.

Delpit, L. (1995). *Other people's children.* Paper presented to the National Reading Conference, New Orleans, LA.

Dwyer, E., & Flippo, R. (1983). Multisensory approach for teaching spelling. *Journal of Reading, 27,* 171–172.

Dykman, R., & Ackerman, P. (1992). Attention deficit disorder and specific reading disability: Separate but often overlapping. In S. Shaywitz & B. Shaywitz (Eds.). *Attention deficit disorder comes of age: Toward the end of the twenty-first century* (pp. 165–183). Austin, TX: PROED.

Fernald, G. (1943). *Remedial techniques in high school.* NY: McGraw-Hill.

Friend, M., & Cook, L. (1992). The new mainstreaming. *Instructor, 101,* 30–34.

Gillingham, A., & Stillman, B. (1970). *Remedial training for children with specific disability in reading, spelling, and penmanship.* Cambridge, MA: Educators Publishing Service.

Grossman, J. (Ed.) (1973). *Manual on terminology and classification in mental retardation, 1973 revision.* Washington, DC: American Association of Mental Deficiency.

Hallahan, D., & Kauffman, J. (1982). *Exceptional children.* Englewood Cliffs, NJ: Prentice Hall.

Kirk, S. (1963). *Educating exceptional children.* Boston: Allyn & Bacon.

Lindsey, J., Beck, F., & Bursor, D. (1981). An analytical-tutorial method for developing adolescents' sight vocabulary. *Journal of Reading, 24,* 591–594.

Mohr, L. (1995). Teaching diverse learners in inclusive settings: Steps for adapting instruction. *Paper presented at the Council for Exceptional Children Annual Conference.* Indianapolis, IN.

National Clearinghouse for Bilingual Education. (1995). *Ask NCBE,* January 20, 1995.

Norton, D. (1995). *Through the eyes of a child: An introduction to children's literature.* Upper Saddle River, NJ: Merrill/Prentice Hall.

Pellicano, R. (1987). At risk: A view of social advantage. *Educational Leadership, 44,* 47–50.

Ramsey, P. (1991). *Making friends in school: Promoting play relationships.* NY: Teachers College Press.

Savage, J. (1994). *Teaching reading using literature.* pp. 324–380). Madison, WI: Brown & Benchmark.

Scarcella, R. (1990). *Teaching language minority students in the regular classroom.* Englewood Cliffs, NJ: Prentice Hall.

Shaywitz, S., & Shaywitz, B. (Eds.) (1992). *Attention deficit disorder comes of age: Toward the end of the twenty-first century.* Austin, TX: PROED.

United States Government Printing Office. (1975, 1977, 1984). *Federal Register, 40, 42, & 49.*

In Conclusion

This book stressed that each young child should receive the best possible program of emergent literacy experiences in the home and other early childhood settings and later an optimum literacy program in kindergarten and the primary grades. All literacy experiences should begin at the child's present developmental level and proceed to the optimum level possible. If this is done, each child can be assured of the most success possible in literacy. This textbook is based on the premise that nearly every child can learn to read, write, and spell with the proper experiences and instruction.

Emergent literacy experiences should begin very early in a child's life and consist of listening to trade books, nursery rhymes, poetry, and other material read aloud regularly beginning in infancy; going on family outings; having a print-rich environment in the home or other early childhood setting; participating in reading reenactments; being exposed to many good reading models; dictating language-experience books and charts; having writing materials in the home and being encouraged to engage in many different types of writing activities; playing school with siblings or friends; participating in art or construction activities; engaging in dramatic play and block play; and using different kind of multimedia.

All of these early literacy experiences should be made meaningful, enjoyable, and relevant for young children and should be presented only when a child is ready for them. It is important that young children participate in as many of these experiences as seem appropriate to ensure that they will be ready for literacy instruction in school.

This text has recommended that literacy instruction in kindergarten be mainly informal, consisting of many of the experiences that were recommended for the home and various preschool settings. It further has encouraged kindergarten teachers to provide literacy instruction for each child that is developmentally appropriate for him or her. For some children, this may be whole language instruction with relevant skills instruction, while for other children it may be the emergent literacy experiences mentioned earlier which they did not have before kindergarten. This textbook did not recommend any type of formal phonics program for kindergarten children, as this type of program is not considered developmentally appropriate or necessary for young children.

A whole language program with relevant, meaningful skills instruction that constitutes a balanced literacy program was recommended for the primary grades. A balanced approach will ensure that the unique strengths of whole language and skills-based instruction can be best utilized while the limitations of both are minimized. A whole language program is excellent because it motivates children and is highly interesting to them. In addition, it involves each child actively and encourages collaboration and cooperation. It also teaches skills in a meaningful manner in the context of real materials. As a complement to that, skills-based instruction can be used to teach the important letter names, sight word, graphophonic (phonic) skills, and word skills in a structured developmental way. This often is important for children who have difficulty learning skills in a less structured way.

Kindergarten and primary-grade whole language classrooms may contain the following elements: a print-rich environment, interactive story reading, predictable books, big books, collaborative groups, message boards, book talks, a writing workshop, and skills that are presented and reinforced within the context of real materials. Classrooms that stress skills often teach literacy skills in isolation and employ games and reproducibles to a large extent. Although some skills-based materials may allow teachers to teach skills very well, their use often does not result in children who either choose to read or enjoy reading. Then one wonders if total skills-based literacy instruction has really been successful despite the children's acquisition of skills. That is why this textbook has recommended a balanced reading program for each kindergarten and primary-grade child that uses the strengths of both whole language programs and skills-based instruction. This type of literacy instruction also may be called interactional. Such a program should be especially designed for each child based upon his or her present literacy level and literacy strengths and weaknesses. Although individually prescribed literacy instruction is important for all young children, it is especially important for young children with special needs that may make learning literacy skills difficult.

Because the individual children in your future early childhood classrooms all will have such varied needs and interests, it will become incumbent upon you to use a variety of approaches, strategies, and materials with them. The development of the optimum literacy program for each child attending an early childhood classroom is indeed a daunting task, but it can be made easier if the teacher has a firm grounding in the elements that can comprise such a program. This textbook has provided sufficient material for future early childhood teachers to make a good beginning in this difficult undertaking. Although you will learn much more in the future from your own pupils and further study, you should now be well prepared to present literacy skills effectively to the children whom you will teach. Your success in this most important endeavor will profoundly influence the lives of many, many children.

ACTIVITIES INDEX

This activities index is provided to make it easier for the early childhood teacher to locate the activities (strategies, games, and reproducibles) that are contained in this textbook. To use the index, simply look up the activity under the proper letter of the alphabet. All of the activities are found in bold print in this index. For your convenience, the other major concepts included in this textbook are included in the Activities Index but are found in standard print.

NAME INDEX

A

Aardema, V., 14, 285
Abrahamson, R., 20
Ackermann, P., 277
Adams, M., 52, 128, 188
Addison-Wesley, 50
Adoff, A., 202, 285
Afflerbach, P., 238
Agard, J., 87
Ahberg, J.A., 14, 85
Alberg, A., 85
Alexander, A., 87
Alexander, M., 20
Alexander, P., 192
Aliki, 65
Allard, H., 84
Allen, J., 84
Allen, L., 141
Allen, R., 43, 46
Allington, R., 134
Alverman, D., 200–201
American Association on Mental Deficiency, 279
American Book, 50
American Psychiatric Association, 277
Ames, L., 39
Anbar, A., 80
Ancona, G., 286
Anderson, H., 86
Anderson, R., 128, 180–181, 188
Anno, E., 87
Anno, M., 86
Antee, N., 140
Archambault, J., 30, 66, 181
Argyle, S., 248, 250
Arno, E., 14, 83
Arnowsky, J., 30
Aruego, J., 14, 20, 114
Asch, F., 14, 30
Ashley, B., 285
Association for Childhood Education International (ACEI), 52
Aukermann, R., 50
Ayliffe, A., 85

B

Babbit, N., 30
Baer, G., 174
Bagban, M., 80
Baker, A., 82
Baker, K., 30
Baldwin, R., 168, 174
Bales, R., 198
Bardot, D., 285
Bare Books, 44

Barnes, C., 287
Barnes, D. 287
Barney, 55
Barrett, J., 30
Barry, K., 82
Bartkowski, R., 86
Bartocci, B., 83
Base, G., 87
Bate, L., 85
Battles, E., 86
Bauman, J., 62, 239
Bayer, J., 140
Baylor, B., 85
Bean, T., 190, 200
Beaty, J., 283
Beck, J., 284
Begaye, L., 285
Beisner, M., 87
Bellugi-Klima, U., 72
Bemelmans, M., 84
Berenstain, B., 157
Berenstain, J., 30, 34, 83, 85, 181
Berenstain, S., 30, 34, 83, 85, 157
Bergeron, B., 9
Bernstein, B., 72
Bernstein, R., 287
Bertrand, J., 238
Besar, M., 30
Binch, C., 285
Bishop, C., 285
Bissex, G., 218
Blair, S., 83
Blaska, J., 287
Blacksma, M., 114, 141
Bloomfield, L., 129
Bolton, F., 30
Bond, G., 44
Bonn, R., 14
Bonners, S., 30, 85
Bonsal, C., 140
Booth, B., 285
Bornstein, K., 83
Bottner, S., 82, 128
Boynton, S., 82, 87
Breimeyer, L., 86
Brenner, B., 141
Brent, R., 62
Bridwell, R., 30, 82
Bright, R., 86
Brooks, L., 65
Brown, B., 72
Brown, M.W., 30, 65, 83, 84, 85, 114, 141, 200
Bunting, E., 87
Buringham, J., 85
Burke, C., 11
Burns, D., 181
Burns, M., 128
Burrows, A., 219

SUBJECT INDEX

A

B

C

T